AGING
&
OLD AGE

AGING

&

OLD AGE

An Introduction to Social Gerontology

BETH B. HESS

County College of Morris
Dover, New Jersey

ELIZABETH W. MARKSON

Boston University
Boston, Massachusetts

MACMILLAN PUBLISHING CO., INC.
NEW YORK
COLLIER MACMILLAN PUBLISHERS
LONDON

Macmillan Publishing Co., Inc.
866 Third Avenue, New York, New York 10022

Collier Macmillan Canada, Ltd.

Library of Congress Cataloging in Publication Data

Hess, Beth B
Aging and old age.

Includes index.
1. Gerontology. 2. Aging. 3. Old age.
I. Markson, Elizabeth Warren, joint author.
II. Title.
HQ1061.H46 1980   301.43'5   79–9969
ISBN 0–02–354100–8

Printing: 2 3 4 5 6 7 8   Year: 1 2 3 4 5 6

32,767

Preface

————•◆•————

The plan of this book is somewhat different from that of many current textbooks in social gerontology. Rather than focusing exclusively on the particular problems of growing old in America today, we have sought to place the current scene in a broader context, considering both the changes that have taken place through the long history of human societies, and the prospects for change in the future. As sociologists, our emphasis is on the larger social systems in which aging takes place. We are also reflexive about the study of aging itself: Why do we study certain aspects of aging and not others? What are the consequences of our findings and the methods used to study old people?

Many issues in the study of aging have a significance beyond helping us to understand the plight of old people today. What, for example, can gerontology tell us about aging in general, or about the experiences of younger people that will affect the way future generations adapt to old age? What can we learn about American culture and values from the study of health care, social services, and institutionalization policies with respect to old people? How do the mind and body grow old, regardless of social context? And what will be the social environment of those entering old age in the twenty-first century?

We begin with a sociology of knowledge approach to the emergence of social gerontology, then describe some of the recurring issues of theory and method, and conclude Part One with a set of conceptual models that will serve as guides throughout this volume.

Part Two deals with the aging body and mind, those processes that were long thought to be inevitable and decremental, and which often represent authentic aging because they are so visible. What will surprise many is how very little we do know about aging and how value-laden or culture-bound so much of our thinking on these matters turns out to be. Institutionalization is one such clouded issue, in which fear and rhetoric often displace serious discussion of the alternatives. Throughout Part Two recent research is presented and assessed, and the implications for public policy are discussed. Biological and psychological events cannot be considered apart from their grounding in social reality, including current theories and practices of professionals.

In Part Three we analyze the social subsystems—or "institutional spheres"—in which old people occupy *statuses* and enact social *roles,* or fail to do so. Following the models developed in Part One, we focus on the *interaction* between the aging individual and the structure of social roles. Each chapter begins with a historical overview of the changes in social structure affecting the status and role of old people, and ends with some thoughts about the future course of aging in that subsystem. The bulk of these chapters consists of description and analysis of the current scene, not only the problematic aspects but the many ways in which America's aged are successfully adapting to the changes of later life.

If there is a theme running through this volume, it is "change," an emphasis on the variable, the emergent, and the modifiable. To some degree, each generation alters its social environment, which then becomes the context of action for a succeeding generation, and so on through time. Most of you are now college students who will be old people sometime after 2020 (a perfect date for looking ahead). What will our society be like then? What will you be like? Gerontologists already know some things about you that will influence your aging and the impact you will have on this society as you move along your life course. We can also make some predictions about the social order in which you will continue to grow old. Some of these guesses may prove correct and others may prove flawed, but you will have one advantage over all those who have aged before you: You will have thought about growing old, learned what to expect, examined the conditions for successful aging, and understood the situation of those now old. Perhaps you will even gain control over the circumstances of your own aging.

One of the most influential and popular recent books on aging was titled *Why Survive?* (Butler, 1974). The answer, we believe, is that old age need not be feared, stigmatized, or ridiculed, as it so often is today. There is an inevitability in death, to be sure, but the last of life, under appropriate conditions, can be a time of repose, of new initiatives, of personal awareness, and of assistance to others. Your task, in adulthood and beyond, will be to ensure that all this is possible.

Because we believe that the surest way to learn is to do, we include in each chapter some suggestions for research projects that can be undertaken by individual students or the class as a whole. We urge you to select at least one project that brings you into direct contact with old people in your community. Only in this manner can the words on these pages have any reality or meaning. Moreover, there is much to be learned *from* as well as about the elderly—and that may be the most important lesson.

Acknowledgments

It is fitting that, as gerontologists, our first set of "significant others" consists of those who first stimulated our interest in aging through their own example: our parents, grandparents, and aunts, especially Yetta and Albert Bowman, Ruby Lee Warren, Elizabeth Jane Rawlings and Rebecca Gray.

Our husbands, Richard Hess and Ralph Markson, were, as ever, models of unflagging encouragement and support. This book is dedicated to our children: Laurence and Emily Hess, and Alison Markson—our hostages to a future that we hope will somehow be better for our efforts to understand the social context of aging.

Professionally, we are doubly fortunate to have had superior role models and mentors—Matilda White Riley and Elaine Cumming. We have benefitted from stimulating colleagues: Anne Foner, Joan Waring, Marilyn Johnson, and Paul H. Wueller. Joanne Stakosch and Alexandra Lukawsky were very helpful readers of the first draft.

Our most immediate debt is to Kenneth J. Scott, our editor, and other members of the superb Macmillan staff: Ellen Gordon, copy editor; David Novack, our production supervisor, and Natasha Sylvester, book designer.

In all these—parents, family, mentors, colleagues, and editors—we have been extraordinarily fortunate. We hope this volume will, to some small degree, redress the balance of gratitude.

B. B. H.
E. W. M.

Contents

PART THREE

Aging in Social Systems

PART ONE

The Study of Aging

1

Social Gerontology: An Emergent Field of Study

Why Gerontology?

In 1970, under the heading "Aged," the *New York Times Index* listed forty-four items. By 1977, the *Times* carried 120 news stories about the aged, and over 150 cross-references to other headings with content on old people. Most of the articles in 1977 and 1978 deal with nursing homes, programs for old people in various communities, housing, crime and transportation problems, statements by politicians deploring it all, and signs of increasing militancy among the aged. Among the more intriguing recent items are the following:

Census Bureau projects that by the year 2030 17% of Americans will be over 65 compared with 10% currently . . . (February 6, 1977)

Plans to establish health facility for elderly New Jersey residents stopped by area residents fearful of daily influx of elderly blacks and Hispanic persons seeking medical treatment . . . (April 4, 1977)

Nevada Senate passes bill allowing manufacture and use of controversial drug Gerovital, said to relieve depression in the elderly (May 6, 1977)

Fledgling gerontology curricula . . . cropping up in universities across the U.S., as median age rises . . . (June 19, 1977)

New York State Supreme Court revokes license of Royal Manor Home for Adults . . . and Paradise Manor Home for Adults . . . charging that homes are dirty and mismanaged . . . (August 18, 1977)

Operators of . . . old age homes threaten to close homes . . . because state officials fail to meet them on proposals for increased reimbursement . . . (June 21, 1977)

New York State Social Services Department obtains temporary restraining order to keep nine adult residential homes from closing . . . because electricity was to be shut off and they could not pay their staff (February 3, 1978)

Hearing scheduled on the shortcomings in America's tangled pension programs (June 23, 1978)

Senate sends Carter a bill raising mandatory retirement age to 70 (March 24 ,1978)

Strengthening political power of older US citizens (October 24, 1977)

Gray Panthers convene . . . (October 29, 1977)

Growing interest in gerontology among college students as a career field . . . (January 18, 1978)

Clearly the old are with us if not "of" us in many ways. Yet as old people come more to public consciousness, the study of aging and old age has become an important new academic specialty. Courses in introductory social gerontology are being introduced into the curriculum of most universities and colleges; students such as yourself are drawn to this field through genuine interest and/or career expectations. How has this all come about? Surely old people have formed an important segment of the population for many decades without attracting such attention.

Why social gerontology now? To answer this question we must explore the conditions under which any social issue is created and dealt with— what is called the *sociology of knowledge* approach.

DEFINING A SOCIAL ISSUE

Contrary to much popular thinking, scientists do not confront an unchanging reality "out there" waiting to be systematically analyzed by researchers who are dedicated to truth alone. The process is more complicated than that. What is studied in any society at a given historical moment is determined by many factors having little to do with the intrinsic qualities of the subject matter. For the most part, such decisions are *political*, involving the allocation of scarce resources and reflecting priorities in the realm of societal values. We need only think of the overhaul of science education in the United States in the late 1950s, less in response to any major change within that field than to the fear that the Soviet Union had surpassed us technologically with the launching of Sputnik. Or, more recently, enormous sums have been spent on federal support of cancer cures, a more popular course, politically, than calling for changes in life-styles that could reduce cancer-related deaths through prevention. Moreover, what can be studied at any one time depends upon what else is known in that society.

If such is the case with presumed "hard" sciences—medicine, physics, and chemistry, for instance—it is even more likely that those who study human behavior will be influenced by their cultural context and historical moment. The question we ask and seek to answer in this introductory section is, "Why did the study of aging and old age emerge in America in the years following the end of World War II?"

There are a number of reasons why these topics would continue to be avoided: old age is associated with losses in physical and mental functioning; it is a prelude to death; old people make us uncomfortable. The ostrich approach—what we don't think about need not distress us—undoubtedly operates at some level to discourage students and practitioners, as well as the general public, from pondering the issues of aging. It is often said of the United States that ours is a nation of youth-worship where effectiveness, vitality, and good looks are highly valued. A content analysis of television and magazine advertising would support this thesis: in 1976, toiletries and toilet goods were the second leading category in terms of net time and program costs for national network advertising. In third place was proprietary medicines, which were largely designed to disguise the effects of normal aging (*Statistical Abstract of the United States*, 1978, p. 847). Much of this emphasis on youthful beauty can be related to a marriage market in which personal qualities are important bargaining chips, perhaps the only ones for women; but much also can be attributed to the perception of young people as *potential* achievers of the American Dream. Old people cannot make the same claim on our hopes and resources.

Therefore, it should not surprise us that old people in America had not been much studied or particularly thought about as a discrete category. Researchers and practitioners tend also to be attracted to subjects and subject matter that have intrinsic appeal (what we often call "sexy" topics). For example, if given a choice of working with very young or very old mental patients, most of us would select the former on the assumption that something of value could be produced—a child could become a productive adult, a future to be salvaged—whereas providing therapy to an octogenerian might be thought to be an exercise in futility. A common belief is that young persons can still be changed, but the old are too set in their ways (You can't teach an old dog new tricks). Less obvious perhaps is the "halo effect," whereby the social evaluation of the client/patient carries over to the giver of services. Thus, those who study successful adult males are accorded higher prestige than those dealing with women, the aged, or even children. *Hard* science and methodologies are deemed more worthy than *soft* subjects and methods, reflecting a general tendency to value masculine traits and virtues in our society. And because the old are primarily female, or, in any event, rarely evoke images of strength and productivity, it has been relatively easy to neglect them and their problems.

What, then, accounts for the surge of interest in aging and old age in postwar America, at least among politicians and some academics, and why has aging recently become a matter of public concern? The emergence of gerontology—the study of old age—is an interesting illustration of the process that C. Wright Mills (1959) has described as the transformation of personal problems into public issues. In general, we would suggest that private troubles become societal issues when a critical mass of individuals is involved and when their problems are defined as stemming from forces beyond their control but which can be dealt with effectively at the public level. The short answer to our question, Why gerontology? is that old people are there in large numbers and their well-being was ultimately defined as a national responsibility. The long answer will take up the rest of this volume. Since there is no easy way to cover all topics at once, we present here a brief overview of the many important long-term (*secular*) trends, each of which is explored in greater detail in later chapters, that account for the concentration of old people in modern industrial societies and make their fate a matter of concern to all citizens.

FORMATION OF THE CRITICAL MASS

Aging of Populations. Modern, as contrasted to preindustrial, societies are characterized by low birthrates and low mortality rates. In simple societies, population balance is maintained by both high birth and death rates, often reinforced by female infanticide (which controls population for two generations). In the course of economic development, many agricultural societies experience the "demographic transition": a phase in which death rates are substantially reduced through public sanitation measures and change in diet, but fertility rates remain very high. Improvements in nutrition and sanitation, long before the medical discoveries that led to immunization, were responsible for declines in infant

Table 1–1. Median Age of U.S. Population *

Date	Age
1800	16.0 **
1850	18.9
1900	22.9
1950	30.2
1976	29.0

* A median is the midpoint of a distribution, i.e., where 50 percent of all cases fall above and 50 percent fall below.
Statistical Abstract of the United States, 1978, p. 25.
** 1800 data for whites only; other years include all races.

and childhood deaths from infectious disease (with the exception of smallpox and diphtheria) in the eighteenth and nineteenth centuries (McKeown, 1978). In turn, this lowered probability of infant death reduced the necessity for bearing large numbers of children so that a few might live. As women limited the number of their pregnancies, both mother and child enjoyed better health. It is this reduction in mortality in early life and during childbirth that accounts for the dramatic increases in average life expectancy of the twentieth century.

As more people survive youth and young adulthood, and fewer infants are reproduced by each couple, the average age of the entire population will rise; this is what is meant by the "aging of populations" in modern industrial society, as illustrated in Table 1–1.

The apparent downturn from the 1950 high median age reflects the very large number of infants born in the postwar decade (1947–1957). Given the very low fertility rates of the past five years, the median age should continue its historic rise for the remainder of this century.

Moreover, since 1900, the rate of increase of the older population in the United States is greater than that of the population as a whole, as indicated in Figure 1–1.

The Aging of Individuals. Another way of looking at the formation of a critical mass of old people is to measure the average number of years that an individual could expect to live at various ages, e.g., at birth, age 20, age 45, or even age 65. This is *life expectancy*, which has shown dramatic increases in the United States in this century.

Most of this gain in life expectancy, as already noted, is accounted for by lowered death rates in infancy and childhood, which were most pronounced between 1900 and 1950. At the older ages, and particularly from 1950 on, the increases in life expectancy have been relatively small. Having survived infancy and the perils of young adulthood (pregnancy for

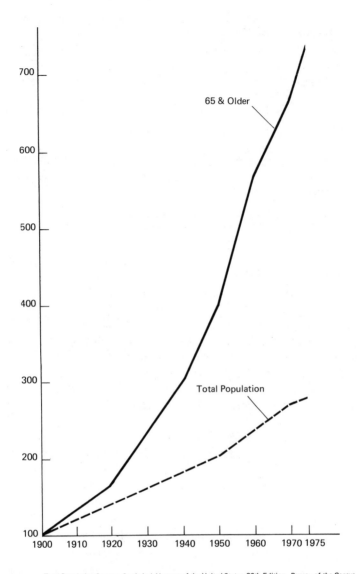

Total Population Source: Statistical Abstract of the United States, 96th Edition, Bureau of the Census, 1975
65 & Older Source: Current Population Reports, Special Studies, Bureau of the Census, Series p-23, No. 59

Figure 1–1. Rate of Increase 65 & Older vs. Total U.S. Population 1900–1975. FactBook on Aging, NCoA, 1978, p. 5.

women, military service for men), life expectancies at age 45 today are not very different than they were in 1880. The life expectancy of one who has survived to age 65 has increased only two to six years in this century.

Increases in life expectancy are not evenly distributed across the popu-

Table 1–2. **Average Remaining Lifetime at Birth and Age 65, by Race and Sex, 1900–1975, in Years**

	1900	1940	1955	1970	1975
Total					
at birth	49.2	63.6	70.2	70.8	72.5
at age 65	11.9	12.8	14.2	15.0	16.0
White					
Males:					
at birth	48.2	62.8	67.3	68.0	69.4
at age 65	11.5	12.1	12.9	13.1	13.7
Females:					
at birth	51.1	67.3	73.6	75.4	77.2
at age 65	12.2	13.6	15.5	16.9	18.1
Nonwhite					
Males:					
at birth	32.5	52.3	61.2	61.0	63.6
at age 65	10.4	12.3	13.2	12.9	13.7
Females:					
at birth	35.0	55.6	65.9	69.0	72.3
at age 65	11.4	13.9	15.5	16.1	17.5

Siegel, Jacob S., "Demographic Aspects of Aging and the Older Population in the United States," Current Population Reports, Special Studies, Series P–23, No. 59, May, 1976. United States Department of Commerce, Bureau of the Census, United States Printing Office, Washington, D.C. Adapted from Table 5–1, p. 26, and Statistical Abstract of the United States, 1978, Table 96, p. 66.

lation. When the data are broken down on the basis of sex and race, fascinating patterns emerge.

Race. The doubling of life expectancies for nonwhites is unquestionably the result of improvements in infant survival and maternal health. In 1900, fewer than 20 percent of nonwhite male infants could be expected to survive to age 65; by 1974, the figure had risen to 53 percent. But these percentages must be compared with the comparable ones for white males: 39 percent in 1900 and 68 percent in 1974. For nonwhite females, the proportion surviving to age 65 increased from 22 percent in 1900 to 70 percent in 1974 (compared to 44 percent and 85 percent for white females). In other words, only half of all nonwhite males born in 1974 can expect to live beyond age 65; two thirds of both nonwhite females and white males will survive to old age; and four fifths of white females will live into their seventh decade. Obviously, the health benefits enjoyed by whites have not been fully extended to nonwhites. Nonwhite males are especially at risk of early death from all causes—natural and accidental.

Sex. Differences in life expectancy by sex have increased for all races, and more so for white than nonwhite. More is said about the *consequences* of this sex differential later, but we now consider in greater detail some of the causes. Many see the lower life expectancy of men as a reflection of the occupational stresses of most male work roles: some men are dehumanized on the assembly line, and others are overburdened with managerial responsibility; in either case, smoking, drinking, and worrying lead to ill health and early death. The traditional woman, on the other hand, sits at home watching television; she may become slightly neurotic, but she lives longer. If this theory is correct, then the entry of women into the full-time labor force should be accompanied by higher female death rates at earlier ages from ulcers and heart attacks, cirrhosis, and lung cancer. At the moment this does not seem to be the case, although it may be too early to detect these changes in mortality rates. In fact, as life-styles have tended to converge for men and women, sex differences in life expectancy have continued to increase! This suggests that women may have always had a potentially longer life span than men, masked throughout most of human history by the physical risks associated with frequent pregnancies. Higher life expectancy for females has been noted even where life-style differences between the sexes are minimal, as in the case of Roman Catholic teaching orders (Madigan and Vance, 1957).

Increases in life expectancy for males are probably best explained as the outcome of their being born to women who have had fewer children and were in better health than heretofore. Such public health improvements as sewers, pasteurization, and better diets, already alluded to as responsible for lowering infant mortality in general, have actually had greater impact on male death rates since these are typically higher than for females. That is, being the more vulnerable sex biologically, males have derived greater benefits from the reduction of infant mortality.

Proportion of Old People. For all these reasons, by the middle of this century, both males and females, white and nonwhite, were likely to live to and through their sixth decade. At the same time, with the striking exception of the decade between 1947–57, birthrates were declining steadily, with dramatic dips during the Great Depression and in the 1970s. These basic demographic processes produce not only sizable numbers and proportions of old people but also encourage the legitimate expectation among younger persons that they will survive to old age. On the other hand, we should not exaggerate the proportion of old people in our society: in 1900 only 4.1 percent were 65 and over; today, the figure is almost 11 percent. Although the proportion of old people has increased almost threefold, this still leaves almost 90 percent of the population who are not elderly.

Since the proportion of old people depends upon how many younger

The Study of Aging

Table 1–3. Per Cent of Population 65 and Over, 1900–1970, and Projected to 2050

Year	Per Cent	Year	Per Cent
1900	4.1	1980	11.0
1910	4.3	1990	11.7
1920	4.6	2000	11.7
1930	5.4	2010	11.9
1940	6.8	2020	14.6
1950	8.1	2030	17.0
1960	9.2	2040	16.1
1970	9.8	2050	16.1

Siegel, Jacob S., "Demographic Aspects of Aging and the Older Population in the United States," Current Population Reports, Special Studies, Series P–23, No. 59, May, 1976. United States Department of Commerce, Bureau of the Census, United States Printing Office, Washington, D.C., p. 9.

persons there are, any shift in fertility has a profound effect on the age composition of the society as a whole, especially since death rates have remained stable for several decades and since large-scale in- or out-migrations appear unlikely. Table 1–3 represents the best guess of the Bureau of the Census regarding the per cent of Americans 65 and over in the years ahead:

How can we speak of a "critical mass" when the proportions of those 65+ will remain under 12 percent in this century? All that these data need mean is that there would be a few million more older Americans each decennial census. Numbers alone do not elevate personal dilemmas to social problems. Had not other secular trends converged to create a particular set of needs among the aged, old age might not have emerged as a distinctive stage of life in industrial societies.

FROM ASCRIBED TO ACHIEVED STATUSES

Much of the rest of this book is devoted to examining the full consequences of *modernization* on the social positions (*statuses*) held by old people, especially those related to the three dimensions of social stratification: power, prestige, and property. In broad outline, the organization of work and families associated with the Industrial Revolution, the spread of public education, and the triumph of individualism have all served to undermine the authority of elders. Although there has been a great deal of erroneous romanticization of the traditional or preindustrial family and of the position of old people in those societies, and an equally overdrawn account of the current plight of the aged, it is probably correct to say that the control over property, work, and family affairs that was once exercised by elders has been greatly diminished.

The breakup of the traditional *extended family* is often attributed to the forces of industrialism, and especially to the introduction of factories to replace home-based (and, thus, family-controlled) production. However, the recent work of historians of the family has done much to dispel the myth of the extended family. It appears that young people had been leaving the family farm and village long before the factories were built, and that the care of parents in old age was far from assured. This pool of landless labor made the factory system possible, and, in turn, the availability of factory employment drew more young people from the countryside, out of range of parental control. In the United States, the supply of unattached workers was dramatically increased by the young (mostly male) immigrants who came, we often forget, as single persons rather than as members of a family unit. The factory system was but one force eroding family controls over the young. In the modern family, bonds of marriage (*conjugality*) became more important than those of blood (*consanguinality*) and choice of a marriage partner is made on the basis of personal attraction rather than on the potential benefit to kinfolk. Moreover, the ability to find employment through the impersonal mechanisms of the labor market further reduces the need for kin support, although at certain stages of industrial development or for certain labor pools, family members find jobs for one another or control the entry into occupations through apprentice programs (Hareven, 1978). In general, however, the more complex the work organization, the more reliance there is on education and talent, i.e., achieved characteristics, though neither is really independent of family background.

Other secular trends further reduce the economic power of elders. As national firms replace small, self-owned businesses, and large-scale agriculture displaces the tenant-farmer and homesteader, not only are fewer men able to hand down a family enterprise, but they themselves, as employees of someone else, are removed from the labor force at some fixed time, often with a drastic loss of income.

What all this means is that most old people today do not have income-producing employment, cannot demand care from relatives, and do not hold positions of prestige. By the late 1950s it became evident that income maintenance, health care, and the provision of social services to the aged were *public* rather than private responsibilities. The Social Security system began to be seen as *the* income support for retired workers or their survivors; the long Medicare battle was initiated; and the groundwork was laid for what would eventually be the Older Americans Act of 1965.

And as old age became recognized as a stage of the life course with special properties, involving many millions of Americans and their offspring, and potentially including all citizens fortunate enough to survive, it became necessary to know more about the process of aging and the condition of being old.

EMERGENCE OF ACADEMIC GERONTOLOGY

Interest in both the process of aging and the condition of being old was confined to a few scholars at a limited number of universities in the 1940s and 1950s. Much of this activity was centered in the state universities of the Midwest where interest was focused on the adjustment of recipients of old-age assistance and other effects of the Great Depression (Streib and Orbach, 1967). The 1960s began with a grand flourish: three major volumes, the first generation of gerontology "Handbooks," which delineated the field, described existing research, and prepared the agenda for the coming decade: Birren's *Handbook of Aging and the Individual: Psychological and Biological Aspects*, Tibbitts' *Handbook of Social Gerontology: Societal Aspects of Aging*, and Burgess' *Aging in Western Societies*. These were followed by Tibbitts and Donahue's *Social and Psychological Aspects of Aging*. As these titles indicate, there was some question as to how to divide the field, a problem that still plagues those attempting to define *gerontology*. The original three-part division—psychological and biological, sociological, anthropological—gave way to the absorption of anthropology into the broader concept of "social aspects"; the division of biology and psychology; and even the combination of psychology and sociology. The latest generation of *Handbooks* 1976-7 consists of three volumes: *Biology of Aging* (Finch and Hayflick), *Psychology of Aging* (Birren and Schaie), and *Aging and the Social Sciences* (Binstock and Shanas).

The production of so many impressive volumes in the early 1960s served two important intellectual functions: they permitted instant access to a whole field of knowledge and provided the basis for courses on aging and old age. The development of curricula often awaits the availability of resource material. It is very difficult to teach a subject until it is readily accessible to students through textbooks (although there are instances of the reverse process, e.g., women's studies). The 1960s were, however, less marked by the introduction of courses in gerontology than continued research and thinking through of the deeper issues. Age is actually an exceedingly complex variable; it has physical and social dimensions, its meaning is socially constructed, its psychological manifestations and correlates are still unclear, and there is no simple way to distinguish how mind, body, social system, and historical events influence one another or have an independent effect on aging individuals.

The 1960s were a period of continued productivity in research and methodology. Dozens of important studies were carried out in the United States and abroad (e.g., Shanas et al., 1968). Old people in the community and in institutions; mental illness and death; the transitions from middle to old age—all, and more, became part of the emergent field of social gerontology. However, both despite and because of the generally high quality of all this activity, the field required consolidation and a set of criteria by which to judge the new abundance of data, and, most of all, it needed a general theoretical framework to organize existing material and shape the direction of further research. An ambitious attempt to achieve these several goals was undertaken by Matilda White Riley and her colleagues in the three volumes of *Aging and Society*. Volume 1, which appeared in 1968, was an *Inventory of Research Findings*, a systematic presentation of carefully evaluated research data up to 1968. Here, in one place, were reliable data on all aspects of aging. Volume 2: *Aging and the Professions* (1969) contained essays on the application of the data to professional practice, and Volume 3: *A Theory of Age Stratification* (1972) presented a model for the study of aging that is described in Chapter 2.

Although critical masses, professional concern, and increasing interest among politicians and foundations were necessary to inaugurate the study of gerontology in the 1950s and 1960s, they were not sufficient to produce an academic specialty in the very different world of higher education in the 1970s. For the latter, extensive funding becomes the primary requirement. The Older Americans Act of 1965 and amended in 1973 and 1978, and the funding activities of departments of the federal government and its research institutes, accelerated the flow of money to colleges and universities and individuals prepared to study the aged, offer courses, create gerontology programs on campus and in the community, and build gerontology centers.

Gerontology in higher education is one of the few academic growth industries, and is not without its growing pains. For example, there is no consensus regarding what is a *gerontologist*: is there a specific body of knowledge to be mastered, or does each separate discipline—biology, sociology, psychology, social work—equip its graduate students with a gerontological overlay? Nor is there consensus on what constitutes a gerontology *program* or *center*; each one established to date appears to be unique. And within the major professional association, the Gerontological Society, an uneasy alliance connects researchers, teachers, and practitioners, whose needs and interests increasingly diverge. At the same time, each group is increasingly dependent on the others in order to do its task well: researchers should be aware of the implications of their work for practitioners, and the latter must know how to apply research findings to their practice. And we who teach gerontology need to stay abreast of the research, to evaluate and integrate new findings into our course work while also remaining sensitive to the concerns of our students for practical applications of their studies.

As might be expected of a new and rapidly developing field of study, there are problems of definition and direction, of theory construction and research methods to be worked through. We explore these issues in the next section.

Doing Gerontology

From our brief overview, the many problems that beset the new field of gerontology can be appreciated. In this section we concentrate on the most important of these: issues of identity, direction, methods, and theory, all of which arise from the distinctive nature of the subject matter. If aging is a process occurring at many levels of analysis, a holistic approach must breach the traditional divisions of academic labor. However, since most gerontologists have been trained in an existing specialty—biological/medical science, psychology, sociology, anthropology, or social work—they have brought to the new field the particular methods and theories by which they have learned to organize the world. It is this multidisciplinary quality of gerontology that presents the most difficult challenge to those who seek to understand the meaning and process of human aging.

PERSISTENT ISSUES

The Question of Identity. As might be expected of any emerging field of study, the first problem is to distinguish a subject matter apart from others, and then to define what falls within its boundaries. Here, again, the proportion of old people in modern societies is crucial. So, also, are the unique characteristics of the elderly, especially those conditions that can be considered problems. In our culture, problems must be traced to causes and thus made amenable to solutions. If solutions are to be found, then much research must be undertaken—it was this void that provided the rationale for the research activity of the postwar decades with its emphasis upon the physical and social difficulties of growing old. But problems of delineating a purely gerontological focus of study were increasingly evident, even as the areas of legitimate old-age concerns expanded and deepened. Growing old begins at birth, and age is a continuous variable, whereas division of the life span into age-defined categories is a *social fact*, culturally derived and historically changeable. Clearly there is no simple way of fencing off old age as a discrete period, or of confining the study of aging to one society or one epoch.

All these confusions are reflected in the diversity of gerontology programs in graduate education: some are found in the school of social work; others in the social science departments; and some in a separate division, department, or school of "human development" or variation on that theme, in which sociologists and psychologists often struggle for control. Some professional schools of nursing and medicine have incorporated gerontology into already existing courses, while others have established specific training for the role of geriatric nurse practitioner, or a clinical rotation in geriatrics. A few programs have become independent degree-granting units of large universities, with a faculty composed of specialists from other divisions. No meeting of the Gerontological Society or the Association for Gerontology in Higher Education is without symposia and sessions on defining a gerontologist or on how to organize the requisite material and training program to generate a "core" curriculum.

If the fact that gerontology cuts across a number of established fields of study, i.e., is *multidisciplinary*, creates confusion only at the organizational level of a college or university we could, literally, consider it an academic problem and pay no further heed. But the range of knowledge required to understand aging and old age leads to difficulties at the substantive level—that is, what shall be taught and how? The basic question is whether or not the relevant findings from biology, psychology, sociology, and history can be combined to create a new product, or must simply be mixed together to give the student a working knowledge of each. This is rather like the difference between hash and stew, and may be just as much a matter of taste. At the moment, most programs and probably all introductory courses have taken the "stew" approach—a little of everything. In the next chapter some theoretical schemes are presented that have the potential for integrating material from the various disciplines.

Many of these difficulties are not unique to gerontology. The two other new academic specialties of the 1970s—Black studies and women's studies—are also interdisciplinary. Age, sex, and race are *ascribed statuses* involving physical differences that are used to evaluate the social worth of individuals and, hence, their access to societal resources. It is impossible to understand the effects of color, sex, and age from a knowledge of only physiological distinctions or the distribution of personality traits. It is becoming obvious to students of human behavior that we are dealing with a seamless web of cause and consequence. In general, genetic traits or body types or physical characteristics are "potentials" that can unfold in a number of ways, within certain limits, depending upon such factors as cultural beliefs regarding beauty or worthiness, socially structured opportunities or obstacles, particular family constellations, and chance events. Moreover, social/cultural environments are subject to change over time, much of it brought about by those attempting to overcome discrimination on the basis of ascribed traits.

Thus, although the multidisciplinary requirements of gerontology are creating confusion and identity problems at the moment, they also provide a challenge. The organization of knowledge and institutional structures to convey this knowledge could become a model for behavioral science in the future. Unfortunately, professional advancement and recognition still depend upon academic research in one traditional discipline, a case of "knowing more and more about less and less." The study of aging thus holds the promise of a field that will break down barriers between different branches of knowledge.

The Problem of Direction. By the problem of direction we mean simply Gerontology for whom? Like the divisions mentioned previously, gerontologists also differ by being primarily engaged in laboratory research, college teaching, or primary health care and social service (similar to the split in psychology between experimenters, academics, and clinicians). Although this diversity can be stimulating and lead to an interchange of information which will make research and practice mutually supportive, problems of priority inevitably arise. Is gerontology to be a "pure" endeavor, with the sole aim of understanding the process of aging? Or, because so many old people have difficulties in adaptation and even survival that are traceable to the social system, ought not the role of the gerontologist be that of advocate for change?[1] Where should federal funds be directed? As described in Chapter 8, the Older Americans Act allocates federal funds for research, for establishing training centers, and for a range of social services. But what priorities will emerge when the money stops flowing?

Short-term grants or contracts for research are known as *soft money*. The principal investigator brings the funds to her/his institution and is able to hire graduate students and other staff. But soft money is precisely that; it melts away over time so that much of academic gerontology is rather precariously anchored. Nor has the outpouring of academic research and publications had an appreciable effect on the daily lives of old people, although the fact that so much is being done has made aging and its problems a matter of public knowledge, and college courses in social gerontology do serve to sensitize growing numbers of young people, to the issues and concerns of the aged. On the other hand, research that could be of value has often been neglected. Estes and Freeman (1976) have pointed out that many of the "good works" mandated by the 1973 revisions of the Older Americans Act—particularly the state units and the

[1] An illustrative example of just such a dilemma occurred when some members of the Gerontological Society objected to holding the 1978 Annual Meeting in New Orleans, Louisiana, a state that had not ratified the Equal Rights Amendment. Since most elderly are women for whom changes in the Social Security rules would be beneficial, and since women have been well represented among gerontologists, the issue of women's rights appeared germane to the Society's goals. However, those opposed to moving the meetings argued that this was a "political" issue and the Society as a professional organization must remain above politics. The meetings were subsequently moved to Dallas, Texas.

nutrition programs—were designed without any preliminary study of their potential effects, many of which have proven to be negative.

A more pervasive problem of direction, however, arises from the fact that almost all these research projects are funded by federal or state government, so that some needs will be met but others will not. Similarly, some kinds of information will be sought, whereas other kinds will not and some people will be favored and some not. Resulting programs and legislation are the outcome of political pressures and interest group politics at all levels of government.

With respect to America's aged, this whole matter of intervention is greatly complicated by the variety of the needs and the extreme diversity of the older population. For example, relatively healthy old people in the community may require very little assistance, whereas those who are ancient and frail should have a range of services. Unlike other modern industrial societies, the United States has not developed a comprehensive system of social welfare throughout the life course, with provisions for the aging and old as an integral part. If it is thought that old people should have more social interaction, money is put into senior centers rather than community facilities for a variety of age groups. Providing Dial-a-Ride rather than adequate public transportation is another example of this process of unintegrated social planning.

Lacking a national consensus or overall plan of action, issues of direction in research and the provision of services, and the link between these, remain unresolved and will continue to be dealt with on an *ad hoc*, temporary basis.

THEORIES OF AGING

One enduring goal of gerontological research has been the discovery of the key to successful aging. Given inevitable declines in physical functioning, what psychological and social adaptations lead to high morale or levels of satisfaction in old age? The issues and dilemmas just outlined are also evident in the construction of theories of aging: the intricacy of dealing with many levels of human behavior, difficulties in conceptualizing old age as a discrete period, selection of variables for intensive study, and the choice of situations requiring intervention.

As is shown in Chapter 5, the assumption that biological aging is a fairly direct and universal process has had to be modified. Social behaviors and personality traits can have physiological effects, and, at the very least, they can affect how an individual responds to an aging body. Social class, ethnicity, rural-urban residence, and other structural variables are associated with variations in functioning and behavior in old age.

Two early theoretical attempts to relate biological, psychological, and social elements deserve detailed mention.

Disengagement Theory.   Using data from the Kansas City studies of the 1950s, Cumming and Henry (1961) proposed that "successful" aging involved a gradual withdrawal from social networks *and* a concurrent tendency for others to lower expectations of the aging person and to reduce interaction with him/her. The process operates at three levels. From a societal perspective, the elderly must be eased out of roles in which they no longer function effectively in order to make way for younger role players. For the individual, *disengagement* is a mechanism for maintaining a balance between the old person's diminished energies on the one hand and demands of role partners on the other. At the psychological level, disengagement refers to a conserving of emotional resources in order to concentrate on one's preparation for death.

Comparing disengaged respondents to persons in their fifties who were fully engaged in social networks, Cumming and Henry found that both groups scored higher on measures of morale than did persons who were caught between full involvement and complete withdrawal. The idea that self-absorbed, passive old people could be said to have aged "successfully" is not an easy one for Americans to accept. Disengagement theory has, as a consequence, been extremely controversial, with most criticism centering on the original claim that disengagement was universal, inevitable, and functionally necessary for both individuals and social systems. Somewhat toned down, however, the concept of a *disengagement process* has proven useful in explaining some patterns of aging, but has not been accepted as *the* unified general theory of aging that was first proposed.

Activity Theory.   In contrast to disengagement theory, other researchers emphasize the positive outcomes of remaining engaged in the world at large and finding substitute roles for those that are lost through retirement or widowhood. There is impressive data to the effect that high levels of social involvement are indeed associated with high morale and other measures of satisfaction. But it is often difficult to pinpoint this relationship. People who are satisfied with life may seek out social interaction, while good health and adequate income may also be a source of both morale and sociability. Moreover, many old people are neither active nor socially involved and still report themselves quite content.

Such contradictions can be resolved by proposing dual processes of *selective* engagement and disengagement. Some roles cannot be easily replaced (spouse), others are often more or less willingly relinquished (worker), and still others can be expanded (grandparent). Health and physical capacities of the old person will inevitably set limits on activity, and much will depend upon what the environment offers. Life experience, the availability of *role partners,* and the values of the era in which the old person was socialized will also affect those activities and networks that are sustained.

These two early formulations—disengagement and activity theories—flawed and relatively simplistic as they may appear, have nonetheless stimulated research and dialogue within the field. Their importance as theories *limited to* old age has often been overlooked. The trend today is toward grand designs that encompass aging in a theory that attempts to organize all social behavior. Thus, sociobiology, exchange theory, symbolic interaction, and life-span development models are being introduced into gerontology. This veritable theoretical bazaar, however, can be confusing to the introductory student (and possibly disillusioning, when one realizes how many ways the same data can be interpreted).

Sociobiology. The basic concept of sociobiology is the *altruistic gene.* Evolutionary forces operate in such a way as to preserve the gene-carrying organism that is beneficial to group survival; not survival of the fittest individuals, but persistence of genetic material is the key. Thus, men are willing to die in battle to preserve their genes (half of which reside in their offspring, and some of which they share with their siblings). As with any theory at such a general level, by explaining everything it often fails to explain anything. Knowing that men will fight for their genes does not tell us much about the War of 1812. The sociobiologist, in a sense, works backwards: from the persistence of a culture trait or pattern of human behavior to thinking through its significance in protecting the gene pool.

For example, Katz (1978) has proposed a sociobiological analysis of the role of the grandmother. Because human females are the only primates to survive in large numbers past their reproductive years, the postfertile female must have some important evolutionary function; this task can only be to care for the children of her son, especially his female offspring since they carry the long-lived female gene. If this is indeed the case, those groups or societies that fail to provide for grandmothers are courting genetic disaster. It may be comforting to know that older women were the true force behind human evolution and survival, yet it is evident from the data on modern families that grandmothers are no longer essential for this purpose—the genes can be protected and preserved through other arrangements. Indeed, as we shall see later, the older woman is held in very low esteem in our society today. This is perhaps in part a sign of biological obsolescence, but it is also heavily influenced by cultural values. Such cultural variation and the capacity of humans to invent an endless number of meanings for their acts suggests a very broad range of action within the limits, if any, set by biology and the evolution of behavior. Nonetheless, sociobiology is an extremely fashionable theory today, and we may expect its application to gerontology to generate considerable controversy.

Exchange Theory. The central ideas of exchange theory, which come from structural anthropology, experimental psychology, and classical economics have been applied at both the societal and interpersonal level. In its broadest application, exchange is based on the *rule of reciprocity*: to receive is to be obligated to return something of comparable value. This principle is thought by some to be the foundation of human society, from the first exchange of marriage partners between bands of prehistoric gatherers to the felt obligation of a middle-aged child to care for an aged parent today. But it is in the analysis of interpersonal behavior that the principles of exchange have been most thoroughly applied. The basic assumption is that each person in an interaction is seeking to maximize benefits while incurring the least cost, in terms of prestige, self-esteem, and other psychic variables.

Thus, the status of old people in the society is partially explained by their lack of exchange value; they have nothing with which to bargain for care or respect, except, of course, for the claim to reciprocity from those whom they nurtured as helpless infants. The rule of reciprocity has no time limit; the obligation to return a "gift" remains in force until the debt is repaid. At the interpersonal level, relationships between the old and young can be explained by asking "Who is getting what and at what cost?" Differences in power and prestige can raise or lower the risks of gain or loss in an exchange, and thus make it more or less likely that individuals will interact with certain others and be comfortable. People tend to continue in relationships that are rewarding and to drop (if possible) those that are too "costly." Individuals with few rewards to offer may have difficulty in getting what they want from others.

Since almost any interaction can be analyzed as an exchange, the theory is potentially very powerful. However, since humans vary greatly in what they count as a cost or benefit, and often change their evaluations to fit necessity ("I really didn't want it anyway"), there are problems in applying the principles of exchange to the full range of social behavior.

Symbolic Interaction. If sociobiology and exchange theory are based on universal principles that can explain everything in general though not necessarily in particular, *symbolic interaction* is rooted in the particular. Symbolic interactionists study what they call *the social construction of reality*; that is, the meanings we give to what we are doing. These meanings are shared by those who are engaged in some regular interaction with one another; indeed, the definitions of the behavior develop out of the conversations that constitute the interaction.

The language of the theater is especially favored in symbolic interaction analysis. Participants in an ongoing interaction are referred to as *role players* or *actors* who "perform parts" that are continually being improvised or reinterpreted as the situation warrants. All this makes it very difficult to assume that the meaning an outside observer attaches to an event will be the same meaning held by the participants. If we wish to understand fully, we must attempt to find out how the actors define their situation. In gerontology, therefore, the elderly themselves must be our guides.

We must also be alert to the informal relationships worked out by actors within formal institutionalized settings. Yet, these relationships are often overlooked in the name of efficiency or what others think is "good for you." The most glaring cases occur in long-term care institutions where, for example, inmates are forbidden heterosexual contact because it would become more difficult for the staff to keep track of the patients. Another example was brought to our attention by an anthropologist, Krtystyna Starker, from participant observations at a senior center. She found that the members recreated the prestige hierarchy of their "outside life" in the men's card games and in the women's preparations for the midday group meal. When a government-sponsored nutrition program was instituted, the women's work was taken over by "experts," and the men's card tables were moved around to suit the convenience of the food servers. Ethnic dishes were replaced by more "nutritious" fare. Not surprisingly, attendance at the center declined, fewer meals were taken there, and what was served was often left uneaten.

Although closer attention to the meanings given by participants would have spared many a well-intended mistake, symbolic interaction studies by their very nature are limited. There is no analysis of the wider social systems beyond the specific setting, or of the sweep of history and cultural/social change. Yet it is always important to know how actors interpret their own experience, a truth we often lose sight of in our need to discover uniformity in human behavior. Thus, the gene-carrying grandmother of sociobiology could actually perceive her care of the grandchild in a number of ways: as an opportunity to have fun, to do her duty, as an incursion on her freedom, as a payoff for her offsprings' assistance, or as a means of maintaining the family line intact.

Life Span Developmental Approach. Whereas it can be argued that each stage of life—infancy, childhood, adolescence, young adulthood, mature adulthood, and old age—presents special challenges, tasks to be performed, obstacles, and opportunities, each life is nonetheless one unbroken line of experience. Therefore, no stage is entirely independent of what has already happened to the individual; even infancy is affected by prenatal maternal health and whether or not the child is desired or planned for. Psychologists have been intrigued with the possibility of constructing schemes of lifelong development, involving patterns of both stability and change in personality, behavior, attitudes, and motivations of individuals.

The dominant theories in contemporary developmental psychology have departed from the Freudian model in a number of important ways. First, Freud's emphasis on the early years and their sexual content has been diluted. Following Erikson, most theorists now see the whole life course as providing opportunities for change and emotional growth: decisions to be made, responsibilities to discharge relationships to nurture or relinquish. Second, and following from the first, the experiences of infancy and childhood need not have permanent effects. Adulthood is not simply a recapitulation of the trauma of weaning and toilet training and Oedipal resolutions. Rather, many intervening events, pure chance, unique constellations of people and places, and historical happenings are able to modify or even drastically alter original psychic structures. Further, human beings continually reconstruct the past and its meaning in the light of the present.

In this perspective, old age may be viewed as a period during which an individual faces a number of new situations: retirement, widowhood, loss of friends and family, physical decrements, chronic illness, and decline of income. But there are also opportunities to find new friends and activities and to develop novel strengths and adaptations. If psychic growth and development are initiated by the need to reintegrate the ego after some major challenge, then old age should be a time of important personality change. This is a very different view from that which sees old people as extremely rigid and unchangeable. But there are also continuities. What is often called "personality" is a consistent style of adapting to experience and approaching others.

This emphasis on both the flexibility and stability of traits make lifespan developmental models more applicable to the study of aging than theories that see personality fixed at the onset of adulthood if not adolescence.

Summary. A theory is a model of how the social world works, a way of organizing variables so that we can understand why people behave as they do, and be able often to predict outcomes. Because human beings have the ability to change their environments and to attach any number of meanings to their behavior, it is not easy to construct general theories. Each of the theories described will help explain some aspects of aging but not others. For example, both disengagement and activity theory are probably correct to some extent; some individuals will have high morale by restricting their life space, and others by maintaining or expanding the social relationships of middle age. More likely, selective disengagement combined with a sense of continuity in one's life will be predictive of "successful aging." If, however, one wishes to understand the world as experienced by old people, some form of symbolic interaction theory is applicable. To explain the status of old people in a given society might involve the principles of exchange theory, whereas continuities in aging from primates to humans would be best understood through sociobiological analysis.

Not only does the choice of theoretical perspective depend upon what the researcher wishes to know but the kinds of questions one asks also determine the type of data needed to answer them.

RESEARCH METHODS

The Link Between Theory and Research. The choice of a research strategy, or *method*, is influenced by many factors. Primary among these is the theoretical model by which the researcher has ordered the world. Today, much research is undertaken to advance professionally or is limited by time and money constraints, or done under contract to government agencies that have specific needs for information. But personal values and professional interests often combine to allow the researcher to study topics of theoretical as well as practical importance.

Ideally, a research design should be guided by a theory that predicts what the data will demonstrate if indeed the theorized relationships are correct. If the data fit the theoretical expectations, that view of the world is supported; if they do not, some revision of the theory is required. In this fashion, theory and research feed into one another, each sharpened by the insights of the other.

The theoretical model of the researcher also influences the selection of method by which to gather data. A test of disengagement or activity theory, for example, requires *interviews* with a sample of respondents who are asked about their social contacts and their feelings (often using techniques for uncovering emotions of which individuals are not always conscious).

Symbolic interaction studies will rely on *observation* or *participant-observation* techniques, where trained researchers systematically record the behavior of all participants in a setting—which clearly sets limits on the numbers of research subjects. This technique does, however, yield data that is rich with the flavor of everyday life, and careful observations often uncover patterns in relationships that are not apparent at first glance or discoverable through questioning. For instance, Stephans (1976) found a variety of social networks among the seemingly isolated residents of a single-occupancy room hotel, and Hochschild (1973) uncovered a web of helping relationships linking elderly occupants of an apartment house.

Exchange theorists are also concerned with patterned interactions, but their interest is in *why* the exchanges take place and how these are maintained: what benefits and costs are involved. Often, the explanation is developed *post facto*; that is, after the event. If the relationships exist and continue, then each participant must be receiving rewards that are judged worth the effort that each puts into the interaction. Observations, questionnaire data, and laboratory experiments are all techniques through which the exchange theorist can test the theory.

Sociobiologists use *comparative* data, drawn from other cultures and other species, to discover regularities in behavior and the persistence of traits across time and space. The anthropological literature and ethology (the study of animal behavior) have provided prime sources for this theory.

The concept of life-span development is more psychological than sociological, and data are derived from *in-depth interviews* with the same respondents at different times in their life. This research design is *longitudinal*, following the growth and development of one set of subjects. These researches are limited by the time factor and the difficulties of keeping the original sample intact. We are just now, for example, receiving data from the latest wave of interviews with subjects who were first studied as children in the 1920s and 1930s, and who are currently entering middle and old age.

There are, of course, many other theoretical perspectives in psychology and sociology. Most of these have not yet generated the research and theoretical clarification of those we have described in some detail. Freudian psychology has little to say about old age, although Freud's influence is seen in some theories concerning death and the dying individual. Behaviorists have been successful in applying the techniques of *behavior modification* to patients in institutions; through carefully planned regimens of reward and the withholding of rewards, some patients have learned to take care of themselves and others. There has been little systematic application of the Marxist/conflict tradition in gerontology, although old people are often included in the category of oppressed minorities and the powerless in modern societies.

Although ideally guided by theory, data collection has been greatly affected by the kinds of questions one can ask of old people, and the availability of older respondents. Another determinant of method is the use to which the data will be put—social workers, practitioners, and activists will expect their findings to be of use to those dealing directly with old people, and are, therefore, likely to concentrate on "social problems." Other researchers will be writing for their academic peers, and be concerned with specifying general, universal, "normal" processes.

In actuality, most research in social gerontology hews closely to the dominant methods of sociology and psychology: survey research for the former, laboratory tests for the latter. This research has produced fairly static data of a cross-sectional nature, but it is relatively simple to conduct and provides a large amount of information in a short period of time—ideal for master's theses, doctoral dissertations, and professional journal articles.[2]

Research is equally important for the undergraduate; there are few better ways to learn a subject than to do it. For this reason, we have devised a number of exercises for students. The experience of fieldwork will help you evaluate the research of others and learn what can and cannot be done well, and will also bring you into contact with old people in your community.

There are, however, a number of problems in doing research in gerontology of which you should be aware before engaging in your own data-gathering projects. Finding respondents will not be easy; establishing rapport takes time; respondents' memories or attention spans will vary greatly; your own attitudes must be examined. Above all, there are great difficulties in the accurate interpretation of the data once it is gathered. We now turn to this subject.

Problems in the Interpretation of Data. Early studies of aging and old age depended heavily on *cross-sectional data* (answers from different kinds of people at one point in time). To find out how the old and the young differed on a given trait, researchers would compare the answers of young respondents to those of old people. In many instances, the differences found were interpreted as effects of growing old, e.g., "the older the respondent the lower the score on some intelligence tests," which was then taken as evidence that cognitive faculties decline with age.

The potential fallacies in such logic became obvious to a number of sociologists and psychologists who were working somewhat independently but toward the same goal of developing techniques that could capture the unique qualities of age as a variable. First, age indexes more than years lived; it tells us when a person was born, what type of *roles* she or he is expected to assume or withdraw from, and at what particular points in the life course she or he experienced certain historical incidents (Elder, 1974). Thus, the way a person thinks or acts is affected by the unique cultural and social setting within which infancy, childhood, and adult years are experienced (*cohort* membership). An individual's attitudes and behaviors are also influenced by changes over the life course in the roles entered or given up, and as experience accumulates (life course sequences). Finally, the particular period in which the person is observed may account for their feelings and actions—as, for example, an economic depression affects wages throughout the society, or a nuclear reactor accident engenders

---

[2] At the other extreme, articles written for the popular press often oversimplify complex issues and unconsciously reinforce stereotypes—as for example, the distorted image of the Black grandmother (see Chapter 9).

a general fear of atomic energy (*period* effects). This latter consideration—current events at the time of measurement is often overlooked as an explanation of findings of historical change.

Moreover, since age is a continuous variable, arbitrary divisions of the life span can produce misleading data. Variations *within* one age range are often greater than *between* age categories, and particularly in the case of the aged. Moreover, age groups are composed of individuals who vary along other important characteristics such as sex, race, religion, ethnicity, and social class.

All studies of older people, especially those comparing the old to younger respondents, are plagued by the problem of selective survival. Over time the birth cohort loses members, so that those who remain are not necessarily representative of all in the original group. In general, individuals with the healthiest constitutions at birth, who have been well fed and well cared for, and who have had access to health facilities, will survive. To the extent that such variables are associated with social class position, many attitude comparisons do not reflect authentic differences by age alone.

The best way to find out how growing old affects the individual is to have measures from the same person throughout her or his life, i.e., longitudinal data. And unless the longitudinal study is repeated on another age cohort we cannot tell whether or not the life course data are historically unique. This could invalidate many contemporary theories of life-cycle regularities (e.g., Levinson, 1978; Sheehy, 1976).

How, then, are we ever to know whether or not attitudes change with age, or capacities for intellectual performance, and role-playing abilities? How can we ever distinguish what is the result of increasing age from what is characteristic of people who entered a society at the same time, or from traits developed as a response to the peculiar times through which one has lived? Riley, Johnson, and Foner (1972) concluded that the effects of age, cohort experience, and time of measurement are inextricably bound together, each affecting the other.

Cohort Analysis. While recognizing such limitations, there are models for the presentation of data that partially overcome these methodological pitfalls. Let us examine the design for cohort analysis (Table 1–4) that appears to be the most powerful thus far developed for studying age-related phenomena. The basic information comes from measurements taken of respondents at different ages at different points in time, either the same respondents interviewed at other times or a series of cross-section studies from different years. We can compare persons of the same age at different time periods by reading the diagonals; or people of different ages at the same time by looking at the columns; and one *cohort* over its life course by reading along the rows. Comparing one row with an-

Table 1–4. Model Table for Cohort Analysis

Birthdate of Respondents	Date of Information Gathering				
	1900	1920	1940	1960	1980
1880–1885	(20–25)	(40–45)	(60–65)	(80–85)	—
1900–1905	(0–5)	(20–25)	(40–45)	(60–65)	(80–85)
1920–1925	—	(0–5)	(20–25)	(40–45)	(60–65)
1940–1945	—	—	(0–5)	(20–25)	(40–45)
1960–1965	—	—	—	(0–5)	(20–25)

Aging → Cohort → Period (directional labels)

Numbers in cells are ages of the respondents.

other indicates something about aging and changing life-course patterns, whereas contrasts in column data indicate period differences or events affecting all the age strata. The diagonals allow us to explore cohort variation. Unfortunately it is not always easy to find data that can be analyzed in this fashion since the same questions or measurements must have been made on similar populations at a number of different time periods. The U. S. Census, archives of polling organizations, and epidemiological surveys have provided much exciting material for cohort analysis, although on somewhat restricted topics.

A fascinating example of the confusion of age and cohort variables was reported by Srole and Fischer (1978). In 1954, Srole had directed an extensive study of the mental health of people aged 20–59 living in midtown Manhattan (Srole, et al., 1962). One of the findings of this well-known project was that rates of mental impairment were higher in each successive age group. The researchers assumed from this cross-sectional study that age was somehow implicated in deteriorating psychological functioning. Srole and his colleagues would have predicted that the younger respondents in 1954 would show increased "mental morbidity" as they aged. In 1974, twenty years after the original interview, 81 percent of those who were still alive and located were reinterviewed with the same battery of mental health indicators. Although it was still true that the older the age group, the higher the percentage of mental impairment, there was *no increase*, and even a slight decrease, in the impairment rates of each birth cohort twenty years later! Contrary to predictions, mental health did *not* decline with age. While 22 percent of those aged 50–59 in 1954 were mentally impaired, only 18 percent of the same respondents showed similar impairment in 1974; and the same pattern was repeated for the other ten-year birth cohorts. With his 1974 data, Srole proceeded to compare different cohorts at the same age; that is, comparing persons aged 50–59 in 1954 with those aged 50–59 in 1974, and so on. For every comparison, among the four age groups, on measures of mental impairment, self-rated health, and psychological maturity, the findings were the same: the more recent the birth cohort, the lower the percentage of impairment, of self-rated illness, and of intolerance. Clearly, it was the experience of birth cohorts and not life stage or age *per se* that accounted for these findings. In a further analysis, Srole and Fischer divided the cohorts into male and female segments. Almost all the improvement in mental functioning was due to changes among women; not only was each entering cohort of women better off on all these measures, but through time the women were more likely to improve their mental function than were men. In other words, the cohort differences occurred in one segment only, a sure sign that one is not dealing with the effects of age (which should affect both sexes similarly at the same ages). In presenting this paper to the Gerontological Society, Srole honestly acknowledged the fallacy of his having assumed an age difference from cross-sectional data. The 1974 findings indicate that each successive birth cohort is better equipped to cope with life's contingencies, and that it is among women that threats to mental well-being are increasingly successfully resisted.

Summary. This introductory chapter has dealt with the two major components of the study of aging: why the subject has emerged as an academic specialty and as a matter of great national interest, and how the gerontological enterprise is carried out. The number of old people, their proportion of the population, and their loss of sources of power and control in a modern society have combined to make old age a problematic aspect of the life course. How are health and income needs to be met? How are individuals expected to live out these final years? What can one do to prepare for one's own old age? Although these are all very personal questions, when they are shared by large numbers they become social problems, the solutions to which become defined as public issues.

To answer these questions and to guide public policy we need accurate and carefully gathered information. Research is being funded and carried out today on all aspects of aging and being old. An enormous body of data has been accumulated, but the numbers require interpretation. The interplay between theory and method that guided the original research design is also crucial to understanding the findings. We have been able to give only a hint of the enormous complexities of this process. Above all, it is important to bear in mind that research findings are often very limited, applying to only a particular population at a particular historical moment. The techniques of cohort analysis are only now being perfected and adopted by researchers. Social gerontology itself is about to come of age.

Research Exercises

As a necessary first step to the other exercises in this book, students should conduct a preliminary survey of the community.

1. Find out how many persons 65 + live in the city, town, or county where your college/university is located. This should be a matter of record from the most recent decennial census, but since the 1970 enumeration took place a decade ago, an attempt should be made to find out about migration patterns over the past ten years.

2. Contact the local Area Agency on Aging (sometimes called the Office on Aging) for a list of programs for the aged, and of clubs and centers where old people gather regularly.

3. Prepare a list of nursing homes or other institutions with large numbers of older patients. Boardinghouses and residential hotels also frequently house the elderly.

After these subpopulations have been identified, you can begin to plan research designs involving any or all of them:

Survey Research. Once you know how many old people are in the community, you can design two-stage area samples, based on the proportions of persons 65 + in each census tract. This procedure is described at the end of Chapter 2. However, before going into the field, a survey instrument must be designed. You should begin thinking about the type of information you want to gather, and how to word your questions. The interview schedule will need to be pretested and revised several times before being taken into the field.

Snowball Samples. Less representative but easier to find than a probability sample, the "snowball" sample can start with a group of participants in a senior center, for example, and then move on to friends and friends of friends. The questionnaire designed for survey research could be used, but the snowball sample affords the opportunity for a more intimate type of interviewing than is possible with respondents on whose door a stranger has knocked. Therefore, you might consider asking fewer but more personal questions. Students should have some training in the administration of in-depth interviews, and, of course, pretest is essential.

Observation. Choosing strategic sites for observation is a challenging experience in itself. Where can a younger person sit unnoticed to observe the everyday interactions of old people? And what should be observed? Checklists must be carefully drawn, and where possible, unobtrusive recording techniques must be perfected. There are also ethical considerations; observations are a form of eavesdropping. But if the subjects are aware that they are being observed, will this subtly alter their behavior? These are important questions that must be considered before research is undertaken. In general, those whom you observe should be given some idea of what is happening and the opportunity to see and comment upon the results of the research. The object of this exercise, after all, is to gather information that will be of some value to you and to them.

If fieldwork exercises cannot be conducted, there are many other types of research: secondary analysis of census data; library searches in historical and anthropological sources; content analysis of magazines, television, novels, and other cultural artifacts; family case studies; and oral histories. One or more of these is suggested at the end of each chapter.

Discussion Questions

In what ways is social gerontology similar to women's studies or Black studies? And in what ways is the study of aging unique?

Under what circumstances could the average age of the population in modern societies be lowered? How likely are these circumstances?

Which of the several theoretical perspectives discussed in this chapter would you use to explain what goes on at a senior center to study retirement, or to understand intergenerational contact?

A national poll reports the following percentages of persons replying that they are "very satisfied" with their marriages:

Age	Per Cent
Under 20	40
20–34	50
35–49	55
50–64	66
65+	72

Can we conclude that people are more satisfied with their marriages as they grow older?

2

Toward a Sociology of Age

————◆◆————

One consequence of the trends described in Chapter 1—the increased visibility of the aged, public concern with their needs, and the development of academic gerontology—has been a renewed interest in *age* itself as a sociological variable. A *sociology of age* embraces more than the fact of age as an attribute of individuals; it deals with age as an element of social structure, as well. Whereas social gerontology focuses on growing old and the state of being an old person, a sociology of age asks such questions as: "How is the society divided into age groups, what is expected of persons of given ages, what roles are available, and how do social actors (role players) acquire or relinquish age-based roles? In what ways are the answers to these questions historically grounded; that is, influenced by a particular pattern of events in that society— wars, famine, industrialization, or emigration, for example? And how is biological aging translated into a succession of social roles over the life course?"

In this chapter we present a series of *models*—ideas about the way in which the elements of a sociology of aging are linked together, in order to place the discussion of aging in a broad but unified context. *Conceptual models* are guesses about the process at work in the real world, and must eventually be tested against the evidence of research. At this moment, the sociology of age is in the stage of theory construction

and self-definition. This chapter presents several schematic representations of the important dimensions of a sociology of age—societal, cul-
tural/historical, and life course.

The Theory of Age Stratification

The most systematic analysis of the links between age and social systems
appears in *Aging and Society*, Vol. 3: *A Sociology of Age Stratification*
(1972) by Matilda White Riley, Marilyn E. Johnson, and Anne Foner.
The theory of age stratification proposes that it is theoretically and prac-
tically fruitful to think of members of a society as being stratified along
the dimension of age in much the same fashion as we assume that attributes of social class divide people into categories or *strata* based upon
how much power, prestige, or wealth they command. In this perspective,
age becomes a basis of control over resources through age-linked *statuses*
(positions available to persons of certain ages), and inequality between
age strata occurs because age is used as a criterion of entry or exit from
potentially powerful social statuses.

SOCIETAL LEVEL PROCESSES

Age enters into social structure at two important points: the population
of any society is composed of its age strata, and social systems are composed of statuses awaiting role players of certain ages. The upper part of
Figure 2–1 diagrams the elements and processes operating at the level of
the society as a whole: the formation of age strata of role players, the
rules governing entry and exit from roles, and the number and types of
roles generated in the various areas of social activity.

Formation of the Age Strata (Element A in Figure 2–1). Although
originally a matter of accident and individual choices, the combination
of births, deaths, and migration patterns at any time period produces for
each society a certain number of people in each age stratum. The age
strata makes up the population pyramids of societies at any given historical moment. Figure 2–2 illustrates the changes in the demographic
profile in our country over the twentieth century. The longer the bar, the
more individuals are in that age group.

Each birth cohort (all those born during a specific period) varies in its
original composition and will change over time as a result of differing
rates of mortality by sex, social class, race, and ethnicity. Cohort members encounter historically grounded opportunities and barriers for filling
social roles as they move through the life course. For example, work roles
depend on the state of the economy; when the economic sector is ex-

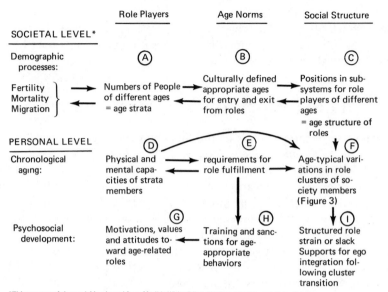

Figure 2-1. Multi-Level Model of Age Stratification Processes.
*This segment of the model is adapted from Matilda White Riley, Marilyn Johnson, and Anne Foner, *Aging and Society*, Vol. 3. New York: Russell Sage Foundation, 1972, p. 9.

panding, people enter the labor force earlier and can move to better jobs, allowing Blacks and women to experience expanded opportunities. As another example, roles in the family sector are influenced by wars, the economy, and changes in divorce laws, among other factors. Therefore, the cumulative experience of the cohort—its fertility, marriage rates, political orientation, labor force participation, and the like—must be placed in its historical context.

Even though all members of a society will experience a given event, the effect will vary by age (as well as sex, race, ethnicity, and social status within the cohort). For example, war has a greater impact on young adults than on older people, and a famine has a greater impact on adult females than on children or adult males (who receive the food that the women forgo). And because each cohort lives through a different slice of history than any other, the flow of cohort members through the system of roles brings change; that is, each cohort modifies the social structure because of its unique experience. Subsequent cohorts are not only different in themselves but move through a changed structure of social roles.

Age Structure of Roles (Element C in Figure 2-1). Age also becomes an element of social structure through its use as a criterion for entry and exit from role-playing opportunities in the institutional spheres of the

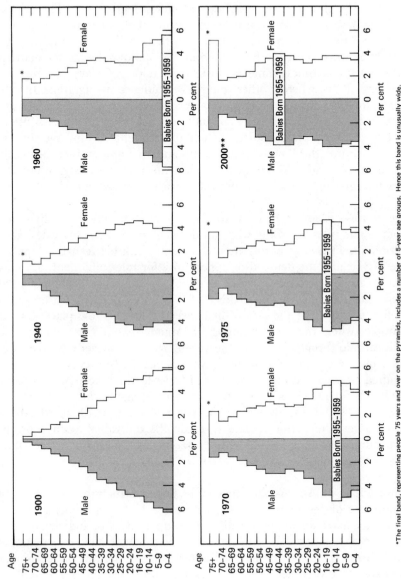

Figure 2–2. Age structure of the U.S. Population in the 20th Century. From: Population Reference Bureau, Washington, D.C.

*The final band, representing people 75 years and over on the pyramids, includes a number of 5-year age groups. Hence this band is unusually wide.
**Assuming a Total Fertility Rate of 2.1, slightly improved mortality and current levels of legal immigration.

society: the economic, political, religious, educational, and family systems. In our society, for instance, laws regulate ages for employment, voting, office-holding, marriage, and criminal responsibility (including a number of acts that are offenses *only* when committed by persons under age 16).

Thus, at the societal level people are arranged in *age strata* (element A) and there is also the *age structure of roles* (element C). The two are probably rarely in balance because of events that occur in the world at large. In a period of economic depression there will be more people than jobs; after wars, there are fewer men of the appropriate age for marriage; and, at various times, some countries will undergo heavy out-migration of young adults, whereas other countries experience in-migration. In other words, the "fit" between *role players* (people able to assume certain positions in the society) and the availability of such roles in the institutional spheres is always problematic, a source of instability in any society. One way to control the flow of role players and to improve the balance between people and positions is to modify the rules regarding appropriate ages for entering or leaving major social roles—the *age norms*.

Age Norms (Element B in Figure 2–1). Every society has a division of labor: some rules regarding who can do what tasks. In many cases, age is a criterion. These age norms are a connecting link between the supply of role players and the demand or opportunity for role fulfillment. Since age norms can be altered more easily than, say, birthrates or economic cycles, they often become the mechanism that reduces potential disorder and conflict arising from the lack of fit between roles and role players, as, for example, when the restless young of America were given an enlarged political role through lowering the voting age. As another example, when the economy cannot absorb young job applicants, the level of education required for entry into the labor force is raised, which keeps young people in schools for longer periods. These changes in age norms at the societal level are a stabilizing device; at the personal level, as discussed later in this chapter, the norms operate to guide the individual's education and preparation for filling age-linked roles, serving as a means of *social control* over behavior.

Implications of Age As an Element in Social Structure. To stress the importance of age in the social structure would be an empty exercise if it did not make an important difference in the lives of individuals. As a member of a particular birth cohort, a person will have experiences at given historical moments that will either enlarge, narrow, or recapitulate the experience of other cohorts, thus accounting for relative stability or change in social systems. Generation gaps are probably less a matter of intrafamily relationships than of differences in cohort experience. In simple societies, almost by definition, the rate of social change is slow; the life course of successive cohorts may vary only slightly, and lacking outside sources of new traits, there is a limited probability of internally induced change.[1]

For technologically complex societies in close contact with a variety of other cultures, the rate of change from both inside and outside the society is increasingly rapid. The life course of cohort members is shaped by these changes, and the cohort itself becomes the vehicle for social change as its members modify the institutional spheres bringing new values, definitions, and capacities to their roles (Riley and Waring, 1978).

As one example of how cohort formation influences the life course of individuals, let us look at the effect of such a simple variable as the number of persons in an age group. It is commonly believed that the remarkable upward mobility of young men during the late 1940s and 1950s testified to high levels of achievement motivation (especially for second-generation immigrants taking advantage of the American educational system). A cohort analysis of the same phenomenon would emphasize the fact that these men were products of a very small birth contingent who were able to take advantage of government-sponsored higher education at the close of World War II, and who entered the labor force at a time of economic expansion. It would be very strange had they *not* flourished. Conversely, the young adults now entering the job market are members of the largest birth cohort in our history, and the failure of many to equal, much less surpass, the success of their fathers is often interpreted as a "softening" of achievement goals. In reality, their mobility potential is inhibited by sheer numbers on the one hand, and the relatively stagnant economy on the other.[2]

Thus, the sociology of age must deal not only with the effects of social systems on aging individuals but also with the independent effects of age stratification on the social system. The emergent academic specialization of age stratification promises to be an exciting new frontier in sociology. But the current interest of most gerontologists centers on the bottom half of Figure 2–1 and on the condition of today's old people.

PERSONAL PROCESSES

The lower segment of Figure 2–1 describes two sets of events that occur as the individual ages: *chronological aging*, with its biological manifestations of increasing and then decreasing capacities; and *psychosocial de-*

[1] These statements are comparative, contrasting preliterate with industrial Western societies. In fact, there is considerable evidence of social change in simple societies, but the rate of change, at least before their discovery by anthropologists, was undoubtedly extremely slow (but see Foner and Kertzer, 1978).

[2] This lack of fit between institutions and role players is brilliantly analyzed by Joan Waring (1975) as the problem of "disordered cohort flow," which in turn creates pressures for adjustments at both the individual and societal levels.

velopment, the series of developmental tasks that provide an opportunity for personality change throughout the life course. The two events are not separate; to be a given age is to be assumed to have certain abilities that are also components of developmental challenges such as identity formation in adolescence, maturity through marriage and parenthood, courage in widowhood, or dignity in dying. Conversely, successes and failures in these crucial growth experiences can affect the manner in which a person ages.

Chronological Aging.   The aging of the organism refers to the growth and subsequent decline of physical and mental abilities (Element D) associated with the performance of required roles. Throughout infancy and childhood, and often into young adulthood, physical strength and intellectual skills are on a generally upward course. Although there is considerable debate over the degree and rate of declines in functioning, adulthood is typically experienced as a plateau period, followed by varying declines in vigor, quickness, sensory sharpness, and other capacities that are described fully in Chapter 4. Our concern in this section is with the relationship of physiological changes to role performance.

In this regard two general points should be made. First, biology is not necessarily an unchanging foundation of individual development. We know that certain aspects of the environment such as diet and public health affect average height and weight as well as life expectancy. Second, because of these factors the link between physiological capacity and role assumption may be *more* tenuous now than at earlier times. For example, the average age of first menstruation (menarche) has been lowered from 16 in the last century to about 12 today. The evidence on menopause is less clear but its onset seems to be occurring at later ages. Thus, we are experiencing the paradox of an increase in the span of *potential* fertility while the period of *actual* childbearing for American women has contracted to an average of five years in their midtwenties. Social behavior in humans thus appears to be increasingly freed from its biological base, contrary to the contentions of sociobiologists.

That most women and men are now quite likely to live beyond the ages of productivity and reproductivity is one of the reasons why old age has become a problem for individuals and social systems. The age norms (Element E) that govern role entry and exit can no longer be clearly tied to the state of the organism, and must depend upon social convention for legitimacy. Thus, retirement is justified as a means of opening up jobs for younger workers rather than by the incapacity of the older worker.

In societies where achievement is believed to have replaced ascription in the assignment of social statuses, arbitrary age norms are likely to generate opposition, as evidenced by the movement to end mandatory retirement rules. Another interesting deviation from age norms has been reported by Presser (1975) with respect to remarriage: second and third marriages are more likely to be characterized by broader discrepancies in age between spouses than at first marriage, including many more instances of wives being older than their husbands.

There are, of course, roles for which age is irrelevant (king or queen), and those for which increased age is a prerequisite (soothsayer, mother superior), and those for which youth was once thought to be essential (long-distance runner). In general, however, we are socialized to a limiting notion of appropriate ages for dating, marriage, childbearing, working, and retirement, and these are tied, however loosely, to assumptions about the capacity of the organism as well as to propriety.

As the individual ages and becomes qualified or disqualified for certain roles, the combination of statuses occupied at any stage of life varies (Element F). Indeed, life stages may be defined as the cluster of roles typically played by persons of different ages. The age structure of roles at the societal level is reflected in the role cluster of aging persons (Figure 2–3). A description of these clusters, and the analysis of transitions between life course stages, is the story of psychosocial development.

Psychosocial Development. Moving from one age stratum to another is accompanied by socialization to age-appropriate behavior ("Big boys don't cry", "Old women lose interest in sex"). Primary socialization, which occurs in the early years, is thought to lay a motivational base for subsequent conformity to role expectations, and many believe that these original orientations to people and roles form a core personality (Element G). There is, however, sufficient evidence of attitudinal and value change throughout the life course to suggest that many personality features are relatively flexible, and that the expression of any one trait is often constrained by the requirements of other roles in an age-related cluster. What this means is that "personality" may be a kaleidoscopic series of role adaptations, some continuous with the past, others representing new adjustments. Further, if the mix of roles varies by life stage, then personality change is built into aging. This is especially possible at those points where major roles are acquired or relinquished or realigned—the transition periods of the life course. Chapter 5 explores the personality changes associated with the transitions of later life.

Age Norms (Element H). Whereas age norms function to control the flow of role players, they are also prescriptions for behavior, expectations shared by members of a society concerning what people of a given age ought to be doing and how they should comport themselves (Neugarten,

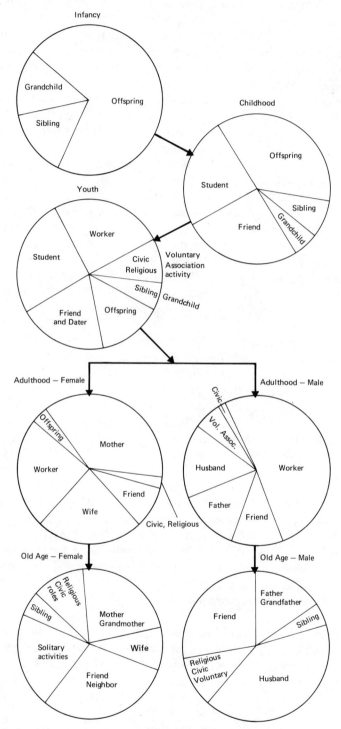

Figure 2–3. Life Course Series of Typical Role Clusters.

Moore and Lowe, 1965). The expression "to act one's age" means precisely to conform to age-based role expectations. Others in the social network will give approval for conformity and express disappointment over failure to act one's age (Riley, Foner, Hess, and Toby, 1968). Particularly important, again, are the pressures exerted at transition points, and whether or not the individual is "on time" in making the required changes in the role cluster. For example, school-age boys who want to cling to their mothers, or older women in miniskirts are both "off time," as are the unmarried thirty-year old, the young widow, or the middle-aged roué.

The Structure of Roles (Element I). At the level of psychosocial functioning, problems often arise from a lack of fit between age-related energies and opportunities to perform the role. Looking first at any single role, actors must be both willing (have the capacities and motivations) to perform and able (having the opportunity to assume the role) to do so. This linkage between social structure and personality yields the following property space for role orientations at any life stage, but has special relevance for old age:

		Able (Can Assume Role)	
		+	−
Willing	+	a	b
(May assume role)	−	c	d

This scheme allows us to predict selective disengagement and the attitude of the actor toward role involvements. Cell a, for instance, describes those fully engaged in a role; cell b, those who are probably unhappy at being denied the opportunity; cell c, those who voluntarily relinquish a role that is still open to them; and cell d contains the voluntary disengagers whose capacities are consonant with the available roles.

But role performances do not occur in isolation; much depends upon the other relationships in the cluster. As Figure 2–3 illustrates, the complexity of clusters varies with the maturation of the organism. The balance between an individual's role-playing capacities and the demands upon these energies from role partners can lead to structured "strain" or "slack." *Role strain* is a familiar sociological concept (Goode, 1960; Wilensky, 1962), evidenced in a number of recent studies which have found that people experience lowered morale and life satisfaction in middle age (see Miller, 1976, for a full review). Such strain may underlie a pervasive sense of "midlife crisis" among American males (Brim, 1976). The concept of *role slack* has been less systematically analyzed, although underdemanded role-playing capacities could account for both the turbulence of late adolescence and the discomfort of many older people.

The Historical Dimension

When we speak of age as a variable in social structure we mean primarily the use of age as a criterion for allocation to social roles. Through these roles the individual gains access to power, property (wealth), and prestige (measured by deference from others). Age strata, therefore, vary in their command over the scarce resources of the group. Considering the enormous variety of cultures and the thousands of years of recorded history, it is not surprising that age, aging, and old age have been treated in many different ways. At the risk of oversimplification, Figure 2–4 represents a model of cultural development from simple to complex social systems. The nature of social life undergoes change as new *modes of subsistence* replace technologically simpler means of exploiting the environment. Major shifts in the economic sphere allow more people to live together permanently and lead to greater division of labor, and thus to increasingly complex social systems. These developments, in turn, affect the process of aging, the meaning of age, and the status of old people.

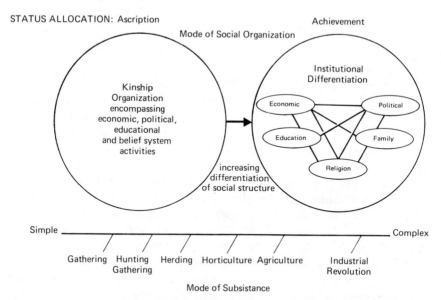

Figure 2–4. A Model of Sociocultural Development. From Hess, Beth B., "A Sociology of Age: What Would it Look Like?" in Mildred Seltzer, Harvey Sterns, and Tom Hickey (Eds.), *Gerontology in Higher Education*, Belmont, CA: Wadsworth Publishing Co., 1978, p. 205.

The Study of Aging

CULTURAL DEVELOPMENT

Patterns of norms and behaviors developed over time to ensure the survival of social groups are called *institutions,* and sociologists have typically described five of these: economic activity, political behavior (order keeping), family formation and relationships, religious beliefs and rituals, and educational tasks (socialization). When faced with the need to solve problems of subsistence, order, reproduction, solidarity, and norm transmission—the essentials for survival—social groups (families, clans, tribes, societies) work out their unique solutions through trial and error, and these successful activities become *social norms* or the "way it is done" for that group. As can be seen in Figure 2–4 we have distinguished simple from complex societies by the degree to which the institutionalized arrangements for fulfilling necessary tasks are carried out as family-based responsibilities or have become separated from the kinship matrix, i.e., *social structural differentiation.* As the food supply becomes more plentiful and secure, more people can remain together over long periods of time. The size of the permanent group and the technology of providing food and shelter and security lead to division of labor, specialization of tasks, and ultimately to the emergence of institutional spheres that are no longer based on kinship or controlled by family members—separate political, educational, economic, and religious areas of activity. The family also changes, and so, therefore, does the status of elders. The shift from an agricultural to an industrial economy is especially important to understanding the status of old people today.

The linearity of Figure 2–4, however, obscures another important process: The U-shaped curve of *familism* of Figure 2–5 (Winch and Blumberg, 1968). Familism refers to the dominance of kin-based considerations in the lives of family members.

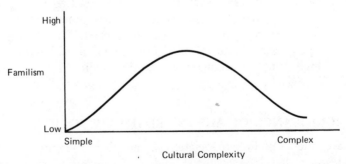

Figure 2–5. Familism and Societal Complexity. Adapted from Robert Winch and Rae Lesser Blumberg, "Societal Complexity and Familial Organization," in R. F. Winch and L. W. Goodman (Eds.), *Selected Studies in Marriage and the Family,* 3rd Edition, New York: Holt, Rinehart and Winston, 1968.

Contrary to much popular sociology, although kinship is the basic organizing principle of simple societies, family controls are not total or necessarily oppressive. Among gatherers and hunters, the nuclear unit of the married pair and their dependent children are relatively free of obligations to other family members, with living arrangements determined by the need to find new sources of game and plants. Where there is little property to pass on, and minimal social distinctions, the power of parents to place children in the stratification system is limited. Therefore, a considerable degree of freedom from family control is found in simple societies.

In horticultural economies, a common pattern is *matrilineage,* where descent is reckoned through the female line (although the mother's brother has ultimate authority). When the groom must also move to his wife's family land (*matrilocality*), he becomes a stranger in her group; under these circumstances power within the marriage is frequently egalitarian. However, hoe agriculture is soon replaced by the plow and possibly by draft animals, and with these comes *patrilineage* and *patrilocality*—male lines of descent and living with the family of the groom—and, ultimately, *patriarchy*—male dominance, in its fullest development. The link between property and patriarchy is almost universal.

Plow agriculture involves large landholdings, domesticated animals, permanent houses and storage places, agricultural surpluses, and the products received in trade. In other words, there is private property, something of value to bequeath to heirs, advantages to be gained from arranging marriages, and important statuses to be conferred on offspring. Under these circumstances, the extended household as a basis for concentrations of power, goods, and labor becomes both necessary and common in societies that are now stratified by social class. The land and its products, once thought of as belonging to the community, are now controlled by the heads of extended households. When we speak of the shift from traditional to modern forms of social life, we are contrasting this agricultural model to the industrial phase of economic development. However, high familism continues to characterize the upper class in modern society as long as property is held or controlled through families. There is also evidence of high familism among the very poor, where resources must be pooled for survival.

THE SIGNIFICANCE OF AGE IN PRELITERATE SOCIETIES

Age Categories.   Preliterate societies vary greatly in the number of discrete age categories that are recognized, and in the degree to which members of an age group interact exclusively with age-mates (*age grading*). Eisenstadt (1956) argues that peer groups are essential in adolescence in those societies in which the indulgent care of children in the family contrasts sharply with impersonal standards of achievement in the larger society. In these cases, the peer group serves as an intermediary social network in which tolerant acceptance by family members is replaced by the interaction of equals judged by general standards, thus preparing the young person for the larger world outside the family.

Most of the anthropological literature on age grading has focused on the transition from childhood to adulthood, a problem-filled passage in many societies at all stages of development. But the recent upsurge of interest in old age and the sociology of age have generated studies of *later life* transitions in preliterate as well as modern societies (Foner and Kertzer, 1978; Stewart, 1977). Moreover, such studies have raised the possibility of intergenerational hostility.

Age Conflict. Obviously, the entry of young males into positions of social power must be accompanied to some extent by a decline in authority of those who previously occupied those statuses, although relatively short life spans probably minimized problems of succession. Conversely, females in many societies *gain* power and prestige through the transition from mother to mother-in-law (at least over the daughter-in-law). The societal and generational conflicts that attend major life stage transitions are not necessarily minimized by rigid age grading (Foner and Kertzer, 1978) any more than when left to the "normal" course of aging in the extended family (LeVine, 1965). When elders must die before juniors benefit from inheritance, there is bound to be intergenerational tension, feelings that may be intensified by the sexual jealousies that Freudians consider to be basic to father-son relations (LeVine, 1965). Avoidance behavior and other patterns of formality between members of adjacent generations are the techniques most frequently devised for handling these tensions in preliterate societies. Another arrangement, characteristic of agricultural societies in the historical period, is the *stem family* in which one son (the eldest, typically) assumes control of the family property in return for maintaining the aged parents in a part of the house or in their own smaller home on the estate (see P. Laslett, 1976).

Care of Elders. The provision of care for an aged parent, which many believed to be one of the positive features of all family systems until recently, has actually been less than an ironclad guarantee. Much depends, as already noted, upon the rules of inheritance and also upon the subsistence level of the group. Turnbull (1970) has described in ghastly detail the dramatic change in Ik families wrought by famine: when resources were plentiful, intergenerational sharing and solidarity characterized the tribe; when the food supply was drastically reduced, both infants and old people were ruthlessly denied sustinance. There is also the example of the Eskimo aged who, although not necessarily set adrift on an Arctic ice floe, expect little from their offspring and make few demands for care.[3] In general, however, the overwhelming importance of kinship relationships throughout prehistory and in agricultural societies has probably ensured the elderly of at least minimal care, a pattern that sociobiologists would argue has served to ensure survival of lineage genes through an understanding that care of the child will be reciprocated in the parents' old age.

STATUS OF OLD PEOPLE

In all but the most impoverished environments, throughout most of human history, elder males have been able to claim positions of power and prestige through their family-based control over property: weapons, land, knowledge, and sons or daughters with whom to contract alliances with other families. Historical religions have further reinforced the status of older men. Émile Durkheim saw belief systems as reflections of the social order; what was really being worshiped was the society itself. The injunction to Honor thy father and mother, to follow the rules laid down by an authoritative priesthood, and to perceive God as a "Father" not only reflect the patriarchal social order of traditional society but serve to socialize junior family members to *filial piety*, the respect and deference owed to a father (or uncle).

This type of authority is strongest in agricultural societies, and begins to wane with the introduction of the factory system and the social relationships of industrialism. We avoid the extensive debate over exactly what constitutes modernization and whether or not it is the cause or effect of industrialization. We have already noted the fragmenting of extended households in the preindustrial period in Western Europe. Whatever transformation was occurring in the family system was soon to be accelerated by the development of the factory, and was later mirrored by the rise of parliamentary government. Max Weber has related these shifts to the profound ideological challenge of Protestant individualism, and Karl Marx believed them to be the requirements of an emergent capitalist class. The important point here is that institutional spheres are *interdependent*; major change in one area reverberates throughout the whole social order.

Table 2–1 summarizes the shifts that have affected the status of old people in the major institutional spheres in modern industrial societies as compared with the traditional agricultural patterns (see also, Shorter, 1975, and Fischer, 1977).

[3] It was this interesting piece of anthropology that doomed a series of federally sponsored social science textbooks for schoolchildren; parents did not feel that this was the type of knowledge to which their children should be exposed; legislators were aghast at the implications of such an illustration of family life.

Table 2–1. Institutional Spheres and Historical Change

	Traditional	*Modern Industrial*
Economic Roles	Owner of land or trade that can be handed on to heirs Experience more valuable than technical competence Social class placement ascribed	Employee, subject to mandatory retirement and pensions Unable to pass along occupational status Recent knowledge and skills more marketable than experience
Family	Control over mate selection Strong kinship obligation Control over inheritance Family as public institution Call on kin for aid, help	Free mate selection Family obligations attenuated more voluntary than not Privatized family life Norm of generational independence Other institutions available for aid, service, etc.
Political	Power accrues with age through control over alliances, and authority over other family members	Achievement-oriented, universalistic norms of political competence
Education	Observation, on-the-job sources of knowledge Elderly as walking encyclopedias	Increasingly longer periods of formal training required Obsolescence of knowledge
Religion	Age confers authority, both from life experience and nearness to the next world	Religion still seen as refuge for aged, and an area in which they may excel
Health/ Welfare	Average life expectancy of four decades Dependent upon reciprocity of kin in times of need	Life expectancies of seven decades, with increasing advantages to women (though greater probability of long widowhood) Public provision for income and health care

Adapted from Hess, Beth B., "A Sociology of Age: What Would It Look Like?" in Mildred Seltzer, Harvey Sterns, and Tom Hickey (Eds.), *Gerontology in Higher Education*. Belmont, CA: Wadsworth Publishing Co., 1978, p. 209.

In Part Three the consequences of modernization in the various institutional spheres are described, but it is apparent that few of these changes, if any, enhance the status of elders.

As will be discussed in Chapter 3, modernization opens the way for junior members of the family to find work and marriage partners without the intervention of elders. Consequently, the power of family heads declines, with a commensurate loss of prestige.

There is evidence that the life course, with its typical age-based role clusters, has undergone subtle changes with modernization. The *meanings* attached to life's stages, as well as the *norms* for entry and exit, have changed. Complexity of social structure is reflected in complexity of roles, singly and in combination. We now turn to a consideration of the life course.

Age Structure and the Life Course

This section pulls together the various themes developed in the preceding pages, placing the study of America's aged in its broader frame, so that we may look to the future with a deeper understanding of the past.

CONSTRUCTION OF LIFE STAGES

If the basic thrust of cultural and societal evolution has been toward increasing specialization and complexity in social structure, a similar process has been occurring with respect to the life course. Today we recognize a number of life-course divisions, each of which has become a field of intensive study by behavioral scientists: childhood, adolescence, young adulthood, mature adulthood, and old age.[4] Such categorization makes sense only if real differences are associated with being at one stage rather than another, such as differences in physiological capacity, access to social roles, and behavior and psychological functioning. Since aging is a continuum, age categories are culturally defined divisions of an ongoing process. That is, life stages are *socially constructed* and not "inevitable" or "natural" (Rader, 1978). But every society has certain tasks to be accomplished, and assigning these tasks on the basis of age, especially when physical capacities are central to their performance, is an extremely efficient mechanism.

Almost all societies have, at the very least, distinguished between adults and nonadults, or, more precisely, between individuals who are deemed capable or not of successfully filling adult roles. The well-known *rites of passage* are public ceremonies signifying this status transformation. Usually applied to males, the rituals mark the end of childhood and the

---

[4] As the typical life span increases and as different cohorts reflect the rate of social change, even these broad categories require refinement. Child psychologists now distinguish the psyche of preschoolers from that of schoolchildren or children who are immediately prepubertal. We recognize an early and late adolescence, with age 15 as a rough line of demarcation. And, as discussed later, there may be stages within adulthood, as well as the important distinction by Neugarten (1974) between the "young-old" (55–74) and the "old-old" (75+).

assumption of adult responsibilities, often involving painful trials and mutilations attesting to one's manhood. Comparable ceremonies for females are rare. Whereas the advent of menarche signals potential fertility, the menstrual discharge is frequently associated with negative forces, and the young female is shunned or otherwise stigmatized. But regardless of the specific treatment, puberty is frequently recognized as a major life-stage transition.[5] So, also, in varying degrees, are marriage, birth, and death.

Beyond these ritual moments, the celebrations of which vary enormously, societies differ in the rigidity of age grading as a mechanism for controlling the flow of role players. In modern societies, the importance of individual achievement should reduce the impact of ascribed characteristics. Ironically, the very diversity of status determinants in complex societies often leads to using a *master status* in order to "place" people. Age or sex (and, in some societies, race), as obvious physical attributes can then become major mechanisms of role allocation by simplifying judgments of social worth and capacities amid the array of other characteristics such as ethnicity, education, occupation, religion, and income.

AGE STRATA AND THE LIFE COURSE

The age stratification system described in the first part of this chapter is composed of persons who occupy age-linked social statuses. The succession of age-based role clusters is commonly viewed as composing a set of *life stages*. Central to both age stratification and life-course perspectives is the assumption that individuals who share cohort membership or life stage are similar to one another in ways that set them off from members of other age/life-stage categories.

These two aspects of age grading are somewhat independent, and each is influenced by history in particular ways. Moreover, the strata are seen cross-sectionally, whereas the stages are longitudinally linked. Figure 2–6 illustrates this crucial difference.

Age strata represent birth cohorts, the size of which are determined by fertility, age-specific mortality, and in- or out-migration. All three of these processes are influenced by other forces: e.g., birthrates follow the business cycle; migration patterns reflect economic and political events; and death rates are sensitive to famine, war, and public health factors. Occupants of age strata are also at particular life stages, defined by the cluster of social statuses that are normally and normatively assigned to persons of given ages. The age norms prescribing appropriate behaviors are also influenced by history. Therefore, membership in a given age group has different

[5] Ariès (1962), however, notes the absence of transitions to adulthood in medieval Europe, children being perceived as miniature adults.

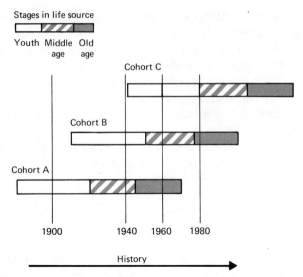

Stages in life source

Youth Middle Old
       age   age

Cohort C

Cohort B

Cohort A

1900   1940 1960 1980

History

Figure 2–6. Processes of Cohort Formation and Aging. From Matilda White Riley, Marilyn Johnson, and Anne Foner, *Aging and Society, Vol. 3.* New York: Russell Sage Foundation, 1972, p. 10.

social meanings through time. For example, teenagers in the Great Depression were expected to contribute to the family income where possible; today they are expected to remain in school until they are suitably trained; in the first instance adulthood was conferred early, in the latter, it is delayed.

DIFFERENTIATION OF THE LIFE COURSE

That conceptions of age differences are historically grounded has been illustrated by Ariès' (1962) social history of childhood. The idea that the child is a distinctly different kind of person than the adult emerges rather late in Western history. Ariès implies that a new way of thinking about childhood was responsible for the fairly recent creation of a child's world of experience, separate from that of adults, in their own part of the home and identified by particular clothing and activities. It could also be argued that the emergence of the Post-Reformation private household, a lessened need for child labor, lowered rates of infant mortality, and the emotional relationships that characterize the modern family led to the new conception of childhood (see Shorter, 1976). In either case, we are dealing with reciprocal causes and effects in the institutional spheres.

More novel than the discovery of childhood is the recent recognition of "adolescence" as a qualitatively unique stage of life (Musgrove, 1964) to be followed by "studentry" (Parsons and Platt, 1972). As the period between the end of childhood and the beginning of adulthood becomes greatly elongated in mid-twentieth-century America, young people in an essentially normless (or *anomic*) situation worked out adaptations to their special conditions of existence—a set of values, behaviors, and artifacts that ultimately become the youth culture of adolescence and college age. The new life-styles are subsequently seen as expressing a distinct life stage.

In the past few decades old age has also become a unique life course stage. The critical mass of old people is one factor; another is the relative *anomie*, just as in adolescence, of rolelessness. Although young people have yet to assume important statuses, the aged have typically outlived productive and reproductive roles. Up to the 1930s there simply were not that many persons in this situation to warrant thinking in terms of a distinct life stage. Today, when faced with the necessity to adapt to changing conditions of living, the aged are developing their own norms and customs and consciousness, i.e., what many would call a proper *subculture of aging* (Rose, 1965).

Actually, old age is not the most recent life course stage to be "discovered" or defined as presenting unique problems of adaptation. Once youth and old age are so considered, the middle years become more distinct in comparison. What was once thought to be an undifferentiated adulthood is now divided into early, middle, and late periods (like the Stone Age). There are conferences, journal articles, and television programs devoted to such topics as "women at midlife" and "male menopause."

Not only is the life course divided differently from one historical epoch to another but the content of the stages also undergoes variation and elaboration. Life-span developmental psychology is concerned with the definition of the emotional and cognitive changes associated with the succession of life stages. But it is the addition or subtraction of social roles that typically initiates the developmental challenge and the need to reorganize personality traits and orientations around the new cluster of roles. This raises again the problem of "off time" transitions and their effect on the course of personality development. Does, for instance, a middle-aged man who loses his job behave and think of himself as a man in the prime of life or as a has-been? Does the widow suddenly cease to have a sexual component in her personality? In other words, how closely are developmental tasks linked to age?

Indeed, are there life stages apart from social history? As Figure 2–6 illustrates, the life course is historically anchored. It means something different to be a youth during wartime than to be either a child at that moment or a youth at another historical period. Thus, some of the presumably fixed, built-in life stages that have been proposed by psychologists may, in reality, reflect the experience of only one cohort (Riley, 1978). As an example, will future cohorts of men have a midlife crisis, or is this a phenomenon peculiar to the cohort of primarily white males who came to adulthood in the early 1940s and experienced a series of rapid transitions: from civilian to soldier to college student to husband and father—all in the space of ten years (Winsborough, 1975)? Or, as members of the small birth cohorts of the 1920s, and parents of the large birth cohort of 1947–1957, do they bear a unique dependency burden of aged parents with few other offspring, and of educating and launching their many young adult children?

It must also be noted that no two birth cohorts age in the same way. Each begins with a unique composition, undergoes a particular history, and reaches old age in a society that has been somehow changed by that cohort's very passage through the institutional spheres. Aging in *all* its dimensions, therefore, is variable. Old age, as the final life-course stage, is affected by all that has gone before in the society and in individual lives. For these reasons great caution must be used in making sweeping generalizations about "normal" aging, especially if the current cohorts of elderly are used as examples. Today's old people are the first to comprise a sizable segment of the population, and among the first to be affected by mandatory retirement provisions, to have means of support apart from reliance on kin, and to expect the provision of a range of services. They are unique also in that they represent the last of the immigrants, of people who reached maturity between World War I and the Great Depression, and who saw their children achieve remarkable social mobility and their grandchildren grow up in the 1960s. To what extent we can use their lives as universal models of aging is debatable, but it is certainly clear that the adaptations and patterns set by these cohorts will become the norms for the old people of tomorrow.

SUBDIVIDING OLD AGE

It is becoming increasingly obvious that the aged are not a monolithic category—that old people vary from one another along a number of identifying characteristics, plus an entire lifetime of unique experience. In fact, there is greater individual variability among these 65+ than there is among people in other age strata (Ragan and Davis, 1978). This means that the range of difference on social and psychological measures is wider for older respondents than for younger ones. There are great differences between persons at the lower and the higher end of the "65+" category in income, health, living arrangements, marital status, and probability of institutionalization. Neugarten (1974) has written of the "rise of the young-old," those from age 55–75, who are neither deprived nor decrepit, and who may very well deny the label of "old person." If the trend toward early retirement continues, the youngest of the "young-old" will share the nonworking status of other elderly but very few additional characteristics.

Age 55–75 may be too broad a category, including as it does many who feel at their peak with large numbers who are aware of the short span remaining to them. It may be necessary for researchers and social activists to think of those 55–64 as in "early old age," 65–74 in "middle old age," and 75+ as being in "late old age." Each grouping has different resources at its disposal and different needs to be met, and probably different levels of functioning.

Whether or not it is accurate to speak of distinct "subcultures" evolving out of these differences is still a moot question. Subcultures are distinctive ways of adapting to the social environment, so that the basic question is, Do these various subcategories of old people have a different experience of life? Or, as Neugarten and Hagestad (1976) ask, Is our society becoming more age-graded? They note trends that reinforce age-segregation but other clues suggest a relaxation of age-based allocation to roles. On the one hand, more legislation is targeted to specific age groups, and age is built in as a triggering mechanism for certain benefits. Moreover, in the world at large, many settings have become increasingly age homogeneous: housing developments, leisure and voluntary activities, grade and high schools, and work places. These have become environments in which one interacts primarily with others at the same age or life-course stage. On the other hand, there has been an influx of "off time" women into higher education and the labor force, older men changing careers, early retirees, and elderly activists. There are many settings in which age lines are blurred in some common activity, and many communities in which old and young are in daily contact.

As our age structure appears to be increasingly age-graded through the identification of age-specific capacities and resources, or challenges and needs, the ultimate result may be to demonstrate the underlying continuity or continuum of aging, and perhaps the futility of categorization. Yet, when so much is in flux, age can become a logical means of rationalizing the distribution of scarce social goods.

Research Exercises

1. Your library should have publications of the World Health Organization and other international data-gathering agencies. Find age pyramids from other countries to compare with that for the United States in 1975. What is the relationship between social/cultural complexity and age stratification? What might be the effects of different age distributions on economic and political institutions?

2. From the anthropological literature select three case studies, one from

a gathering/hunting or pastoral society, another from an agricultural society, and a third from a society in the process of industrialization. Compare the treatment of the elderly, their position in the kinship structure, and other relevant variables on which information is available for all three societies.

3. If the class is undertaking a random probability sample survey, steps should be taken to select the sample. The first step involves defining the study population—all those 65 + in a city, country, standard metropolitan area, state, or other geographical area. Data from the last decennial census are on file in most municipalities and larger political divisions, which indicate how many persons 65 + were in each census tract at the time of enumeration. If there have been no radical changes in the population since the census, you can assume that old people are distributed in the same fashion at this time. Therefore, if there were 50,000 old people in the study population at the last census and you decide on a 2 per cent sample (1,000 respondents), 2 per cent of the number of old people in each Census tract must be contacted. Census tracts are further broken down into numbered blocks. With a set of maps (one for each census tract), use a table of random numbers to select the specific blocks to which interviewers will be sent with instructions to begin at one corner and go from house to house until an older respondent agrees to be interviewed.

For example, if five hundred old people are assumed to be in Tract 408, ten interviews are required; ten blocks are then selected by the use of random numbers, and students are dispatched to get one interview from each block (back-up blocks are similarly selected in case no interview is obtained in the first chosen).

The sample survey *questionnaire* should also be in the preparation stage. The interview schedule should take no longer than one half hour to administer under ideal conditions. Begin with basic background data such as age, sex, race, marital status, educational attainment, ages of children, place of residence, ethnicity, and religion. Sections should be prepared on health status and medical care, income and expenses, religious and political participation and attitudes, measures of self-esteem and attitudes toward aging, uses of leisure, and family interaction. If completed in time, data on these sections can be used for discussion when relevant chapters are reached. However, the construction of questionnaire items is itself a means of learning what is important in the study of aging.

Discussion Questions

List several violations of age norms. How do others react and why?

In what ways do social events influence biological aging? Do changes in the organism affect the social system?

Why do you think so many Americans believe that old people were better treated in the past than they are today?

Do you think that age will increase or decrease in importance as a basis of role allocation? Why?

3

Beliefs About
Aging and Old Age

———◆———

Grow old with me!
The best is yet to be.
The last of life, for which the first was made.
  —Robert Browning, "Rabbi Ben Ezra,"
  stanza 1.

An aged man is but a paltry thing.
A tattered coat upon a stick, unless
Soul clap its hunch and sing, and louder sing
For every tatter in its mortal dress.
  —William Butler Yeats, "Sailing to Byzantium,"
  stanza 2

In Perspective

Although both poets quoted were describing the same experience—old age— it is obvious that each perceived this last segment of the life course from different vantage points. In the first quotation, old age is painted in romanticized, Norman Rockwell strokes, where the joys of the golden years are delineated. In contradistinction, the second excerpt calls forth a stark, near-pariah —emaciated, poverty-stricken, lonely, and eccentric—a tableau of our own inevitable aging and death. The differences in these two depictions of old age highlight the ambiguity with which it is viewed in our society where common sense and folk wisdom tell us that it is desirable to live as long as possible—but that it is better to be young than to be old! The dictates of the youth orientation of American culture indicate that aging and old age are to be dreaded and personally avoided for oneself; that the old are less attractive, less mentally acute, and less worthwhile than younger people. Political and social conservatism are usually associated with growing older; in the late 1960s and early 1970s, this perspective was summarized succinctly by the adage: "Never trust anyone over 30!"

There is thus little question that the aged are regarded unfavorably relative to the nonaged. In fact, the aged have been described by some sociologists as a minority group precisely because they are subject to negative stereotyping, discrimination, and social and economic disadvantages. Whether or not the aged possess other minority group characteristics, such as a distinct subculture and group consciousness, is, however, open to extensive debate. (For a discussion of the aged as a minority group, see Rose, 1965; Butler, 1975.) As an integral part of an age stratification approach to gerontology, where theoretical emphasis is placed on societal structures and processes that flow from and characterize age strata, a further look at the ways in which old age is viewed both by the young and old is important and provides the focus for the remainder of this chapter. What does our theoretical model (Chapter 2) tell us about attitudes and beliefs regarding aging and old age?

SECULAR BELIEFS ABOUT OLD AGE AND SENIOR ESTEEM

Are old people of different societies accorded the same general degree of social esteem, or does this vary by the type of society? And, do cultural beliefs about the last portion of the life course influence actual social roles of old people? In 1960, Burgess suggested that a variety of dynamic social trends during the twentieth century have had an adverse effect upon the elderly in Western nations. These include (1) increased urbanization; (2) substitution of home production by factory production; (3) emergence of the conjugal family; (4) rise of complex bureaucratic organizations; (5) increased leisure time; and (6) extension of life expectancy (Burgess, 1960). Burgess has suggested that these social trends have led to specific social consequences for the aged. First, the insecurity of old age has become pronounced; prolongation of life for more people often leads to greater anxiety and fear about mental and physical disability and to the probability of declining levels of both real income and of income in comparison with younger age groups. Second, loss of priority in the family and of the power associated with seniority, resulting from the decline of the extended family, has led in turn to the greater likelihood that the old will rely upon impersonal organizations as help sources. Third, the old of today are more likely to experience "roleless roles," that is, where there is little for them to do in our expanded leisure (and prepackaged food) era (Burgess, 1960).

To what extent do our current cultural beliefs about old-age substantiate or repudiate Burgess's statements? Are the old indeed viewed as relatively unproductive surplus workers, with too much leisure time but an inability to fill it, tormented by anxieties about their declining physical and mental functioning, and turning for sustenance to public institutions in the absence of family ties? The evidence, which is reviewed throughout much of this book, suggests that this is an inaccurate view of the now-old. Yet an oversimplified view about the declining status of the elderly in contemporary society appears to be held by many.

As Burgess would agree, the relative esteem of the aged has varied according to the society. Although the findings are not clear-cut, the majority of investigators have reported findings that support the premise that *attitudes* toward old people are most favorable in simple societies and decrease with increasing industrialization (Cowgill, 1968; Parsons, 1942; Shelton, 1965; Streib, 1968). However, as noted in Chapter 2, this linear assumption obscures much variation.

In a recent cross-cultural analysis of esteem of the old as related to societal socioeconomic complexity, Sheehan (1976) examined data on forty-seven nomadic, tribal, and peasant societies (described prior to substantial Western contact). The nomadic, or geographically mobile, bands were characterized by few material resources and an emphasis on survival and youth. Not surprisingly, the esteem of old people was low. Life was so uncertain and short that there was little opportunity for role differentiation. With little material wealth to accumulate or control, and limited accumulation of knowledge, these bands were relatively egalitarian across both age and sex categories. In tribal societies that have a more complex social organization, the elderly were held in moderate to high regard. As we have seen, a distinguishing feature of tribal societies is that economic, familial, religious, and political behaviors are all organized along lines of kinship, and age is one of the means by which power and rank are assigned. Although being young is valued, for youth is associated with prowess as a fighter, the old men in tribal societies commanded extensive political power. In the most complex of the three types of societies, the peasant and agricultural, "heightened socio-economic development may combine with the security of a relatively productive and peaceful environment" (Sheehan, 1976, p. 436) to promote very high prestige of old people, especially men. As governors of labor and finance, as overseers of ceremonial and religious rites, and as preservers of the heritage of the past, the few old men who lived until old age were indeed village elders (Sheehan, 1976). When old women do have power in preliterate societies, this is most often due to witchcraft; in almost all such societies studied, old women are viewed as possessing both magical powers and evil motives (Gutmann, 1977).

As societies began to industrialize, however, age-based power came to be challenged. The family or clan, once the source of social and political order as well as economic production, dwindled as the primary source of social organization. Transformation of the economy, such as that brought about by the Industrial Revolution, brought changes in other spheres as well. As the locus for work was transferred from the home to the factory or business, the material bases of power and authority of "the elders" were substantially reduced and shifted to more impersonal agencies such as the workplace, the school, and other extrafamilial settings. No longer was the skill or knowledge of the past of the old particularly needed.

This last point is a critical one, for, at the same time that Western industrialized nations, and ours in particular, have moved closer and closer to a work ethic, where personal worth is based on capacity to work and ability to earn rather than on age-status or hereditary rank, an age stratum has essentially been declared superfluous. Sources of traditional authority possessed in a peasant society have been parceled out to a variety of other social institutions over a period of centuries whereas, at the same time, technological innovation has made the labor of old people (and youths) less and less necessary. Moreover, the life expectancy of people at birth has increased dramatically since the turn of the century (Chapter 4). This increase in life expectancy has been more pronounced for women than for men, and in the majority of societies— whether nomadic, tribal, or peasant—women have been accorded less esteem than men at all ages. That elderly women now comprise the great majority of old people in contemporary society may color the relative prestige of the aged as a whole. In the mass media today, for example, the old woman is most often portrayed as a sexually unattractive nag (Livson, 1977). This trend is also reflected in popular jokes, where old women are almost the exclusive targets of jokes about the physical undesirability of aging (Richman, 1977). The predominance of elderly women has had an impact on our general expectations and beliefes about old age—at least to the extent to which sex stereotypical behavior is supported. A general spillover of behavioral norms and expectations from the majority sex to the minority would not be implausible.

SECULAR BELIEFS ABOUT OLD AGE AND FEAR OF DEATH

Among many preindustrial societies, the old were given special veneration not only because they controlled property and deployed labor but also, very importantly, because they represented linkages both with the past and with the gods and thus with the sacred. As religions became more formalized and bureaucratized, a class of priests developed, curtailing the role of the individual elder as spiritual mediator. Yet the old maintained some of their sacred aura, perhaps because they were considered too old to be interested in worldly temptations or perhaps because their advanced age was associated with authority.

As Western cultural values and social institutions have been recast from the traditional bases of first the clan and then the rule of the absolute or exceedingly powerful monarch into more modern forms, increased *secularization* has occurred and rational law-based authority replaced older, traditional sources of authority such as the family, tribe, or priesthood. Rational/legal authority thus represents a value shift away from the importance that was once accorded the sacred. Instead of obeisance to the deity, loyalty is now required to the secular values of patriotism and nationalism.

During the Middle Ages, by all accounts, life was indeed nasty, brutish, and short, except for the fortunate few members of the upper class, and relatively small value was placed upon individual autonomy or personal freedom. Indeed, both concepts threatened both the foundations of feudalism and the authority of the church. Wars were frequent, epidemics of disease were not uncommon, and life was hard. Death was very much a part of life and likely to occur at any age. As Ariès (1962) has pointed out, popular medieval art depicted "steps of the ages" or rows of figures, showing the various ages from birth to death, standing on a double staircase, with steps going up on one side and down on the other. In the center, however, ready to greet members of *any* age group, stood the skeleton of the Grim Reaper, Death, with his scythe.

The Reformation and the Age of Enlightenment not only did much to reduce the power of the church in general and of any one religious group in particular; it also set the stage for increased secularization, that is, the proliferation of tolerated religious groups served to deemphasize and defuse the power of any particular sacred belief system. As options in their present life expanded, people no longer depended on the next world as the source of justice, and this world became more enticing. With the emergence of the Industrial Revolution, greater emphasis was placed on materialism and acquisition of goods and capital; with improved production techniques, there was, after all, far more for the fortunate few to possess and for the remainder to hope to acquire—if not for themselves, perhaps for their offspring.

The combination of a shift from relatively absolute traditional authorities, such as the feudal lord or monarch or clan head and a single church, to more diffuse and differentiated sanctions also led to increased participation by members of a society in its various social institutions. This participation enhanced attachment to earthly and temporal value systems as individuals became able to exercise greater control over their fate. Thus, the elderly as spiritual mediators and links with the next world seem far from everyday involvement in the here-and-now world of accumulation of capital and pursuit of success. Activism, rather than mystical contemplation or concern with the next world, came to characterize Western culture by the end of the nineteenth century, when all of society seemed malleable to scientific efforts.

Belief in activism has shaped the mythology of old age that we espouse at the present time. Death, probably only a welcome guest at the height of periods of mystical orthodoxy as in the early Christian era, is doubly unwelcome, for it represents not only the cessation of life with all its earthly rewards but also is the epitome of inactivity and the end of becoming and being. Today death is uncommon among younger age groups in our society. Rather than standing in the center of the staircase and equally accessible to all stages of life, Death has moved determinedly toward the end of the stairs and awaits the old. Salter and Salter comment:

> To the young, aging and death are tied together in one unattractive package. As Malveaux and Guilford put it, the attitudes of many students toward growing old can be encompassed by the three Rs of "Repudiation, Repugnance and Repulsion." (1976, p. 232)

As death has become less an everyday event, it has probably also become more feared—and the elderly along with it. The activist-youth-oriented emphasis of our culture is also associated with an interest in the new, the novel. Ability to adapt to constantly changing situations is valued. Such adaptability is, however, bought at a price—a high propensity for anxiety and for tension. It may be argued that avoidance of the elderly is a way of eluding anxiety about one's own mortality and of reducing tension about the possible newness and novelty of one's present interests and pursuits. One study of college students and their attitudes toward aging as related to death anxiety found that the items most significantly correlated to level of death anxiety were those relating to one's own fears about personal aging (Salter and Salter, 1976). Young people who feared that in their own future aging they might experience inadequate income, unpleasant life-style changes, and loss in strength and vigor were those who were most afraid of death (ibid.). These students were also, interestingly enough, unlikely to express support for a preretirement education program, a health services delivery program, a home property tax relief program, and a guaranteed minimum income program—all of which were resolutions of the 1971 White House Conference on Aging—although they were likely to support the idea of a national awareness campaign! One may wonder to what purpose the national awareness campaign would be conducted, since it was not viewed by these students as related to any policy recommendations.

Summary. A combination of factors, including a shift from a traditional, family-based power to a rationalized authority structure, where the family as the unit of social organization is sacrificed for the nation and state, and where increased emphasis is placed on personal freedom and individuality as well as earthly pleasures, have all tended to diminish the relative esteem in which the elderly are held. The increased diversity of society and the multiplicity of choices and skills tend to reduce the power and authority of the old. Their managerial skills, work skills, and ability to act as mediators with the sacred, lose significance in an activist, youth-oriented society where change is valued. Most importantly, the increasingly large numbers of old people in the population are not perceived as potential leaders by virtue of their particular survival skills. Instead, the old are now viewed by the young as symbols of death and inactivity.

Current Issues

AGE APPROPRIATE NORMS FOR BEHAVIOR

Ideas of what being a child, a young adult, or an old person means are some of the most unspoken "givens" in any society. Like fish asked to describe water, we tend to be in a quandary when we are asked to reflect upon the properties of each life stage; like the fish in water, such qualities are unquestioned. But, as we have suggested, the culturally defined content of these age statuses varies from culture to culture and from one time period to another. Within the broad limits of biological capacity (which is, incidentally, far more diverse than our own cultural views lead us to believe), sex and age statuses are socially designated rather than being biologically decided.

Each society develops a model of appropriate age statuses and successive life phases that are simply "taken for granted" as the basis of behavior. Through this process of internalization (learning the rules and making them yours) individuals are directly and indirectly pressured into "acting their age." Eventually many of these age-appropriate definitions of behavior take on the force of what Robert Merton (1957) has termed the "self-fulfilling prophecy" whereby people act as they are expected to act. It is for this reason that beliefs about old age are of particular interest in looking at aging and old age.

Social norms are one means by which age-appropriate behavior is conveyed and learned. Every society has norms for age-appropriate behavior. Age is, after all, one of the bases for ascription of status. It is also a basic dimension affecting both the shape of the social structure and social interaction. Norms, essentially rules for the right and proper way of doing things, apply not only to the way in which acts or events should be performed but also to their timing. Age norms, like other types, may be either *proscriptive*—"thou shalt not" or *prescriptive*—"thou shalt."

The ordering of life events through age norms is most often prescriptive, although a proscription may be implied as well. For example, as stated in Ecclesiastes: "to everything there is a season . . . a time to be born, and a time to die . . . a time to every purpose under the sun" (3: 1, 2). Age norms thus operate both as "prods" and "brakes" upon behavior, hastening or slowing down specific events and allowing people to compare their own performance against these "social clocks" (Neugarten, Moore, and Lowe, 1965). Norms, thus, are specifically linked to certain types of age-related behaviors, and sanctions to ensure conformity may be invoked against the "deviant" who does not act one's age.

What consensus about age-appropriate behavior exists in American society? The results of a series of sample surveys, reported by Neugarten, Moore, and Lowe (1965), are shown in Table 3–1.

Data from the same study also suggest that personal belief in the validity and relevance of age-related norms increases throughout the life course and that age is an appropriate criterion by which to evaluate behavior. Interestingly, as with age identification, individuals are likely to allow themselves more latitude about age-appropriate behaviors than they are to other people; young men, in particular, perceive fewer age constraints governing appropriate behavior than do their female counterparts. This latter finding probably reflects the importance our culture has traditionally accorded to "getting married at the right age" for women, and to the "right age" at which to bear one's first child (Neugarten, Moore, and Lowe, 1965).

As Neugarten and her associates caution (1965), their data are based on a sampling of a middle-class segment of the population, and the norms reported would be expected to vary somewhat by level of education, income, occupation, race, and ethnicity. Yet the basic life events with which they are concerned are no less normatively prescribed in other social class or ethnic groups, although the timing may differ.

What are the appropriate norms for behavior in old age? As Wood (1971) pointed out, "The norms for behavior in old age in society are far from explicit" (p. 77). The elderly have been described as "roleless" (Burgess, 1960), with almost no role proscriptions about proper standards (except to avoid bizarre behavior), and only a few prescriptions for preferred role behavior (Rosow, 1967). To a large extent, the lack of norms

Table 3–1. Consensus in a Middle-Class Middle-aged Sample Regarding Various Age-related Characteristics

	Age Range Designated as Appropriate or Expected	Per Cent Who Concur	
		Men (N = 50)	Woman (N = 43)
Best age for a man to marry	20–25	80	90
Best age for a woman to marry	19–24	85	90
When most people should become grandparents	45–50	84	79
Best age for most people to finish school and go to work	20–22	86	82
When most men should be settled on a career	24–26	74	64
When most men hold their top jobs	45–50	71	58
When most people should be ready to retire	60–65	83	86
A young man	18–22	84	83
A middle-aged man	40–50	86	75
An old man	65–75	75	57
A young woman	18–24	89	88
A middle-aged woman	40–50	87	77
An old woman	60–75	83	87
When a man has the most responsibilities	35–50	79	75
When a man accomplishes most	40–50	82	71
The prime of life for a man	35–50	86	80
When a woman has the most responsibilities	25–40	93	91
When a woman accomplishes most	30–45	94	92
A good-looking woman	20–35	92	82

Neugarten, Bernice L., Moore, Joan W., and Lowe, J. C., "Age Norms, Age Constraints and Adult Socialization," *American Journal of Sociology*, Vol. 70, no. 6, 1965, pp. 710–717.

for appropriate behavior in old age is the result of the very large recent increase in numbers of elderly in the population and to the type of economic and family organization of our society. In the past, as has already been noted, only small numbers of old people survived; this was the case as recently as half a century ago. Thus, the issue of age-appropriate behavior for the old in 1900 was relatively inconsequential; there were simply not enough old people whose behavior required social control. Most remained in the labor force until they were no longer able to work or until they died.

There is some evidence that old people themselves are more conservative about age-appropriate behavior in this last portion of the life course than are young or middle-aged adults. In a series of items designed to evaluate perceived appropriateness of old-age behaviors, Wood and O'Brien (cited in Wood, 1971), found that the old were less inclined than younger adults to approve of "a retired couple who wears shorts when they go shopping downtown" or "a recently widowed woman of 65 who buys a red convertible." They also assumed that younger people were more intolerant of these behaviors than the young themselves reported.

The greater conservatism of old people suggested in the Wood study is probably a reflection of age cohort differences rather than of age itself. The now-old of today were socialized in an era when modesty was highly valued, when self-restraint and discipline were inextricable components of the work ethic that governed much of their lives, and when achievement rather than self-expression was one's life goal. As future cohorts age, it will be interesting to see the extent to which norms for age-appropriate behavior in old age develop or change or disappear altogether. Certainly our experience with large proportions of old people in the population is too new for us to conclude that old age is by definition normless in our society. As Wood notes:

> evidence for the emergency of norms for mobile, leisure oriented kinds of behavior in retirement is growing. We are witnessing increasing numbers of persons retiring well before age 65 who are in good physical condition and who have had much more experience with leisure and mobility than earlier generations of older persons. It may be expected that some of these persons will be "pioneers" in creating new and different life patterns in retirement. (Wood, 1971, p. 77)

As the age for retirement becomes more flexible as a result of recent legislative changes, the emergence of new norms for old-age behavior is likely. In the past when retirement was mandatory by age 65 for a majority of workers, little attention was paid to the abilities or interests of members of the labor force as they made retirement more or less feasible (Chapter 7). The greater latitude provided by the options of early and late retirement can be expected to stimulate the development of behavioral norms founded on performance in tasks and on aptitudes in using employment and leisure.

PERCEPTIONS OF OLD PEOPLE

A wealth of research has been undertaken over the last twenty-five years or so to assess ways in which older people are perceived by the general population. The majority of these studies, however, were handicapped by the types of samples used (most often college students), by the types of instruments used (generally noncomparable), and by the very detail with which their findings were reported. As a consequence, comparisons of changes in attitudes toward old age over time and among various age groups is extremely difficult. (For further discussion of methodological problems in studies of perceptions of aging, see McTavish, 1971.)

How the Young View the Old. Because of their accessibility as an audience, much work on attitudes toward aging has used college students as respondents. Although the findings are somewhat contradictory, the preponderance of data suggests that there is considerable adherence to negative stereotypes about the aged. In an early and influential study of 142 psychology graduate students, for example, Tuckman and Lorge (1952) reported that at least one third of their respondents perceived old people as stubborn, touchy, engaging in frequent quarrels with their children and relatives, bossy, and meddling in other people's affairs.

A later study (Golde and Kogan, 1959), which focused on the attitudes of undergraduate college students, also provided support for the premise that young people have a negative perception of the old. At least one in every five respondents surveyed espoused one or more of the following statements:

When I am with an old person, I feel negative feelings.
When I am with an old person, I feel passive, subordinate.
The thing I like least about old people is irritability.
When an old person is walking very slowly right in front of me, I feel pity.

In addition, although 58 percent of the students in this study indicated that their relationships with their grandparents had been satisfactory, another 23 percent said that their relationships had been unsatisfactory (Golde and Kogan, 1959).

Nor is there any reason to believe that attitudes toward the elderly as reported by the young have become any more favorable in recent years. For example, an article by Weinberger and Millham (1975) reported that college students continue to express negative attitudes toward the elderly and to view old age pejoratively. Although the evidence is mixed, contact with an old person appears to be a mediating factor; for example, students with living great-grandparents endorse fewer negative stereotypes about the aged than do those with living grandparents only (Bekker and Taylor, 1966). As has been found for many other areas of attitudes and beliefs, greater contact with, or knowledge of, a group of people and their diversity tends to demystify the group and to reduce stereotypical thinking.

Age As a Factor in Beliefs About Old Age. There is conflicting evidence regarding the influence of age itself on perceptions and stereotypes of old age. McTavish (1971), for example, reported results from a 1965 national survey to the item, "Old People Are Annoying"; 36 percent of all respondents agreed, with the following variation by age:

Table 3–2. Per Cent agreeing with the statement, "Old People Are Annoying"

Age Group	Per Cent Agreeing
17–29	37
30–39	25
40–49	34
50–59	40
60–69	51
70–99	40

McTavish, Donald G., "Perceptions of Old People: A Review of Research Methodologies and Findings," *The Gerontologist,* Vol. 11, no. 4, Part II, 1971, p. 99, table 2.

What this table suggests is that respondents in their thirties, who are entering their productive middle years, are most favorably disposed to the old, a pattern that continues for people in their forties. Among those in their fifties, however, less favorable attitudes toward the old are held—perhaps as respondents have had to cope with their own parents' health and fiscal problems. The young-old (60–69) express the *most* unfavorable attitudes toward the old, whereas the attitudes of the old-old are similar to people in their fifties. It is clearly the young who are most likely to give favorable answers! Since McTavish does not cross-tabulate age with income and education, it is difficult to tell whether this finding is the result of age or of the effect of these other two variables. However, other tables suggest that the latter may be the case, as people of lower incomes and educational levels were also most likely to view old people as annoying.

Additional evidence that younger groups of adults have negative attitudes toward the old is available from the Harris survey (1975). As Table 3–3 indicates, those under 65 are more likely to see the 65+ population as relatively passive than are those 65+.

The general public aged 18–64 were much more likely to exaggerate the proportion of time that "old people in general" spend in such inactive pursuits as sitting and thinking, just doing nothing, and socializing with friends, than were those 65+.

Negative stereotypes not only influence the general population but also affect members of the stereotyped group. Much of the self, that is, the totally acting person, is formed through the actions and reactions of others to us. In that sense, we can think of the self, as Charles Horton Cooley suggested many years ago, as a looking glass.

Cooley viewed the self as developing within a context of social re-

Table 3–3. Public Who Think "Most People Over 65" Spend "A Lot of Time" Doing Specified Activities

Activity	Public, Aged 18–64	Public, Aged 65+	Net Difference
Sitting and thinking	66%	42%	−24%
Socializing with friends	53	42	−11
Gardening or raising plants	47	34	−13
Sleeping	42	25	−17
Just doing nothing	37	27	−10

Louis Harris and Associates. *The Myth and Reality of Aging in America,* National Council on Aging, Washington, 1975, p. 60.

lationships. The *"looking-glass"* or *reflexive* self is marked by three principal elements: (1) one's own imagination of one's appearance to the other person; (2) the imagination of the other's judgment of that appearance; and (3) some sort of self-feeling, such as pride or mortification. Schematically, the relationship between these various elements is shown in Figure 3–1:

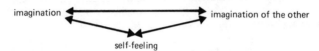

imagination   imagination of the other

self-feeling

Figure 3–1.

George Herbert Mead, the social philosopher and friend and colleague of Cooley's, elaborated on Cooley's concept of the looking-glass self. For Mead, language was the major means by which the self is created. Basic to discussions about the self—and beliefs about the aging or aged—is the assumption that the self is a social product, arising out of social interaction. According to Mead's reasoning, the person learns, essentially through language, to hold the attitudes of others. In so doing, one begins to regard one's self as a social object and to formulate lines of action accordingly. Stated differently, each individual internalizes other people's responses to himself or herself and is thus able to think about and to act upon these responses.

Key to the concept of the "looking-glass" or reflexive self is the assumption that social interaction by definition is dynamic rather than static or fixed: I interact, therefore I am. We have spent some time on the concept of the social self because it provides a fruitful framework to evaluate the force of belief systems about aging on old people, as well as upon other age strata. Individuals, at all ages, mesh their behavior with that of others; we do not follow a preset singular plan of action.

Beliefs About Aging and Old Age

The framework of the looking-glass self is also useful in considering changes in the self. The self is an open-ended social product, that is, we tend to see ourselves as others see us, but to alter some of these beliefs according to current experiences. The significance of stereotypical beliefs about old age thus becomes highlighted; not only do younger people hold often fallacious beliefs about old age but these negative images will be adapted and internalized by old people themselves. As the following data indicate, this is indeed the case.

Table 3–4. Comparison of Personal Activities and Belief Reported By Public 65+ and How Public+ Thinks "Most People Over 65" Are

Activity/Belief	Personally Engage in Frequently or Believe	Think True of Most 65+	Net Difference
Sitting and thinking	31%	42%	−11
Sleeping	16	25	− 9
Just doing nothing	15	27	−12
Are very useful members of own community	40	32	− 8

Louis Harris and Associates. *The Myth and Reality of Aging in America*, National Council on Aging, Washington, 1975, pp. 59, 60, 63.

From the preceding table, it is evident that people 65 + tend to view *themselves* in a more favorable light than they regard *most* people over 65, suggesting that the old have internalized some of the negative beliefs about old age that are held by society in general. The theory of *cognitive dissonance* (Festinger, 1964) predicts that attitudes toward anticipated or apparently inevitable events tend to become more favorable as exposure to the events increases. In fact, old people do have a more favorable view of those 65 + than do people between the ages of 18–64, but the elderly nonetheless share common perceptions of "most old people"—perceptions from which they excuse themselves whenever possible. By personal exemption, the individual 65 + may still maintain a sense of self-respect by interpreting cultural messages about the elderly to apply to others but not to one's self. This suggests a kind of *pluralistic ignorance*, where individuals incorrectly assume that each is alone in holding some belief, when, in fact, many others share that same belief.

Age Identification.   There is an emerging literature indicating that older people often deny their own aging, clinging instead to perceptions of themselves as "middle aged" or even "young" (Riley and Foner, 1968; Blau, 1973). Their reference group, that is, the group against which many old people compare themselves, is that of younger people rather than the culturally stereotyped images of members of their own age cohort and stratum. Recent empirical work on denial of one's age found that age identification is closely related to a variety of factors: self-assessment of one's worth in comparison to older and younger people in general, level of education, and health (Bultena and Powers, 1978). In a study of 235 noninstitutionalized Iowa residents, who were interviewed in 1960 and in 1970 and at least aged 60 at the time of the initial interview, only 25 percent identified themselves as "old" or "elderly" in 1960. Seventy per cent indicated they were middle-aged (although all were over 60 at that time); and an additional 5 percent did not answer the question (Bultena and Powers, 1978). By 1970, when all respondents were 70+, the proportion identifying themselves as middle-aged had decreased dramatically to 32 percent—a decrease of 48 percent—and the number who viewed themselves as elderly or old had increased commensurately to 63 percent— an increase of 38 percent (Bultena and Powers, 1978). Interestingly, although other research has suggested that there are sex differences in age identification (Peters, 1971; Ward, 1977), the Iowa study did *not* find significant differences between men and women. Instead, altered life situations, especially declines in physical health and independence, "made retention of a middle-aged identity problematic" (Bultena and Powers, 1978, p. 753).

That fewer people would identify themselves as middle-aged once past the age of 70 is hardly a surprise. What is of particular note and relevant to understanding the force of secular belief systems about old age is that chronological age is only one of many factors influencing identification of the self as belonging to a specific age group. Retention of youthful self-image is also dependent upon physical health and the belief that one is relatively better off than other members of one's age cohort. It is thus not hard to understand why many elderly may "make fools of themselves" by acting younger than their chronological age dictates in our society, or why the most rapidly expanding medical specialty is cosmetic surgery, including facelifts, breast and buttocks lifts, and eye pouch removal, primarily for aging women.

Despite the importance of social definitions of life course stages, a person's self-conceptions and behavior are not limited to one's current chronological age. Through the processes of reflection and internalization, one learns the cultural images of *all* life stages, so self-esteem and behavior both reflect and anticipate standards of appropriate behavior. Once legitimized, roles and beliefs about oneself are not easily abandoned, often persisting as a source of gratification and a means of relating to other people in a comfortable fashion. For example, the former athlete may, in early old age, view himself or herself as "just a little out of condition" but not as incapable of game play. When overwhelming physical evidence and the responses of others indicate that this self-view is no longer tenable and is an impediment to meaningful social interaction, the athlete is forced to redefine her/his self-image accordingly. Redefinition of one's age identification is, however, a gradual and interactive process at any age, and is perhaps most difficult in old age.

ATTITUDINAL STABILITY IN OLD AGE: ANOTHER MYTH?

It is part of our folk belief system that you can't teach an old dog new tricks, implying that old people are likely to be accompanied to their deaths by a lifelong collection of prejudices and beliefs. Much social science research has been based on the premise that attitudes, values, and beliefs tend to stabilize and become less amenable to change as part of the aging process. This view reflects the assumption that a basic personality is formed relatively early in life—an assertion that has been dominant until recent attention has been paid to personality change throughout the life course. Although the "fixed at five" view of personality is no longer tenable, there are several reasons, as Glenn (1978) has pointed out, to expect values and attitudes to stabilize after young adulthood. One of the major reasons is "the dense spacing of significant life events in early adulthood and the wider spacing of those events thereafter" (Glenn, 1978, p. 5). Events such as completing school, leaving the parental home, commencing a career or occupation, marrying, and becoming a parent generally occur within a relatively short time span. After this period of intense resocialization and change, the individual typically experiences fewer major life changes. There is also some reason to believe that inherent changeability may decrease with age; proponents of this view cite physiological slowing down and intelligence changes associated with the aging process, both of which are discussed later in this book. Still other social scientists have suggested that values, attitudes, and beliefs tend to stabilize as a way of reducing ambiguity; "some authors seem to believe in a kind of 'attitude inertia,' by which attitudes, once established, tend to perpetuate themselves" (Glenn, 1978, p. 4). Existing beliefs and attitudes, too, may be reinforced by experience; accordingly, their resistance to change varies as a function of the amount of experience that constructed and strengthened them (Glenn, 1974; Glenn, 1978).

A number of studies appear to confirm the thesis that old people become more rigid as they age (see Riley and Foner, 1968, for a review). Yet most research on aging and attitudinal change has been cross-sectional and thus has not taken account of educational and experiential differences among age cohorts. The few cohort studies that have been made, however, deal with changes in *birth cohorts* rather than with changes in specific individuals over time and thus do *not* provide a measure of the ways in which particular groups or persons stabilize or vary.

Although several important cohort studies support the aging-stability thesis (Nunn, Crockett, and Williams, 1978; Cutler and Kaufman, 1975; Glenn, 1974), new evidence has been presented by Glenn (1978) that calls this thesis into question. Presenting data dealing with racial, ethnic, and religious tolerance and intolerance—presumably deeply ingrained beliefs which are highly resistant to change—Glenn (1978) found that responses changed substantially between 1959 and 1969. Percentage changes in five age cohorts who were asked their willingness to vote for a Catholic, Jewish, or Black president are presented in Table 3–5, in which the level of education of respondents is controlled.

As Table 3–5 shows, when education is controlled, the data do not really support the age-stability hypothesis. Those in age cohorts 4 and 5, the oldest two groups, were, on the whole, no less open to change than those in the younger age cohorts. Between the years 1959 and 1969, rapid social change occurred. A Catholic president, John F. Kennedy, had been inaugurated, the Civil Rights movement had emerged as a major change force, and several Jews had been elected to Congress. The impact of events (a period influence) has affected the attitudes of all age groups. Table 3–5 clearly demonstrates that older people are sensitive to social changes that challenge long-held and deeply ingrained prejudices. It is impossible to conclude on the basis of limited evidence such as this study that attitudinal stability is *not* enhanced with age, but we can question the thesis that older people are unshakably set in their ways and beliefs. As each successive age cohort is better educated, low education may be the crucial factor in explaining "attitudinal inertia" rather than age. The "old dog/new tricks" saying indeed may be yet another fallacious belief about age in our culture.

Table 3–5. Change in Reported Willingness to Vote for a Catholic, Jew, and Black for President As Reported on a Gallup Poll, 1959 and 1969, by Age Cohort and with Level of Education Controlled

| | | | Per Cent Change, 1959–69 | | |
| | Age in | | Non-Catholics willing to vote Catholic President | Non-Jews willing to vote Jewish President | White willing to vote Black President |
	1959	1969			
Cohort 1:	20–29	30–39	+18.4	+14.6	+10.3
Cohort 2:	30–39	40–49	+20.7	+ 9.8	+ 8.3
Cohort 3:	40–49	50–59	+18.1	+12.3	+22.5
Cohort 4:	50–59	60–69	+25.3	+14.4	+20.4
Cohort 5:	60–69	70–79	+13.7	− 7.4	+15.7

Norval D. Glenn, "Aging and Attitudinal Stability," paper distributed at Roundtable, American Sociological Association Meetings, 1978, tables 6, 7, 8.

POPULAR MESSAGES ABOUT GROWING OLD

Television Speaks. In a country where there are more television sets than people, one in four persons between the ages of 18 and 64, and one in three aged 65+ spend "a lot of time" watching television (Harris, 1975). It seems reasonable to ask what message is conveyed about aging and old age through this medium. As Hess (1974) commented, television and other media have generally overlooked the very fact of the growth of the older population as a major and varied segment of our society. Past research, though limited in amount, suggests that the elderly, when presented on television, are portrayed in negative stereotypical terms (Marshall and Wallenstein, 1973). When attention is turned to the aging and old in prime-time dramatic programs, at least one study (Arnhoff, 1974) has shown that old people are depicted as increasingly evil, failures, and unhappy. Sex stereotypical differences are highlighted as well; 40 percent of the males portrayed were shown as successful, happy, or good in comparison to 10 percent of the women. Furthermore, women have relatively little mastery over their fates; as Arnhoff pointed out, most males who fail do so because they are evil, women do so because they age. The message—broadcast loud and clear—is evident.

When the portrayal of the aged in a variety of program categories is evaluated, the aged do not fare much better. In a random sampling, all kinds of programs during a six-week period in 1976 were analyzed at different times of day, seven days a week (Harris and Feinberg, 1978). People over age 60 were most common on news and talk programs, which drew about 10 percent of their characters from this age category. Comedy show characters age 60+ accounted for the next most frequently appearing group (9.5 percent). Although moderate to high degrees of authority and esteem characterized about 40 percent of the aged 60+ characters observed, this was the result of the preponderance of senators, congressmen, and other public figures on talk shows and the news. Only rarely were women 60+ with power and authority depicted. In dramatic shows, there were few portrayals of effective old people, and romance among old people was totally absent, thus perpetuating the cultural beliefs that both intellectual and sexual capacities deteriorate in old age. Poor health among the elderly was a frequent theme. In commercials, for example, bad health and the diminished authority of older women as compared to men predominated—despite the fact that the majority of the target audience for many products are older, relatively healthy women!

In another study of television portrayals of old people—in programs and commercials—Ansello (1978) found that elderly persons accounted for 6.3 percent of all characters. Older women were most likely to be seen on daytime television, especially in commercials where they "extoll tried-

and-true ways of doing things." Clearly, the aged are seen as unengaging characters on television; they remind us of the ambiguities, discomforts, and deprivations commonly associated with the last portion of life, and arouse anxiety about death.

Old Age in Novels. Novels, too, provide a rich source of information about cultural beliefs and stereotypes and tend to be more in the forefront of new ideas than television. To what extent are the elderly stereotyped in fiction? Peterson and Karnes (1976) evaluated a series of books, published from 1922 on, that received the Newbery Medal as the outstanding piece of adolescent literature of the year, and found that although older characters were not consciously discriminated against, they tended to be only "partial people." Although sex stereotyping was very common— men were employed, women were portrayed as wives, mothers, and grandmothers with no employment or community involvement—there was little overt negative stereotyping of old people. Rather, the older characters were tangential to the main characters in the books studied, and were useful only for their relationships with the "important people" in the story. As Peterson and Karnes (1976) commented: "They are there, but nobody seems to notice."

In an extensive study of age in literature by Ansello and his colleagues (Ansello, 1977), the least sophisticated depictions of aging were found in literature for the youngest readers (preschool to fourth grade). As might be expected, sex-role stereotyping was significant, with female characters passive and nurturant rather than "directive" or physically exertive. Older women were much more likely than men to be described as "sad," "poor," and "dear"; the men were usually described as "wise" and "smart," but also as "foolish" and "crazy."

In adult fiction, eighty-seven novels, issued by commercial publishers in the United States during 1950–75, were identified that had a protagonist over 60 years of age and presented a narrative primarily from the perspective of this person (Sohngen, 1977). An analysis of these novels indicated that their social emphasis was essentially on WASP (white, Anglo Saxon Protestants) middle-class elderly. A variety of themes was presented, the most common of which was retirement. Life reviews, reminiscences, the meaning of life and its ironies, however, accounted for the largest category of themes. "Fairy Godmother" and "Adult Nancy Drew" novels were also found. Problems of living, such as generational power struggles, institutionalization, and segregated living, too, received attention (Sohngen, 1977). Relatively few novels, however, dealt with sexuality in old age.

Loughan (1977), evaluating "the new naturalism"—novels of old age— proposed that although the protagonists in contemporary novels of old age display both energy and self-assertive sexuality, they nonetheless face an inevitable process of degeneration and decay. All their energies are expended in keeping alive, bounded by the tedium of daily existence:

> Sammler recognizes with horror the implications of his lack of body power: "He was old. He lacked physical force. He knew what to do but had no power to execute it. He had to turn to someone else . . . Sammler was powerless. To be so powerless was death. And suddenly he saw himself not so much standing as strangely leaning, and as a past person." (Loughan, 1977, quoting from Saul Bellow's *Mr. Sammler's Planet*, 1970)

Summary. Presentation of the old on television and in novels appears to differ. On television, a more popular and conventional medium, the elderly are rarely depicted in positions of power or prestige unless they happen to be public figures on a news or talk show. Women are generally regarded as losing rather than gaining authority as they age, and poor health for both sexes is a common theme. In novels, the presentation of old people varies according to the audience for whom the book is intended. In adolescent literature, sex stereotypes abound, but the old are not overtly stereotyped. Neither, however, are they "part of the action." In adult novels, old people as protagonists are apparently increasing, and a multiplicity of common themes are treated. Absent, however, are novels dealing with the Black aged, Hispanic aged, and elderly of other minority groups. Focus is on the middle-class, relatively well-educated white Protestant. The vigor of characters varies—some are very active indeed—but the essential picture conveyed is one where old age has few positive features to offset its bleakness and unlovely aspects.

Prospects

At the present time, old age is still regarded with fear and misgiving by the majority of our society. Much of this is no doubt a heritage of our past experiences with preceding age cohorts of old people who had limited education and whose socialization has been markedly different from our own. Emphasis on activism and on the work ethic have also made us cling to a jaundiced view of the elderly as superfluous people who have outlived their peers and careers. As we have discussed, most of our beliefs about age are time bound and culture bound, and much of what we think we know about the aged and about old age is not necessarily true. Although old people cannot evade the myths about aging, they do not necessarily see themselves in these contexts.

As we have more experience with better educated, healthier age cohorts of old people, we shall probably find that many of our current beliefs are as inappropriate or brutal as the custom of placing one's elderly relative upon an ice floe seems now. At the moment, however, negative stereotypes abound that promote *gerontophobia* ("fear of old people") and *necrophobia* ("fear of death").

Research Exercises

1. Prepare a *photo essay* from magazine and newspaper advertising and copy to illustrate images of the elderly. What messages are being conveyed to readers regarding aging and being old? How do these images contrast with those of younger people? Are there differences by the type of magazine or newspaper?

2. Systematic *content analysis* of television programs and advertising requires a schedule for viewing and a checklist of items to be recorded. Particularly important would be a catalogue of roles, i.e., who does what at which ages. Also, sex differences in age norms and role expectations should be noted.

3. The sample survey questionnaire developed by the class should be ready for pretest, with a group of students taking different sections to try out on any older respondents willing to assist.

Discussion Questions

How applicable are the following sociological concepts to the material in this chapter?

"Looking-glass Self"
"Pluralistic Ignorance"
"Self-fulfilling prophecy"

Debate the question: Are Old People a Minority Group?

How many "good things" about growing old can the class list? Is there agreement on these items? What are the "bad things" about growing old?

PART TWO

—◆—

Aging Bodies and Minds

4

The Aging Organism

Aging is a process that begins when we are born, ends when we die, and occurs at varying rates among different people. The aging process diverges even within each of us for our body organs do not age at the same rate; that is, it is possible at age 25 to have the heart of a person of age 20, the muscles of a 35-year-old, and so on. In youth, the bodily changes associated with aging are viewed with excitement—growing taller and stronger, getting new teeth, and developing secondary sex characteristics are hallmarks of growing up and of achieving readiness to take on new, more complex social roles. There comes a time—sooner rather than later in our youth-oriented society—where bodily changes are viewed less positively. Few people welcome the sight of their first gray hairs, wrinkles, or abdominal paunch. As Sontag (1972) has commented, "After thirty-five, any mention of one's age carries with it the reminder that one is probably closer to the end of one's life than to the beginning" (p. 29).

It is also evident that there are sex differences in growing old, not only because of biological differences but also as a result of social distinctions; "for most women, aging means a humiliating process of gradual sexual disqualification" (Sontag, 1972, p. 32) whereas getting older may actually act in men's favor. Masculinity has traditionally been associated with assertiveness, competency, autonomy, self-control, and power—all of which are qualities that are enhanced by achieving maturity (if not old age). Femininity, on the other hand, has been associated with passivity, helplessness, quiescence, noncompetitiveness, and warmth—qualities that are, incidentally, often attributed to "good" children.

Changes in physical appearance caused by aging have different implications for women than for men. Erosion of the physique is generally undesirable for everyone—but especially for women. A sample of television commercials broadcast during evening hours brings this home clearly: Oil of Olay (guaranteed in several languages to help maintain youthful, soft skin); Geritol (a vitamin supplement that promises women they will become not older, only better); and Playtex girdles, removing those unsightly bulges and thus allowing the fortyish woman to dart around the house in her wedding dress of twenty years ago. And women, even famous ones, are given less latitude to be anything *but* old once cosmetics, pills, and girdles have ceased to disguise their age. In the popular media, the older man with a younger woman is considered normal; the older woman with a younger man is a (perhaps perverse) rarity. For example, in the March 28, 1978, personal column of *The New York Review of Books*, the following ads appeared:

Male professor, 51, 5'10", divorced, personable . . . looking for an intelligent, independent, humane, somewhat younger woman.

and, more to the point:

Attorney-writer, 55, 5'11", divorced, empathetic, seeks long-term friendship on all levels with bright, civilized, sensuous, slim, woman, 35–45. Photo, please.

Advertisements indicating that a personable, empathetic or any other kind of fortyish or older woman was seeking to meet a younger man are more scarce; during the specific week in question, there were no such ads.

The way in which men and women perceive their own capacity for self-care in old age differs as well. In one study of persons 65+ who were asked to rate their ability for self-care, men were far more likely to report themselves as independent than were women (Markson and Grevert, 1972). Interestingly, age was a factor; although similar proportions of men and women in their sixties rated themselves as independent, once they were over 70, men were much more prone to see themselves as independent (eight in ten men as compared to a little more than half the women). This held true regardless of actual level of physical impairment. Put another way, regardless of disability, old men clung to the notion of being able to care for themselves. Their self-images retained a "masculine," that is, self-assertive core, where they saw themselves as capable of maintaining active roles despite objective evidence to the contrary. The importance of this finding is underlined by evidence suggesting that old people who perceive their health more favorably (whether or not they are correct) are also more likely to have higher morale, greater satisfaction in life, and less depression (Riley and Foner, 1968).

What are some of the actual physiological changes that occur in old age, and are there differences between men and women, between whites and nonwhites, and among those of different socioeconomic backgrounds? The remainder of this chapter focuses on changes in the body, functional capacity, and patterns of mortality in old age.

Physiological Changes in Old Age

PHYSICAL DECLINE

Although there is considerable individual variation in the decrement of function of human organs over time, there is a gradual diminishing rate of efficiency of the body. Leaf (1973, p. 52) has said that the average person at age 75 has 92 percent of one's brain weight at age 30, 84 percent of the basal metabolic rate, 70 percent of the kidney filtration rate, and 43 percent of the breathing capacity. In other words, there is a gradual slowing down of the body. Cardiovascular function also changes with age; even in the absence of pathology, the output of the heart and heart strokes themselves decrease, the net effect of which is that the heart has to work harder to achieve less. Muscle tone and strength also decline; peaking at between the ages of 20 and 30, they then decrease gradually throughout the remainder of one's life (Weg, 1976). Skin wrinkling, too, is obviously associated with aging and is apparently the result of loss of subcutaneous fat tissue, decreasing skin elasticity, and exposure to sun and weather. Hair becomes gray and thinner—again as a result of the slowing down of the body—in this case, a reduction in the number of pigment-producing cells.

Loss of sensory activity—vision, hearing, taste, smell, and touch—have also been observed in old age (Weg, 1976). The extent to which these changes are inevitable is not fully understood; for example, the reduction in taste and smell may be the result of such factors as malnutrition and ill-fitting or nonexistent dentures.

As our sampling of television commercials shows, using dentures is almost synonymous with growing old. Slightly over half of those 65 or older are edentulous, that is, have lost all their teeth. By age 75, about three fourths of the American population are toothless. Edentulousness is not, however, inevitable in old age; it is strongly related to low income and its correlate, low education. Much of the tooth loss of old age could have been prevented if these individuals had access to adequate dental care throughout their lives. Furthermore, there have been recent changes in the art of dentistry; in the past, it was believed that certain chronic diseases such as arthritis could be alleviated by pulling teeth, and little attention was given to preserving teeth. Tooth decay, a major reason for tooth loss among those without dental care, slows down after about age 30 or 35; gum diseases then become the major source for tooth problems. Both sources are preventable.

Allied to the physical changes associated with the aging process are vision decrements that are common in middle age and old age. Among people 12–17 years of age, for example, only 22 percent have defective vision (defined as less than 20/40 without correction). This proportion actually decreases thereafter until about age 45 at which point defective vision increases. By age 75–79, 85 percent of the population has less than 20/40 vision. Although defective vision is the norm in old age, serious visual deficits are much more rare, affecting slightly more than 7 percent among those 65–74 and 16 percent of those 75+. Not only is the incidence of blindness and other serious visual difficulties greater the older one lives, but the incidence of blindness is twice as high among nonwhites as whites, and the rate of absolute blindness is three times greater. Of the approximately 500,000 legally blind people in the United States, about half are over 65.

Hearing loss, too, is common in old age. Seventy-five percent of those aged 75–79 have hearing difficulties as compared to 19 percent in the 45–54 age group. Impaired hearing associated with the aging process is known as presbycusis and is first noticed in loss of acuity in the higher tone ranges—a process that begins in early adulthood (Corso, 1971). Most aged retain a level of hearing that is sufficient for normal living, however, and only about 7 percent of old men and 5 percent of old women have severely limiting hearing problems.

Summary. There is a gradual slowing down of the body with age. Some of this is subject to control or retardation; for example, muscle strength and tone can be regained and maintained with an exercise regime of six to eight weeks among both older men and women. Such exercise not only improves muscle tone but results in improved cardiovascular function and general energy level (Weg, 1976, p. 84).

NUTRITION

Although Americans are very "diet conscious," they pay little attention in general to good nutrition. Weight loss diets are found in paperback and hardcover books, magazines and newspapers; food advertisements fill much of our newspapers. But relatively little attention is given to nutritional procedures that may ward off the more deleterious effects often occurring in the aging process. Indeed, the little research that exists on nutrition and aging comes primarily from laboratory experiments, so that we know more about the nutrition of aging rats than of people. Faulty nutrition and dietary habits, however, have been impiicated as factors in the development of chronic disease among human populations. For example, arteriosclerosis is related to saturated ("animal") fat intake, and reduction in saturated fats in one's diet with a concomitant increase in polyunsaturated (vegetable) fats may decrease cholesterol levels. This is not as straightforward as it first seems, for the body manufactures cholesterol as an indispensable element in the physiological functions of the body; the cholesterol in food thus may not be as responsible for raising the level of blood cholesterol as that made by the body in response to the food taken and other factors not fully understood. Whether diet prevents heart attack is unproven; as Bignall (1976) observed:

> This is as illogical as observing that the incidence (of coronary heart disease) is greater in men who are bald and deducing that they would benefit from wearing a wig. . . . to show that lowering the serum-cholesterol is beneficial then he must contrast the risk of C. H. D. between a group of men with a high cholesterol who have had it lowered and a group with a high cholesterol which is allowed to remain high. (p. 1034).

Fiber in the diet, it has been suggested, may prevent bowel cancer, diverticulosis (weakening of the intestinal wall), and a variety of other gastrointestinal complaints. Refined sugars—common in most sweets and many other packaged foods—have been implicated in the development not only of tooth decay but diabetes and possibly heart disease (Yudkin, 1978). Nor is salt free from blame; sodium intake has been related to hypertension, a poorer prognosis in congestive heart failure, certain liver disorders, and excessive fluid retention. Overweight itself exacerbates a number of chronic illnesses, including arthritis and certain kinds of heart disease.

What, then, is an optimal diet? At the present time, there is no firm answer. Although the "recommended daily allowance" (RDA) of vitamins, minerals, protein, fat and carbohydrates is accepted, this represents the *minimum* requirements to prevent nutritional diseases. The *optimal* dietary requirements to maintain peak health and functioning are poorly understood. Some investigators, such as Nobel Prize winner Linus Pauling, have suggested that the body requires very large amounts of vitamin C if it is to ward off the common cold, other respiratory disorders, and possibly cancer. This claim remains highly controversial, although there is emerging evidence that large doses of this vitamin may reduce incidence or shorten the duration of the common cold (Anderson, 1972; Coulehan et al., 1974; Wilson and Loh, 1973). Niacin, Vitamin E and other vitamins have also been heralded as wonder drugs and their lack in our

Table 4–1. Recommended Daily Dietary Allowances for Selected Age Groups According to the Food and Nutrition Board, National Academy of Sciences—National Research Council

Age	Weight (lbs.)	Height (inches)	Calories	Protein	Calcium	Iron	Vit. A	Thiamine	Niacin	Vit. C
Male										
9–12	72	55	2,400	60 gms.	1.1 gms.	15 mgm.	4,500	1.0 mg.	16 mg.	70 mg.
35–55	154	69	2,600	70	0.8	10	5,000	1.0	17	70
55–75	154	69	2,200	70	0.8	10	5,000	0.9	15	70
Female										
9–12	72	55	2,200	55	1.1	15	4,500	0.9	15	80
35–55	128	64	1,900	58	0.8	15	5,000	0.8	13	70
55–75	128	64	1,600	58	0.8	10	5,000	0.8	13	70

The Merck Manual of Diagnosis and Therapy, Rahway, N.J.: Merck Sharp & Dohme Research Laboratories, Table 50, p. 1721, 1966.

current diet lamented. But firm and constant empirical evidence has failed to find a panacea for either major or minor illnesses; simply not enough is known about the role of diet in prevention of illness. Faddism rides rampant.

It has been suggested, however, that the recommended daily dietary allowance differs for various age groups, as may be seen in Table 4–1.

Taken from a widely used physicians' manual of diagnosis and therapy, Table 4–1 indicates that some variation in nutritional needs is expected according to age, sex, height and weight. The requirements detailed are included not to be taken slavishly, but rather to highlight the point that the metabolism and level of activity of a person, as well as age, should be taken into account in considering nutritional needs. The 20-year-old hockey player who weighs 128 pounds may have greater nutritional needs than her 130 pound male age peer who spends much of his time playing chess; likewise the tennis-playing 75-year-old man will have different nutritional and dietary needs than his t.v. watching counterpart. The question of optimal nutrition, as previously noted, remains unresolved.

What other factors influence nutrition? Living alone—and, as discussed in this chapter, women usually live longer than men, thus having a greater chance of widowhood—is often associated with poor nutrition. Since eating is a social as well as physiological function, preparation of a meal simply for one's self may be cursory and inadequate. Old men who live alone may not know how to cook and thus rely on fast foods, which may contain insufficient minimal dietary requirements. Physical incapacity, too, may interfere with nutritional intake; the physically impaired person may find it difficult to prepare a meal and eat it. To remedy this situation, nutritional programs have been developed under Title III of the Older Americans Act. Yet nutritional programs at senior centers have met with mixed success; some critics of specific centers have commented that inadequate attention is paid to the ethnic preferences of the groups attending the meal program. Accordingly, much of the "balanced diet" is viewed as unattractive.

Institutionalization, too, contributes to poor nutrition. In some nursing homes and other institutions for the elderly, the food, like that at some colleges and universities, suffers from batch cooking, heating on steam tables, and choice of cheaper rather than more nutritious foods. Again, ethnic and racial preferences may be ignored in an institutional setting.

Lastly, income plays a significant factor in dietary composition. Many of the elderly live on fixed incomes and are unable to purchase the more expensive items such as meat and fish. The problem of a low, fixed income may be compounded by lack of access to transportation so that the old are forced to buy their groceries at the closest store to their residence; thus they may not be able to shop around for the best buy on a diet which meets minimal dietary requirements.

STRESS

One of the more intriguing areas of inquiry dealing with the physiology of aging has been in the area of stress. Proposed by Selye (1956), stress is defined as "the state manifested by a specific syndrome which consists of all the nonspecifically induced changes within a biological system" (p. 54). Observing that any type of environmental change—pleasant or unpleasant—that requires an individual to adapt to a new or altered physical or social environment may produce bodily changes in the organism, Selye proposed the following network: event → alarm reaction → resistance by the organism → exhaustion. This theory, known as the general adaptation syndrome (GAS), postulates that after an initial alarm reaction following a stimulus, a stage of resistance occurs as a result of cortical activity in the brain that in turn has an effect on body metabolism. If stress continues, the person enters stage three—exhaustion—which is a kind of premature aging in which bodily reserves are depleted. Stress, then, is an event that produces changes in the bodily maintenance or psychic ease of an individual. That physiological or environmental stress plays a decisive role in lowered bodily resistance has been demonstrated in laboratory studies involving both people and animals; it is also of increasing interest in explaining the onset of various types of illness.

Stress is a deceptively simple concept, however. It is intuitively easy to understand how unpleasant events may be upsetting and produce physical changes (for example, lowered resistance to colds during exam time) and emotional depression. Following the Great Blizzard of 1978, when an unprecedented amount of snow fell in New England, the aftermath of the storm-related severe flooding and home destruction that occurred in seaside towns was observed to produce depression and agitation among residents of communities that had been badly damaged by the storm. These effects were strongly pronounced seven months after the actual storm itself (*Boston Globe*, August 6, part 1, p. 1). On the other hand, positive changes—such as a better job, a lengthy vacation, and so on—may be as disturbing as disasters, as has been recently demonstrated (see, for example, Holmes and Masuda, 1974). The mechanisms by which people respond to stress are still poorly understood, however, and it has been suggested that an important element in the relationship of illness to understanding stress as it relates to the development or exacerbation of illness is to distinguish clearly among the physical health, psychological state, and actual events that occur among people (Dohrenwend and Dohrenwend, 1974). The manner in which stress may relate to the development of chronic disease is thus incompletely understood. The following paragraphs analyze one chronic disease, hypertension (high blood pressure), within a possible framework.

Hypertension.   Hypertension is of increasing concern because of its relationship to heart disease and strokes. Data on the extent of hypertension indicate that its incidence is indeed associated with the aging process. In 1971–74, at the time of a major national study of high blood pressure, there were an estimated 23.4 million Americans between the ages of 12 and 74 with hypertension (Advance Data, 1976). The prevalence rate of the disease increases drastically with age; 0.8 percent of those in the 12–17 year age group have hypertension as compared to 40.7 percent between the ages of 65 and 74. Not only is hypertension a disease of older age groups but the psychosomatic medical literature suggests that it is a physiological response associated with an emotional attitude of being prepared to meet all threats, where "You feel you may be attacked and hurt at any instant; it may be painful, it may be dangerous, you feel you are in danger. You're threatened every instant, you have to watch out" (Graham et al., 1962, pp. 160–161.). Keeping this thought in mind (for which there is, incidentally, experimental evidence), let us look at some of the social characteristics of people who develop hypertension.

Paradoxically, in younger age groups, hypertension is more prevalent among men than women, but by the time one reaches age 55, the risk of hypertension is greater among women than men. Thirty four percent of women aged 55–64 have hypertension as compared to 32.3 percent of men; by age 65–74, this difference is more distinct (43.9 percent of women as compared to 36.6 percent men of that age). Proportionately more blacks than whites have high blood pressure (22.2 percent as compared to 15 percent); white men have the lowest rates of this disease (12 percent) and black women the highest (25.9 percent). Hypertension is also associated with low income and levels of education; people who did not go to high school are twice as likely as college graduates to be hypertensive, and those with incomes of less than $5,000 yearly are almost twice more likely to have this disease than those with incomes of $10,000 or more.

In old age, the difference associated with race (itself confounded by the low socioeconomic status of many black aged) and sex are even more obvious. About one in four white men aged 65–74 has hypertension as compared to slightly more than one in three black men (25.4 percent versus 38.1 percent). White women more closely resemble the rates found among black men; about one in four white women (40.2 percent) has hypertension as compared to half the black women (50.5 percent). Clearly the chance of having hypertension rises with low income, limited education, and being either black or female. Black women are in the highest risk group. How, then, do these social characteristics of hypertensives relate to stress? It seems not too far-fetched to propose that the combination of low socioeconomic status and minority group membership contributes to a feeling of being under attack and watchful; the poor and socially disadvantaged actually experience more threats—both environmental and social—than the well-off and more powerful. A recent study has evaluated the development of hypertension among black and white women to determine the extent to which work load—and overload—work satisfaction, reported strain about work performance, and evaluation of one's performance relate to high blood pressure (Harenstein, Kasl, and Harberg, 1977). The findings suggest that housewives who reported tension about their housework and who were critical of their own performance as housewives were very likely to have high blood pressure. Also at high risk of hypertension were working women with a strong commitment to their work role and who were dissatisfied with their own work achievement. This study reveals important information about the impact of social pressures—economic, minority status, and sex roles—as well as possible personality factors on hypertension. The nature of the development of hypertension, especially the biological processes involved and how these interact with social stresses, is still vague. This is true of other chronic diseases as well; the particular mechanisms by which stress may produce disease are not well delineated. Apparently as one grows older, the ability to withstand physiological and environmental stress is substantially reduced (Shock, 1976). Growing old here refers not to chronological age so much as to organ age, which is itself influenced by genetics, life-styles, and nutrition. The ways in which one's biological state, including one's genetic inheritance and one's personal and social situation, relate to the development of most disorders in old age remains to be unraveled.

CHANGES IN REPRODUCTIVE CAPACITY

One age change that is universal to women is menopause, the permanent cessation of menstruation, which usually occurs between the ages of 48 and 52. Approximately 27 million women over the age of 50 in the United States have gone through menopause; they have an average life expectancy of twenty-eight or so more years (Jones, Cohen, and Wilson, 1973). There is, incidentally, no equivalent to menopause among men, for there is no specific time after puberty in males when they are infertile as a result of age-related changes (Masters and Johnson, 1966). Indeed, some men have normal testosterone levels (the male hormone responsible for gonadal activity) at age 80 or beyond (Vermeulen et al., 1972).

When menopause occurs, the ovaries stop producing about 90 percent of their secretion of hormones—the best documented example of hormone decrease during aging in humans (Finch, 1976). The process of cessation of ovarian function is still not fully known other than that estrogen levels drop significantly. Menopause as the onset of infertility among women is widely recognized and perhaps has been enjoyed by many women in the past as a welcome relief from childbearing. This release was bought at a price, for it suggested that a woman was neither sexually interesting nor had value in producing sons (Cooper, 1975). Much mythology still surrounds menopause. During the nineteenth century, for example, the mythologies of menopause and menstruation were closely linked. One gynecologist of that period described women as "a moral, a sexual, a germiferous, gestative, and parturient creature" (Collins, 1976). Menstruation was thought to be a process by which women were relieved of toxic substances; menopause, therefore, indicated that a woman was no longer getting rid of evil toxicities which thus remained trapped inside her.

> During the greater part of the thirty years of sexual activity a woman loses from four to six ounces of blood every month. The system is now so thoroughly accustomed to this drain that to stop it suddenly . . . we would naturally suppose would be followed by untoward consequences. This we find in reality to be the case, even though the cessation of menstruation at the change of life is a perfectly physiological one. (Shirk, 1884)

Since the woman's body was no longer able to eliminate waste products through menstruation, it was also proposed that waste products were eliminated through the skin in "unnatural sweats"—the so-called "hot flashes" of menopause (Shirk, 1884). Today this theory is dismissed as ridiculous, yet menopause remains not much better understood. As Finch (1976) has put it, "One of the major questions biologists are asking at present is how many of the phenomena of aging in women are the result of this loss of hormones" (p. 64). The cultural stereotype of the menopausal woman is of a person prone to depression, anxiety, loss of confidence, and lack of sexual interest. The one common symptom, felt among a majority of women during menopause, is hot flashes; the demonstrable physiological sign is a decrease in urinary excretion of estrogen, usually followed by atrophy of genital tissues. Contrary to popular belief, a woman's body does continue to produce estrogen after menstruation ceases, although it does so at lower levels than during the reproductive years (Clay, 1977). Finch has raised the question of whether the ovary ages (and menopause occurs) because of intrinsic changes and depletion of ova or because of changes in brain signals sent to the ovaries. Experiments on rats suggest that the latter theory may be correct; when the ovary of an old mouse is transplanted to a young one, the old ovary regains its youthful function. Experiments with electrodes implanted in the brain of rats also indicate that stimulation of the brain of a rat may reactivate the ovary. This suggests that the brain may indeed control reproductive aging among females, and that the ovary may be "jump started" by stimulation of the portion of the brain controlling the endocrine system (Finch, 1976).

While manufacturers of estrogen describe menopause as a "deficiency disease" that lends itself to symptomatic control through estrogen replacement therapy (Collins, 1976), such treatment is controversial. There has been relatively little research on the effects of estrogen replacement even though it is now known to have serious side effects. That menopause is a normal developmental phase for women (Clay, 1977) is only beginning to be recognized in the gynecological literature (see Bart and Sculley [1972] for a content analysis of modern gynecological textbooks that display some rather old-fashioned views of female patients). Many of the "problems" associated with menopause are social rather than physiological; for example, the frequent anxiety and depression experienced by older women are most likely the result of surviving in a culture that becomes less supportive of women as they grow older (Collins, 1976; Clay, 1977; Livson, 1977; Reitz, 1977).

What are the implications of menopause—an apparently natural change of aging—for the aging process itself? Osteoporosis, a disease of the bones whose major effect is fracture, is, for example, four times more common in women than in men. Old age increases the risk of fracture, especially among women. The loss of estrogen that occurs after menopause may be related to the incidence of osteoporosis, yet the evidence is inconclusive (Heaney, Eisenberg, and Johnson, 1973). There are differing views of whether heart disease is accelerated in women after the menopause, and it is also not clear why men have a greater incidence of certain types of heart attacks than women. In sum, an age-old phenomenon common to all women in midlife remains as mysterious as ever. What makes it occur? What is its impact on the development of disease in later life? What is the differential contribution of male versus female hormones to the development of, or insulation from, chronic diseases in later life? As more research is done on the aging process, it should become easier to determine which chronic diseases, if any, are inevitably associated with the aging process, and which are related to hormonal changes, to stress, to diet, and to genetic factors. At the present time, there is just not enough information to say more than that the elderly are prone to chronic disease. This is discussed at greater length in the following section.

Health Status

THE FRAMEWORK OF DIS-EASE

Health and illness are straightforward words, and it seems pedantic to attempt to define them. Yet both words have been given different meanings in each particular society and time period. Health and illness are historically grounded since both are consequences of social problems and represent problem-solving endeavors that have succeeded or failed in the past. The occurrence of anthracosilicosis—an occupational lung disease very common among coal miners—is historically linked to the evolution of the use of coals as fuel. Though anthracite coal solved many fuel problems for a while, it had unanticipated social consequences—lung disease among miners who inhaled dust. The recognition of silicosis as a specific occupational disease is also linked to the rise of trade unionism. Although "miner's asthma" had been observed for many generations, it was not until miners became unionized that health benefits for this condition were sought. Prior to that time, the disease was considered a natural, if unpleasant, occupational risk.

Health and illness are culturally circumscribed as well; what is "normal" or healthy is defined by the society in which it occurs. This is not to say that diseases are not real or that specific agents or pathogens may not be identified, but, rather, that each society itself defines, in light of its values, how the condition is to be viewed. Whether the condition will be considered a "polite," socially acceptable one, such as arthritis, or an "impolite one," such as venereal disease, is inextricably related to social values and moral judgments. Indeed, whether the disorder is recognized as a disease varies. In some societies certain medical conditions are empirically demonstrable as disease, yet they go unrecognized. Yaws—a disease with skin lesions that ulcerate, causing nodes and disfigurement—is so common in some tropical regions that people without its blemishes are considered odd looking. Likewise, conditions that might be identified as severe mental illness by Western psychiatrists are viewed as possession by evil spirits by a Puerto Rican spiritualist.

Within our own society, what is considered illness will vary according to occupation, age, and sex of the afflicted person. A skin rash on the hands may be an itchy nuisance to a teacher but a major health problem to a cook; hoarseness is a bother to an accountant but disabling to an opera singer. To summarize: health and illness are dynamic concepts that change with time, social circumstance, and social values. One useful way to think of health and illness among the old is within a "dis-ease" framework; "if we take disease literally as the absence of ease, then we must of course ask: whose ease? and In what context?" (Wilson, 1970, p. 6). Disease is not randomly distributed among the population, but varies greatly according to age, sex, socioeconomic status, residence, and habits. Although there are marked discrepancies in the health of the old and young, as is later examined at some length, several dimensions are also common to disease in all age groups (Antonovsky, 1972). First, all diseases have at least one of two socially undesirable consequences—they are painful to the individual, or second, they handicap one in exercising faculties—mental or physical—for performance of social roles. Furthermore, diseases are characterized by both a kind and degree of acuteness-chronicity with a certain level of threat to life. Finally, diseases are generally recognized by the medical institutions of the society as needing care under their direction.

ACUTE AND CHRONIC CONDITIONS

The concept of dis-ease and the common denominators of all diseases together provide a useful framework to look at health status in old age. The focus on functional limitations, degree of pain, chronicity, and type of medical care or other health services one may require from the community, emphasizes function rather than pathology. Most old people exhibit one or more signs of pathology associated with the aging process; the important task has become that of tracing the patterns of incapacity that follow.

Types of disease vary according to age group; for example, as shown in Table 4–2, the incidence of *acute* conditions of all types declines with age.

Table 4–2. Incidents of Acute Conditions Among the Noninstitutionalized Civilian Population, 1975 (Rate per 100)

Condition	0–5	6–16	17–44	45+
Infective and parasitic	55.4	33.7	20.1	9.1
Respiratory				
upper	142.9	81.3	51.7	29.3
other	70.9	62.4	58.0	32.1
Digestive system	14.6	14.3	10.7	6.0
Injuries	49.5	43.9	38.7	24.6

Statistical Abstract of the United States, 1977, p. 113, Table 176.

Children under six years of age are most likely to have acute conditions of any type, and the incidence of acute medical conditions declines steadily thereafter.

Chronic conditions, however, increase with age. Over three-quarters of the population 65 and over have at least one chronic disease, half have two or more chronic diseases, and slightly more than half of the old have had to limit their activity as a result of chronic medical problems. As Table 4–3 shows, this limitation of activity varies by sex. Men are more likely than women to have an activity limitation, as well as to be limited in one or more major activity.

SEX DIFFERENCES

Paradoxically, whereas women have more chronic conditions in every instance except for heart conditions, they have less activity limitations than men. Men are more prone, perhaps, to "killer" conditions such as heart

Table 4–3. Activity Limitation Among People 65+ by Sex and Selected Chronic Conditions (1974)

	Per Cent		Male–Female Difference
Limitation	Men	Women	
Heart condition	25.2	22.2	+ 3.0
Arthritis/rheumatism	15.6	29.4	−13.8
Visual impairments	8.6	10.7	− 2.1
Hypertension without heart disease	6.0	10.9	− 4.9
Mental and nervous	3.0	3.8	− 0.8
Severity of limitation			
No activity limitation	50.3	56.9	− 6.6
Activity limitation	49.7	43.1	+ 6.6
In major activity	44.8	35.3	+ 9.5

Statistical Abstract of the United States, 1976, Table 177, p. 114.

disease, whereas women are more likely to have arthritis/rheumatism and hypertension. Women are more vulnerable to chronic disease, but less disabled.

There is a wealth of evidence that indicates that women in younger age groups have higher rates of acute disease, and more disability days, and that women restrict their activity and stay in bed more than men. A variety of explanations for this sex-linked difference in illness behavior have been proposed that are related to social roles of men versus women. Women, who are permitted greater latitude to express their feelings and to show physical weakness more than men, may be more likely to say that they are ill at the sign of the first symptoms of an illness, whereas men who are imbued with an ethic that discourages infirmity and loss of strength, may ignore symptoms of illness until they become disabling. Then, too, housewives have been alleged to have fewer time constraints than working men or women and thus are more able to take time out to be sick. In any case, slowing down and seeking medical attention when acutely ill at younger ages may promote longevity; women who utilized health services more heavily at earlier age levels apparently have benefited from this by early diagnosis and control of chronic conditions in old age (Verbrugge, 1976). Biological factors, too, probably play a role; women throughout their lives have higher rates of illness than men but lower death rates. Madigan, who compared two Roman Catholic teaching orders with essentially similar contemplative life-styles in order to explore the contributions of biological versus social factors in the longevity of the two sexes, found that though sex differences were reduced between

The Aging Organism

them when the life style was similar, women still retained a biological advantage (Madigan, 1957). This biological advantage, incidentally, is found in other species, such as in rats.

RACE DIFFERENCES

Significant socioeconomic differences associated with minority group membership also affect the extent of disability that is felt among those 65 and over. Overall, blacks are more likely to have some limitation of activity as a result of a chronic condition; 52.8 percent of the black aged, 45.9 percent of the Hispanic aged, and 44.6 percent of the white and other racial group aged had such limitation in 1976. Much of this, however, is the result of the heavy concentration of blacks in families with an annual income of less than $5,000 per year; 56.0 percent of the black aged as compared to 39.2 percent of the Hispanic, and 34 percent of the white and others 65+ lived in these low-income families. When family income is taken into account, as shown in Table 4–4, the relationship between minority group membership, limitation of activity, and number of disability days becomes weaker. In each group, the higher the level of family income, the lower is the average number of days of bed disability, at least until a certain level above the poverty level is reached. For low-income people, especially those in minority groups, their level of disability may in fact be underenumerated. (For further discussion, see Chapter 7.)

Table 4–4. Limitation of Activity and Days of Bed Disability, by Minority Group and Family Income (1976 Data)

Limitation of Activity Caused by Chronic Conditions	Per Cent 65+ limited activity			
	Total U.S.	Hispanic Origin	Black	Other (including White)
Income less than $5,000	53.4%	46.0%	59.4%	52.7%
$ 5,000–9,999	43.1	42.2	46.5	42.9
$10,000–14,999	39.6	58.3	41.2	39.0
$15,000 or more	38.7	60.0	40.7	38.2
Days of Bed Disability Per Person Per Year	Average no. days in bed			
Income less than $5,000	16.9	33.5	19.7	15.9
$ 5,000–9,999	14.6	17.4	19.7	14.2
$10,000–14,999	11.4	0.8	0.9	12.3
$15,000 or more	13.1	—	14.8	13.2

Advance Data from Vital and Health Statistics of the National Center for Health Statistics, no. 27, April 14, 1978, Tables 2 and 4.

AGE DIFFERENCES

Age, too, is a significant factor in activity limitation; only 42 percent of those aged 65–74 were limited as compared to 56 percent of those 75 years of age or older(*Health*, 1976–77). In general, the "young-old" have the fewest incapacities; according to a study by Shanas et al. (1968)[1], persons 65–69 functioned very well, with close to seven in ten reporting that they had no difficulties at all in such activities of daily living as going out of doors, walking up and down stairs, washing and bathing, dressing and putting on shoes, and cutting toenails. By age 75–79, there is a marked change in physical capacity, with an increasingly large number of people of both sexes who experience major and minor difficulties in physical functioning. Among the old-old, aged 80 or over, close to a half of the noninstitutionalized old reported some difficulty in major tasks. Forty-two percent had difficulty walking stairs, 34 percent could not cut their toenails (a homely but essential task, also indicative of ability to bend and manipulate one's arms and legs); another 19 percent had difficulty in washing and bathing. Fewer had difficulty in dressing and putting on shoes (13 percent) and in getting around the house (11 percent). Again, old people with the lowest incapacity scores were more likely than other old people to have a relatively high income.

Despite the rise in functional incapacity associated with age, there was no decline in the proportions who felt that their health was good; about the same percentage in every age category classified their health as good. The more mobile an old person is, apparently the more likely he/she is to say that his/her health is good. This is not surprising; attitudes toward health are an indicator of general morale and sense of well-being, of which physical fitness is an important component. Interestingly, old people in their midseventies tend to be somewhat depressed about their health; once over 80, however, people are optimistic, perhaps because they are members of a biological and psychological elite. As Cumming and Henry observed in their studies of the old:

> Through the interviews of the seventies there runs a thread of pessimism which sometimes borders onto irritability and self pity. . . . Among the eighties there is less complaining and more chirpiness, sometimes a mood of using up the last days of life in tranquility and sometimes a genuine carefree quality. (1961, p. 201)

As Shanas et al. pointed out, those people who feel that their health is poor are far more likely than others to express feelings of loneliness and alienation, possibly as a result of depression. Those who survive into their eighties may never have been prone to the depression found among many of those a bit younger. There is some indication that subjective,

---

[1] This section is drawn from the work of Shanas et al. (1968).

psychosocial data provided by old people is a significant predictor of mortality, one that is more accurate than the medical opinion provided by their family physician in judging life expectancy (Wimmers and Mol, 1975). The real, if difficult to delineate, "will to live" seems a key factor in predicting the course and the end of the aging process for both men and women.

The Sick Role in Old Age

Despite the apparent good spirit in which most aged take the normal decrements in health and physical functioning associated with the aging process, the occurrence of incapacitating illness is a significant life event. Being sick is not an isolated event at any age but, as Talcott Parsons (1958) has observed, a distinct social role, characterized by certain rights, obligations, and privileges. These include a release from everyday role responsibilities, in return for which the sick person is expected to define his or her state of ill health as undesirable and time limited, and to seek appropriate medical treatment in order to bring about a speedy recovery. The sick role differs from many other social roles—wife, husband, parent, worker—in that it is only conditionally legitimated; staying in the role is discouraged, for illness may provide an inviting, if unconsciously motivated, relief from the tension of one's life.

For the old who have outlived their jobs and their spouses and friends, or who are witnessing a dropping away of social ties, the sick role may be an attractive alternative to carrying on as before. As we have shown, old age is generally a devalued status in our society, and feeling "old" is marked by both a sense of physical and behavioral changes in one's self and by an awareness of ill health, disability, and weakness (Blau, 1956; Suchman et al., 1958; Phillips, 1956). The aged who are retired, widowed, never married, and without friends or contacts with relatives are also those most likely to "feel old" and to be concerned with their health. Illness and disability are more accessible in old age precisely because of declining physical function, and may also provide some elderly with a central social role at a time when other roles have been relinquished or are unsatisfying (Parsons, 1960). Illness and disability are also ways of getting attention and care from others. Secondary psychological gains may be gotten as well; being sick lends a rationale for centering concern primarily on one's self and on one's own body.

But illness or disability in any age group is a highly charged emotional experience that raises questions about the prospect of recovery, death, lingering disabilities that worsen, and about the meaning of life itself. In this fashion, disease disturbs one's sense of what Erikson (1963) has called ego identity, that is, "the accrued confidence that ability to main-

Aging Bodies and Minds

tain inner sameness and continuity is matched by the sameness and continuity of meaning for others." As discussed at greater length in the next chapter, old age has been described as a time of ego integrity versus despair. In the former, personality reintegration, an awareness of relatedness to others and a sense of selfhood, are the positive outcomes of the developmental challenge of old age. In despair, however, awareness of personal deterioration, withdrawal of emotional expression, and depression may occur. It is thus not surprising that following surgery, old people often experience a marked and progressive mental deterioration. Such decrement, which occurs postoperatively in about one in four aged patients, was correlated to loss of an accepting, comfortable home environment. It was also most common among the oldest old (Titchner, Zwerling, Gottschalk, and Levine, 1958). Disabling depression, which often lasted several months after surgery, was frequent; some aged felt completely powerless to resist external stress or threats.

As is discussed in Chapter 6, most old people view institutions as the last resort for the treatment of medical problems, and fear institutionalization as a prelude to death. Yet incapacitating disease often invites placement in a nursing home or other facility from which a frequent method of release is death. Once in the institution, the old are even more isolated—spatially, socially, and psychically—from their everyday lives and often are dependent upon their caretakers for their basic life needs. The old person who is isolated from former activities is also often denied social supports in learning how to phase out life and to die.

There is a little agreement about how the aged feel about death in general or their own deaths in particular, probably because there is relatively little real cultural preparation for, or interest in, this event. Indeed, old people in general are hesitant to define *any* of their personal problems as suitable for outside help. Keeping a stiff upper lip and not depending on others or expressing need is part of the work ethic with which they were brought up. In turn, medical personnel are less likely to refer physically ill older people for consultation even when such a referral would be appropriate (Ginsberg and Goldstein, 1974; Kuraski, White, and Schratz, 1979), perhaps because the old are going to die soon anyway and referral is a waste of scare resources that might be expended on a younger person.

An attitude of therapeutic nihilism clearly often prevails in medical treatment and nursing care facilities for the old. Old people are more likely to die from minor ailments in a nursing home or institution than if they are left to live in the community even in adverse home conditions (Blenkner, 1967). Once in the sick role, the old run a calculated risk—that of becoming locked in the role and shunted off to an institution that cares only for their basic physical needs. They also are likely to be overmedicated with psychoactive drugs—often, for the convenience of their caretakers rather than in response to their own needs (Green, 1978). These may be the unanticipated consequences of sickness in old age. Rosow (1967) has pointed out that old people are well off when they are married and living with a spouse, still at work, have no major loss of income, and remain in relatively good health. For old people who become seriously sick, it is unlikely that these conditions are met, and they are at high risk of dying. The following sections review the reasons and conditions in which old people die.

Death

MEASURES OF MORTALITY

Although the probability of death for any living creature is exactly 100 percent, there are obviously some differences in the frequency with which people die within any given time period as well as the average probability of living a specified period of time. These averages can be measured with some accuracy for people with specific social characteristics.

Mortality Rates. The simplest measure of death is the *crude mortality* or *death rate*, which is defined as follows:

$$\frac{\text{Total number of deaths within specified time period}}{\text{Total population within that time period}} \times 1,000$$

Put another way, the crude death rate gives a statistic that is an overall rate at which people die in a given time period.

Of more use is the *specific death rate* that measures the mortality of subgroups which can then be compared. Some examples of specific death rates are disease specific, age specific, sex specific, and race specific. These are calculated as in the following example, which gives a formula for age and sex specific death rates among white men:

$$\frac{\text{Number of white men, age 65–74, dying of heart disease, 1975}}{\text{Total number white men, age 65–75, in 1975 population}} \times 1,000$$

If one wished to calculate a comparable figure for, say, white women who died of heart disease in 1975, this may be done by simply inserting the appropriate data.

As expectations of living until old age have increased, the mortality rate in old age has become very large, as the following table, which shows mortality rates by age during 1976, demonstrates.

Life Expectancy. Life expectancy differs from the death rate in that life

Table 4–5. Mortality Rates for Different Age Groups, by Race and Sex, 1976

[Refers only to resident deaths occurring within the United States. Rates per 100,000 estimated population in specified age group]

Age	Total			White			All other		
	Both sexes	Male	Female	Both sexes	Male	Female	Both sexes	Male	Female
Rates per 100,000 population									
All ages [1]	889.6	1,007.0	778.3	899.4	1,010.4	793.6	824.8	983.5	680.0
Under 1 year	1,595.0	1,762.6	1,419.0	1,356.2	1,511.8	1,192.1	2,781.5	3,012.4	2,542.2
1–4 years	69.9	78.2	61.3	64.1	71.9	55.9	96.9	107.5	86.1
5–9 years	34.8	41.0	28.3	32.7	38.3	26.9	45.1	54.8	35.4
10–14 years	34.6	44.0	25.0	33.7	42.8	24.2	39.5	49.9	29.0
15–19 years	97.1	139.9	53.2	96.0	138.1	52.6	103.3	149.8	56.9
20–24 years	131.3	198.4	64.4	120.0	182.4	57.0	199.5	300.1	107.2
25–29 years	129.3	187.2	72.4	110.9	159.8	61.8	254.8	389.9	139.3
30–34 years	144.8	196.5	94.5	122.4	164.2	80.9	297.8	436.6	180.7
35–39 years	198.4	261.6	138.6	168.4	219.2	119.2	405.0	580.5	261.8
40–44 years	313.4	406.0	225.3	271.9	352.2	194.0	601.1	811.3	426.1
45–49 years	498.1	647.8	356.3	450.0	586.6	319.0	863.6	1,138.3	625.6
50–54 years	767.7	1,017.3	536.8	706.8	940.9	488.4	1,280.3	1,683.3	928.6
55–59 years	1,175.0	1,578.0	807.2	1,107.7	1,496.4	757.0	1,796.6	2,352.8	1,312.6
60–64 years	1,822.8	2,496.3	1,230.5	1,743.6	2,407.9	1,157.7	2,579.2	3,371.4	1,917.0
65–69 years	2,541.5	3,586.9	1,712.8	2,486.7	3,542.9	1,651.5	2,990.0	3,963.4	2,229.2
70–74 years	3,948.3	5,433.7	2,856.4	3,824.1	5,340.8	2,721.9	5,335.2	6,394.1	4,452.1
75–79 years	6,186.7	8,263.3	4,850.6	6,102.6	8,246.8	4,745.3	7,131.4	8,428.5	6,132.6
80–84 years	9,034.4	11,521.1	7,632.5	9,183.4	11,774.4	7,743.4	7,394.7	9,010.0	6,333.6
85 years and over	15,486.9	17,983.9	14,312.1	16,068.5	18,767.6	14,823.3	10,018.5	11,519.1	9,175.2

[1] Figures for age not stated included in "All ages" but not distributed among groups.
Advance Report, Final Mortality Statistics, 1976, DHEW Pub. PHS 78–1120, 26:12, Supp. 2, March 30, 1978, Table 1.

expectancy reflects the average length of life remaining to a person at any given age. (The procedure for calculating life expectancy is complex; those interested should read L. Dublin et al., *Length of Life: A Study of the Life Table.*)

Table 4–6. Selected Life Table Values, by Color and Sex: United States Death-Registration Areas, Selected Years 1900–74

Life Table Value and Year	Total	White		All Other	
		Male	Female	Male	Female
Life expectancy at birth:					
1974 (est.)	72.0	68.9	76.7	62.9	71.3
1973	71.3	68.4	76.1	61.9	70.1
1972	71.1	68.3	75.9	61.5	69.9
1970	70.9	68.0	75.6	61.3	69.4
1960	69.7	67.4	74.1	61.1	66.3
1900	47.3	46.6	48.7	32.5	33.5
at age 20:					
1973	53.4	50.5	57.7	44.9	52.6
1900–1902	42.8	42.2	43.8	35.1	36.9
Per cent reaching age 65:					
1973	72.9	67.5	82.2	51.0	68.1
1900–1902	40.9	39.2	43.8	19.0	22.0

National Center for Health Statistics, *Vital Statistics of the United States*, Vol. II, Mortality. Selected years.

Life expectancy is affected by such variables as race and sex; for example, white males born in 1900 had an average expectancy of 46.6, while white females averaged 48.7. Nonwhites had a lower life expectancy—14.1 less years for men and 15.2 less years for women. By 1960, life expectancy at birth had increased dramatically—by 22.4 years. Again, there are racial and sex differences; whereas the increase in life expectancy at birth was most pronounced during that period for nonwhites—28.6 for men, 32.8 for women—there is still a noticeable racial differential. By 1974, this had narrowed to 4.0 years between white and nonwhite men, and 5.4 years between white and nonwhite women. The lower life expectancy among nonwhites reflects low income and low parental education, both of which are associated with diminished life chances. For example, among families with incomes of less than $3,000 per year and with less than eight years of formal education, the infant mortality rate is about 140 percent greater than the national average. A study of Native American reservations highlights some reasons for the connections between race, socioeconomic factors, and life expectancy. On the reservations, infant mortality was 41.8 per 1,000 as compared to 25.3 for the general population. People were subjected to extreme overcrowding—an average of 5.4 people per home as compared to 3.2 for the general population. Furthermore, about three quarters of those living on reservations got their water from a potentially contaminated source (a focal point for infectious diseases), and over eight in ten had inadequate toilet facilities. Not surprisingly, their rates of infectious death were many times higher (USDHEW, *Indicators*, March 1964). Inaccessibility of health care, too, creates excessive mortality; in 1969–70, the maternal death rate among Native Americans was 1.4 times higher than among non-Indians (Slocumb and Kunitz, 1977).

By 1973, the proportion of people who reach the age of 65, whether white or nonwhite, had, however, increased dramatically. In 1900 only about 42 percent lived until their sixty-fifth birthday as compared to 72.9 percent in 1973. Much of this leveling off is the result of changes in the infant mortality rate, which is, as has been discussed, the greatest contributor to life expectancy. Yet despite our medical technology and relatively high standard of living as a nation, our life expectancy at birth is lower than that found in many other countries, as may be seen in Table 4–7. As the table also shows, this is especially marked in male life expectancy. The United States ranks nineteenth for men, seventh for women.

That our society has a lower life expectancy than a number of other societies reflects the existence of pockets of extreme poverty in this country. Almost one in five Americans lacks access to health care, is malnourished or underfed, and lives in conditions of physical risk and deprivation. Wide differences in income are associated with wide differences in life expectancy. The implications of this on old age are clear; those of lower socioeconomic status, many of whom are Black or Hispanic, are less likely to have a chance to grow old. When they do, as we have seen, they are apt to have a higher rate of limiting disabilities.

Life Span. Although life expectancy has changed markedly within the last eighty years, the life span is not really different. Recent media reports have suggested that a scientific breakthrough is imminent that will mean significant prolongation of the life span, that is, the biologic limits to which we are able to survive. Yet despite intriguing reports that suggest forms of diet—eating yogurt is a current favorite—allows one to live productively in good health to age 130 or so, we know that this is more fiction than fact. The touted longevity of Old Testament biblical figures such as Methuselah and that of people in portions of the U.S.S.R. is more the result of inaccurate record keeping, different ways of counting time, and faulty recollection—all perhaps with a heavy dose of wishful thinking and Soviet propaganda—than to demonstrable evidence (Medvedev, 1974; also, Mazess and Forman, 1979, on Ecuador.) To date, there is no proof

Table 4–7. Life Expectancy at Birth by Selected Countries and Sex

Country	Data Period	Sex		Years, More Female Life Expectancy
		Male	Female	
Sweden	1972	71.97	77.41	5.44
Norway	1966–70	71.09	76.83	5.74
Netherlands	1972	70.8	76.8	6.0
Denmark	1970–71	70.7	75.9	5.2
Japan	1972	70.49	75.92	5.43
Israel	1972	70.14	72.83	2.69
Switzerland	1969–70	69.21	75.03	5.82
Germany, Democratic Republic	1969–70	68.85	74.18	5.33
Bulgaria	1965–67	68.81	72.67	3.86
Canada	1965–67	68.75	75.18	6.43
Ireland	1971	68.58	72.85	4.27
France	1960–62	68.5	76.1	7.6
New Zealand	1960–62	68.44	73.75	5.31
Australia	1964–67	67.92	74.18	6.26
Italy	1968–70	67.87	73.36	5.49
United Kingdom	1968–70	67.81	73.81	6.0
Belgium	1959–63	67.75	73.51	5.76
Greece	1960–62	67.46	70.70	3.24
United States	1972	67.4	75.2	7.8

National Center for Health Statistics. Data adapted from Tables CD.I.22a and 22b, *Health: United States, 1975,* U.S. Government Publication HRA 76–1232.

that the actual life span of either men or women has increased or decreased since ancient times! What has changed is the *proportion* of people who survive to old age.

SEX AS A FACTOR IN LIFE EXPECTANCY AND MORTALITY

From the preceding discussion of life expectancy and death rates, it will be apparent that there is a definite difference between men and women. The weaker sex with respect to both prenatal and infant mortality, men have shorter life expectancies throughout the life course (but not shorter life spans). This seems both biologically and socially based. The male social role, with its emphasis on aggression and exposure to greater physical risks, has been thought to play a part. First, men tend to smoke, drink, and drive more than women do; lung cancer, accidents, and homicide have been more common among men as causes of death than among women. Men traditionally have been exposed to greater occupational hazards; sports, leisure activities, and work-related travel allow for greater possibility of disease and death. There is some hint that this is changing, although the data are inconclusive. Suicide, for example, which is most common among men over 65, appears to be increasing among women within the last two decades, but whether this is a real difference or merely a random fluctuation remains to be seen. The incidence of lung cancer is also increasing among women. Not very long ago, it was hypothesized that the hormonal differences between the sexes might insulate women somewhat from this disorder, causing the lower death rates that were observed. Recent evidence, however, suggests that this is not the case; as smoking has become more socially acceptable among age cohorts of women—especially professionals (Dicken, 1978)—lung cancer in women has also increased. Some investigators have proposed that as women enter more stressful occupations their heart disease rate will more closely parallel that of men. The "type A" personality, characterized by ambition, single-mindedness, and devotion to work, has been observed among men and is positively related to the likelihood of a heart attack (Friedman and Rosenman, 1974). Although functional for success, the "type A" personality can be dangerous to one's health. Whether career-oriented women will develop this sort of predisposition for heart disease remains to be seen.

In addition to these social factors relating to death, there is evidence that genetic factors act to boost women's life expectancy. Higher fetal death rates and congenital deformities have been consistently found for males than females, and it is believed that women have greater resistance to degenerative diseases, especially cardiovascular, because of their production of estrogen. At this time, it is not known whether the genetic endowment of women is the decisive factor in their greater longevity or whether this advantage will be modified by social and cultural changes.

MARITAL STATUS

Not only are there sex differences in life expectancy and in mortality but there are also differences related to marital status. As with physical disabilities, the lowest death rates among adults are found among the married. Widowed, divorced, and never married fare worse at all ages but most obviously among the old, as Table 4–8 shows.

The elderly of both sexes who are widowed are more likely to die than their age peers who are married, and those who are separated, divorced, or never married are most likely to die. There are interesting differences between men and women; among those aged 55–64, for example, married men are about twice as likely to die as married women although the married among both sexes are at a lower risk of death. As Durkheim suggested many decades ago, marriage insulates against death. The support function and mutual aid aspects of the marital relationship are of particular interest. Among the now-old who were socialized before 1920,

Table 4–8. Death Rates per 1,000 among Married, Widowed, and Others, by Age Group and Sex (1962–63 Data)

Marital Status at Death	Men			Women		
	55–64	65–74	75+	55–64	65–74	75+
Married	20.0	42.3	95.6	10.3	21.6	68.8
Widowed	38.1	72.5	146.5	14.5	33.7	100.9
Other	42.6	96.5	190.6	16.4	45.9	152.1

U.S. Public Health Service Publication 1000, Series 22, no. 9, p. 6, 1969.

marriage has most likely involved a sex-role-related division of labor where men had the primary responsibility as wage earners from which they drew much of their identity. Women were responsible for management of the home and for socioemotional and caring functions. Females may also have worked during part or all of their marriage, but their primary role was that of housewife/mother (Oakley, 1974). Traditionally then, marriage has been a different experience for the two sexes. For men it has had a replenishing support function that maintains their capacity to work; for women it is a sphere of interpersonal engagement (Glick, Weiss, and Parkes, 1974). This may be clearly seen when the meaning of widowhood for the two sexes is examined. After the death of a spouse, women are likely to feel personal loss and abandonment and men to feel dismemberment, as if a part of their own body had been cut off. Not surprisingly, adaptation to bereavement also differs between men and women. Women may compensate for their loss by going out to work and finding new interests. The newly widowed men, however, feeling as if part of themselves has been amputated, have an interrupted work pattern and find it difficult to step back into former roles (Glick, Weiss, and Parkes, 1974). Widowed men, too, tend to take poor care of themselves and are more likely to drink to excess than those still married (Schneidman, 1973). The separated or divorced man likewise is in a high risk category.

Although it is clear that marriage in some way insulates people from premature or untimely death, it is a more powerful shield for men than for women (Gove, 1973). Perhaps this is related to the differences in the meaning of marriages in the past for the two sexes. As definitions of roles within marriage change, as well as marriage and divorce patterns themselves, with future age cohorts, it will be interesting to determine the extent to which marriage continues to enhance life expectancy. If, as Schneidman (1973) has suggested, much of the high mortality among today's nonmarried and widowed old—especially old men—is subintentional suicide, that is, where "the decedent plays some partial, covert, latent, submanifest or unconscious role in his own demise" (p. 29), this pattern should change as greater androgeny (nonsex-role linked behavior) becomes prevalent within and without marriage.

CAUSES OF DEATH

Since 1900, marked changes in causes of death have taken place. As one might expect, given the change in life expectancy, there has been a decided drop in deaths from acute illnesses in old age and an increase in deaths from chronic disease. Ranking the ten leading causes of death, from highest to lowest, for 1900 and 1976, the shift is as follows:

1900	1976
1. pneumonia and influenza	1. diseases of the heart
2. tuberculosis	2. cancer
3. gastroenteritis	3. cerebrovascular diseases
4. diseases of the heart	4. accidents
5. cerebrovascular diseases	5. influenza and pneumonia
6. chronic nephritis	6. diabetes mellitus
7. accidents	7. cirrhosis of liver
8. cancer	8. arteriosclerosis
9. diseases of early infancy	9. suicide
10. diphtheria	10. diseases of early infancy

By the end of 1976, four of the ten leading causes of death at the turn of the century were no longer common. The three leading causes in 1976 were all chronic diseases associated with the aging process. Gone are tuberculosis and gastroenteritis as major killers. Pneumonia, once known as "the old man's friend," though still a major cause of death, had dropped from the leading cause of mortality to fifth on the list. As may be seen in Table 4–9, the leading cause of death among the old is heart disease; about 44 percent of those 65+ succumb to this disorder. Cancer of various types is the cause of death for another 18 percent, probably reflecting both the effects of aging and exposure to conducive environmental factors. Men are slightly more likely than women to die of cancer—19 percent of men and 16 percent of women 65+. The third leading cause of death among the aged is cerebrovascular diseases (strokes), which account for 13 percent of the deaths of these people. Women are slightly more likely than men to expire from this cause—16 percent as compared to 11 percent. These three broad categories of disease account for three quarters of all deaths among those 65 and over. As perusal of the death rate material in Table 4–9 illustrates, the major causes of death shift with age. In childhood and early adulthood, accidents, suicides, and homicides are the leading precipitants of death, followed by cancer. By age 35–44,

Table 4–9. Death Rates, by Selected Causes and Age Groups. 1976

Cause of Death	Total	<1 yr.	1–4	5–14	15–24	23–34	35–44	45–54	55–64	65–74	75–84	85+
					Age Group (Deaths per 100,000)							
Malignant neoplasms	175.8	3.2	5.3	5.0	6.5	14.5	51.5	182.0	438.4	786.3	1248.6	1441.5
Diabetes mellitus	16.1	.3	.1	.1	.4	1.8	3.9	9.8	28.4	70.0	155.8	219.2
Heart diseases	337.2	23.1	1.8	.9	2.6	8.5	50.8	199.8	552.4	1286.9	3263.7	7384.3
Cerebrovascular	87.9	4.4	.7	.6	1.2	3.4	11.5	31.4	85.8	280.1	1014.0	2586.8
Arteriosclerosis	12.3	.9	0	0	0	0	.2	.9	5.2	25.8	152.5	714.3
Pneumonia and flu	28.8	64.8	3.9	1.0	1.5	2.4	5.4	11.6	26.3	70.1	289.3	959.2
Bronchitus, emphysema and asthma	11.4	2.3	.5	.2	.2	.5	1.3	6.0	23.0	60.7	101.4	108.5
Cirrhosis of liver	14.7	1.1	.1	0	.3	3.7	16.9	35.0	47.6	42.6	29.3	18.0
Diseases of infancy	11.6	818.5	.1	0	0	0	0	0	0	0	0	0
Accidents*	46.9	41.4	27.9	17.0	59.9	43.5	37.1	39.9	47.7	62.2	134.5	306.7
Suicide	12.5	0	0	.4	11.7	15.9	16.3	19.2	20.0	19.5	20.8	18.9
Homicide	9.1	5.6	2.5	1.1	12.4	16.5	14.3	10.0	7.3	5.3	5.3	4.9

* Up to the age of 35, the majority of deaths caused by accidents are motor vehicle; among those 35–54, deaths are fairly evenly distributed between motor vehicle and other types of accidents; in the 65–74 group, accidents due to causes other than motor vehicles are about 2:1, and by 75+, very few motor vehicle accidents account for accidental deaths.

Advance Report, Final Mortality Statistics, 1976, DHEW Publication PHS 78–1120, vol. 26, 12, Supplement 2, March 30, 1978, Table 6.

heart disease ranks second—replacing cancer—and by age 45–54, heart disease ranks first with cancer second. By age 55–64, heart disease is the leading cause of death, cancer second, and cerebrovascular illness third.

Much of the difference in patterns of mortality is the result of the fact that, until recently, people rarely lived long enough to die of a chronic disease from which they may have been suffering for some time; acute infections were the cause of death. This may be clearly seen in the "Bills of Mortality, London, 1665," shown in Table 4–10, which were compiled during an epidemic of plague. Plague was by far the leading cause of

Table 4–10. Causes of Death, Listed on The Bills of Mortality, London England, for the Week of 26 September–3 October 1665

The Diseases and Casualties this Week.

Abortive	4	Palsie	1
Aged	42	Plague	4929
Ague	3	Plannet	1
Bloody flux	1	Plurisie	1
Cancer	1	Purples	1
Childbed	14	Rickets	12
Chrisomes	7	Rising of the Lights	8
Consumption	103	Rupture	1
Convulsion	60	Scowring	2
Dropsie	33	Scurvy	5
Drowned at St. Magdalen		Spotted Feaver	63
Bermondsey	1	Starved at Nurse (at St. Maudlin	
Feaver	201	in Old Fishstreet)	1
Flox and Small-pox	3	Stilborn	9
Flux	1	Stopping of the stomach	6
Frighted	1	Suddenly	3
Gangrene	1	Surfeit	24
Grief	3	Teeth	92
Griping in the Guts	28	Thrush	2
Jaundies	4	Timpany	1
Imposthume	4	Tissick	3
Infants	18	Ulcer	1
Killed by a fall at Stepney	1	Vomiting	1
Kingsevil	1	Winde	4
Overlaid	1	Wormes	13

Christned { Males 75 / Females 67 / In all 142 } Buried { Males 2801 / Females 2919 / In all 5720 } Plague 4929

Decreased in the Burials this Week   740

Parishes clear of the Plague   6   Parishes Infected   124

Reprinted in *Milbank Memorial Fund Quarterly (Health and Society)* 55, no. 3 (1977), p. 404.

death; other infectious diseases also were prevalent. "Feaver" (fever), "consumption" (tuberculosis), "spotted feaver," and such gastrointestinal disorders as "griping in the guts," "stopping of the stomach," vomiting, "winde," and "wormes" were listed as causes of death. It is interesting to notice that only one person died of cancer, and forty-two died from old age. It is also intriguing to notice differences in diagnosis—such disorders as "purples," "rising of the lights," "kingsevil" (probably scrofula, a form of tuberculosis causing skin lesions), "overlaid," "chrisomes," and "plannet" do not exist as current disease classifications. This is of some pragmatic interest, for as we become more knowledgeable about currently prevalent chronic diseases such as cancer, perhaps the nomenclature we now use may seem as quaint as that used in seventeenth-century mortality data.

As discussed earlier, excess mortality among men is almost universal. In our society, heart disease is the major killer for men. Within the period 1952–77, there have been increases in certain disorders causing death among men in old age that do not extend to women to the same degree: diseases of the respiratory system, including lung cancer, chronic bronchitis, emphysema, and other lung disorders. There also have been increases in arteriosclerosis and other diseases of the circulatory system among white men. Among nonwhite males, increases in death rates for lung cancer and genital and urinary cancer have occurred. Leukemia, diabetes, anemia, bronchitis, motor vehicle accidents, and homicide have also been increasing among nonwhite males as a cause of death. The reasons for these differentials in causes of death are complex; exposure to greater physical risks, stress, hormonal differences, racial differences (especially, for example, in the anemias), and environmental factors are all believed to play a part.

The decline in acute and infectious diseases as ranking causes of death is largely the result of a rise in real income and standard of living (Fuchs, 1974)—a significant feature of which has been a better diet—improvements in public health and hygiene standards, and to a lesser extent, immunization and medical therapy (McKeown et al., 1975; McKeown, 1976). Paradoxically, the sudden and continuing rise in medical care expenditures—from 4.5 percent in 1955 to 8.4 percent of the Gross National Product in 1975—began *after* about 92 percent of the decline in mortality from infectious diseases had already occurred (McKinley and McKinley, 1977).

The extent to which medical measures have contributed to declines in mortality from infections is open to continuing debate. A comparison of the data following the introduction of efficacious medical interventions (antibiotics for bacterial infections, inoculations for disorders such as polio) has shown that only 3.5 percent of the decline in death rates from ten common infectious diseases since 1900 can be attributed to specific medical interventions and technology such as inoculations and drug therapy. Put another way, these diseases were already declining at a rapid rate prior to the introduction of new therapeutic modalities (McKinley and McKinley, 1977). Perhaps the net effect of antiinfectious treatment has been to postpone death for the least fit, thus extending the duration of chronic conditions. As Gruenberg (1977, p. 19) has suggested, chronic diseases and disabilities have become more common precisely because technology has allowed us to defy death's claim over the old, sick, and weak—or at least to postpone death's claim. The result of this is that people survive to much older ages to die of chronic diseases. The situations in which people die are discussed in the following section.

Attitudes and Circumstances Surrounding Death

Despite the many technological improvements in public health and health care within the last fifty years or so, death eventually comes to all. Since the reduction of infant and childhood mortality, the old are *the* group most likely to die. This is probably not a welcome thought at any age, and perhaps some of our own cultural aversion to the old reflects their impending death. As noted in earlier chapters, the United States is an instrumental society where work and activity are valued as ends in themselves; death is the epitome of cessation of productivity and of stillness. Furthermore, if religion is an expression of ultimate concerns, then physical health is decidedly a religion in the United States with the physician as priest (Kalish, 1969). Death, therefore, is an antireligious act, the final insult, as it robs us of what we most worship—life and health. Also, Americans have a great respect for technology and its ability to modify or manipulate the physical environment. Death, too, should lend itself to manipulation and obsolescence. When President Nixon declared a "war on cancer" in the early 1970s, it was thought that a society able to put a man on the moon should be able to "conquer" cancer, the second leading cause of death.

These three interwoven beliefs—activity, health, and manipulation through technology—give substance to the fabric of American life. Yet they also produce a pattern with an oversocialized view of humanity, where natural acts, such as death and to a lesser extent, giving birth, are made unnatural and are medicalized. Put another way, as both the acts of dying and giving birth have become less common life events, both phenomena, essentially disruptive to a technologically oriented and mobile society, have been increasingly viewed as best handled by medical and technical personnel in special facilities.

GOING AND COMING—SOME PARALLELS BETWEEN GIVING BIRTH AND DYING

There is, as shown in literature ranging from *Romeo and Juliet* to *Love Story*, a link between sexuality and death; both are forces within us that threaten our personal sense of self by leading beyond it. (It is perhaps no accident that, after Adam and Eve knew one another sexually, they became mortal.) Although sexuality and death are opposite sides of a coin in fantasy (Mednick, 1977–78), literature and mythology, there is a greater parallel between the acts of giving birth and of dying—at least in the ways in which they are handled. Both imply an invasion or threat to the integrity of the body; both are seen as appropriate for medical intervention and management. What are some other similarities between these two processes?

Locus. Although it is more comfortable for people to die in their own homes, this is seldom accomplished. The majority of deaths (somewhat over six in every ten) from any cause occur in an institution, most often the general hospital (Lerner, 1970). Birth, too, although more comfortably accomplished at home, occurs most often in the general hospital or nursing home. Neither of these facts is surprising in view of the modern definition of birthing and dying as being within the purview of the medical profession. Yet they highlight the point that shifting birth and death to an institutional setting serves to underline their unnaturalness and inappropriateness to everyday life. One may question whether institutional care, with its panoply of sophisticated equipment and expertise, is required in "routine" births and deaths if alternatives were available, but certainly a hospital or other institutional setting permits greater control over these two acts, the actor (or actress) and the family.

Management by Professionals. Both giving birth and dying may be bloody and difficult processes. Since most of us have had no opportunity to witness either event, it is not surprising that technical skill is considered requisite for both. There is, of course, a price paid for this; as Margaret Mead observed:

> No primitive society leaves the mother alone, nor does any leave her alone among strangers. It remains for modern civilization in the isolation of cities and suburbs to leave a woman approaching childbirth all alone. (Mead, quoted in Arms, p. 84, 1975)

Simply put, the woman giving birth or the person dying is stripped of the emotional supports provided by friends and family. What is substituted instead is "detached concern" or "nonemotional involvement" of the hospital staff. To a large extent, significant others may be excluded because of the fear of technical personnel that they will be disruptive or cannot "take it." But physicians, nursing staff, and other health care workers also have anxieties about death. Often these are resolved in treating a terminal or dying old person by being more detached than concerned (see, for example, Sherizen and Paul, 1977). Nor is care of the old, dying person at home encouraged by medical personnel; perhaps because death is so unwelcome, it is assumed that dying at home is inappropriate for both the old person and her/his family.[1] Uncomfortable and lonely deaths would seem the rule rather than the exception.

Emotional Responses. Although the act of giving birth is not readily comparable to that of dying with respect to emotional meaning to the person undergoing the experience, some responses are common to both. Suzanne Arms (1975) describes typical reactions of women undergoing childbirth, including loneliness, fear, frustration, humiliation, degradation of the body, and loss. These are not unlike the feelings reported among dying patients (Kübler-Ross, 1969; Schneidman, 1973). It is suggested here that some of these feelings are related to lack of appropriate emotional supports for people undergoing either experience.

Social Death. Birthing and dying in an institution may often involve social death. As noted by Kastenbaum (1969; 1977), social death begins when treatment personnel lose their concern for the individual as a human being and treat the patient as a body; that is, those behaviors one would expect directed toward a living person are absent. One is not consulted about his/her wishes or preferences. With terminally ill patients, such behavior occurs most often when patients are unconscious, or semiconscious (Sudnow, 1967). To a lesser extent, the terminally ill but conscious patient and the woman experiencing childbirth could be said to undergo social mini-deaths. They are most often "acted upon," with little explanation about the need or outcome for various procedures. In fact, there is some indication that dying patients are systematically deceived about the purpose of many medical procedures for fear that they may become upset. It is well documented that few dying patients are told they are in fact dying (Glaser and Strauss, 1965; Glaser and Strauss, 1968; Quint, 1967), although there is some indication that most people would prefer to know if they were dying (Kalish, 1969). Certainly people's feelings about how to handle death vary, but treating the dying patient as an unworthy possessor of such news denies sentience.

[1] One interesting exception is the *hospice* concept, where the terminally ill are maintained in the home as long as possible (nurses and other trained staff make daily visits and spell off family members for hours or even days). Patients who require intensive care are moved into the hospice, which resembles a motel more than a hospital, and family members are encouraged to remain in the room. The hospice movement may become more bureaucratized as a reflection of Medicaid, Medicare, and other third-party payment requirements for reimbursement.

After-the-Fact Recognition. One last relevant parallel between the acts of birthing and dying is the recognition of the significance of the event after the fact. That is, the actual act of dying or of giving birth is shunned by most of the intimates of the person concerned; after the act is accomplished, however, those who know the new mother or knew the dead person gather around to give their emotional support. Despite the popularity of natural childbirth (itself an interesting term, lending credence to the postulate that we regard most childbirth as *un*natural), many expectant fathers have been known to say that they just couldn't witness anything like birth; they wouldn't want to see anything so disgusting. Similarly, few people, except those closest or most obligated to the dying person, wish to watch death take place. After the event, however, several things occur. First, in the case of birth, the new baby is "shown off" through the window of a nursery and the mother is visited; in the case of death, the corpse is "shown off" in a viewing, and the family of the deceased is visited. Second, gifts may be presented; flowers and candy are sent to the new mothers, clothes and toys are sent to the child. In the case of death, flowers are sent to the deceased, and flowers, candy, and food are presented to the survivors. The act of dying before and during its occurrence is shunned (Kalish, 1966).

WHO DIES WHERE

Status and Illness. Uncomfortable, lonely deaths are also a reflection of the social status and type of illness of the dying old person. Although most old, and, in fact, most people in any age cohort, presently die in a hospital or nursing home, the type of institutional facility in which they terminate their lives and the quality of care they received are variable. The right *not* to die in a hospital is also partly a function of social status and diagnosis.

Social Status. As Gruenberg has pointed out, "the paradoxical fact about death is that it is at once the great leveler and the great discriminator" (1977, p. 18). Rank has its privileges throughout life, and the way in which one dies in old age is no exception. "A president, king or prime minister will receive more attention than a drunken derelict. There will be more personnel mobilized, more equipment used, more expense tolerated to save the life . . ." commented one physician and student of dying (Lasagna, 1970). The poor elderly are rarely accorded "heroic treatment." In fact, the poor, dying patient may be treated as biologically dead prior to actual death; the eyes may be forced closed and the body wrapped while the person is still breathing, for it is more difficult to work on a dead body than a live one (Sudnow, 1967). How the person who is biologically alive but gives no indication of continued existence should be handled is a complex legal and policy issue beyond the scope of this discussion. That medical heroics are *differentially* applied, according to the age and perceived social status of the person, is the point here.

Imputed social value is also a significant factor in determining the sort of care a dying patient will receive. The judgment of a nurse that a patient is unattractive, of low social status, and poor moral worth may often condition the way in which one is handled during terminal illness (Quint, 1967). The alcoholic, the prostitute, the "bum," the criminal, and the welfare mother all have low social worth and are not accorded the same care and concern by medical personnel as, say, the respectable-in-appearance middle-aged man (Sudnow, 1967).

Age, itself a status, also influences the kind of care the dying patient receives. As childhood mortality has become less common in the United States (16 percent of all children under one year of age died in 1900 as compared to about 2 percent in 1970), the death of a child impresses us as most tragic because the child has not yet had a chance to live (Kalish, 1966; Kalish, 1969). One is impressed with the helplessness and relative purity of the child. In a society such as ours, where childhood is pro-longed as a preparation for a productive, achievement-oriented adulthood, the child essentially has not had an opportunity to "become." Old people, however, have low social value (Glaser, 1966; Glaser and Strauss, 1964) and often their death is regarded by others as a release from the aches, pains, and tedium of old age.

The poet Rainer Maria Rilke commented on patients dying in a Paris hospital:

> Now they are dying there in 559 beds. Factory-like, of course. Where pro-duction is so enormous an individual death is not so nicely carried out, but then it doesn't matter. . . . Who cares anything today for a finely finished death?

A "finely finished death" is, however, more available to the rich and independent than to those of low social worth. The old and the poor, with the exception of southern Blacks, are most likely to die alone, with-out social supports by significant others or concerned personnel (Sudnow, 1967). They are also likely to die in an impersonal, sometimes unpleasant institution such as a public hospital, mental hospital, and most recently, as is discussed in Chapter 6, the nursing home.

Even the rich or famous may have difficulty dying a "finely finished death" with significant others around in the locus of one's choice. A few people, such as Aldous Huxley, have refused to end their lives in an in-stitutional setting and follow the prescribed dying trajectory (Glaser and Strauss, 1967). Huxley chose to accept his death from cancer with the help of LSD and his wife as a supporting guide (Huxley, 1968). The poor have none of these options. One old man, dying from terminal cancer, attempted suicide in a nursing home; he was immediately sent to a mental hospital, placed under security precautions, and died seventeen days later, still under security lest he kill himself (Markson, 1971).

Type of Illness. Not only does social worth determine the supports available to the dying old person but so also does the disease from which one is dying. As life expectancies have increased and communicable diseases decreased, the length of terminal illnesses have significantly changed. Heart disease, cancer, and vascular lesions affecting the central nervous system are leading causes of death; patients with cancer or vascular lesions are more likely to die in a hospital than are those with heart disease. To some extent, this finding reflects the pattern of the illness; heart disease is more sudden and less predictable than cancer. Yet there is some indication that the chronicity of the disease itself has a deleterious effect on the amount and type of care given the patient; as Lasagna (1970) noted, the patient with intractable pain is a constant reminder that the doctor's skills are limited. Since few clinicians enjoy the role of ineffectual therapist, they prefer to concentrate their efforts on more "interesting" patients or on the process of the disease itself. Certainly patients with cancer are currently viewed with well-grounded pessimism.

Yet, as Susan Sontag has pointed out, cancer has been singled out as the most loathsome disease, and as indicative of some sort of moral or health care failure of the individual. Treatment for cancer may parallel an exorcism; whether the patient dies or not, what is necessary is to get rid of the demon cancer (Sontag, 1978).

Not only the disease but the site and origin of the disorder can affect the type of care and support structure that are available to the patient. One may wonder if the recent rash of "leukemic" books and films, such as *Love Story*, may not indicate a fascination with the "clean death," an aversion to "dirty deaths" such as cancer of the ileum, a distinction that is reflected in the supports offered to patients.

Since Americans are generally unwilling to talk about dying, and doctors are no exception, medical personnel frequently prefer to treat dying persons as if they were going to live (Duff and Hollingshead, 1968; Glaser and Strauss, 1965; Glaser and Strauss, 1968). Strauss and Glaser have described the system of "closed awareness" (1965) which surrounds most dying patients. There are at least five important conditions that must be satisfied to maintain this system of closed awareness. First, the patient does not recognize signs of impending death; second, the physicians and other medical personnel do not tell the patient; and third, the family must assist secret keeping, with records kept in an office, discussions about the patient's prognosis made in her or his absence, and so on, and finally, patients must have no allies able to tip them off (Glaser and Strauss,

1965). This system, of course, may break down with signals from the staff, family, or others.

It is very difficult to reverse this process, to generate a system of "open awareness." Kübler-Ross (1969) has pointed out and Strauss and Glaser have shown that the basic response to death is a resounding no! for most people. Thoughts of our own death bring a profound ego-chill, the sudden awareness that our nonexistence is entirely possible. Within the last few years there has been a swing toward "forced awareness" in some settings, where the dying person may be *required* to confront her or his impending death whether or not this is appropriate for the individual concerned. The routinized application of "death awareness" may, as Kastenbaum (1979) suggests, be as damaging to some as no news is to others. Yet, at least some of the people who have been told of their approaching death have been able to use this knowledge to achieve a "finely finished death" (for example, Johnny Gunther [Gunther, 1963] and Charles Wertenbaker [Wertenbaker, 1974]).

In sum, then, closed awareness would appear to function, in most cases, against the interests of patients by denying or reducing the opportunity to use their remaining time to best advantage.

SUMMARY

In aging, there is a gradually diminishing rate of efficiency of the body. There is, however, considerable individual variation in human aging; even within the same individual, all organs do not age at the same rate. Although some slowing down of bodily function in old age seems inevitable, decremental change may be retarded or controlled through exercise, proper nutrition, and good dental and medical care.

Socioenvironmental stress plays an intriguing albeit incompletely understood role in both the process of aging and the development of disease. The evidence to date suggests that stressful life events result in lowered resistance of the body to acute disease, and facilitate development of various chronic illnesses, including heart diseases. The exact mechanism by which stressful events lead to disease is, however, not yet understood. Nor is it known why some people under stress may develop one type of illness, others under comparable stress be prone to other diseases, and some remain disease free. Probably a combination of factors, including biological predisposition, meaning of the event(s) to the specific individual, and coping mechanisms mediate the relationship between stress and illness. Although much has been written descriptively about aging and decrement in function, relatively little has been unraveled about causality.

For example, menopause is universal among women and, although much mythologized, its importance, other than cessation of reproductive capacity, remains incompletely known. What is clear is that menopause is unique to women; there is no parallel inevitable change in reproductive capacity among men associated with growing older.

Indeed, the definitions of health and illness themselves are dynamic, changing with time, social circumstances, and social values. Disease literally designates an absence of ease, and may be operationally defined as encompassing conditions that are painful or handicapping in one's performance of social roles, which range along a continuum of acuteness/chronicity, and which are considered within a specified society as requiring treatment. As we have discussed at some length, disease is not randomly distributed in the population but rather varies according to age, sex, socioeconomic status, and life style.

Since 1900, there has been a marked decrease in acute illnesses among all age groups but especially among those 65+. Concurrently, chronic diseases have increased. Interestingly, women are more likely to develop one or more chronic diseases but, when they do, they are generally less disabled. This difference may reflect the greater utilization of medical care by women than men; early diagnosis and treatment may postpone disability. Sex-linked biologic differences may also play a role. Racial and ethnic differences in disability, too, have been observed, yet the evidence indicates that socioeconomic position rather than race/ethnicity explains much of the variation.

Despite the almost universal expectation of physical decrement in old age, being sick is a difficult and highly charged emotional experience for the old. Illness raises questions about one's prospects for recovery, probability of increased disability, the likelihood of death, and the meaning of life itself. For some elderly who have relatively few social roles left or whose available roles are ungratifying, the sick role may be seductive, for it provides a new role. Tarrying in the sick role, however, is likely to be unrewarding. A general attitude of therapeutic nihilism—often unwarranted—dominates much medical treatment for those 65+, and this attitude may indeed hasten further physical decline and death.

Closely allied to patterns of health and disease is mortality. Today, the likelihood of reaching at least age 65 is very high; in 1973, 72.9 percent of the eligible birth cohorts did so. Yet this is a relatively new phenomenon, unparalleled in history. Much of our great life expectancy is a result of rises in income, standard of living, and public health and hygiene measures—all of which have been significant in reducing acute illnesses that accounted for much of the mortality observed in the past. Chronic diseases—heart disease, cancer, and cerebrovascular disease—now account for three fourths of the deaths among the 65+.

Men have shorter life expectancies than do women, and this is especially noticeable among men who have been widowed, divorced, or never married. It was suggested that for both sexes, marriage insulates against death but this seems particularly true for men, who tend to react to bereavement with less resiliency.

As death among younger age groups has become less common, the old have been singled out as *the* group that is going to die. Death and the act of dying thus are no longer commonplace events that occur at any age. As part of our general cultural aversion to death, which, after all, represents the apotheosis of stillness, our society has tended to remove the dying person from home and place her/him in a specialized institution such as the hospital or nursing home. Although this minimizes disruption to the lives and activities of friends and relatives of the aged dying person, it also reduces the opportunity for anticipatory socialization to one's own death and for the care of the dying person. For the individual who is dying, the opportunity to use the last of life productively or happily in familiar surroundings is denied by institutional management.

Despite the many changes in life expectancy within the past century, there has been no change in life span. More and more people now are surviving to old age, but there is no reliable evidence that the length of life that seems possible for humans to live has changed an iota since ancient times. Whether new scientific discoveries will change this prospect for succeeding age cohorts remains to be seen. The impact of changes in sex-stereotypical behavior on patterns of disability, disease, and mortality among future age cohorts is another intriguing prospect. As the distinction between appropriate behavior for men versus women becomes more blurred, will their forms of illness and death more closely approximate one another? Or, are the marked differences currently observed part of the biologic potential of the two sexes? These remain among the unanswered questions in the study of human aging.

Research Exercises

1. A *content analysis* of obituary notices may reveal interesting patterns by occupation, level of education, marital status, ethnicity, and place and primary cause of death (when given). If your local board of health permits access to death certificate records, data from several years can be collected and analyzed for these variables as well as for evidence of monthly and seasonal patterns.

2. Prepare an annotated *bibliography* on the extensive social science literature on death and dying.

3. *Interviews* with health care providers—visiting nurses, physicians, hospital and clinic staff, and the like—provide insights into their perceptions of the older patient. Also of interest is their preparation for treating the elderly since most nursing and medical schools have only recently introduced or expanded curricula on aging.

4. When data from the *sample survey* are available, analyze the health sections.

5. *Inventory* the health care facilities for old people in your community.

Discussion Questions

Debate the question: Is there a right to die?, i.e., should a patient have the right to refuse "heroic" life-sustaining measures, and are others bound by the patient's choice? Should there be a law concerning this issue?

How inevitable are sex and race differences in aging?

What would be the consequences (social and personal) if there were a breakthrough in the extension of the life span—if, for example, large numbers of people lived to age 120?

5

The Aging Psyche

George Bernard Shaw, a master at successful aging, is credited with the following exchange upon visting his eye doctor: "I am pleased to tell you, Mr. Shaw," the oculist said "that your vision is completely normal."

To which Shaw, never known for his modesty, replied, "Then, in this one sense I am just like everyone else."

"No," replied the physician, "very few people have normal vision." This anecdote highlights the problem of evaluating psychological changes in aging, for what *is* normal in old age (or, for that matter, at any other point in the life course)?

Successful aging may be viewed from a variety of perspectives, including a statistical norm—what most people do—or, in the case of eyesight, an ideal that few reach. Consideration of aging and its psychological dimensions involves many levels of analysis—intellectual functioning, psychomotor ability, changes in self-esteem and personality, and psychopathology. Since gerontology is a new field, each of these topics has problems in definition and direction, theory construction, and research methods that have by no means been resolved.

Furthermore, the diversity of old people makes it difficult to make any generalizations about the criteria for growing old successfully. Indeed, many theories of old age have been developed on the basis of distinct populations in a specific age cohort or geographic locale. For example, research on age changes has been undertaken in the Midwest, where the population studied was predominantly white, middle-class, and Protestant (see, for example, Cavan, Havighurst and Burgess,

1949; Cumming and Henry, 1961; Havighurst, Neugarten, and Tobin, 1975). In a similar study in California, the population studied was, again, predominantly middle class but interested in moving to a retirement community (Lemon, Bengtson, and Peterson, 1972) and in a study of the aged in the South, those included were volunteers representing a microcosm of the population of one southern community (Palmore, 1970; Palmore, 1974). Yet three quarters of old people live in cities and are heavily concentrated in the northeastern United States where the ethnic composition, economic structure, and life-styles differ from the South, Midwest, or retirement communities in Southern California. Within the field of gerontology as a whole, relatively little attention has been given to normal aging processes among the minority aged, to urban-rural differences, sex differences, or socioeconomic differences. Age cohort variations, too, are only recently being explored. Our knowledge of personality and intellectual changes in old age thus reflect the values of the definers of these dimensions, the availability of research subjects, and the ideals of our culture.

Changes in Ability and Intellect

Old age is often viewed as a period of declining intellectual ability and a slowing down of responses that occur as results of physical frailty and psychomotor changes. Decreased performance on speeded tasks has been delineated by some as the hallmark of aging (see, for example, Birren, 1970). The neuropsychologist Donald Hebb has commented in this vein: ". . . the elderly are also considered a brain injured population . . . some test data showed the same pattern that appears with brain damage: no loss in vocabulary or information into the 50s and perhaps the 60s, but a steady decline in other areas . . .", (1978, p. 20).

Indeed, much research indicates that there is a decline in learning ability, motor response, and intelligence among the elderly, but there is increasing evidence that these differences may be the result of cohort variation rather than actual decrements of function that are inextricably related to old age. Many studies comparing the old and the young have been cross-sectional, and the elderly have had less education and stimulation throughout their lives than have their younger counterparts. Even in carefully designed studies, such factors as sampling error, unreliable tests, individual differences, and personal variability have rendered the definition of *normal change* difficult. What is invariably related to growing old thus remains hazy. Some of the more significant intellectual changes are reviewed in the remainder of this section.

REACTION TIME AND SENSORY MOTOR RESPONSES

Birren (1970) has proposed that "slowness of behavior is the independent variable that sets limits for the older person in such processes as memory, perception and problem solving" (p. 126). Results of experimental studies with the elderly have consistently shown that reaction time, that is, the elapsed time between presentation of a stimulus and the beginning of a person's response, declines slightly but definitely with age (Riley and Foner, 1968; Jarvik and Cohen, 1973). It has been suggested that these changes are indications of reduced central nervous system functioning. Further changes in the nervous system leading to such slowing down are *not* considered under the voluntary control of the individual (see Jarvik and Cohen, 1973, for a more extensive review and discussion).

There is, nonetheless, considerable variation in reaction time among individuals that is related to physical training as well as to age. Botwinick and Thompson (1968) divided young adults into two groups—athletic and nonathletic—and compared them to older adults. They found that, whereas the reaction time of old people was slower than that of the young, the elderly more closely resembled the nonathletic young adults than the athletes. Clearly, environmental factors, such as level of accustomed exercise and nutrition, play a part.

A decrement in ability to perform complex sensory motor tasks in old age has also been noted. Again, there are various reasons for this change. Factors such as physical health and level of sensory impairment (vision, hearing, taste, touch, smell) need to be controlled before any extensive conclusions about "normal decline" are drawn. Moreover, the role played by such variables as motivation and interest in the tasks on which one is being tested is not completely understood. Many experimental studies involve tasks to which younger people, especially students, are particularly attuned, and that lie outside the experience of older people. Experimental or laboratory studies have a ready pool of captive undergraduates to act as subjects; it is more difficult to entice older people into such studies that also may be of less intrinsic interest to them. Serving as an experimental subject may be required of the undergraduate as part of the coursework, and also provides the student with the opportunity to learn about the nature of such work. These factors, often acting as powerful motivating forces for the student, are absent for the older nonstudent who sees no direct personal benefit (other than perhaps pecuniary reward) in participating in such studies.

INTELLIGENCE

Thurstone, one of the pioneers of intelligence testing, commented that intelligence can be defined as what was measured by I.Q. tests. This pragmatic definition of intelligence has dominated most research on intellectual ability and the aging process. As Baltes and Labouvie (1973) have pointed out, most psychologists "concentrate on this performance or product (consequent) aspect of the intelligence construct and neglect those areas of research that are primarily aimed at conceptualizing intelligence as an inferred process-construct" (p. 159). Stated differently, little attention has been paid to intellectual processes that may produce behavioral stability in old age, or where apparent loss can be well compensated (Schaie, 1972).

The most common framework within which intellectual change associated with the aging process has been examined is the cross-sectional study, in which persons of different ages have been compared through test results such as the Wechsler-Bellevue Adult Intelligence Test. Because they dealt with cross-sections of the population, these studies have not really considered *changes* in intelligence but rather differences between different age cohorts. According to Baltes and Labouvie (1973), the evidence for age cohort differences in I.Q. is very strong. Since different age cohorts vary with respect to their level of education, opportunity, life experiences, and physical health, their scores likewise will differ. To date, the majority of cross-sectional studies have strongly supported an "age-decrement" model of intellectual functioning. In general, I.Q. has been shown to peak in the late teens and early twenties (consistent with physiological growth and change, as well as with student status) and then to decline with age. The following diagram, based on Bromley (1966), shows relative age differences for several intellectual functions measured by the Wechsler-Bellevue Scale.

As Figure 5–1 shows, certain intellectual functions have been observed to decline at a gradual rate from about age 20 or so, whereas others do not. Intelligence is not unitary; rather, there are intelligences (Botwinick, 1973). On tests such as the Wechsler, a distinction is made between verbal intelligence and performance or psychomotor intelligence. The verbal sphere encompasses comprehension, arithmetic, similarities, vocabulary, and ability to recall digits; the performance area includes such tasks as picture completion, arrangement of pictures in a logical sequence, block design, and assembly of objects. The performance items involve *speed* of psychomotor response, and decline early in life. Verbal skills, however, tend to peak in early middle age and stay constant until about age 65 or 70.

This pattern of decrement in abilities may provide a partial explanation of why optimal achievement in some occupations occurs early in life but late in others. In fields such as mathematics, significant contributions tend to be made by young people. For example, Charles Fefferman, recipient of the Fields Medal for his work in mathematics, became a full professor at the age of 22 and before the age of 30 had received the Salem Prize, the Waterman Award, and other honors for his work in mathe-

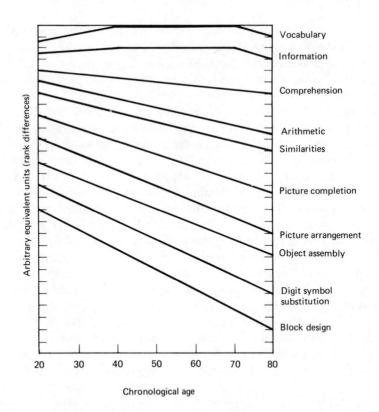

Vocabulary

Information

Comprehension

Arithmetic

Similarities

Picture completion

Picture arrangement

Object assembly

Digit symbol substitution

Block design

Chronological age

Figure 5–1. Relative Age Differences and Decrements in Intelligence on Subtests of the Wechsler-Bellevue Intelligence Test (expressed in rank units of relative difference). D. B. Bromley, *The Psychology of Human Aging* (Baltimore, Md.: Penguin Books, 1966), p. 226.

matics (*Science,* November 10, 1978, p. 612). In literature, the arts, philosophy, and the law, where personal experience and accumulated knowledge are significant, accomplishments may be made much later in life or continue throughout the life span. Thus, Sophocles wrote the Greek tragedy *Oedipus Rex* when he was 75, Verdi composed *Falstaff* when over 80, and Vera Stravinsky, widow of the composer Igor Stravinsky, had a successful art exhibition, including recent paintings, and published a book at age 90!

It is unclear to what extent decremental changes in intelligence depend on actual age-related brain change. The evidence suggests that *brain weight* begins to decrease at about age 30, presumably as a result of alterations of neurons or nerve cells in the brain. However, there is no agreement about whether actual brain *cell loss* is a concomitant of aging. There are at least three different and contradictory sets of findings: (1) *no* cell loss associated with aging can be observed (Van Buskirk, 1945); (2) brain cell loss occurs *early* in life but *not* later (Diamond, 1978); (3) brain cell loss occurs as a result of aging (Brizzee, 1973). As further studies of the aging brain are undertaken, these discrepancies may lessen or be resolved. Until then, many beliefs about necessary brain changes and age-linked decrement in intelligence are open to challenge.

The role of *genetic* factors in intelligence—an unresolved debate for any age group—may also influence intellectual performance and decline in old age (and explain such achievers as Sophocles). The existence of genetic determinants in the decline of intelligence is unproven but is strongly suggested by the parallel intellectual decline observed among identical twins in old age (Kallmann, 1961). This genetic potential may, however, be modified by physical disease; among identical twins whose intellectual abilities had been virtually equal, physical illness produced sharp distinctions in their intellectual capacities (Jarvik and Cohen, 1973).

The relationship between *cardiovascular disease* and intellectual impairment has also been explored. Much of the functional loss in intelligence observed among old people may not be an inevitable feature of aging itself but rather a reflection of failing health status and its effect on the ability to process information (Thompson and Marsh, 1973). Intellectual decline has, in fact, been most pronounced among old people who were about to die. Thus, physical states that are precursors of death are strongly related to, and perhaps cause or interact with, reduced intellectual performance on tests; certainly diminished accomplishment on a series of performance tasks seems an accurate predictor of death (Botwinick, West, and Storandt, 1978).

With those who are at a higher risk of dying because of physical illness—and among any group of old people—*motivation* is a core factor that is difficult to control in a research design. It is plausible that the elderly in poor health have less interest in test material that requires reproduction of digits, picture arrangement, arithmetic solutions, or other usual measures of intellectual prowess. Instead, their energies are drawn into themselves, and they are more concerned with their own sensations and perceptions than with outside stimuli. This occurs among the well elderly as well; for example, Donald O. Hebb commented on his own aging as follows:

> The third major cognitive effect (of aging) I've observed is to me the most interesting and surprising: a major shift in motivation. For 35 years, research and the problems of behavior were everything to me. . . . Today I have none of that drive, that engrossing, dominating need to fiddle with and manipulate ideas and data in psychology. . . . In areas other than psychology, I am just as pigheaded—that's how we say "motivation" where I came from—as ever; in my continuing fight to put a small 10-acre farm into better shape, for example (1978, pp. 22–23).

Summary. The problem of measuring intelligence in older people is complex for several reasons. First, there is no universal agreement on what intelligence is. Second, much of the work on intelligence in old age has been cross-sectional and thus has not taken account of differences between the various age cohorts studied. Third, even tests standardized for older people should be interpreted with caution; they are relatively new. There is an extensive and technically sophisticated literature on the nature of intelligence, its components, and changes throughout the life cycle. Readers interested in the details should consult the *Handbook of the Psychology of Aging* (Birren and Schaie, 1976) or *The Psychology of Adult Development and Aging* (Eisdorfer and Lawton, 1973). It seems clear that personality factors such as interest, rigidity/flexibility, and caution affect test scores (and perhaps actual achievement) in old age. Some of the common personality characteristics in old age that are salient psychic dimensions of aging are described at greater length in the following section.

The Aging Personality

What do we know about how aging affects the personality? Again, much of the information we have is based on cross-sectional studies that limit generalizability about what *must* be in old age. There is, however, a wealth of studies describing what some groups of elderly *are*. Some of this evidence supports popular stereotypes of the aged. For example, on the basis of an extensive review of the literature, Riley and Foner (1968) reported that, in general, old people are more rigid, have a lower tolerance of ambiguity, and are more dogmatic than younger people. To some degree, this lack of flexibility and need for definitiveness may reflect duration in the role; as old people accumulate experience in a role, they are less likely to want to deviate from it. Recent longitudinal work, such as that done by Maas and Kuypers (1974), indicates that throughout the life course, there is a strain toward constancy; that is, each individual attempts to maintain an equilibrium in values, attitudes, norms, and habits as he/she ages. Old age thus reflects and expands upon what had begun in the earlier years, although developmental change may also occur. Likeness in life-style between early and late adulthood is more common for men than for women, for women experience a variety of role changes as they marry, bear children, and so on, which, in turn, influences their style of life. Women, on the other hand, are more likely to maintain certain personality tendencies than are men; this is especially true for women who have been plagued by feelings of self-doubt, depression, and anxiety in their younger years (Maas and Kuypers, 1974). Cohort differences, too, may play a part in personality among the now-old; those 65+ who were socialized before 1920 were reared in a more predictable environment in which power relationships, traditional family roles, and values were both well-defined and rarely subject to question.

The now-old are also more restrained, less impulsive, and more cautious, especially in new situations, than are the young, and they have been reported to be more conforming and passive (Riley and Foner, 1968). Again, this may reflect age-cohort differences in socialization and in opportunity; those 65+ today were adults during the Great Depression of the 1930s and during World War II. Neither of these eras, with their great pressing social problems, encouraged individual autonomy. Indeed, because of economic and political pressures, there was often relatively little range for the personal self-realization that has become the hallmark of generations reared and entering adulthood under the aegis of Dr. Spock. Although our culture has always stressed independence, it has also stressed conformity. Independence has been translated as self-reliance rather than deviation from the norm.

The relatively low education and occupational statuses of people now 65+ has also contributed to the restraint, caution, and rigidity that has been observed as characteristic of them. Ample evidence indicates that lower socioeconomic status is related to an attitude of fatalism and authoritarianism. Put another way, the eras in which the now-old were socialized as children minimized the likelihood of strong feelings of internal control, that is, the feeling that one is able to control the course of one's life through one's own actions. Sex-role differences, too, may contribute to the observed personality characteristics of the now-old. Until around 1970, most studies of the elderly did not report on sex differences, probably reflecting a masculine bias in gerontological writings. Yet, because of the distinctly prescribed sex-appropriate behavior that was stressed by both the parents and peers of those now 65+, obvious gender-linked personality aspects exist. For example, recent studies indicated that middle-aged women have significantly less internal control than their male counterparts (Palmore, 1974), but better self-rated health, more social contacts, and greater sexual enjoyment enhance their feelings of self-mastery. Physical appearance, too, plays a part in perception of one's own control (and perhaps other personality variables); women 65+ who were rated as attractive by interviewers in a large-scale survey were more likely to feel that they could control their lives through their own actions (Campbell et al., 1976). Among men, however, height was the decisive factor (Campbell et al., 1976).

SELF-ESTEEM

Personality, like intelligence, in old age cannot be understood without reference to the first three quarters of the life span. One major dimension of personality of interest to sociologists and social psychologists has been self-esteem; that is, how people feel about themselves and view themselves in relationship to others. Self-esteem is also an important antecedent of well-being and of social behavior, for the person with low self-esteem is more likely to be depressed, to experience anxiety, and to have difficulty in interpersonal relations.

Despite the fact that most of us tend to think of ourselves as more or less constant throughout our lives, our self-esteem is apparently not fixed in childhood. Rather it is subject to a series of developmental changes, influenced not only by our childhood experiences but by social expectations, roles, and role changes. What happens to self-esteem in the aging process? Common sense would lead us to believe that the self-esteem of those 65+ (and at any other age) is at least partially contingent upon the regard with which one is treated. The old, as discussed in Chapter 3, are viewed with a not unjaundiced eye by the young. Paradoxically, on the basis of cross-sectional data, the now-old are generally likely to regard themselves as favorably, if not more so, than do younger people. In Riley and Foner's (1968) review of the literature, the old as compared to the young are less likely to admit shortcomings in themselves, more likely to feel adequate in their marriages and as parents, more likely to consider themselves as having better moral worth, and about equally as likely to feel that their job performance has been at least adequate. These findings again point to the importance of persistence in the role; as the elderly have more experience and more commitment to the pattern of life they have lived, they are perhaps less likely to be introspective and certainly less likely to want to change or vitiate their past performances and beliefs. Young people, growing up with self-change workshops, personal growth handbooks and seminars, and greater emphasis on personal development and change as legitimate endeavors may differ considerably from the now-old with respect to some of these findings. If personal growth and self-realization are internalized as legitimate foci for one's energy, we would expect that the old of 2020 might spend much of their time in such leisure activities as consciousness raising, yoga, encounter groups, and so on—much as about 13 percent of those now 65+ spend time going to a senior citizen's center or golden age club (Harris, 1975).

Recent cross-sectional data from the Harris (1975) survey for NCoA underscore the point that the elderly regard themselves in a positive light. However, whereas old people may not view themselves as pejoratively as the young think they might, certain groups of old people have lower self-esteem than others. There seems to be no "typical" self-esteem pattern in old age; instead, a variety of social and psychological factors influence self-perceptions in old age, much as they have throughout the preceding portions of the life course.

Race. As Table 5–1 shows, according to NCoA survey data, elderly whites tend to exhibit higher levels of self-esteem on a variety of items

Table 5–1. Self-Esteem Ratings by Those 65+ by Race

	Per Cent 65+ Agreeing with Item			
Self-Esteem Item	Total	White	Black	White–Black Difference
Very warm and friendly	72%	73%	69%	+ 4
Very wise from experience	69	70	63	+ 7
Very bright and alert	68	69	54	+15
Very openminded and adaptable	63	64	51	+13
Very good at getting things done	55	56	45	+11
Very physically active	48	50	31	+19
Very sexually active	11	10	11	− 1

Louis Harris and Associates, *The Myth and Reality of Aging in America*, Washington, D.C.: National Council on the Aging, 1975, p. 149.

than do Black age peers. Sixty-nine percent of the whites 65+ as compared to only 54 percent of Blacks in the same age group saw themselves as very bright and alert. Similarly, 56 percent of the whites surveyed described themselves as very good at getting things done whereas only 45 percent of the older Blacks agreed with this statement. In only two areas does the self-esteem of Blacks approach or exceed that of whites: being friendly and warm, and being sexually active. Both sexual activity and warmth/friendliness are expressive behaviors that are less valued in an instrumental, activity-oriented society such as ours.

That Blacks have lower self-esteem on the majority of items shown in Table 5–1 is a reflection of their minority group status in our society. For the now-old, the relationship between the two races has been essentially a political one where whites viewed themselves as superior and Blacks as inferior. Changes in the opportunity structure for Blacks should produce more positive self-images among future Black age cohorts. That this is beginning to take place is substantiated by NCoA data on self-esteem among those 18–64 years old. Although younger whites still have a more positive self-regard than do Blacks on some items, both races aged 18–64 are about equally likely to describe themselves as very good at getting things done (Harris, 1975, p. 150); this indicates a sense of increased mastery among younger Blacks.

Socioeconomic Status. Those more advantaged with respect to education and income are insulated from a variety of social and personal ills, as has been discussed throughout this book. The uneducated are considered of less social worth in any age group, and the disadvantaged now 65+ are prey to lower self-esteem. Drawing upon NCoA data, educational level has a definite effect on self-esteem in old age:

Table 5–2. Self-Esteem Ratings by People 65+ and Level of Education

Self-Esteem Item	Total	Per Cent Agreeing with Item		
		Some High School or less	High School Graduate or some College	College Graduate
Very friendly and warm	72%	72%	74%	70%
Very wise from experience	69	60	73	67
Very bright and alert	68	64	73	81
Very openminded and adaptable	63	59	71	64
Very good at getting things done	55	53	58	62
Very physically active	48	43	55	62
Very sexually active	11	11	11	10

Louis Harris and Associates, *The Myth and Reality of Aging in America*, Washington, D.C.: National Council on the Aging, 1975, p. 151.

As may be seen in Table 5–2, old people with some high school or less were *less* likely to see themselves as very wise from experience, very bright and alert, very open-minded and adaptable, very good at getting things done, and very physically active than were those who had graduated from high school or had college educations. Aged Blacks in the survey were disproportionally represented among those with some high school or less; 74 percent of Blacks as compared to 42 percent whites had some high school or less, and 62 percent of Blacks had a seventh-grade education or less. The combination of low educational attainment and minority group status apparently interact with one another to produce the very low self-esteem noted among elderly Blacks.

Education is a salient variable for self-esteem in younger age groups as well; the self-regard with which those 18–64 viewed themselves closely resembled that of people 65+ when level of educational attainment was taken into consideration (Harris, 1975). Education, not age, appears to influence one's level of self-esteem. As future, better-educated age cohorts reach old age, self-esteem may be expected to increase beyond that noted among the now-old.

Sex. At all ages women rate themselves lower than men on self-esteem (Turner, 1977). Among younger women, this is probably related to women's acceptance of the traditional definitions of femininity in which passivity and nonassertive behavior are emphasized. But, as Turner (1977) has pointed out in an extensive review article, women rate themselves lower on global measures of self-esteem and on character and ability items. Even in their traditional roles of spouse and parent, women view themselves more negatively than do men (Turner, 1977). Women are also more self-critical—and self-criticism is a correlate of self-esteem—perhaps because of early sex-role training where greater latitude is permitted for introspection, verbalization of feelings, and admission of symptoms (Turner, 1977). The "domestication of the middle-class American woman" (Slater, 1976), too, may play a part, for, as Philip Slater has observed, the role of the housewife is characterized by emotional and intellectual poverty as well as isolation in which her task is to produce an outstanding child:

> The only way she can feel she's putting a proper amount of effort into the task is by cultivating the child's natural entropic tendencies to make more housework for herself; or by upsetting and then comforting the child so she can flex her nurturance and her therapeutic skills. . . . Naturally this creates a great temptation to induce such crises, indirectly and, of course, without conscious intent. (1976, p. 71)

Oversocialization to the feminine role thus would seem to promote self-criticism and, concurrently, low self-esteem. Interestingly, however, as women age, their self-esteem more closely resembles that of men. As Neugarten (1975) has pointed out, women but not men define themselves in terms of events within the family cycle, and middle age is a period of launching children out in the world. Middle age is also a time of increased sense of personal freedom and a satisfying change in self-concept (Neugarten, 1975). Men in midlife, however, "take stock" of their careers thus far and may experience increased job pressures or job boredom (Neugarten, 1975). The aging woman thus is more likely to describe herself as more assertive, competent, independent, and effective in her relationships with others than the younger woman. In short, after the "empty nest," women shift from a less "feminine" to a more "masculine" self-concept (Turner, 1977). The self-esteem of women thus seems to be dependent upon their life events, whereas for men, socioeconomic status and achievement are more salient determinants (Turner, 1977; Maas and Kuypers, 1974). This is especially true for the highly feminine, other-oriented woman, whose late life self-esteem is inextricably related to her marital status and contacts with children. Those women who have put all their emotional eggs in one basket—motherhood—are especially prone to depression and are more vulnerable to changes in life-style (Bart, 1970).

Shifts in old age from a more negative, stereotypically female self-concept to a more masculine—or androgynous—self-regard are not without perils. There is really no legitimate role for the strong, old woman. Aggressive older women are viewed with alarm by both younger women and by their spouses. As Slater (1976) has summed up the problem:

> If women behave in ways that seem to imitate men, we call this masculine; but, if customs change, and certain activities get redefined as appropriate

for women, are they "masculine" for doing them? Suddenly we realize we've stumbled on a powerful weapon for "keeping women in their place." It's really a very old and familiar weapon, used with great effect against minority groups. It begins with a stereotype—"women can't think logically," for example. If a woman then shows a capacity for logical thought, she's stigmatized as "masculine." (1976, p. 75)

The now-old are caught in a dilemma; women, once into middle and old age, have more positive self-concepts but little cultural and institutional support for expression of this new sense of self. Future age cohorts, socialized to more androgynous sex roles, are likely to have less gender-related discrepancies in self-esteem and to experience fewer tensions in old age when they flex their instrumental and expressive attributes.

SELF-CONCERN

As people age, Neugarten (1975) has observed, they move toward more "egocentric, self-preoccupied positions and attend increasingly to the control and satisfaction of personal needs" (p. 140). She also stressed that it is impossible to state whether this increased sense of "interiority" is an inherent quality of the aging process or a reactive property (Neugarten, 1975, p. 141). Certainly the elderly have been reported to be more introverted and more concerned with physiological functioning than the young (Riley and Foner, 1968). This is not particularly surprising given the relatively greater declines in physical functioning of the elderly, and in their ability to perform daily tasks. Responses to the 1974 NCoA survey indicate that those 65+ are about twice as likely to see poor health as a very serious problem for themselves as compared to people 18–64.

The elderly also have symptoms indicative of some sort of mental illness, usually of a minor nature and encompassing such psychoneurotic symptoms as hypochondriasis and depression. Sickness at any age is characterized by greater egocentricity and concern with bodily functions, and a number of old people have their bodily concerns firmly rooted in reality rather than in sheer hypochondria. Although the number of aged with psychiatric disorders is unknown, Busse et al. (1970) observed that only 40 percent of 222 noninstitutionalized people 60+ who were studied at Duke University could be considered "normal," that is, free from depression, hypochondria, or other mental disorder including psychosis. Furthermore, there is an indication that impending physical decline may increase the likelihood of depression (Busse et al., 1970). Elderly hypochondriacs, though relatively free from physical pathology, had many more symptoms than the "normal" group (Busse et al., 1970). This picture is not as bleak as it first sounds, for " a number of elderly people with psychoneurotic reactions of varying degrees are still able to maintain a reasonably acceptable adjustment in society" (Busse et al., 1970, p. 83).

That many old have psychoneurotic symptoms is a reflection of lifelong personality patterns as well as age or cohort crises; younger people in the general population have also been found to have very high rates of psychiatric disorder (see, for example, Srole et al., 1962), and there is no reason to believe that aging should make one *less* neurotic or *less* prone to psychic distress. The added stresses of poverty, loss of friends and spouse through death, and biological decrement—coupled with attitudes toward aging in our culture—may, however, be sufficiently trying to induce psychic symptomatology.

If this were the case, what is "normal aging?" A number of studies have addressed this issue, and none has fully resolved it. Some of the current approaches are reviewed in greater detail in the following section.

Views of the Normal Aging Process

SOCIAL EXPLANATIONS

As discussed in Chapter 1, a variety of approaches to old age have been proposed, including activity theory, disengagement theory, continuity theory, subculture theory, and the sociobiological perspective. A key notion in many formulations has been that of *adjustment* to old age rather than a developmental or life-course approach. The early work of such researchers as Cavan, Havighurst, and Burgess (1949), for example, essentially was concerned with what makes for "adjusted" aging. Postulating that old people are not very different from middle-aged people, the individual who aged optimally was one who maintained usual activities as long as possible, found substitute roles for relinquished ones, and maintained social involvement.

Role theory was used in early works, such as Phillips (1956) and expanded upon by Blau (1973), to provide a framework to predict adjustment in old age. Adjustment referred primarily to goodness of fit between the perceived needs of old people and the extent to which they were able to satisfy their needs within the social structure. For Phillips (1957), involvement in fantasy, absentmindedness, daydreaming about the past, and thoughts of death were considered indicators of maladjustment and not part of "normal" old age. Reaching the age of 70, retirement, and death of a spouse were all viewed with equal weight as negative role changes that could contribute to maladjustment.

A challenge to activity theory and its assumption that action is equivalent to adjustment was the disengagement theory (Cumming and Henry, 1961), which used activity theory as a straw man and, in turn, was used as a whipping boy (see Cumming, 1975, for further discussion of the point). As originally formulated, disengagement theory may be summarized by its first two postulates: "Although individuals differ, the expectation of death is universal and decrement of ability is probable. Therefore, a mutual severing of ties will take place between a person and others in that society" (Cumming and Henry, 1961, p. 211). And, "Because interactions create and reaffirm norms, a reduction in the number or variety of interactions leads to an increased freedom from the control of the norms governing everyday behavior. Consequently, once begun, disengagement becomes a circular or self perpetuating process" (Cumming and Henry, 1961, p. 211). In the controversy surrounding this theory—considered an apologia for neglect and inactivity by some (see, for example, Blau, 1973; Gordon, 1975)—an additional postulate (number 6) of the theory is often forgotten: "Because the abandonment of life's central roles—work for men, marriage and family for women—results in dramatically reduced social life space, it will result in crisis and loss of morale unless different roles, appropriate to the disengaged state, are available" (Cumming and Henry, 1961, p. 215). Cumming and Henry thus were proposing that old age was not a continuation of middle age, but rather a distinct period in the life cycle with age-appropriate activities, which were different in quality and quantity from those in earlier ages. As should be evident, this theory remains controversial precisely because it has emphasized the decline in activity that may occur in old age (for a recent critique of disengagement theory see Hochschild, 1975; also see *International Journal of Aging and Human Development*, Vol. 6, No. 4, 1975, special issue on disengagement theory.)

Interestingly, disengagement theory made the first explicit recognition of sex differences in aging. Based on the age cohort that they studied, Cumming and Henry observed that women's roles are essentially unchanged from girlhood to death; women are socioemotional leaders who throughout their lives only change the details in their essentially expressive approach to the world. Men, on the other hand, are asked to make major role changes in old age; trained to be instrumental leaders and to work, their retirement has a tinge of failure to it. Furthermore, because they have been trained to be task- rather than person-oriented, men may find it difficult to strike up relationships after retirement or widowhood, and they have little contact with role models of the same sex from whom to learn. The retired man or widower must find new male role models or learn from women—an unaccustomed activity in adulthood. Accordingly, women, because of the sameness of the feminine role throughout life, may become "family representatives" after retirement. Because of the differential death rate, women have more female role models from which to draw, and this persists through widowhood when they have a reference group of other widows readily available. Growing old thus is an easier task for women than for men precisely because the social restraints imposed upon women do not provide discontinuity in old age; they go from "a little too much constraint to just the right amount of freedom," whereas men go from "too much of the one to too much of the other" (Cumming, 1963, p. 389). Whether growing old is indeed an *easier* task for women than for men in our society remains to be seen; certainly it is a *different* process. The higher rates of mortality and physical disability, and, as discussed later in this chapter, heightened risk of suicide among men 65+, indicate that old age is qualitatively different for the two sexes. Men are more disabled, but women have more disabilities; women live longer but, as shown later in this chapter, have greater prevalence of certain types of mental illness. To what extent these differences are biologically determined or socially based is also an unanswered question.

PERSONALITY AS A VARIABLE

Personality, too, plays a vital part in the modes of aging for both men and women. Noting that neither activity theory nor disengagement theory was adequate to account for individual differences in successful aging, some researchers have proposed that personality may be a key factor (Havighurst, Neugarten, and Tobin, 1964; Neugarten, 1965). Drawing upon earlier formulations by Frenkel-Brunswik and her associates (Reichard, Livson, and Peterson, 1962), these researchers in the Kansas City Study of Adult Life looked at both men and women to find a personality dimension that would fill this gap (Havighurst, 1968). They derived four basic personality types: (1) the *"integrated,"* who included activists and selective activists with reduced activity, as well as the successfully "disengaged" or happy rocking-chair contingent; (2) the *"armored defended,"* encompassing those who denied the aging process as well as constricted individuals who differed from selective activists in that they had less integrated personalities; (3) the *"passive-dependent,"* who included persons seeking succor from others as well as the apathetic; and (4) the *"disorganized."* The various types of integrated personalities reported high levels of life satisfaction; as did the subcategory of armored-defended who denied the aging process. The constricted reported high or medium life satisfaction. Only the apathetic and unintegrated reported medium or low satisfaction with life. Havighurst concluded: "Of the three dimensions on which we have data—activity, satisfaction, and personality—personality seems to be the pivotal dimension in describing patterns of aging and in predicting relationships between level of activity and life satisfaction" (p. 23, 1968).

A slightly different approach was suggested by Cumming (1963) who proposed a "temperamental variable, basically biological" (p. 379) as critical to style of aging. Assuming two ideal types, *impingers* (extroverts) and *selectors* (introverts), the degree to which an individual more closely resembles one type over the other will affect modes of growing old. The impinging personality, with need for interaction with others and a strong press for dominance, is likely to be active and perhaps in early old age appear younger than age peers. But, as physiological decrements occur, he/she will become progressively less able to impact the social situation, and suffer anxiety and panic when this happens. "(Their) problem in old age will be to avoid confusion," noted Cumming (1963, p. 380). In contrast, the selector, who may have been considered withdrawn when younger, will seem age-appropriate when old. Precisely because of this reserve, however, the older person may become listless and disinterested in the environment: "(Their) foe will be apathy rather than confusion" (p. 380).

Numerous other attempts have been made to delineate specific characteristics of the last portion of life. Whereas psychoanalytic theory has tended to regard adult personality as constant, the work of Erik Erikson is a notable exception. Outlining eight developmental stages that stretch from birth to death, Erikson (1963) has proposed two stages of particular significance to growing old: *generativity versus stagnation*, which involves either a sense of fulfillment in life based on one's achievements to date or a feeling of inertia and stasis, and extends from relatively young adulthood into old age; and *integrity versus despair*. In this last developmental phase, the individual becomes increasingly aware of one's own mortality and either comes to terms with one's own life as well lived and inevitable or becomes despondent and anxious.

More recently, Butler (1975) has criticized Erikson's formulation and proposed a model, drawing from the work of Neugarten (1974) as well as his own, that defines several characteristic tendencies among the old. Butler hastened to add that these tendencies are neither inevitable nor are they to be found in the same degree among all individuals. Briefly, Butler observed the following. First, there is a change in the meaning of one's sense of time—quality rather than quantity is important and a sense of the "here and now" dominates. A shift in perception of the life cycle also occurs, which includes: subjective awareness of death, the notion of the life course as an unflooding process of change, the experiencing of time as finite in human terms, a feeling of life experience or "knowing what it is all about," an accumulation of factual knowledge, and a sense of stages or phases of life. Also heavily emphasized by Butler is the importance of a "life review," that is, a progressive return to consciousness of past experiences and an active attempt to reconcile past life crises (perhaps one of the functions of reminiscence). Attachment to the familiar, and desire to leave a legacy, transmit power, and preserve continuity are also important personality traits of the old person. Finally, old age should encompass a sense of serenity and a capacity for growth (Butler, 1975).

COMMONALITIES

Are there any common patterns that may be woven from these particular theoretical strands? A dominant thread running through all the formulations is the fact of approaching death or physical decline. Just as one may speak of common areas of concern in adolescence, there are general concerns in old age. Yet, as in adolescence, there are also sociostructural diversities that color and modify, such as level of education, economic position, ethnicity, sex, rural-urban differences, and age cohort. Personal attributes, such as personality or temperament, physical condition, and level of energy, also modify or influence one's perspective. Given the immense diversity of aged along these dimensions, it is clear that there is no single satisfactory theory of normal aging. What we have instead is a series of approaches that, when put together, imply a "different strokes for different folks" model, the commonalities of which may be summarized as follows:

Congruency with Personal and Sociostructural Characteristics	Persistence of Old Role Activities		
	No Change	Modified	New Activities
Congruent	+	+	+
Incongruent	−	−	−

In other words, an old person may continue in accustomed activities without any reduction in those activities, may continue in part of these activities or modify them, or may choose new (including "rocking chair" as well as active) pursuits. What is key is not the activity but the *congruency of the choice* with social and personal characteristics of the chooser, so that a sense of consistency and continuity is maintained, where old people sustain themselves on their own terms. Obviously, an old person can move from one category to another in this scheme, as one's social situation or personal needs change. The retired college professor, for example, may continue to teach on a visiting professorship basis and to write for some years, but as his/her life situation (including health) alters, may find this incongruent with his/her needs and feel dissatisfaction. With luck, this person will then move into another pattern, which is more self-congruent.

That this does not happen in old age as a matter of course is also clear. The following psychological evaluation of a normal, 65-year-old woman highlights some of the dilemmas of growing old.[1]

Evaluation: Rita Brown

Date of birth: 5/10/13
Marital status: married (second marriage)
Occupation: retired teacher

Tests administered: Wechsler Adult Intelligence Scale (WAIS); Strong-Campbell Interest Inventory; Personal Orientation Inventory; Who Am I; How Old Am I; Threats to My Old Age; Life Satisfaction Index

[1] We should like to thank Sara Goodman, Boston University, for providing the psychological evaluation from which this report is excerpted.

Results of Testing: On the Wechsler Adult Intelligence Scale, Ms. Brown received a full scale score of 139 which places her in the very superior range. Her earlier group intelligence tests had yielded scores between 138–141, and she was surprised to see a consistent score. (During administration of the WAIS, tasks which required memory or speed made her anxious. She remarked, "you see, my memory is poor" or "You see how slow I am getting.") She commented after hearing her test results, "I guess some things get better and others worse."

While she had worked as a teacher in early childhood education, her highest occupational interests lay in the physical and social sciences and in art. She commented, upon reviewing her experiences: "I did an adequate job in all the jobs I've had but never really enjoyed them or felt fulfilled. . . . It's a career over with, which was pursued mainly to put my children through college and medical school. It lacked enjoyment and satisfaction."

In response to 5 "who am I" questions, Ms. Brown described herself as (1) a strong woman; (2) capable; (3) independent; (4) fearful of death of loved ones and of myself; and (5) passing time—no goals. With respect to items on "How Old Am I," she indicated that what she liked about her age was "the freedom from financial and child rearing responsibilities. I like the option of doing many things that please me." In response to what she disliked about her age, she stated: "I dislike losing physical and mental agility and feeling too old to have long term goals." Her preferred age is 30, because "I would like to be old enough to make mature judgments and young enough to pursue any area of development." A consistent theme that emerged in both test and self report material is that time has run out, and that it is too late to pursue formal intellectual pursuits or a new and more satisfying career.

On the life satisfaction index items, Ms. Brown indicated a high degree of life dissatisfaction with no expectations for happy events in the future. She also demonstrated a holding-on, "don't let anything more happen to me" life pattern.

In sum, Ms. Brown is a very intelligent and articulate woman who feels that life has cheated her intellectually and emotionally. Cheated of her occupational goals, she feels that she vicariously achieved through her two sons who became physicians. She described herself: "I am a three time loser—I failed vocationally, I spent a lifetime catering to men, and I lost a son" (who died 4 years ago, at age 32).

This case evaluation hints at some of the problems felt by one woman around the time of her sixty-fifth birthday. As is evident from her description of herself, many of her old role activities were not particularly satisfying to her. Because of the particular family situation and more general expectations for her age cohort, she was not able to pursue her real occupational interests while she was young; they were not considered appropriate for women of that generation. At age 65, she feels that she was cheated, but she is unable to switch to more satisfying pursuits. Although she is disappointed and bitter, she still maintains a feeling of self-worth and of personal competence.

Not all old people are as fortunate as Ms. Brown, however, and may experience profound psychological distress in old age. In the following section, some of the more common psychopathological problems that present themselves in old age are delineated.

Pathology and Deviance

Much behavior that appears abnormal from a psychological or psychiatric viewpoint is not necessarily considered odd from a sociological perspective, where deviance is seen not as a property of the acts themselves but in terms of the meanings that others attach to the behavior. Focus on the deviant case provides information about what is normal, customary, and expected behavior since most of the script for both deviant and non-deviant roles is derived from group experience. Much of our knowledge of the norms and values of any given culture is based on examination of specifically prohibited or disapproved behavior that by its very existence tells us what falls within the socially acceptable range. In psychology and psychiatry, as well, much of what is considered normal has been derived from observation of people who deviated from usual or customary behavior. Freud, for example, based his theory of normal psychosexual development upon illustrations of pathological deviation. A review of psychopathology that appears distinctly related to being old thus sheds light upon normal and abnormal aging. Some of the more common mental disorders noted among those 65+ include depression and chronic brain syndromes, both of which are discussed in the following sections.

DEPRESSION

Until recently, depression in old age has received sparse attention, perhaps because of our general cultural aversion to old age and treatment of the elderly. Although effective treatment of depression in younger people has become commonplace, an attitude of psychotherapeutic nihilism has pervaded approaches to this disorder—and to most mental changes—among the old. Freud, for example, singled out the aged as a group that was inappropriate for the psychoanalytic method: "owing to the accumulation of material, so much time would be required that the end of the cure would be reached at a period of life in which much importance is no longer attached to nervous health" (1959, p. 245). In short, why bother, since alleviation would come at a time when one has little time remaining—which also deprives the therapist of the experience of "success"! The current equivalent is the belief that old people are too inarticulate for the "talking cure."

Later theorists have challenged this assumption, especially since personality development as "ongoing" rather than "fixed at five" has become a prevalent concept. Erikson (1963), as noted earlier, delineated old age as the final stage of ego development, whose task is that of identity versus despair; the aged individual comes to terms with her/his life as inevitable, has a sense of relatedness to humanity in general, and faces the prospect of death with a degree of calm acceptance. Despite criticism by many gerontologists of Erikson's precise description of old age, the last stage of life is now viewed as a distinct developmental period—and probably a series of subperiods related to the age and physical condition of the specific person.

Recognition of depression in old age has also been influenced by the development of new techniques with which to treat it. As Gurland (1973) pointed out, the introduction of antidepressants has been followed by the acceptance of many minor "old age" complaints, such as constipation and early morning waking, as being caused by depression. The utilization of antidepressants and psychotropic drugs has been a mixed blessing, however, for many of the side effects of psychotropic medication produce symptoms such as trembling, shakiness, restlessness, and excess salivation, which, in turn, are thought to be bizarre and associated with the aging process. Advertisements by zealous pharmaceutical companies, combined with a belief that psychotropic (mood changing) drugs can "cure" the older patient—or at least make caretaking easier—has contributed to excessive medication of this age group (Green, 1978). The history of medicine is replete with similar examples of the availability of the cure leading to increased recognition of the disease, and of the cure instituting new patterns of symptoms.

The prevalence of depression in old age is unknown. As with any illness or personal crisis, only those cases in which people seek help or in which large-scale sample surveys reveal a specified condition are identified. The old are slow to seek help, largely because of their belief in self-reliance and self-determination associated with the work ethic in our culture. There is evidence that depression is very common in old age, however, and that it is related to many of the changing circumstances accompanying growing old. The death of close friends and relatives, decrements in physical functioning, and loss of major social roles have all been identified as factors that probably contribute to, if not cause, depression (Gurland, 1973).

Cath (1972) has proposed that the depression of the aged is not covered adequately by the concept as generally applied to younger people, for in the old it is complicated by *depletion*, that is, "an intermediate step between depression and other complex conditions subsumed under the name senility" (p. 302). Simply put, growing old in our society very often involves a loss of mastery over portions of one's life when previous problem-solving strategies are no longer readily available or effective. Loss of old coping mechanisms tends to deplete one's energy and to shift focus away from accustomed roles and activities. Attention is then placed more and more on one's own sensations, feelings, fears, and despondency. Much of the egocentricity that has been attributed to the old may reflect social changes, in which past role relationships are disrupted but no new roles are sufficiently attractive or available to engage people at a time when they are closer to the end of life than to the beginning.

Allied to depression in old age is vulnerability to suicide. As Table 5–3 shows, suicide rates rise with age. Although suicide is the third most common cause of death (after accidents and homicides) among the 15–24-year-old age group, the rate of suicide in this age group is considerably lower than that among the other age groups.

As Table 5–3 illustrates, those in the 75–84-year-age group are most vulnerable to suicide. The suicide rate, however, differs according to sex. At all ages, as Figure 5–2 shows, men are more vulnerable to suicide, and this is particularly pronounced in old age. For women, suicide peaks among those 45–54 (the empty-nest and menopausal years that are associated with frustration and disillusionment for many), then declines in the 55–64 year age group, and drops further with increasing age. For men, suicide rises more or less directly with age, reaching its height among those 75–84, and declining very slightly thereafter.

Although relatively little systematic analysis has been undertaken re-

Table 5–3. Suicide Rates per 100,000 Population by Age Group, 1976

Age Group	Rate per 100,000 in Age Group
Less than 1 year	0
1–4 years	0
5–14 years	.4
15–24 years	11.7
25–34 years	15.9
35–44 years	16.3
45–54 years	19.2
55–64 years	20.0
65–74 years	19.5
75–84 years	20.8
85+ years	18.9

Advance Report, Final Mortality Statistics, 1976, DHEW Publication PHS 78–1120, vol. 26, 12, supplement 2, Table 6.

Aging Bodies and Minds

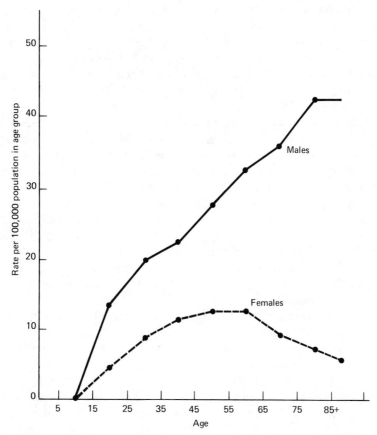

Figure 5–2. Suicide: Death and Death Rates, by Age and Sex: 1970 (National Center for Health Statistics Data). *Facts of Life and Death,* 1974, Table 41.

garding different crisis points in the life course for men and women, suicide rates as a gross indicator of severe depression indicate that women become depressed at an earlier age, perhaps as a result of role changes relating to their sexuality and childbearing functions. Men are more likely to become depressed at the ages of retirement, postretirement, and physical impairment. As future age cohorts, with more flexible and diverse role repertoires, grow old, it will be interesting to see whether this sex-typed pattern of severe depression persists.

ORGANIC BRAIN SYNDROMES

Despite the apparent frequency with which the old experience depression, the most commonly *diagnosed* psychiatric problem among those 65+ has been organic brain syndrome. Part of this is no doubt a result of the state of the art. As Barry Gurland, a psychiatrist concerned with mental disorders in old age, has put it, psychiatric diagnosis is "often used merely as an administrative tool to qualify the patient for insurance benefits or for admission to an institution" (1973, p. 353). Gurland also noted: "Furthermore, there is still the frequent belief that diagnosis in the elderly is likely to be an untreatable organic brain syndrome no matter what his symptoms are" (1973, p. 353).

Yet psychiatric diagnosis is often unreliable. Vera Norris (1959) in a study of mental illness in London found only a 68 percent level of agreement among psychiatrists on patients diagnosed as schizophrenic; on senile dementia and cerebrovascular psychosis, the two leading organic mental illnesses of old age, agreement was even lower: 53 percent and 29 percent, respectively. Similar differences have been observed in other studies. For example, Blum (1962), in a review of diagnostic consistency among psychiatrists, reported diagnostic *disagreements* statistically significant at the .001 level in proportions of patients whom different clinicians had assigned to organic versus nonorganic categories. Such a difference would occur as a result of chance in 1 in 1,000 cases, thus emphasizing the point that diagnosis is an art rather than a science.

In psychiatric diagnosis, two broad categories of organic brain syndromes are distinguished: acute brain syndromes and chronic brain syndromes. *Acute brain syndrome* occurs at any age; is often reversible; and is caused by a variety of agents, including head trauma, infection, or other disease processes such as diabetes, anemia, malnutrition, or congestive heart failure; by substances such as lead or other chemicals; or by drugs and alcohol. *Chronic brain syndrome,* on the other hand, occurs most often in old age, is believed to be irreversible, and is marked by physiological degeneration in the brain upon autopsy. These changes include thickening and hardening of cerebral blood vessels, an increase in the supporting tissue of the brain and spinal cord; loss and damage to nerve cells; wider convolutions in the brain and fluid filled spaces; and the appearance of so called "senile plaques" which are small irregular dark blobs, detectable through staining and microscopic techniques (Bondareff, 1959; Corsellis, 1962; Busse, 1962). Clinically, it has been difficult to differentiate the two most common types of chronic brain syndromes—senile dementia and cerebral arteriosclerosis—and often the distinction is made on the basis of the age of the person and the speed with which symptoms occur. Nor, as Jarvik and Cohen (1973) have observed, is the relationship between degree of physical symptoms, physiological changes, and behavior symptoms clear. Characterized by memory loss, deterioration of intellectual function, and emotional instability (Butler and Lewis, 1977), chronic brain syndrome remains an intriguing disorder precisely because its hallmark is impaired memory.

MEMORY LOSS

When a younger person forgets a name, the date, or to do something, she/he is usually described as absentminded, preoccupied with other thoughts, or busy with specific tasks. The old who forget similar information are portrayed in dissimilar terms, and are often dismissed with comments like: "She must be getting old" or "I wonder if he is getting a little senile." Because memory loss is popularly associated with the aging process, the old are given less license to forget, and lack of recall is viewed as indicative of irreversible and pathological changes in the brain.

Although such organic changes are indeed symptomatic of psychosis in old age, they also occur in brains of people who do *not* have organic psychosis and who function normally until their death. Organic changes thus appear to be a necessary but not sufficient cause for senility. Memory loss in old age—as at any age—is intriguing precisely because of the many reasons for its occurrence. Furthermore, popular belief to the contrary, there is some reason to believe that memory loss is not a natural, that is, inevitable, consequence of growing old. As Diamond (1978) has pointed out, there is growing scientific evidence that profound structural changes or cell loss do *not* occur in the brain with aging if one lives in a reasonably stimulating environment:

> In the absence of disease, impoverished environment, or poor nutrition, the nervous system apparently does have the potential to oppose marked deterioration with aging. There has to be some reason for the remarkable human beings who keep their brains in good condition for almost ten decades. As Krech (personal communication) quips, "he who lives by his wits, dies *with* his wits." (1978, p. 70)

The implications of this statement are far-reaching, for with good health care, adequate income maintenance, and increased (and personally appropriate) stimulation, senility may become a rarity.

The French neurologist Delay (1970) has suggested that memory loss, regardless of its cause, is patterned and progresses from the loss of social memory, the culturally shaped and shared ideas, expectations, and explanations we make of the world; to autistic memory, a blending of fact and fantasy; to sensory-motor memory, the simple recollections of how to walk, eat, control bowel function; and so forth. Memory loss is thus a loosening of social constraints on rational or normal behavior, and symptoms of memory loss are dependent upon the personality and social situation of the specific individual. *What* is forgotten is therefore a psychosocial product, for recollection is not a simple reproduction, like a photograph, but rather a reconstruction, like a painting, of the past based on individual and social experience.

There is some indication that human memory and recollection function somewhat like a very sophisticated computer which records, remembers, and searches for information, makes comparisons and associations, and combines these processes to solve problems. Thus, forgetting at any point in the life span normally occurs because of temporary loss of information in a growing network of new learning (*information overload* in computer terms) or because of a faulty association procedure. Various investigators, from Freud (1924) to the present day, have proposed that memory is primarily associative. That is, successful locations of linking, or apparently linking, paths in the network of memory allow us to feel that we have understood a particular event or series of events. Sometimes this process is not straightforward. We have probably all had the experience in which we are talking to a friend about some recent happening but suddenly begin to ramble on in a long, only tenuously connected story. At this point, we wonder, "Now, how did I get onto that?" This is an illustration of associative memory at its height.

Forgetting, too, is common to all of us and usually refers to a failure to remember some event or item that we want to remember or are expected to remember. Forgetting most often takes place when any of the memory links is blocked. If this blockage continues, one is likely to try to replace "missing links" through compensatory mechanisms such as evasiveness or fabrication in an attempt to restore the appearance of connections between events and to conceal from others that one has forgotten.

In recollection among all age groups, there is a strong interpretive element in the events to be remembered. The mind does not work like a tape recorder where every sound is registered; rather, it is more like a student attending a lecture course in which she/he notes key phrases and concepts while ignoring or screening out others. One aspect of this selective recording is that, in general, pleasant or interesting experiences are more likely to be retained in memory than ordinary ones. Happy episodes are more likely to be remembered as taking up more time; they also occupy a larger storage space in memory than do unhappy ones (Ornstein, 1970). Experiences in which one is deeply involved are also more often retained in great detail along with all their possible outcomes; once they are well past, however, the whole interval becomes "chunked over" or condensed in memory (Ornstein, 1970).

When the old are preoccupied with events of the past, there is a tendency to think of this in terms of organic change, that is, undue recall of past memories coupled with inability to absorb new information. Recent memory is problematic as one grows older, for ability to recall may become impaired. Yet there is evidence that old people may not have difficulty in learning new information or in storing it. Rather, information retrieval is impaired (Schonfield, 1965). The issue is by no means resolved (see Arensberg, 1973, for a more extensive review). The old seem to have difficulty in recall when meaningless or unconnected information is involved, yet they are as good or better than young people at remembering material in which some kind of suggestive connection exists between the substance and their own experience. In fact, when an older person sees links between the item/event to be recollected and one's self, he/she may perform as well or better than a young person! (Istomina et al., 1967; Cohen, Silverman and Shmovonian, 1970).

Memory thus is primarily evocative rather than informational. Recalling the past is not a tidy process of retrieving information from neat storage compartments but rather an imaginative recreation of past experiences. This may be related to some of the difficulties of the elderly in dealing with immediate or recent past events, where new information, although absorbed, may not be as personally relevant or important as past events.

Both a sense of the past and an idea of the present are important because they affect anticipation of the future; they are also related to successful aging. For example, centenarians who have successfully dealt with their own pasts tend to have plans for the future, but those with difficulty in recalling their pasts are unlikely to have a sense of themselves beyond a day-to-day survival (Costa and Kastenbaum, 1967). Reminiscence in old age, too, promotes better adjustment and a maintenance of ego integrity (Boylin, Gordon, and Nehrke, 1976). Although the ultimate boundary of all our futures is death—and this is especially pressing for the old—the paradox of successful aging is that it apparently requires awareness without panic of the presence of death so that one may reorganize life to make the most of the time that remains. Muriel Spark, in her perceptive novel, *Memento Mori*, describes the significance that confrontation of one's own mortality has for successful living:

> If I had my life to live over again, I should form the habit of nightly composing myself to thoughts of death. I would practice, as it were, the remembrance of death. There is no other practice which so intensifies life. Death, when it approaches, ought not to take one by surprise. It should be part of the full expectancy of life. Without an ever present sense of death, life is insipid. You might as well live on the whites of eggs. (1967, p. 153)

As is discussed at some length in Chapter 4, death is an unwelcome topic for most of us; it is something to overcome rather than to accept. Yet the ability of many old people to project themselves into the future is apparently impaired by their fear of death (Bascue and Lawrence, 1977), and this in turn promotes memory loss. There is, for example, some indication that people in institutions have a time perspective that is more concerned with the past than that found in their noninstitutionalized contemporaries—perhaps reflecting their anxiety about the lack of a felt real future for themselves (Fink, 1953); they are also more likely to die. The past is gone (and sometimes depressing to remember), the present is fleeting, and the future is a nonnegotiable death. Memory loss may provide a respite from this bleakness.

Memory, Roles, and Personality

How does this relate to "normal" personality in old age? We are suggesting that memory loss may be related to social roles and to role loss. Social roles are, as discussed throughout this book, a mechanism for integration of life events. When few meaningful roles or experiences remain in the life of the old, memory becomes increasingly important as a source of selfhood. Yet this is a double-edged sword, for, with few present roles enabling one to put personal experiences into a framework, memory is likely to be constructed of past, unintegrated events. Put in sociological terms, memory loss in old age is a coping mechanism. When few external resources and satisfying activities are available as a basis for constructing and interpreting reality, one is thrown back on one's inner resources. As with the person marooned on a desert island, life is now exactly as one sees and structures it; many of the formal structures—work, active parenthood, and so on—are of diminished importance. In this sense, much memory loss in old age is a social disease, "caused" by an uninteresting or unrewarding environment.

The degree of variety in past life experiences is also a significant factor in memory loss. Rates of diagnosis of chronic brain syndrome are higher among those of lower socioeconomic background. Martin Roth (1971, personal communication) has proposed that there are no truly senile dowager duchesses, for those of upper-class background seem better able to cope with whatever impairment is present. When impaired, the upper-class elderly have had lifelong experience in handling diverse social situations; their behavior is defined as eccentric, perhaps, but not mad. Put another way, the breadth of experience and education of the middle and upper classes insulates the old of this status to some extent, enabling them to maintain generally successfully coping mechanisms. A history of processing varied environmental social cues can be called upon, and a wide range of responses to various social situations has become habit. Although elderly persons may be more constricted in the number of available roles than are those at younger ages, they have larger role repertoires upon which to draw. As one well-educated elderly woman (a graduate of Bryn Mawr College) was described:

> "My dear, I'm going to be 75 in October and I haven't much (time) left"—and there's so much she still has to do. . . . "Don't ask me how I do anything, sweetie . . . just thank the Lord I'm still here to do it." Isabel Burger, generally known as "Dearie," topping a 50 year career teaching creative drama to and for young people with this new attempt to apply the

technique with older people. . . . (*Bryn Mawr Alumnae Bulletin*, Summer, 1978, p. 5)

Not all people are as fortunate as this woman; their lives have been more circumscribed. The following woman, aged 78, had been admitted to a mental hospital because of memory loss and difficulties in coping:

I had a wonderful life till my husband got sick. My husband was sick 16 years and I took care of him. And I never even knew that he was that sick. He had all kind of heart trouble and I . . . then, when my son, when my— my husband is dead about 18 years and I still dream about him 'cos I loved him. And my son is only dead a couple of years. I went to the hospital, Memorial Hospital, and they took his leg off, and they took his hip off. And I kept going and going and I kept up fine that he shouldn't see my eyes red or anything—I put on such a front. But when I got alone after he passed away . . . (she starts to cry). (Excerpt from taped psychotherapy session, Bronx State Hospital)

A major difference in these two women's lives is opportunity. In the same age cohort, one has had a college education, has been able to pursue her own career and interests, and has enjoyed an adequate income throughout her life. The other has limited education (less than seventh grade), low income, and was overwhelmed by the deaths of her husband and son. Her adaptation to this situation was considered neither normal nor eccentric by those who sought her commitment to the state mental hospital.

Women are especially likely to be diagnosed as having a chronic brain syndrome, including cerebral arteriosclerosis and senile brain disease in old age; the ratio of women to men with this diagnosed disorder is 2:1. Part of this is certainly a reflection of their greater life expectancy. Gruenberg (1977) has estimated that cerebral arteriosclerosis has its highest rate of prevalence between age 65–74 and senile brain disease at age 80. Both disorders are apparently increasing, according to Gruenberg (1977), who has hypothesized that this rise is the result of a reduction of mortality among the frail and infirm who otherwise might have died earlier of infectious disease. But, as was discussed in Chapter 4, age-specific mortality, on the average, is higher among lower socioeconomic groups and among men, which leads one to speculate about how the nature of the life experiences of the poor, especially women, may relate to memory loss or so-called organic changes.

In American society, women's roles have traditionally been less susceptible to a sudden termination or abrupt change than have men's. The process is likely to be gradual. The impact of role loss through attrition— the gradual dropping away of roles as children leave home, retirement occurs, spouse dies, and so forth—seems particularly intriguing. Despite the fact that at least one third of the women now 65+ worked at least part of their married lives (see Chapter 9), domesticity has been the defining feature of the female condition in our society. A woman's identity has been defined by her role within the family and by her husband's occupation. For the working- and lower-class women, the career pattern may indeed be employment-wife/mother-employment, but the major source of gratification and sense of self have been in the familial roles. Other sources of self-esteem, although real (see, for example, Atchley, 1976), were not culturally legitimated. And, as discussed throughout this book, old women are likely to have lower incomes, more years of widowhood, and less employment—in short, less stimulation—than men. They are also more likely to be diagnosed as mentally ill throughout the life span, although whether this is the result of differences in actual prevalence or reflects sexist diagnostic practices is an unresolved debate.

In a now classic experiment on college students, Heron (1957) and his associates isolated young people in a room where they underwent prolonged exposure to a boring environment. Thus began the theory of sensory deprivation, for the students became depressed, irritable, and disoriented, and they had impaired cognitive thinking and even hallucinations. For the poor, lonely, and isolated with a limited repertoire of experiences from which to draw, much memory loss may be a response to sensory deprivation. If indeed, as Erikson (1963) has proposed, old age is the final stage of ego development, satisfactory living conditions and opportunities for personally meaningful activity seem crucial. Identity, after all, requires a sense of comradeship with others, whereas egocentricity is allied to despair. Memory loss in old age may be an adaptive, if not functional, response to a confining, unrewarding present and past.

Prospects

Although much has been written on what happens to the aging mind and personality, relatively little is known about how many of the characteristics observed among the now and past old are hallmarks of the aging process. Knowledge about the inevitability of many of the changes associated with growing old is time-bound, limited to specific age cohorts, and is usually studied cross-sectionally, and this knowledge is also limited by the state of the art. As more sophisticated research designs and measurement techniques develop, answers may emerge to such questions as: Is there an age-linked decrement in intelligence? if so, under what conditions? What practical implications does this have for actual intellectual functioning in a variety of real life (rather than test) situations? Our knowledge of the way in which the brain changes, as well as the significance of these changes for behavior, will also be enhanced.

Much of the data available on personality in old age is also both temporally and culturally limited. Perhaps our cultural aversion to this last period of the life cycle has encouraged normative judgments about the healthy personality in old age. As pointed out earlier, relatively little research has focused on the poor, the minority groups, and the foreign-born elderly, and, until recently, upon the differences between men and women as they aged. Although we cannot predict with great accuracy what the varieties of aging personalities in the future will be, it is evident that they will be somewhat different from those observed among the now-old.

Future cohorts of the elderly, like current and past ones, will take into old age the values, habits, sex-role training, and sources for self-esteem developed over the years that are part of their particular epoch. These will be different among the old of 2020, for trends may be seen among those who are now young adults that may promote different psychological patterns than are current among the now-old. Greater emphasis on androgyny for both sexes, increased career activity for women outside the home, and the removal of mandatory ages for retirement should all have an impact upon the way in which people grow old. What will be the effect of increased emphasis on personal growth, in lieu of the work ethic, on intellectual and psychic functioning?

Increased life expectancy and availability of health care to enable greater periods of physical fitness argue for greater levels of active participation in a variety of roles from which self-esteem may be derived and promoted. The growing number of very old pose an interesting opportunity to determine whether decreased interest and intellectual activity are associated with the inevitable running down of the human organism or a result of understimulation in environment. What, for example, will the impact of greater educational attainment be on self-esteem? on memory and recall?

The environment in which people grow old will also have changed. Public support of more programs for the aged, such as senior citizen centers, medical programs, home help programs, educational opportunities, and so forth can be expected to have an effect not only on the old themselves but on the way in which they are viewed and regarded. Their sheer force of numbers will perhaps create an awareness of their heterogeneity.

Research Exercises

1. From the published autobiographies and memoirs of famous people and writers, preferably from a variety of historical and cultural contexts, write an *essay* on their perception of aging, recollections of midlife changes or crises, intimations of mortality, and so forth. Are there regularities in the aging experience across time and space?

2. Conduct *interviews* with couples in their sixties on their past and present sex-typed behaviors. Do they perceive a shift toward androgyny?

3. Administer parts of a standard adult intelligence test to a convenience sample of persons 18–75. Analyze your findings for age differences. What items discriminated the most? Which discriminated the least?

Discussion Questions

Discuss the cultural stereotyping involved in the concepts of "little old ladies" and "dirty old men."

Is it possible to devise an age-free intelligence test?

What steps can one take to minimize the effects of memory loss?

What types of personality traits are more or less likely to change with age?

6

Institutionalization—
Sin, Cure, Or
Sinecure?

————•◆•————

Despite divergent ideologies, values, and social institutions, most contemporary industrialized countries face similar problems in financing, organizing, and delivering care to people who for one reason or another are not able to care for themselves in old age. As birthrates have decreased and life expectancy has grown, a guarantee of at least a minimal amount of service to the old has been of increased concern, as has been a reduction in the glaring inequities in treatment. In most countries, including the United States, the particular types of care available for the dependent elderly have not been organized to fit a well-delineated and rational plan of action. Rather, like other social arrangements, such as the family, educational systems, and so on, treatment facilities are influenced heavily by the economic structure and societal values of the culture of which they are part. Institutionalization has become a prevalent modality for delivery of service to dependent old people in the United States. Although institutional care in old age is, as discussed later, a personal crisis for the elderly, it is largely socially instigated. The following section reviews some of the reasons for the growth of nursing homes, geriatric wards of mental hospitals, and other extended care residential facilities for the elderly.

Perspectives

Until relatively recently, both elderly people in institutions and institutions earmarked specifically to care for the old were uncommon. In the United States in 1910, only about 80,000 people 65 and over were in institutions of all types; by 1970, about one million elderly people were living in nursing homes, old-age homes, and mental hospitals.

A major reason for the increase in the numbers of old persons in custodial care facilities is the greater life expectancy of people in contemporary Western society. At the beginning of the Christian era in Rome, in contrast, the average life expectancy at birth was about 22 years of age. By the 1600s, the average had increased another ten years—to age 33. Until the twentieth century, relatively few people lived to be old, and those who did were more likely to be economically well off and physically healthy— a biological and social elite (Antonovsky, 1972). As, however, acute infectious diseases have declined as leading causes of mortality in the United States and other industrialized nations, more and more people are likely to spend part of their old age in a nursing home or other congregate care facility for the aged.

Although only about 5 percent of those 65 and over are in an institution at a given point in time, this is essentially a cross-sectional view that tells little about the actual likelihood of living and dying in a nursing home or its equivalent. Recent work by Kastenbaum and Candy (1973) and Palmore (1976) indicates that this rate greatly underestimates an individual's chances for institutionalization. It is likely that around one in four older Americans will be placed in an extended care facility of some kind prior to death.

Institutional care of the aged is not, however, a new phenomenon. The Elizabethan Poor Law of 1601, which laid the basis for much welfare legislation in the United States as well as in England, distinguished between the aged and impotent poor, children, and the able-bodied poor. Aged and impotent poor and children without financial resources were cared for together in an almshouse or poorhouse, where custodial care was provided under the supervision of the municipality. This kind of undifferentiated institution permitted not only close supervision of the moral worth of those receiving relief but an economy of scale. The quasi-penal character of the poorhouse, described eloquently in the nineteenth century by Charles Dickens, was by all accounts unpleasant but ensured relatively cheap and safe isolation of the infirm, the elderly, and other nonproductive members of society. Hospitals, too, served this function for the ill of all ages. Benjamin Franklin, describing the need for a public hospital in Philadelphia, noted that such a facility would guarantee a place where people who had "lost their senses" or had a tendency to wander aimlessly and frighten their neighbors might be confined. Franklin also commented that it would be cheaper to care for the sick in one central location than to send help to their homes (an idea that has persisted in social policies surrounding delivery of care in contemporary society). Furthermore, argued Franklin, the establishment of a hospital for the indigent of all ages would relieve the middle class of seeing the poor die in the streets (Franklin, 1754).

Where, one is tempted to ask, were the families of the aged and infirm poor during the seventeenth and eighteenth centuries? With depressing regularity, commentators on the American social scene lament the death of the multigenerational or extended family and suggest that the growth of nursing homes is an indication of the withering away of family ties. Yet, as detailed in Chapter 2, industrialization and modernization have narrowed the social and economic functions of families over several centuries. (See also Berger, 1971.) The disintegration of the feudal state, the decline of clan or family as a basis for political power, the rise of cities, and the increased mobility of populations moving from the country to cities to seek work all had profound implications for the structure of the family. With the emergence of capitalism, division of labor, and industrialization, added emphasis was placed on economic or market relationships rather than on traditional ruler-ruled and familial ties. With greater potential for individual self-expression and freedom came a loosening of the family as a basis for social stability and regulation. One's position in the economic structure rather than place in the family became a crucial indicator of status and life chances.

It was precisely such social change that occasioned passage of the Elizabethan Poor Law in 1601 and subsequent social legislation in Britain. The elderly were relatively unaffected at that time; since there were few old people in the population, no special concern need be given to their care. If they were self-sustaining, the elderly might live as they chose; if they were indigent, they were placed in a poorhouse or public hospital. A similar pattern developed in America. But even though more people survive to old age, we have not really developed new ways of caring for them in the United States; instead, we have expanded and improved services based on a very old model (with a few exceptions, discussed later in this chapter).

GOALS OF INSTITUTIONALIZATION

Institutionalization of persons at any age has several goals. The first and most obvious is the provision of treatment or service to those who are judged incompetent to care for themselves. Whether institutional care is always the most efficient or effective means of treatment for younger people suffering from a variety of problems, including physical handicaps (Roth, 1967), criminal behavior (Palmer, 1973), or mental illness (Szasz,

1970) is still a topic of controversy. There is also question about whether institutional care for the elderly is most appropriate (Brody, 1976; Curtin, 1976).

A second, less explicit, goal of institutionalization is to isolate people of low social worth from the mainstream of society where their presence might be disruptive to ongoing social relationships. Franklin's statement—that the public hospital relieves the middle class of seeing the poor die in the streets—highlights this point; at one time or another, the criminal, the handicapped, the retarded, the mentally ill, the poor, the old, and the dying have all been recipients of services in isolated custodial settings. For example, the geriatric service of state mental hospitals has often been used as a hiding place to die for the elderly poor. Markson (1971) examined the records of 174 patients, all of whom were 65 or older, who were admitted to a state mental hospital during an eight-month period. This hospital, which admitted all persons referred, apparently served as a terminal care facility; 64 percent of the 174 patients had one or more major physical diseases detected at the admission examination; less than half were able to walk without assistance, 11 percent were in wheelchairs, and 19 percent were on stretchers (one third of whom were comatose) when admitted. A fourth of these 174 people died within thirty days after admission.

A third and infrequently expressed goal of institutionalization of the elderly or other special groups is to make *their* lack of productivity as wage earners economically and socially productive to others. To maintain any long-term care facility, both treatment and supportive staff is required. Institutions employ a number of ancillary personnel, such as kitchen help, administrative and clerical workers, aides, and cleaners. Table 6–1

Table 6–1. Proportion of Full-Time Staff Employed in Nursing Homes by Broad Occupational Category, 1973–74

Occupational Group	Proportion in Category
Total, all full-time employees	100.0%
Administrative and medical staff	3.8
Therapeutic (including Occupational Therapist, Recreational Therapist, Social Worker)	1.8
Registered nurses	7.4
Licensed practical nurses	8.8
Aides	46.3
All other	31.9

Jeannine Fox Sutton, *Utilization of Nursing Homes, United States: National Nursing Home Survey, August 1973–April, 1974.* Vital and Health Statistics Series 13, no. 28, Washington, D.C.: U.S. Government Printing Office, 1977 (DHEW publication no. (HRA) 77–1779). Table Q.

shows the broad occupational categories of workers who were employed at nursing homes in the United States in 1973–74.

Within the past twenty-five years or so, the labor market in health has changed radically. Between 1950 and 1970, for example, the number ·of employees in health care rose from 1.7 million people (2.96 percent of all employed labor force) to 4.3 million (5.6 percent of the employed labor force). In nursing homes, too, staff has been expanding; in 1964 there were 44 full-time employees of all types per 100 nursing home residents. By 1973–74, there were 66 full-time staff per 100 residents (Sutton, 1977). In some communities, providing and maintaining an institution for the elderly, infirm, mentally retarded, or mentally ill may be the only major industry. For example, studies of the closing of state hospitals have indicated that one of the major results of such phaseouts is widespread unemployment among members of the community in which the facility was located (Keenan, 1974; Dingman, 1976). Maintenance of institutions such as the nursing home, chronic hospital, or geriatric center creates jobs; by residing therein, the otherwise economically unproductive clients of such facilities become productive. Payment for their care may be borne by public or private funds, but much of these monies are recirculated to other members of society in the form of salaries, wages, and other payments.

THE PROBLEM OF GROWING NUMBERS

The effects of larger numbers of old people in the population on extended care facilities became obvious by the 1940s. Public mental hospitals received a large number of elderly, often because there was no place else for them. By 1946, using the public mental hospital as an old age facility had become so common that one physician estimated that about 24 percent of all people over 60 years old in the United States were likely to be placed in a mental hospital (Thewliss, 1946). Overinstitutionalization of the aged in inappropriate facilities was soon evident. In 1961, ·for example, although psychiatrists rated as "certifiable" 89 percent of the patients 64 years or older who were in mental hospitals in New York, they observed that the suitability of mental hospitalization in over one half of these cases would be questionable were other facilities available (Goldfarb, 1961).

Within the past twenty years, however, the use of the mental hospital as a terminal care facility has declined. A variety of studies (Lowenthal, 1964; Lowenthal et al., 1967; Epstein and Simon, 1968; Markson et al., 1971) have shown that many old people in mental hospitals were not very different from people who managed to get along outside the hospital or from patients in nursing homes. Accordingly, most states have begun to screen and refer the elderly to facilities other than mental hospitals;

policies vary from state to state and within states. Between 1962 and 1972, the rate of first admissions to state and county mental hospitals dropped from 163.7 per 100,000 people 65 and over to 69.2 (Meyer, 1973). Within the same time period, passage of Medicare and Medicaid legislation provided mechanisms for funding nursing home care for the elderly. Medicare, also known as Title XVIII of the Social Security Act (1965), basically provides limited national health insurance for those 65 years or older. Federal financing for most forms of hospital care are provided, although the elderly patient must pay a fixed amount or deductible before Medicare coverage begins. Provisions for long-term institutional care include 100 days in a skilled nursing home, provided this follows hospitalization for a condition where extended care is recommended by a physician. Further limitations require that a person must have been in a hospital for at least three consecutive days before the admission, that she/he must be admitted to the nursing home within fourteen days after leaving the hospital (or twenty-eight days if no bed is available), and that a utilization review or professional standards review board must approve of the stay. Medicare thus was designed to provide somewhat limited service for specified medical conditions.

Medicaid, also implemented in 1966, differs from Medicare in several respects. Designed to provide coverage for the medically indigent, it is a welfare rather than an insurance program; that is, a "means test" and restrictions on income and property are imposed as eligibility criteria. Limitations on eligibility vary from state to state. Each state not only determines individual eligibility for Medicaid benefits but also licenses and inspects nursing homes that may receive patients under the program. Medicaid provides more liberal coverage for long-term nursing home care

Table 6–2. Growth of Nursing Homes and Sources of Primary Payment 1964–1974

Nursing Homes	1964	1969	1973–74
Number of residents (in thousands)	554	815	1,076
Beds per 1,000 people 65+	32.2	45.2	55.2
Primary source of payment for care			
Medicare	—	3.4%	1.1%
Medicaid	—	13.3%	47.9%
Public assistance	47.0%	36.5%	11.4%
Other	54.0%	46.9%	39.7%
Average monthly charge per resident	$185.00	$335.00	$479.00

Statistical Abstract of the United States, 1978, Health and Nutrition, Table 166; Sutton (1977), Utilization of Nursing Homes, United States: National Nursing Home Survey, August 1973–April 1974. Washington, D.C.: U.S. Government Printing Office (DHEW Publication no. HRA 77—1779).

than Medicare and, as may be seen in Table 6–2, has become increasingly important as a source of primary payment.

Institutional care for the elderly of any kind is not cheap. Although comparable data for mental hospitals are not available, National Center for Health Statistics data for nursing homes indicate that the average total monthly charge per resident in 1973 was $489 in proprietary, (i.e., profit making) and $456 in nonprofit (church, government, and other nonprofit) facilities. Sutton (1977) has reported that costs ranged from $0 to over $1000 per month in 1973–74; about two thirds of the facilities surveyed charged less than $500 per month, and 3 percent were over $1000 per month. Since 1969, charges have increased on the average of 11 percent per year; using this as a basis for estimated costs, current costs for proprietary homes would average $758 per month and $707 for nonprofit homes (and are rising as you read this chapter).

Current Factors Promoting Institutional Care

Although considerable governmental and private allocation of money and manpower has been channeled into institutional care of the elderly in hospitals, nursing homes, personal care homes, and homes for the aged, neither Medicare nor Medicaid has proved to be a panacea in old age. Shulman and Galanter (1976) observed that "the nursing home industry is a disaster, well documented by innumerable investigations and reports" (p. 130). Recent congressional hearings indicated that the "personal care" or "adult home," which does not provide nursing care but nonetheless serves many old people who need supervision, may be dangerous and inappropriate for many residents (U.S. House of Representatives Select Committee on Aging, 1977). The mental hospital, too, has been scored as a house of death (Markson, 1971) and, as always, expensive, inefficient, frequently antitherapeutic, and never the treatment of choice (Mendel, 1976). To what extent are these criticisms valid? And, whether these criticisms are valid or not, what social function does institutionalization of the elderly play? Before examining the processes and effects of institutional care, it is important to consider several broader social issues relating to being old in America.

AGEISM AND LOSS OF ROLE

In American society a man's value has been traditionally assigned by his real or apparent social contribution and achievement, of which occupation and wealth are the most common indices. In the case of a woman, the status of her father and her husband is crucial. Furthermore, ours is an instrumental, activist society in which work is valued as an end in itself; faith in the virtues of action and the sin of inaction runs deep. Death, the apotheosis of inactivity and the cessation of achievement, remains an unwelcome and dreaded confrontation. The elderly lose on both counts; not only are they less active than the young but they are prime candidates for death.

Put another way, if social value is measured by productive capacity, the worth of old and retired persons is low. Nor is it that their production is needed in our society. As Irving Rosow has adroitly observed, "The aged are a problem precisely because we are such an affluent society" (Rosow, 1962). The labor of old people is not needed; the nation is too affluent and individuals are too self-sufficient to need to rely upon the elderly. The lack of a socially productive role for the elderly, combined with their greater infirmity, has led to the definition of old age as a problem, preferably one that is amenable to corrective or palliative treatment. The passage of Medicare illustrates this point. Designed as a compromise move between the proponents of national health insurance for all ("socialized medicine") and the supporters of individual, fee-for-service medicine, Medicare was enacted because even those with polarized views found that they could agree on special help for the aged.

Yet, since old age is accorded lower social value than youth, the elderly still tend to receive less care and consideration when they become handicapped or ill. Relevant here is Alex Comfort's statement:

> One wonders what Archie Bunker would feel about immigrants if he knew that on his sixty-fifth birthday he would turn into a Puerto Rican. White racists don't turn black, Black racists don't become white, male chauvinists don't become women, anti-Semites don't wake up and find themselves Jewish—but we have a lifetime of indoctrination with the idea of the difference and inferiority of the old. (1976, p. 4)

In illness, the older person with heart disease, cancer, or other major disease is less likely to receive the same sort of intensive care for as long a period as a younger person. (One wonders whether the decision to disconnect Karen Ann Quinlan from her respirator would have created controversy had she been 79 rather than 19.) The old person is also more likely to be transferred to an extended or long-term care facility whenever possible (Medicare provides for 100 days of such benefits for retired people), thereby freeing up a bed in the short-term, active treatment hospital where younger patients are more likely to be treated.

SOCIAL CLASS AND INCOME

In addition to age, social class, a crude indicator of which is income, is critical in determining the kind of care one will receive. For example, although Medicare is based on the premise that medical care should be available to *all* Social Security recipients on a nondiscriminatory basis, a recent analysis of Medicare payments by Karen Davis (1975) showed that benefits are not distributed equally among income classes. Old people with incomes above $15,000 per year received 45 percent more days of hospital care on the average than did lower-income persons with similar health conditions, and twice the payments for physician and other services. In addition, the average reimbursement for each physician's visit was 50 percent higher among the high-income as compared to low-income people. This suggests, in part, a tendency among higher-income elderly to receive higher-quality and more specialized services. Wildavsky (1977) has dubbed this the "axiom of inequality," where "the wealthier aged, who can afford to pay, receive not merely the same benefits as the aged poor but even more, because they are better able to negotiate the system. Class tells" (p. 110).

The elderly of low social status are also likely to be placed in a "deprived institution" (Riesman and Horton, 1965), such as the mental hospital. In a study of 348 referrals to two state mental hospitals serving the New York City area, 86 percent of those referred for inpatient care as compared to 59 percent of the general population had not gone beyond elementary school. Their occupational status parallelled their low educational status; 77.7 percent were at the bottom of the occupational scale (Markson and Hand, 1970).

RACE AND ETHNICITY

Both race and ethnicity are salient factors influencing the kind and quality of care that is received in old age. Manard, Kart and van Gils (1975) reported an inverse relationship between the proportion of nonwhite elderly in the general population and the proportion in old-age institutions. States with large nonwhite populations are generally characterized by low institutional rates in such facilities. Much of this is associated with discriminatory practices in admission and utilization of different types of facilities. As Kart and Beckham (1976) have pointed out, elderly Blacks predominate in state mental hospitals (which are not old-age institutions per se although about 30 percent of their inmates are 65 +); whites predominate in nursing and old-age homes. For the Black old, the problem seems not to be one of keeping *out* of an institution but of *receiving* appropriate care when required (J. Jackson, 1973; H. Jackson, 1973). Various hypotheses about the low rates of nursing and old-age home utilization among nonwhites have been proposed that complement the discriminatory practices of some facilities; these include a concentration of nonwhite elderly in geographic areas that have low institutional rates in general—southern states, for example (Manard, Kart and van Gils, 1975)—and age distribution (nonwhites have lower life expectancies than whites in America), so that few really old nonwhites survive to be institutionalized (Manard, Kart and van Gils, 1975). Poverty, too, plays a role; despite the passage of Medicare and Medicaid, states with a high proportion of very poor aged tend to have low rates of nursing home use, reflecting the relative poverty of these states. The major growth in nursing homes has been of proprietary and profit-making facilities, and these are most likely to develop in relatively affluent areas where there is capital to invest. In areas in which such institutions are scarce preference is probably given to the relatively well-off old, whereas the poor, minority members, and other less socially valued people are screened out. Finally as discussed in Chapter 9, old minority women are likely to live with their children and grandchildren where they act as babysitters, housekeepers, and the like. When minority women become ill or frail, they have resources within their household upon which to rely for social support and physical care—until their situation becomes impossible.

For the white ethnic aged, the rationale for institutionalization is somewhat different. The foreign-born elderly differ from the foreign born in the general population; first, there are more of them proportionately. In 1970, for example, 15 percent of those 65 + were foreign born as compared to 5 percent of the general population. Elderly foreign-born are more likely to reside in the northeastern United States and to have come from eastern or southern Europe than their younger counterparts. Poverty, low socioeconomic status, and foreign birth compound the probability of their being institutionalized in a mental hospital (Markson, 1979).

Data for New York City (Markson, 1979) indicate that not only are the foreign-born old overrepresented in institutions (59 percent compared to 43 percent in the 65 + population) but those who receive institutional care are most likely to come from eastern and southern Europe, precisely the ethnic groups who have been most successful since their immigration. In 1972, the highest family incomes were found among those of Russian, Polish, and Italian extraction—$13,929, $12,182, and $11,646, respectively— in comparison to the median family income for all Americans regardless of origin of about $11,000 (Thurow, 1976). This may well illustrate the social costs of upward mobility. Although those ethnic old who are most likely to be institutionalized are people who have been sufficiently advantaged to survive to old age, they have nonetheless failed to move up in the class structure themselves. Their children, however, have fulfilled the American Dream.

The changing nature of the white ethnic family is also relevant. Although, as discussed in Chapter 9, the first generation of an ethnic family may be very tightly knit, the second generation has been expected to succeed both in the majority culture and to retain strong ties with their heritage. Choices must be made, upward mobility can often be won only at the price of rejection of parts of one's ethnic background. This rejection may include the extended family of first-generation ethnics. As one elderly Russian-born woman described her contacts with her family:

> My son, he comes up every Sunday. I bring him up in good shape. He's a businessman . . . He has two stores—dresses, coats—like the Macy's (large department store). His wife . . . she's good, like a diamond; a dress she brings me, a coat, everything. They have plenty, two good stores. I don't have nobody. He (my son) can do what he wants. I told him: "So, I have something wrong with me—Mamma (will) go die. Put me away in the hospital. Please, do me a favor; I can die; I got nobody." He's got plenty; the truth, he's got plenty. (Markson, 1979)

Summary. Comfort has proposed that "old people become crazy for three reasons: because they were crazy when young, because they have an illness, or because we drive them crazy" (1976, p. 4). To this list, must be added a fourth: minority group members are likely to be labeled as crazy as a way of getting cheap, long-term, and available care. The assumption behind this is that mental hospitalization is cheap whereas home help or nursing care is expensive—an erroneous assumption since the funds just come out of different pockets. But the elderly who are sent to a public mental hospital are usually poor, and in areas with large black or foreign-born populations, they are likely to be from an ethnic or racial minority. Native-born whites, on the other hand, are likely to be placed in a nursing home or old-age home.

SEX

At age 70, the average American woman can expect to live 13.6 more years, the man 10.5 years. Because of these sex differences in life expectancy, as women grow older they are likely to find themselves in the company of other women as age peers or alone. To be white, female, middle class—all factors enhancing life expectancy—living alone and having one or more physical disabilities increases the likelihood of entering a nursing home.

In 1973–74, there were 238 women to every 100 men in nursing homes. Women were overrepresented in these facilities in comparison to their numbers in the general population. Despite their greater preponderance, as Table 6–3 indicates, the reasons for which women are admitted to nursing homes do not differ appreciably from those for men. Table 6–3, which is based on nurses' judgments of reasons for admission, gives testimony that physical disability is the major reason for admission—at least as perceived by nurses; about 81 percent of the 318,100 men and 757,700 women in nursing homes fell into this category. Another 11.6 percent were apparently admitted because of behavioral problems; for both

Table 6–3. Primary Reason for Admission to Nursing Homes by Age and Sex, 1973–74 (in per cents)

	Male				Female			
	<65	65–74	75–84	85+	<65	65–74	75–84	85+
Primary Reason for Admission								
Physical	57.7	77.3	83.1	86.4	60.8	76.2	83.1	86.4
Social	5.7	5.7	6.1	7.7	5.4	5.3	6.4	7.1
Behavioral	35.3	15.8	8.5	5.3	32.7	17.6	9.6	5.6
Economic	—	—	—	—	—	—	0.9	0.9

Utilization of Nursing Homes: U.S. National Nursing Home Survey, August 1973– April 1974, Vital and Health Statistics Series 13, no. 28, Table 3.

sexes, this reason was more common among younger (less than 65 and 65–74) age groups.

Why, if there is little difference in reason for admission between men and women, are women overrepresented in these facilities? As we have seen in Chapter 4, women live longer than men, and the risk of institutionalization rises with age and associated infirmities. Thus, whereas women have fewer limitations of physical activity than their male counterparts, their longer survival increases the chance of institutional care. For example, cross-sectional 1970 census data shows that, whereas at any one time only about 5 percent of the old are in an institution, this rises sharply with age; at 85 +, 19 percent are residing in such a facility. Economic and social supports play a role as well. Elderly women are far more likely than old men to live alone; 36 percent of women 65 + and 41 percent of women 75 + lived alone in 1975 as compared to 14 percent of men 65 + and 18 percent 75+ in 1975. Aged women are also more likely to have incomes below the poverty level; in 1974, their median income was $2,400, which is almost less than half the median income of $4,500 for men 65 +. Men, who are generally somewhat older than their wives, also are likely to be taken care of at home until their impairments become so marked that their spouses cannot cope, or until their death. When women become impaired, they have few supports upon which to draw. They are likely to be widowed, and maintaining a household is already financially difficult because of their lower income. When incapacity strikes, Medicare is available to pay for their institutional care, but no comparable income maintenance programs are available to allow elderly women to remain at home with extensive support services. Paradoxically, the least advantaged group economically—black women living alone—are also the least likely to receive nursing home care, but are

Aging Bodies and Minds

probably the most likely to be placed in a state mental hospital when physical faculties and support networks falter.

Institutionalization and Deinstitutionalization

THE NURSING HOME INDUSTRY

Health services and specialties are expanding at a rapid rate in the United States, but nursing homes are the most rapidly expanding portion of the health system. Between 1963 and 1973–74, nursing homes increased by 131 percent, although since 1969, their growth has slowed down to an average of 9 percent per year. Despite this rapid increase, in 1973–74, 72 percent of the nursing homes had waiting lists with over 152,000 people on them. The actual number of people seeking admission to nursing homes is probably somewhat less, since some applicants were on more than one waiting list. On the other hand, many were not on the list who could benefit from skilled nursing care.

As indicated in Table 6-4, about 74 percent of nursing homes are proprietary, 20 percent are nonprofit, including those that are church related, and the remainder are owned by the federal, state, or local government. Table 6-4 includes both personal care homes, which are essentially residential facilities providing some personal care, and nursing homes in which one or more registered or licensed practical nurse is employed.

How good is the care provided in nursing homes and homes for the aged? The answer would seem to be that it varies according to the home.

Table 6–4. Type of Ownership of Nursing and Personal Care Homes by Number of Homes, Residents, and Staff: Resident Ratio, 1973

Type of Ownership	Number of Homes	Residents	Ratio of Full-Time Staff: Residents
Government	960	95,390	.67
Proprietary	10,987	692,222	.54
Nonprofit			
church	793	67,333	.53
Other	2,133	156,147	.57

Nursing Homes: A County and Metropolitan Area Date Book, 1973. U.S. Public Health Service, Health Research Administration, National Center for Health Statistics, Table 4.

One of the most outspoken critics of the nursing-home industry, Mendelson (1975), has criticized proprietary homes on the grounds that they are ridden with "high profits and patient abuse, with government as a silent accomplice" (p. 52). Concealed ownership, in which the operator of the nursing home is identified but the owner is not, has, she suggested, enabled kickbacks and income tax evasion. Other abuses include cutting the costs of patient care in order to make a profit, giving kickbacks to pharmacies; overdrugging of patients; "gang visits" by a physician who "dashes through the nursing home in a couple of hours, then bills Medicaid for sixty or seventy-five or ninety patient visits" (Mendelson, p. 187); performing unnecessary services, and overbilling by dentists, physicians, optometrists, pharmacists, and other providers of services to nursing home patients. Although the government is responsible for the inspection and certification of nursing homes for Medicare and Medicaid, "all of these procedures take time, and the process can be turned off at any of the stages" (Shulman and Galanter, p. 132). Inspection of nursing homes has been lax and ineffective in a system that is conducive to bribery at all levels.

Although a variety of studies have examined the relationship between ownership of the institution and level of care (Townsend, 1962; Holmberg and Anderson, 1968; Levey et al., 1973), no clear findings have emerged. Rather, the quality of the home is affected by the source of payment, structure of the home itself, and sociocultural patterns. To summarize: some proprietary homes are excellent, others are extremely poor. Similarly, some public, government-owned facilities are outstanding, others are not. Each type of facility has its peculiar problems of abuse and corruption— the proprietary home to maximize profits, the public facility from the inertia of bureaucracy and capriciousness of appropriations.

The extent to which nursing-home care is appropriate to all those who are currently receiving it is another topical issue, although most data on this issue are fragmentary or represent "guesstimates." Mendelson (1975) has presented data indicating that 297 out of 378 patients in Michigan nursing homes did not require skilled nursing care. In New York City, between 53 percent–61 percent of the Medicaid patients surveyed did not need to be in nursing homes (Mendelson, 1975). Testimony before the House Select Committee on Aging in 1977 indicated that an estimated 15 percent–20 percent of the individuals in nursing homes in Texas do not require such care (U.S. House of Representatives, Select Committee on Aging, Committee publication no. 95–98).

Overutilization by the elderly has been noted in mental hospitals as well. In New York City, over one third of the old people in two mental hospitals were judged to be able to return to the community if there were group homes, a day-care center, or some extended supervision in the home available. Interestingly, another third were judged suitable for nursing-home care because they had minimal psychiatric symptoms, but their physical condition required nursing care (Markson, Kwoh, Cumming, and Cumming 1971).

ENTERING AN INSTITUTION: THE TERRIBLE CHOICE

Whether or not an excellent institution is available and appropriate, entering such a facility is difficult both for the old person and her/his family. Institutionalization occurs most often because of a failure in coping mechanisms; either the old person's physical needs are so great or behavior is so disruptive that existing familial and social resources are taxed. If support networks are not established in the community, there is no recourse other than the nursing home or public institution.

Most old people hold negative views of institutionalization and would prefer to live at home with friends or relatives. For example, a 1962 national survey of noninstitutionalized old people found that only 3 percent of those 65 + would most like to live in a home for the aged; 61 percent liked this plan least of all (Shanas, 1962). There is no reason to believe that public acceptance of such facilities has increased markedly in the years since. "Almost all older people view the move to a home for the aged or to a nursing home with fear and hostility . . . All old people—without exception—believe that the move to an institution is a decisive change in living arrangements, the last change he will experience before he dies" (Shanas, 1962, p. 102). Institutionalization is perceived by the old person as a rejection by friends and family and as a place to die (Shanas, 1962; Tobin and Lieberman, 1976).

For members of the old person's family, too, the decision for a relative to enter a nursing home or other facility is not an easy one, and some experience feelings of grief that are even more traumatic than the actual death of the old person. Institutionalization, as discussed in Chapter 4, is a social death; the actual physical act of dying is thus anticipated and rehearsed.

More resistant to institutional living are old people with offspring or living with their children, and old people living with their spouses (Shanas, 1962). This is not surprising, for elderly with social supports will cling to them until this is no longer possible or feasible. Not only are old people who have viable social supports less willing to enter an institution but they are less likely to do so. Individuals with minor memory lapses or mild confusion may be absorbed within the family and protected. But when family protection is absent, they may be unable to care for themselves adequately without additional resources. Ability for self-care, it has been suggested, distinguishes the institutionalized old person from the noninstitutionalized one (Lowenthal and Berkman, 1967). The availability of adequate and appropriate home-care services and the ability to locate and pay for them can prevent institutionalization of many elderly. Once again, social status rather than physical/mental status differentiates who receives what kind of care.

RELOCATION

An old Russian proverb states: A boat trip on the Volga is soothing to the nerves. Although a change of locale may indeed have therapeutic results in some instances, this does not seem to be true for the institutionalized elderly. For example, mortality rates among those 65 + in nursing homes were slightly over five times the death rate for the U.S. population in that age group (Sutton, 1977). Why, since placement in a nursing home or other long-term care facility is assumed to be beneficial for the individual, should it so often be a prelude to death? Part of the explanation lies in the fact that such facilities are used for terminal patients; those who enter have already begun to die. Yet at least one investigator (Blenkner, 1967) has suggested that relocation itself may be sufficiently stressful to cause death among some old people, who, like captive wild animals cannot live in a different environment and flourish. Although the relocation of patients has been studied extensively, most studies have serious research design problems. Numbers tend to be small; little is told about how the study groups were selected, and there are few comparisons with the mortality of noninstitutionalized elderly who are similar on salient background or health characteristics. To design such research would not be that difficult; to implement it, however, would be both expensive and time-consuming.

The evidence suggests that mortality rates are excessively high among old people within the first year of institutionalization and that much of this occurs within the first one to three months following relocation. Yet relocation can be beneficial for some; Carp (1968) in a study of urban relocation found that a voluntary move to objectively better living conditions resulted in increased life satisfaction, morale, frequency of social contacts, and enjoyment. This finding has been observed in institutional settings as well; some old people entering or relocating from one facility to another experienced enhanced ego effects. Turner and associates (1967) and Novick (1967) reported that the postrelocation death rate among chronically disabled elderly residents was lower than the rate of the old hospital for the year preceding the move, presumably because their new environment was more attractive and convenient.

The *degree* of change seems also to be a significant factor in postrelocation mortality. Radical environmental change from one locus to another may produce higher mortality, greater pessimism, and a decline in ability to relate to other residents or to staff (Bourestom and Tars, 1974).

Physical condition, however, may be a better predictor of mortality than the extent of environmental change. In a study of 2,174 chronic mental patients, of whom almost one fourth (N = 494) were 65 years or over, Markson and Cumming were unable to find any linkage between moving and mortality among the relatively physically well elderly or among other age groups. Nor was any connection found between cause of death (e. g., possibly stress-induced heart attack) and time since relocation. Mortality of relocated elderly did not differ significantly from that of geriatric patients attending a day hospital or of patients in two state hospitals where no transfer or relocation had occurred. When relocated patients were compared to all geriatric state hospital admissions within the year in the state, significantly *more* of the admissions died; the same held true when relocated patients were compared to all chronic (that is, in hospital for two or more years). Change in setting made relatively little difference to these patients; transfer from an inactive hospital with little environmental stimulation to an active one had no impact on death rates. It should be kept in mind, however, that all the patients relocated had been selected for transfer because they were physically healthy; those with known risk factors were screened out (Markson and Cumming, 1976).

The very ill, the frail, and those with brain impairment or dysfunction are likely to be affected adversely by relocation. Blenkner stated:

> When there is evidence that the older person's intellective capacity, his memory and his orientation to time, place and person are seriously impaired, his chances of survival following relocation are considerably lower than that of a person who shows no or only minimal signs of such impairment regardless of how emotionally or socially disturbed or maladjusted such a person may be. (1967, p. 103)

Furthermore, she suggests, casework and transitional services do not reduce mortality. To the contrary, intensive casework is associated with placement in an institution and with a higher death rate. Killing with kindness is the implication.

Yet the very helpless, those with chronic brain disease, and the apathetic are precisely the people who are most likely to be admitted to a nursing home or other long-term care facility in old age. To old people in these categories, perhaps a blanket warning should be issued: social research has determined that institutionalization is dangerous to your health.

DEINSTITUTIONALIZATION

Keeping old people out of nursing homes or mental hospitals has been the goal of many concerned with the welfare of old people. Examination of contemporary literature is replete with horror stories about the conditions within nursing homes (see, for example, Mendelson, 1975; Curtin, 1976) and mental hospitals (Allen, 1974; Reich and Siegal, 1973). The physical conditions and quality of food in nursing homes have been attacked as have the depersonalization and dehumanization of patients once they are placed in the institution. Feelings of powerlessness, deprivation of credibility, restrictions on freedom of movement, lack of personal privacy, and a feeling of invisibility or being unworthy of account as a person seem endemic (Rosenhan, 1973, Curtin, 1976; Gubrium, 1975) as well as actual physical abuse (Stanford, 1973). To avoid continued dehumanization, many experts now advocate deinstitutionalization for the mentally ill, the juvenile offender, the mentally retarded, and other traditionally institutionalized populations who could be cared for in the community if supportive services were established. Deinstitutionalization in the human services field has become a buzz word, usually used to refer to a "process involving two elements: (1) the eschewal of traditional institutional settings . . . and (2) the concurrent expansion of community-based services for the treatment of these individuals" (Bachrach, 1976).

As discussed earlier, many old people who at one time would have been placed in a mental hospital have been rechanneled into nursing homes and other congregate care facilities. At the same time, many old long-term mental patients have been released to group homes, single-room occupancy settings such as welfare hotels, and domiciliary care facilities. Some mental patients have been transferred merely from one mental hospital to another as a facility, no longer needed for younger, acute patients, was declared "redundant" and closed down (Marlowe, 1976; Markson and Cumming, 1976; Markson, 1976). Financial exploitation of ex-patients by community caretakers and inappropriate placement and conditions of abject deprivation resulting in death have also been reported (U.S. House of Representatives, 1977). Deinstitutionalization, never an issue about which people were neutral, has polarized public opinion: there are those who support it strongly because of the adverse affects of institutionalization, and those who argue against it as untimely, dysfunctional, and creating more social problems and individual misery than it solves. Nor is community-based care necessarily a less expensive alternative than institutionalization (Tobin, 1978).

Moving the elderly mental patient out of institutions has had mixed results. As one would expect, *any* relocation is traumatic and potentially life endangering to a few people (see preceding discussion). In many instances, adequate screening criteria to reduce relocation risk prior to moving were neither used nor contemplated (see, for example, Marlowe, 1976, for an account of the experience in a California hospital dealing predominantly with geriatric mental patients who ranged from being normal to extremely confused). As Bachrach has observed:

The deinstitutionalization movement can best fulfill its promise if certain conditions are met . . . (1) there is a thorough understanding of the functions which they (institutions) serve in American life; (2) consensus is reached as to which of these functions should be continued or discontinued, or which new functions should be added; (3) effective alternatives are established in community settings for the accepted functions; and (4) sufficient time is allowed for the systematic and orderly implementation of new programs and transfer of functions. (p. 64)

Although this extract was written specifically about mental hospitals, the points made are relevant to institutional care for any age cohort with a variety of problems requiring care. Much of the controversy surrounding deinstitutionalization of the elderly mentally ill patient has, for example, resulted from a lack of planning, short time frames, patchy supervision of programs, and inadequate mechanisms for funding alternative care. Nor have state and local governing bodies devised safeguards to prevent some of the problems that are currently found in nursing homes, such as inadequate supervision, inability to control profit making, and neglect of patients. As the network of service delivery agencies, whose establishment is provided for under Title III of the Older American's Act (see Chapter 8), emerges and receives sufficient funding, the distinction between institutionalization and deinstitutionalization may be blurred and a continuum of services will be provided.

The Institution and Its Alternatives

ARE INSTITUTIONS BAD BY DEFINITION?

Congregate care facilities for the elderly are total institutions (Goffman, 1961) in which diverse human needs are handled by a bureaucratic organization that promotes group living rather than individuation. As Goffman describes the total institution:

A basic social arrangement in modern society is that the individual tends to sleep, play and work in different places, with different co-participants, under different authorities, and without an over-all rational plan. The central feature of total institutions can be described as a breakdown of the barriers ordinarily separating these three spheres of life. First, all aspects of life are conducted in the same place and under the same single authority. Second, each phase of the member's daily activity is carried on in the immediate company of a large batch of others, all of whom are treated alike and required to do the same thing together. Third, all phases of the day's activities are tightly scheduled, with one activity leading at a prearranged time into the next, the whole sequence of activities being imposed from above. . . . Finally the various enforced activities are brought together into a single rational plan proportedly designed to fulfill the official aims of the institution. (p. 6)

Total institutions may be categorized into several groups according to their purpose. Nursing homes and homes for the elderly, poor, or infirm are designed to care for those who are perceived to be both incompetent and harmless; mental hospitals manage people who are incompetent but may be harmful to themselves or others. Jails, boarding schools, colleges, camps, armies, and monasteries also are total institutions. What is common to them is that they are essentially resocializing institutions, designed to change people and their sense of selfhood. The designation of total institution is not, as Goffman pointed out, a value judgment but a way of noting the underlying structural design that is common to all (Goffman, p. 124). Total institutions, in other words, need not have negative effects. Most of the evidence about congregate care for the elderly, however, indicates that this is less than an ideal solution for them; change is often negative rather than positive.

Over twenty years ago, Scott noted some striking differences, aside from mental impairment, between institutionalized and noninstitutionalized elderly. Observing that the elderly in nursing homes have been described as functioning at a lower level of adjustment, and having more physical health problems and difficulties, more neuroses, more contracted life spaces (including less social contact with family or friends), and fewer leisure activities, as well as being more likely to feel useless, Scott concluded that a low level of adjustment was not related to nursing home life per se but rather reflected a constellation of factors, including poor adjustment prior to admission (Scott, 1955). Tobin and Lieberman (1976) have elaborated upon this point, suggesting that much of the negative portrait of the elderly institutionalized person may be the result of relocation, preadmission affects, and the process of selection as well as the totality of the institution. The impact of some of these variables has already been discussed; certainly it seems clear that successful aging is more likely to occur when there is relatively little discontinuity of life patterns between late maturity and old age. Some of the negative effects of institutional care reported among the elderly occur because ties with the familiar world and existing role relationships are ruptured. A new kind of institutionally appropriated behavior must be learned.

With the forced relinquishment of old roles imposed by institutional placement, what does the institution offer the patient? With notable exceptions, the answer would seem to be, very little. The basic requirements for adult socialization—that new values and behaviors be inculcated—are generally not met. Residents are required only to accept the requisite medical and nursing care passively. No behavioral expectations, other than for increasing mental and physical dysfunction, are held

(Bennett and Nahemow, 1965). According to a study of forty nursing homes in the Detroit area in which residents were observed during twenty-four one-hour segments, more than half of the residents' time was spent doing nothing. Contacts with staff were relatively sparse; fewer than one in four residents received *any* nursing staff contacts at all (Gottesman and Bourestom, 1974). Time is passed rather than put toward some well-delineated goal as in an active resocializing institution. There seems to be no particular aim. Like the legendary French Foreign Legion, relatively few get out of nursing homes except by death. Unlike the Legion, there are no tasks to perform in nursing homes that are essential to the maintenance of the social cohesion or purpose of the group.

DIFFERENCES IN OUTCOME BY LEVEL OF TOTALITY OF CARE: A CASE STUDY[1]

The following case study is a report of attempts to assess and compare changes in mental and physical status of 255 elderly patients who had been admitted to five different programs for the mentally impaired. All elderly were capable of self-care and comprised two major subgroups as follows.

1. This subgroup includes forty-four elderly patients transferred from Gotham State Mental Hospital to sheltered living arrangements. They were matched as nearly as possible on selected variables with two groups of patients who remained at Gotham State and Earls Court State Hospitals and were not transferred. All three facilities served the New York City metropolitan area. The Gotham group had thirty-six patients; the Earls Court had ninety-one.

2. This subgroup includes thirty-five outpatients at Spartacus day care center and another forty-nine inpatients in Illium Mental Hospital. Both facilities served a medium-sized city in upstate New York and its environs.

The hospital ward structure and treatment programs within each subgroup also varied with respect to content and degree of activity, ranging from sex-integrated sheltered living in the community to treatment on sex-segregated, locked geriatric wards. Differences in the facilities studied are summarized according to an index of institutional totality. An average (mean) score of 3.0 on this index represents maximum totality, and a mean score of 1.0 denotes minimum totality. Ratings of each facility were based on observations by the field staff and on interviews with staff members about the types of program and patient behavior expected. Each of the major subgroups of the study population of 255 included patients

[1] This section is based on research undertaken by Elizabeth Markson, Isabel McCaffrey, and Elaine Cumming (NIMH Grant no. 16498). Names of the facilities are pseudonyms.

in one facility with a low average score and another with a high average score:

Treatment Facility	Mean Totality Score
New York City	
Sheltered living	1.7
Gotham State	2.3
Earls Court State	2.9
Upstate New York	
Spartacus Day Hospital	1.8
Illium State	2.9

The researchers were interested in finding out whether or not outcomes for elderly patients differed with respect to the level of the totality of the facility. At the outset, each of the 255 patients was interviewed, and data was gathered about the patients' physical and psychological state, including evaluations of their mental status, ability to perform activities of daily living, self-assessment of health, and contentment. Hospital case records also were abstracted to obtain supplemental information about mental condition, physical illnesses, length of institutional stay, and other background details.

A second wave of interviewing was conducted after a lapse of approximately 14.5 months. By that time, however, thirty-four patients had died and another forty-five had left their original study groups and moved back to their own homes or other community facilities. The remaining 175 patients who were still under treatment, were then reinterviewed.

Despite the variation in degree of totality of the settings, therapeutic programs, and geographic locations, analysis of data indicated no clearcut superiority of one program or setting over another. Rather, some facilities favored one kind of gain for the elderly, others another; none was a panacea, and each had certain drawbacks for some patients. Neither the "deinstitutionalized" group in sheltered living nor the never-institutionalized in the day hospital program fared much better than their counterparts in predominantly locked geriatric wards of three state hospitals. Ability for self-care and contentment, two indicators of functioning and well-being, are discussed in detail in the following paragraphs to highlight some of the problems that are currently being faced in the delivery of care to the old who need it.

Precisely because the elderly are prone to physical disorders associated with the aging process, physical health and ability to function are crucial for this age group. Indeed, for old people, taking care of one's self may be, as Simon, Lowenthal, and Epstein (1970) have suggested, the functional equivalent of work performance (a commonly used criterion of successful therapeutic outcome) among younger people. One measure of outcome used in the study was increment or maintenance of ability to take care of one's daily needs. There were no significant *group* differences in either initial or follow-up scores according to the level of totality of the setting. However, when each person served as her/his own control, and initial and follow-up ratings were compared, old people in the two more total settings, Earls Court and Illium, demonstrated a significant decrement ($p = <.05$) in their ability for self-care.

One means by which the impact of a treatment program upon the old may be usefully viewed is the degree to which their views of their own capacities agrees with that held by those who are most intimately charged with their care. Adjustment is thus a two-way process in which one may be considered adjusted to a situation if expectations for oneself are congruent with those held by those around one. Put another way, if an old person considers herself/himself unable to perform certain activities, she/he is adjusted if she/he convinces those around that her/his view of herself/himself is correct—whether or not she/he meets objective criteria of disability. A comparison of staff ratings and self-ratings on ability to perform activities of daily living among the elderly in the five settings suggests that, if congruency is a measure of adjustment, very few old people were adjusted to the settings in which they were initially interviewed. Upon follow-up, patients' self-assessments and those by staff were closer (patients saw themselves as less competent), but they were still far from perfect. Neither the more open, alternative settings of sheltered living or day care, nor the relatively total locus of inpatient care promoted agreement between patient and staff views of the same person. Clearly, if scores on ability to care for one's self may be regarded as rudimentary representations of self-image (or image of the other), there was a lack of consensus between old people and their caretakers in each of the institutions regardless of the level of totality.

Contentment at its grossest level is a measure of psychological well-being. Self-reports of contentment have been used by many investigators and have a face validity. In this study, self-reports of contentment were used as pragmatic indicators of how old people assessed their global experience in the different facilities. It seemed likely that people in the less total environments would report more contentment; the freedom of the environment allows for greater role satisfaction and for more roles to be played. However, there was little relationship between the level of totality of setting and the level of happiness reported by respondents. Forty-four per cent of those in sheltered living (the least total environment) as compared to 65 per cent of those at Earls Court (one of the two most total institutions) reported that they were content during a follow-up interview; in no case were there statistically significant differences among the sites. Nor was change in level of self-avowed contentment related to the type of setting in which these old people lived; in fact, very similar proportions—ranging between 43 per cent and 53 percent— indicated no change in contentment between initial interview and follow-up. It seems clear that contentment was not related to the totality of environment.

There is a suggestion that old people in many of the four settings studied are less happy than older people in the general noninstitutionalized United States population. Information from a national survey (Gurin et al., 1960) of the population 55 years of age or over indicates that 82 per cent say they are content; only 46 per cent of the old people in the five institutions surveyed were content. If, as Gurin et al. have suggested, contentment is a reflection of the gratification derived from an individual's central relationships, it is not surprising that old people in the settings studied were less happy. In each setting, the social support provided by a true significant other was not present, nor, given the nature of the settings, could it be. As in the lifeboat of a large ocean liner, people had come together for a common purpose, but without any previous ties to others "in the same boat."

A second reason for lower rates of contentment found among these institutionalized elderly seems to be their mental status. Specifically, those old people who experienced no decrement in memory between initial and follow-up interviews were also more likely to report that they were content than those whose memory declined, and this finding was statistically significant ($p = <.001$). So much for the "happy senile"; the results indicate that discontent is associated with *greater* memory loss.

What do the results from this study tell us that is relevant to total institutions and level of totality as they affect the old? First, it is clear that those in the more open programs were no worse off than their counterparts in the closed environments; moreover, they enjoyed greater freedom of movement and environmental stimulation. An allied point is that a less total, less costly, and more community-based situation could care for most old people as effectively as an inpatient mental hospital or nursing home. That there is no strikingly clear-cut superiority of one type of facility over another with respect to the dimensions of outcome reviewed previously raises some question about the general nature of programs for elderly patients.

Prospects: Unresolved Issues in Institutional Care

Although a variety of rehabilitative and treatment modalities, including therapeutic milieux (Donahue et al., 1960, Gottesman and Schneider, 1963), group occupational and social techniques (Cosin, 1958), enrichment of social environment (Mishara, 1971), and individualized treatment of excess disabilities (Brody et al., 1974) have been used with the institutionalized elderly, the evidence hints that the positive impact of even very carefully designed programs has been of limited duration. That "the best is none too good" poses an awkward but important question, felt keenly by gerontologists and those involved in the treatment of any disabled group of people: "What is a successful program?"

Certainly humanitarian values mandate that attempts to upgrade living conditions and to provide effective therapy are preferred to a futilitarian approach. Since 1965, legislation such as Medicare, Medicaid, and the Older American's Act has underscored this concern, and gaps in the new service structure as well as older ones have been the subject of congressional and individual inquiry. Yet the basic reality is that most programs are inappropriately geared to anything other than meeting basic needs for food, shelter, custody, and short (sometimes serendipitous) alleviation of the varieties of disability associated with being old. Perhaps, if we can do no better, this is enough. But a lingering sense of discontent remains.

Why, for example, has so little been done to enable the elderly to remain at home? One reason that the required coordinated community services have been slow to develop may be that too large a social emphasis has been placed on institutions as solutions to the problems of deviants, including the mentally and physically disabled of all ages. There is no reason to think that old people who need help in self-care differ from other old people about their feelings toward institutionalization. For example, a study of protective care projects indicated that the most frequent services requested by the elderly needing help in self-care was for a homemaker (Gold, 1972). The United States has lagged behind many other nations in developing home help services for the aged; when countries are ranked according to the number of home help per 100,000, the United States falls in group C (2 to 18 per 100,000), along with France, Israel, Japan, and Austria, although our demographic profile is closer to countries in Group A—Sweden, Norway, the Netherlands, and Great Britain—where there are 100 or more homemakers available per 100,000 (Beattie, 1977).

Summary. Although public intervention on behalf of the aged is considered more legitimate than for other age groups or categories of needy people (MacDonald and Martin, 1972), the elderly who require care are still treated as "worthy poor" whose needs are not quite respectable. Many real services required by old people do not come to the surface unless the family is ill-equipped financially to provide care or when there is no family at all. Social responsibility is only tangentially extended to provide good care for all old people, and it has been easy to avoid the issue of unified and comprehensive community health services. Many people are in institutions because it is profitable for them to be there, and because more appropriate facilities do not exist in the community.

Allied to the lack of appropriate community facilities for many elderly is the structure of financing of care. There is some suggestion that the present system of private ownership of care-giving facilities impedes the provision of high-quality care, although the record of public institutions has been far from perfect. Nor have old people and their relatives been potent lobbyists for change; as poor, needy, infirm, or confused consumers, they have been disadvantaged in demanding service geared to maintaining themselves in the community as long as possible. Federal and state funding has tended to be earmarked for partial or total institutional care or for program planning; limited funds have been appropriated for home help, home nursing, or hot meals.

Furthermore, the patchwork design and financing of existing services makes it difficult to deliver comprehensive care that would enable the impaired elderly to remain at home. But there is a need for institutional care; even with an abundance of community-based services, a small proportion of the old will require this type of care at one time or another in their lives. The legacy of Title III may be to enable appropriate, coordinated, and integrated services to be delivered to the old at home or in an inpatient facility. Rational funding and curbs on overspending and cost increases are crucial.

GLOSSARY OF TYPES OF INSTITUTIONS

Adult Home: provides personal supervision (to varying degrees), room, and meals, but does not employ one or more nurses on its staff nor provide nursing care. Generally, residents are required to be continent, capable of basic self-care, and to be able to walk or use a wheelchair or walker without help.

Facility: used to denote a variety of institutions that provide long-term care, including nursing homes, homes for the aged, mental hospitals, and adult homes.

Mental Hospital: a facility to which people of all ages are admitted because of alleged mental disorder. The majority of old people in mental hospitals are there because they either grew old in the hospital, having been admitted when they were much younger, or because they became depressed or confused, or developed other personal, health, or social problems in old age. About 30 per cent of the inpatients in mental hospitals are 65 +.

Nonprofit Homes: a facility that employs one or more nurses on its staff and is operated on a nonprofit-making basis, either by a church, fraternal order, government, or other organization.

Nursing Homes: a nursing home provides nursing service, the extent of which varies according to facility, but one or more nurses is employed on the staff.

Old-Age Home: usually denotes a dormitory-like facility where old people live in one location and receive meals there. In the majority of old-age homes, nursing care is not provided, although some have an infirmary to which the bedridden or very confused may move.

Old-Age Institution: a generic term used to encompass nursing homes, adult or personal care homes, and old-age homes. In short, a facility established specifically for the elderly.

Personal Care Home: Synonym for adult home.

Proprietary Home: a facility that is operated on a profit-making basis, it may be owned by private individuals, corporations, businesses, physicians, or other individuals or groups. It is a business venture.

State Mental Hospital: Owned and operated by the state in which it is located, the state hospital usually contains both geriatric wards and a medical-surgical ward.

Research Exercises

1. Part-time employment in a nursing home provides the opportunity for *participant observation* of the social system of the home and the interaction between patients and caretakers. What role do the relatives of the patients play? Interviews with students who have worked in nursing homes may be more feasible.

2. Interviews with the staff and volunteer "friendly visitors" at state institutions can often be arranged, although questions of confidentiality and professional ethics may be involved. However, much information is a matter of public record; getting access to the information will be the challenge.

3. In the mid-1970s a number of federal, state, and local investigations into nursing home operations were conducted. Many documents can be bought from the U. S. Government Printing Office and others are available from state legislative and investigative bodies. Newspaper accounts are also plentiful. Report on the data uncovered, and the outcomes of the investigations.

4. Inventory the long-term care facilities in your community. Give the number of these facilities and the type of services rendered, costs, patient characteristics, auspices, and so on.

Discussion Questions

Should private enterprise be involved in the delivery of nursing care to the elderly?

Many, if not most, Americans believe that nursing homes would be unnecessary if families were willing to care for their aged relatives. Is this a valid argument?

Can total institutions rehabilitate?

Why are there so few halfway houses for released patients in the community?

Is home care less expensive than residential care?

PART THREE

———◆◆———

Aging in Social Systems

7

The Economics of
Aging

In Perspective

In our historical model, with its emphasis on the economic substrate of social life, the transition from agricultural to industrial economic systems is critical to the status of the elderly. In preindustrial societies, many old people could retain control over the means of production or access to economic positions through the ownership of land, through their skills, and through trade. In their roles as heads of families, the elderly were responsible for the social placement of offspring.

The factory system entails a radical change in economic roles and their consequences for family relationships and household structure. The division between home and work was a novel element in the lives of workers, although for some time family units were employed together in the factory. The separation of a work place from a home place, both physically and psychologically, is the hallmark of the modern economy. This means that a family typically no longer "owns" its means of production, but instead one or more adult members of the family become employees. The number of dependents who can be supported by wage labor is usually restricted to spouse and children, and this unit must be responsive to the vagaries of the labor market. The family must be able to move to where the jobs are and to be free to experience social mobility without obligations to support other kinfolk.

As employees, industrial workers and managers cannot transfer their job directly to an offspring, although they can attempt to prepare their children for certain posts. And as "hired hands" the employees are subject to unemployment and discharge by employers, procedures that the unionization movement sought to make less arbitrary.

Modern industrial economies are also characterized by extreme specialization and technological complexity. Over time, the demand for unskilled labor is replaced by that for trained personnel. Education and vocational preparation become the entry level requirements (whether or not they are actually necessary for performance). In these respects, the most recently trained may have higher labor market value than older workers whose skills have become obsolete. In any event, the ability of younger persons to find their own path through the educational system and into the labor force makes them that much freer of parental or kin-based ascriptive placement in the economic system.

One last secular economic trend deserves consideration. In advanced industrial societies, both capitalist and socialist, small business tends to be replaced by larger firms, leaseholds and family farms by agribusiness and mechanization (which is more efficient for larger areas), corner stores tend to be replaced by chains, and so on. Self-employment of the kind that allows one to work for as long as one desires, and which can be passed intact to heirs, is increasingly rare. Young and old alike sell their services in an impersonal market that undergoes rapid change in the type and distribution of required skills.

In essence, the economic bases of social stratification that were so favorable to old people in preindustrial societies are almost completely reversed in the modern industrial order. This, in juxtaposition to the dominant value of independent achievement, creates problems of self-esteem, as well as of power, for contemporary old people. And the fact that so many old people are outliving their productive roles has made their status a social issue.

Current Scene

The economics of aging can be reduced to the consideration of work, retirement, and income, about which there is a wealth of empirical data. What the tables do not tell us are the subjective dimensions of all three of these economic factors. We depend on smaller studies for an understanding of such variables as the importance of friends at the work place, whether or not retirement was desired, adequacy of income, and so forth. We attempt to weave together both the qualitative and quantitative information on the economic status of old people.

LABOR FORCE PARTICIPATION

Work. It is often said of America that the Puritan work ethic is the corner-stone of our value system, that work as a "calling" (a sacred task) has made productiveness an essential component of self-esteem, especially for men, and that success at one's calling is the measure of personal virtue ("worth" in both senses of the word). When asked what produces a healthy psyche, Freud replied, "lieben und arbeiten"—love and work—but the Puritans who founded our society feared that earthly love would detract from both work in this world and the love of the Lord. Only recently has the "love" aspect of life achieved legitimacy as a goal comparable to that of work. The current cohorts of old people were primarily socialized into a more traditional view of work, and hard work at that. One's job and competency in the task were, and are, sources of personal gratification (intrinsic satisfaction) for a large number of those now-old.

This identity-conferring aspect of employment has typically been applied to men, but there is increasing evidence that many women are as attached to their work roles as are men. We forget, also, in glorifying the mythical past, that immigrant and poor women worked long hours in mills and factories, in mom-and-pop stores, and in domestic service. Many women were the major economic support of their families during the Depression. As Tables 7–1a and 7–1b indicate, many remain in the labor force through late adulthood and early old age.

Table 7–1a. Labor Force Participation Rates (Per Cent) by Age and Sex: 1960–1975, and Projections to 1990

Male	1960	1965	1970	1975	1980	1990
16–19	58.6	55.7	57.5	60.2	62.0	62.6
20–24	88.9	86.2	85.1	84.5	84.5	82.7
25–34	96.4	96.0	95.0	94.1	94.3	93.7
35–44	96.4	96.2	95.7	94.9	94.7	94.0
45–54	94.3	94.3	92.9	91.9	90.5	89.3
55–64	85.2	83.2	81.5	74.7	73.8	69.2
65+	32.2	26.9	25.8	20.8	19.4	16.2
Female						
16–19	39.1	37.7	43.7	49.0	51.3	54.9
20–24	46.1	49.7	57.5	64.0	67.5	74.7
25–34	35.8	38.5	44.8	54.4	58.4	66.0
35–44	43.1	45.9	50.9	55.7	58.1	63.4
45–54	49.3	50.5	54.0	54.3	56.3	59.9
55–64	36.7	40.6	42.5	40.7	41.6	42.2
65+	10.5	9.5	9.5	7.8	7.7	7.2

Statistical Abstract of the United States, 1976, p. 355.

Table 7–1b. Worker Proportions for the Population 65 Years Old and Over, by Age, Race, and Sex: 1950 to 1990

(Figures are monthly averages. Total noninstitutional population)

Age, Race, and Sex	1950	1955	1960	1965	1970	1975	1980	1990
All Classes								
Male								
65 years and over	45.8	39.6	33.1	27.9	26.8	21.7	20.1	16.8
65 to 69 years	(NA)	57.0	46.8	43.0	41.6	31.7	29.9	26.1
70 years and over	(NA)	28.1	24.4	19.1	17.7	15.1	12.9	10.3
Female								
65 years and over	9.7	10.6	10.8	10.0	9.7	8.3	8.0	7.5
65 to 69 years	(NA)	17.8	17.6	17.4	17.3	14.5	14.4	13.9
70 years and over	(NA)	6.4	6.8	6.1	5.7	4.9	4.4	4.1
Blacks and Other Races								
Male								
65 years and over	45.4	40.0	31.2	27.9	27.4	20.9	(NA)	(NA)
65 to 69 years	(NA)	(NA)	(NA)	(NA)	(NA)	(NA)	(NA)	(NA)
70 years and over	(NA)	(NA)	(NA)	(NA)	(NA)	(NA)	(NA)	(NA)
Female								
65 years and over	16.5	12.1	12.8	12.9	12.2	10.5	(NA)	(NA)
65 to 69 years	(NA)	(NA)	(NA)	(NA)	(NA)	(NA)	(NA)	(NA)
70 years and over	(NA)	(NA)	(NA)	(NA)	(NA)	(NA)	(NA)	(NA)

Siegel, Jacob S., "Demographic Aspects of Aging and the Older Population in the United States," Current Population Reports, Special Studies, Series P–23, no. 59, May, 1976. United States Department of Commerce, Bureau of the Census, United States Printing Office, Washington, D.C., p. 51.

Examining the percentages of males in the labor force between 1960–75 in Table 7–1a, we find a consistent decline that is most marked in the two older age categories. The slight increase in participation rates for the very youngest group of workers (those under 19) in 1975 probably reflects declining college enrollment with the end of the military draft, as well as increased college costs. Projected figures for 1980 and 1990, based on a continuation of these trends, indicate that the labor force at the turn of the next century will contain only half the proportion of older workers as in 1960. The most precipitous decline in the proportion of older men workers has occurred since 1970 for men 55–64, fewer than three fourths of whom are expected to be in the labor force in the future. Many of these men will have left employment for reasons of health or because they have become eligible for retirement benefits, but others have chosen to retire with only partial benefits (see the next section). Some of the decline in labor force participation for this age group is attributable to unemployability. It is very difficult for men over the age of 45 to find new employment. They expect higher salaries, are perceived as less trainable, and will have fewer years to contribute to the cost of their pensions than is the case for younger employees.

The patterns for women, in contrast, are very different from those of the men, increasing steadily at all ages under 65. Contrary to popular assumptions, this trend has not been sudden—in 1940, 27 per cent of adult females were in the labor force; this rose to 35 per cent during World War II, dropped to 30 per cent in 1947–48, and then began a small steady climb for each subsequent year. What is remarkable is that the increases are almost entirely made up of married women, even those in the age range 20–34 when many women are also occupied with child rearing. Between two thirds and three quarters of the women in this age group will be employed in 1990. Once in the labor force, it seems that women are as disinclined to leave as are men. This is especially so at the age level 55–64, where male rates continue to drop, while those of women remain fairly stable, in spite of the fact that women are eligible for full retirement benefits under Social Security at age 62. Women at these ages are more employable than males because their jobs usually require less skill and more experience, because they are thought to be more dependable than young women, and, in any event, they do not cost as much in potential retirement benefits as do men.

An additional difference between male and female employment patterns is shown in Table 7–2, regarding the effect of marital status. Married men have higher participation rates than single and "other" men at all ages, whereas for women it is the married who are least likely to be employed at any age. The reduction in women's labor force participation at age 65 + is largely accounted for by the retirement of single females, presumably because they have had a full work life and are better protected by pensions than in the past.

As for the distribution of full- and part-time workers among those 65 + who are still in the labor force, more than half the men but only one third of the women are in full-time jobs. Many of these elderly job holders are self-employed. Professionals, such as attorneys and physicians, and persons owning their own businesses, can practice as long as clients and patients and customers desire their services. Other older persons may be able to practice on a free-lance basis those skills that are still in demand.

Since continued employment is associated with being married, high education, self-employment, and good health, it should not surprise us that minority males are less likely than white men to be employed in late adulthood and early old age. If it is difficult for a middle-aged white male to find reemployment, the problem is doubly severe for the minority job-seeker.

Black women, compared with white women, however, are *more* likely to be employed at all age levels. Among the many reasons for this are

Table 7-2. Labor Force Participation Rates, by Marital Status, Age, and Sex: 1960 to 1976

(Percent civilian labor force of noninstitutional population)

Year and Marital Status	Per Cent Male					Per Cent Female				
	16–19 years	20–24 years	25–44 years	45–64 years	65 and over	16–19 years	20–24 years	25–44 years	45–64 years	65 and over
1960: Married, spouse present	91.5[1]	97.1	98.7	93.7	36.6	27.2[1]	31.7	33.1	36.0	6.7
Single	42.6[1]	80.3	90.5	80.1	31.2	30.2[1]	77.2	83.2	79.8	24.3
Other[2]	68.8[1]	96.9	94.7	83.2	22.7	43.8[1]	58.0	67.2	60.0	11.4
1965: Married, spouse present	88.0[1]	96.4	98.5	92.6	31.0	30.6[1]	37.1	36.2	39.5	6.7
Single	40.9[1]	75.7	89.0	78.1	23.2	28.8[1]	72.9	82.4	76.1	22.4
Other[2]	77.8[1]	96.6	93.8	80.8	18.7	42.1[1]	59.2	67.2	61.6	10.5
1970: Married, spouse present	92.3	94.7	98.0	91.2	29.9	37.8	47.9	42.7	44.0	7.3
Single	54.6	73.8	87.4	75.7	25.2	44.7	73.0	80.5	73.0	19.7
Other[2]	68.8	90.4	92.3	78.5	18.3	48.5	60.3	67.2	61.9	10.0
1973: Married, spouse present	93.4	95.4	97.6	88.6	24.8	43.5	52.7	46.4	42.9	7.2
Single	58.4	77.6	85.9	70.9	20.8	48.6	72.9	79.6	69.1	16.5
Other[2]	77.8	89.9	92.0	74.4	15.8	44.4	63.0	67.7	60.3	9.0
1974: Married, spouse present	94.4	96.2	97.6	87.7	24.2	44.9	55.3	48.1	43.3	6.8
Single	59.4	78.7	86.0	70.8	20.2	49.9	73.1	80.2	69.2	13.3
Other[2]	72.0	93.6	92.7	74.4	16.1	46.2	65.6	69.0	59.9	8.5
1975: Married, spouse present	92.9	95.3	97.3	86.8	23.3	46.2	57.0	50.0	43.8	7.0
Single	57.9	77.9	86.0	69.9	21.0	49.6	72.5	80.3	68.3	15.8
Other[2]	70.6	88.8	91.1	73.4	15.4	47.6	65.3	68.9	59.0	8.3
1976: Married, spouse present	93.5	95.6	97.2	86.1	21.9	46.9	57.3	52.0	44.3	7.0
Single	58.2	79.1	86.5	68.8	20.7	50.3	73.8	81.4	69.6	15.6
Other[2]	79.2	92.3	91.2	71.5	13.6	49.6	64.4	71.2	58.2	8.3

[1] 14 to 19 years old.

[2] Includes widowed, divorced, and married (spouse absent).

Statistical Abstract of the United States, 1978, p. 391.

the greater proportion of nonmarried minority women, their availability for low-wage employment (often without Social Security coverage), and the lesser threat that Black women compared to minority males appear to present to white employers.

In the Harris (1975) Survey,[1] among persons 65 +, the sex and race distribution of employment status, was as follows:

Table 7–3a. Current Employment Status

	Public 65 and Over				
	Total Per Cent	Men Per Cent	Women Per Cent	White Per Cent	Black Per Cent
Employed full-time	3	5	2	3	2
Employed part-time	9	12	7	9	10
Unemployed	6	1	8	5	7
Housewife	17	—	30	18	10
Retired	63	82	50	63	71
Other	2	—	3	2	2

Louis Harris and Associates, *The Myth and Reality of Aging in America*, Washington, D.C.: National Council on the Aging, 1975, p. 83.

Data from the U.S. Department of Labor for the same year permit us to specify employment status by age group of older persons. See Table 7–3b, p. 188.

Job Performance. Older workers are frequently thought to be less productive than younger ones, but this is one of the most difficult areas of research to evaluate because of the confusion between "real" aging effects and cohort differences in skills, training, and education. Much depends on what job tasks are being measured: those requiring experience actually favor older workers, whereas those depending on endurance and strength or speed will often place the older person at a disadvantage. Furthermore, not all abilities decline in the same way or at the same rate, and no two individuals will be affected similarly.

Under these circumstances, it is much easier to set an arbitrary age for

[1] This was a national probability sample of persons 18–64 and 65+ conducted by Louis Harris and Associates in 1974 for the National Council on the Aging which published the findings in a volume *The Myth and Reality of Aging in America* (1975). The data provide one of the few systematic attempts to explore attitudes on aging of younger respondents, as well as from the aged themselves. Organizations such as Louis Harris and Associates are able to provide scientifically sound estimates of the population in general from carefully selected samples of a few thousand respondents.

Table 7–3b. Employment Status of the Public by Age, 1974 Per Cent Distribution

Status	Age			
	55–64	65–69	70–79	80 and Over
Employed full time	38	4	3	1
Employed part time	10	14	8	3
Retired	18	61	63	69
Unemployed	10	4	7	6
Housewife	22	15	18	20
Other	2	2	1	1

Elizabeth Meier, "Over 65: Expectations and Realities of Work and Retirement," *Industrial Gerontology* 2 (2):95–109 (Spring 1975).

displacement from the labor force than to try to match persons to jobs or retrain employees or make agonizing decisions regarding who stays and who goes. Actually, many of the decrements in job performance reported for the current cohort of older workers can be traced to lower levels of educational attainment and lack of technical training in their early work experience, conditions that are less likely to characterize incoming groups of older workers.

There is little question that many job environments and specifications could be reshaped to assist older workers to compensate for functional losses. These workers could also be retrained or transferred to other tasks, if employers were willing to make such investments. It is probably more profitable to hire younger workers at lower wages and with more years to contribute to pension plans. So although industrial psychologists have worked out details for *functional retraining*, there is no compelling need for employers to adopt such programs in today's labor market.

Attitudes Toward Work and Working. Do older people want to work and how do they feel about their employment? The answers to these questions are often taken for granted. Of course everyone wants to work, and everyone is able to find something to like in his/her work; after all, it is better to work than to do nothing or get handouts. Let us look at the data from the Harris (1975) Survey on the desire of the elderly for employment.

As Table 7–4 indicates, the wish of the elderly to continue work is related to retirement income: the lower the income level, the more one needs to work. It is a cruel paradox that the low earners are least able to secure employment or remain in the labor force. Even so, 68 per cent of those with annual incomes under $3,000 further indicated that they would definitely *not* consider returning to work if asked, even for a job that "suited you well." Almost four fifths of all those 65 + were "not

Table 7–4. (Base: The 69 per cent of respondents 65+ who were retired or unemployed)

	Total Per Cent	Income			
		Under $3,000 Per Cent	$3,000– 6,999 Per Cent	$7,000– 14,999 Per Cent	$15,000 up Per Cent
Would like to work	31	43	31	20	23
Would not like to work	65	54	64	76	74
Not sure	4	3	5	4	3

Louis Harris and Associates, *The Myth and Reality of Aging in America*, Washington, D.C.: National Council on the Aging, 1975, p. 89.

interested at all" in retraining for employment, and only 11 per cent believed that they had skills they would like to use if given the chance. Nor did these respondents rate job opportunities as a problem for themselves personally—one quarter of both retired and employed believed that this was a "somewhat" or "serious" problem. These findings are not very different from those reported by other researchers. There is a minority of old persons who desire to remain in the labor force, most of whom desperately need the additional income, but the great majority prefer not to work.

Barfield and Morgan (1978a, 1978b) reporting data from a longitudinal study of retirement being conducted at the University of Michigan Survey Research Center found that economic/financial factors determined the decision for early retirement, but that being able to afford an extended retirement may vary by cohort history. Extra pensions and the end of mortgage payments influence the early retirement decisions of men, whereas current income and the completion of responsibilities to children affect the plans of women. The nonmarried are more likely to plan for early retirement than the married. However, the percentage at different ages who intend to retire *early* does not show a consistent pattern between 1967 and 1976, leading to the conclusion that expected work life earnings, inflation effects, and pension benefits, all of which fluctuate from cohort to cohort, are more important than age itself or a presumed value change toward self-fulfillment with each younger cohort.

As for satisfaction with work among those still employed, Table 7–5 indicates that worker satisfaction tends to rise with age, and that the overall percentage has risen from the 1958–62 period to the mid–1970s. But we must bear in mind again that by the time a worker is over age 50 a long selective process has taken place in which unhappy workers have shifted jobs or dropped out of the labor force. Many older workers will

Table 7—5. Satisfied Workers as Per Cent of Total Workers: 1958 to 1976

[Survey questions asked were variants of "How satisfied are you with your job (or your work)?" Figures for "satisfied" combined responses such as "very satisfied," "somewhat satisfied," and "fairly satisfied"]

Worker Characteristics	Survey Research Center Surveys[1]			National Opinion Research Center Surveys				
	1958	1969	1973	1962	1964	1972[2]	1975[2]	1976[2]
Male	81	88	91	84	92	85	90	87
Female	(NA)	81	89	81	(NA)	86	87	87
White	(NA)	86	90	84	92	87	89	88
Black and other	(NA)	77[3]	85[3]	76[3]	88[3]	78	85	79
Under 21 years	(NA)	75	77	59	88	55	85	51
21–29 years	74[4]	76	84	74	87[5]	76	82	84
30–39 years	79[6]	88	92	82	93[7]	88	88	91
40–49 years	85[8]	87	94	84	92	89	92	89
50 years and over	90[9]	91	96	88	94	92	93	93
Education: Grade school	88	88	93	83	94	86	88	84
High school	77	86	89	81	90	85	90	88
Some college	81 }	81	88	86	89	83	90	87
College degree	}	85	91	90	94	88	85	92
Graduate work	}	91	96	84	93	87	84	86

NA Not available.
1 University of Michigan.
2 Respondents include some unemployed.
3 Blacks only.
4 21–34 years.
5 21–30 years.
6 35–44 years.
7 31–40 years.
8 45–54 years.
9 55 years and older.

1958–1969 and 1973, U.S. Dept. of Labor, Manpower Administration, Research Monograph No. 30; 1972, 1975, and 1976, National Opinion Research Center, Chicago, Ill. unpublished data. Statistical Abstract of the United States, 1978, p. 208.

also indicate job satisfaction simply because they are pleased at being employed. Although Blacks are clearly less satisfied than whites, which is no doubt a function of occupational distribution of the races, the Black percentages are actually high considering the lower wages they earn and the low-status jobs they hold. And whereas females are slightly less likely to be as satisfied with their jobs as males, probably for the same reasons as Blacks, their percentages are rather close to those for men, which suggests more attachment to employment than is typically attributed to women. In fact, when researchers have bothered to find out, the data indicate that women care about their jobs in much the same way as do men: for income, for companionship, and for self-worth (Atchley, 1976; Fox, 1977). It is difficult to tell if these attitudes are new or a change from the past because women were rarely questioned on labor force attachment. It was simply assumed that their lives revolved around home and family.

When evaluating these attitudinal data, it is also important to bear in mind the social psychological process of "cognitive consistency"; individuals tend to bring feelings into line with their experience. Those who say they enjoy their work spare themselves daily pain, and the older person who is without employment need not endure frustration if she/he can claim to be "not at all interested" in a job. However, it is contrary to most evidence to say that the wish to work is a paramount need or interest of older people. Indeed, the importance of work "as a calling" may be diminishing among all age groups. These observations, though, are made at a time of relatively high unemployment; it is impossible to guess what the demand for jobs would be if the supply were greater. At this moment, however, it appears that the structure of the economy will continue to change in ways that reduce the demand for older workers: diminished opportunities for self-employment, increased need for newly trained technicians, and an expanding pool of younger workers at the entry levels. These may be thought of as conditions "pushing" older workers out of the labor force. But there are also many "pulls": secured pensions, health factors, a wish to enjoy leisure after a lifetime's work, among others. The pushes and pulls have combined to produce a rather new phenomenon in Western history: a majority of elderly who are not engaged in productive labor, and who occupy the status of retired person.

RETIREMENT

What has made contemporary aging and old age so very different from its manifestations in agricultural and preliterate societies is the phenomenon of retirement. There is perhaps an additional irony in the fact that the older population is numerically larger than ever, composing a proportionately greater segment of the population, with each cohort being better educated and possibly in better health. Yet, with each successive cohort today, a lower percentage is in the labor force, from age 55 on for males, and later for females, as shown in Tables 7–1a and b.

Questions relating to retirement—who retires, when, and why— are not as simple as they seem. Among the important factors to consider are mandatory retirement provisions, Social Security and other pension systems, the state of the economy, personal health and motivation, and cultural level values. Any one person's decision on whether or not to retire may be affected by any or all of these considerations, as well as by unique circumstances such as family obligations or pure chance.

Mandatory Retirement. Mandatory retirement refers to the provision in labor contracts or regulations of an employing institution that, at a given age, an employee *must* retire. By making such requirements universal, i.e., applicable to all, these rules help employers and union representatives avoid the difficulties of deciding who should go and who can stay. Mandatory retirement also permits younger workers to enter the labor force (thus increasing union membership). Knowing just when one must retire is also thought to benefit the older worker by removing uncertainty and forcing one to plan ahead.

Mandatory retirement has recently become a major target of those who believe that such policies represent a form of age discrimination; that unless it can be shown that age itself affects a person's ability to do the job, such limits on employment are unjust and possibly illegal under the Fourteenth Amendment's guarantee of equal protection of the laws. Although an end to mandatory retirement has been a central goal of the Gray Panthers, a small but very vocal group of activists, it was not until the cause was espoused by such "establishment types" as Representative Claude Pepper of Florida and other legislators with large numbers of elderly constituents, that the Age Discrimination in Employment Act was amended in 1977 to raise the retirement age ceiling from 65 to 70, with temporary exemptions for tenured college professors and for those whose retirement incomes would be above $27,000 excluding Social Security.[2] It is not known how many will take advantage of these extra years of employment; as Figure 7–1 illustrates for one company, the trend has been for both wage and salaried workers to retire *before* the mandatory deadlines.

What the new amendments to the Age Discrimination in Employment Act may best accomplish is the enhancement of employment opportunities for persons age 45–60 who often experience great difficulty finding jobs after becoming unemployed. On the other hand, younger workers will find their chances for advancement curtailed, and this is the

---

[2] Federal employees, who are already exempt from such provisions, may remain at their employment indefinitely.

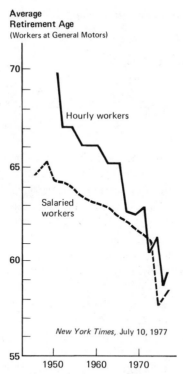

**Average
Retirement Age**
(Workers at General Motors)

Hourly workers

Salaried
workers

New York Times, July 10, 1977

Figure 7–1. New York Times, July 10, 1977.

decade when the large number of persons born between 1947 and 1957 are entering and establishing themselves in the work force. Jobs are also being sought by women and minority group members, so that career opportunities for young white males will be subject to a number of new contingencies. One possible outcome is a resurgence of race, sex, and age prejudice and conditions pitting the three relatively disadvantaged groups against each other.

Mandatory retirement provisions, especially when negotiated in return for pension rights, had been an important bargaining chip for trade unions. The influx of new workers would add to union membership, management could have greater internal flexibility and a lower wage scale, and both unions and management would gain additional contributors to pension plans (many of whom would not remain with the company long enough to become recipients). But Congress was not moved by these arguments.

It remains to be seen how many older workers will continue in the labor force beyond age 65. Most informed projections are quite low—between 200,000 and a half million, and then only to age 68. Between 1960 and 1976, workers increasingly left the labor force at earlier ages:

The Economics of Aging   **193**

Table 7–6. **Per Cent Working Or Looking for Work**

	50–54	55–59	60–64
1960	94.8	91.6	81.2
1976	89.9	83.6	63.7

New York Times, July 10, 1977.

This trend, however, may be in the process of being reversed under the inflationary conditions of the late 1970's. A Louis Harris poll conducted in 1979 found increasing proportions of workers indicating that they would not take early retirement, or even retire at 65 when they were entitled to Social Security benefits, because of financial considerations (Harris, 1979). These findings do not contradict the data on desires to retire, but simply reinforce the importance of retirement income as a crucial factor in the decision to leave the labor force.

Voluntary Retirement. In the 1974 Harris survey sample (see Table 7–3b), fewer than half the respondents 55–64 were in the full- or part-time labor force and eighteen percent had already retired, with an additional 10 percent looking for work. Fully one third of men between ages 60–64 had left the labor force before their eligibility for Social Security and other benefits, although probably with a partial pension. Moreover, almost twice as many retirees *perceive* that they have done so voluntarily than feel that they have been forced out. This is more true of women than of men, of whites than of Blacks, of high income earners, and those with post-secondary education. Again, the less advantaged individuals, for whom work income is crucial, seem to be forced to leave the labor force, whereas those with initial advantages have the ability to choose when to retire.

On the other hand, there is much research evidence to suggest that *when retirement income is assured,* those with the least satisfying employment indicate greater readiness to retire. That is, low occupational status, low income and low education—the factors associated with tedious work—enhance the attraction of retirement (Jaffe, 1972). Conversely, well-educated, high-income earners with intrinsically satisfying employment—precisely those whose retirements would be least problem-filled—are less likely to retire early. In other words, when trying to generalize about "the older worker" and retirement, the "pushes" and "pulls" will vary by education, income, and type of job. Whatever makes employment rewarding reduces the appeal of retirement, and vice versa.

Why Retire? For those who have some choice about this decision, or perceive that they do (which may be another instance of cognitive consistency), the availability of retirement income is paramount. Also important are health status, the ability to continue doing the job, fear of demotion, or an actual layoff. Older workers who are laid off will be able to collect unemployment insurance for several months, after which the decision to retire from seeking employment can be attributed to lack of opportunity. Those in danger of a job shift that could be interpreted as a loss of status might choose to retire instead.

The decision to retire for health reasons is most difficult to evaluate. Is this voluntary or involuntary retirement? The researchers' judgment on this point will make a great difference in the data. This is why Jaffe states that most men retire involuntarily, and the Harris (1975) study finds the contrary (in this research most of those wishing to work cited poor health as the reason for not doing so, but it was left to the respondent to decide whether his/her retirement was chosen or forced).

It is highly unlikely that any of these reasons would constitute a sufficient motive for retirement in the absence of basic income maintenance through Social Security, savings, or private pension plans.

INCOME IN RETIREMENT

As we have seen, income adequacy is *the* crucial determinant of whether an older person retires or continues to work. Social Security, private pensions, veteran's benefits, savings and securities, and earnings from full- or part-time employment are the major sources of income in old age. In addition, the very poor can receive food stamps and Supplemental Security Income (SSI), which, in 1974, replaced the Old Age Assistance programs of the original Social Security Act.

Sources of Income. Table 7–7 lists the variety of income sources of "older units" in 1971, by race. Most old people have more than one source of retirement income, as is indicated further in Table 7–8 for 1975.

Social Security refers to a federal program, begun in 1937 to mitigate the ravages of the Depression by providing limited health care and minimal incomes to unemployed older workers, survivors of deceased workers, and the disabled of any age. The original legislation was the Old Age, Survivors, Disability, and Health Insurance Act, or OASDHI.

What was intended as a relatively small-scale, stopgap system of *social insurance* has grown over the past forty years into a complex and costly agenda for income maintenance and medical care, as Table 7–9 illustrates.

This growth, and the change of purpose it signifies, are at the root of what is now considered to be the "crisis" of Social Security. The original term *social insurance* was intended to reassure those who saw Social Security as the first growth of creeping socialism. The basic thesis was that employers and workers would contribute during the work life of an indi-

Table 7-7. Per Cent of Elderly Units with Money Income from Specified Sources—1971

	Black (N = 1,913,000)	White (N = 19,541,000)
Per cent with income from:		
Earnings	43	44
Income other than earnings:		
Retirement pensions	67	76
OASDHI (Social Security)	65	72
Government employee	2	6
Private pension/annuity	6	15
Public assistance	30	7
Income from assets	13	53
Other unearned income *	11	13

* Includes unemployment insurance, workmen's compensation, veteran's benefits, alimony, contributions from family and others, and miscellaneous.
Adapted from *Social Security Bulletin* (July 1977), p. 34.

vidual who would receive in retirement a benefit pegged to that contribution. But as more individuals retire earlier and live longer than was the case decades ago, and the system has expanded to cover workers in employments that were not originally included, and benefits have continually been raised to parallel the cost of living, most beneficiaries of Social Security are receiving far more than they contributed. The one exception is married women who contribute as employees but receive benefits through their husbands' entitlements. In general, more people are getting more from the Social Security System than originally envisioned, and Social Security has functioned as a means of redistributing income from workers to nonworkers and to reduce the incidence of poverty among the elderly. Social Security is probably less of an insurance than a social welfare system, but it is still financed through a payroll tax. Although the fiction of paying one's own way is maintained, the reality is that the Social Security trust fund is dependent upon current contributions. This is the source of today's concern over the financial soundness of the system as the ratio of contributors to beneficiaries has changed with the demographic trends that have been previously detailed.

In 1978, 21.5 million retirees and their dependents and 7.5 million survivors of beneficiaries received Social Security benefits, as did 5 million disabled workers of any age. To support these recipients, 110 million workers contributed to the system, a ratio of three to one, which is ten times lower than that in 1940 when 35 million workers paid in, while 1 million received benefits. The current "dependency crunch" is clearly affected by the age of retirement, so that one outcome of raising the age

Table 7–8. Per Cent Receiving Different Income Sources Among Families and Individuals Aged 65 and Over—1975

	Families	Unrelated Individuals
Earnings		
Wage or salary income	41.7	13.5
Nonfarm, self-employment income	7.5	2.4
Farm self-employment income	5.9	2.1
Income other than earnings		
Property income, total [a]	64.4	53.8
Social Security and railroad		
retirement income	90.9	90.1
Supplemental Security Income	8.4	13.9
Public assistance or welfare	2.7	2.1
Veterans, unemployment and		
workmen's compensation income	12.3	8.6
Retirement income, total [b]	35.7	22.9
Other income, total [c]	2.9	2.2
No income	.1	.8
Selected Combinations of Income Sources		
Earnings	49.6	17.5
Earnings and property income	3.3	1.5
Government transfer payments	94.5	95.1
Public Assistance or SSI or both	3.8	15.1
S.S. or retirement income or both	92.8	92.1
S.S. or SSI or both	92.1	92.5
	100. [d]	100. [d]

[a] Interest, dividends, net rent, estates or trusts.
[b] Private pensions, annuities, military retirement pensions, federal employee pensions.
[c] Alimony or child support, regular contributions, other.
[d] Detail does not add to total because some families have more than one of the types of income specified.
Unpublished U.S. Census data in *Fact Book on Aging*, NCoA, 1978, p. 56.

of mandatory retirement is that elderly employees will continue to contribute rather than withdraw money from the system. However, the influx of younger workers into the labor force over the next decade should keep the *dependency* ratio relatively stable through this century and up to about 2030. (See Chapter 9.) At that time the baby boom cohort will be entering old age and the labor force will be composed of their own very small crop of offspring. But warnings of impending collapse of the Social Security System should be tempered by the realization that productivity could rise without additional workers, and that payroll taxes are not the only way to finance Social Security or any program of income transfers.

The major objection to financing Social Security through a tax on the wages and salaries of current workers and their employers is that this

Table 7-9. Social Welfare Expenditures under Public programs, Selected Fiscal Years, 1950-76 [1]

[In millions]

Program	1950	1960	1965	1970	1971	1972	1973	1974	1975	1976
						Total expenditures				
Total	$23,508.4	$52,293.3	$77,175.3	$145,855.7	$171,907.9	$191,357.0	$213,941.8	$239,313.6	$286,521.9	$331,366.3
Social insurance	4,946.6	19,306.7	28,122.8	54,691.2	66,368.7	74,809.4	76,165.5	98,953.0	122,947.4	146,592.5
Old-age, survivors, disability, and health insurance	784.1	11,032.3	16,997.5	36,835.4	43,122.8	48,229.1	57,766.6	66,286.6	78,429.9	90,440.7
Health insurance (Medicare)				7,149.2	7,875.0	8,819.2	9,478.8	11,347.5	14,781.4	17,777.4
Railroad retirement	306.4	934.7	1,128.1	1,609.9	1,928.9	2,141.2	2,477.5	2,692.6	3,085.1	3,499.6
Public employee retirement	817.9	2,569.9	4,528.5	8,658.7	10,226.0	11,920.4	14,010.8	16,677.5	20,118.6	24,425.0
Unemployment insurance and employment service	2,190.1	2,829.6	3,002.6	3,819.5	6,665.3	7,651.0	6,065.9	6,661.6	13,871.2	19,699.9
Railroad unemployment insurance	119.6	215.2	76.7	38.5	49.6	86.0	45.2	25.6	41.6	148.2
Railroad temporary disability insurance	31.1	68.5	46.5	61.1	53.0	42.1	34.9	31.5	32.9	78.6
State temporary disability insurance	72.1	347.9	483.5	717.7	773.1	783.7	848.2	915.4	989.5	1,049.2
Hospital and medical benefits	2.2	40.2	50.9	62.6	68.4	68.3	69.8	70.7	72.9	73.6
Workmen's compensation	625.1	1,308.5	1,859.4	2,950.4	3,550.0	3,955.8	4,916.5	5,662.3	6,378.7	7,251.2
Hospital and medical benefits	193.0	420.0	580.0	985.0	1,090.0	1,185.0	1,355.0	1,600.0	1,860.0	2,125.0

Social Security Bulletin (January 1977), p. 5.

method of raising revenue is "regressive," i.e., takes a proportionately larger part of the income of low-wage earners than of the more affluent. This is because the tax is paid on only part of earned income—the first $3,000 in 1937, raised up to $13,200 by 1972, and currently $17,000. Thus, an individual earning $15,000 pays Social Security taxes on *all* this income, whereas someone making $35,000 a year pays taxes on only half his/her total income. However, the very low-wage earner will receive proportionately more in retirement than she/he put into the system compared with the more affluent, but many low-wage earners do not live to collect. Jackson (1976) points to the statistics on life expectancy of Black males to demonstrate that their contributions often exceed the Social Security benefits they receive. She fails to note that proportionately more nonwhite than white males receive disability payments and leave dependents.

Those concerned with income redistribution believe that a much more equitable—fair and universal—method for funding the Social Security System would be from general revenues collected through a progressive tax on incomes, with high incomes assessed at a higher rate than low incomes. If the present system were continued, raising the taxable base to $25,000 would tend to equalize the proportional contributions of different level wage earners. Conservative economists, on the other hand, who are concerned with capital formation and investment, argue that the money collected this way leads to dissaving, i.e., less money deposited in banks to be used for loans and mortgages and the like.

Although the American worker may complain of this tax bite, and moves are underway in Congress to rescind the latest rate increase (without, however, reducing benefits), few have bothered to consider the alternatives: putting away enough from current earnings to pay for one's own old age, or contributing a share of each paycheck to the care of one's aged parents. Both of these possibilities have been estimated by Jaffe (1975) to require the diversion of one third of work life earnings for most workers. From this perspective, the present 6.05 rate for employees, or 12.10 if the employer's contribution is considered a worker loss in take-home pay, is a bargain. Other economists point out that if an entering worker today invested the withheld amounts privately, the rate of return in old age would probably be greater than the Social Security benefit level at that time. As a practical consideration, however, the collection of contributions through withholding removes the issue of how to spend current income from argument within the family and between generations.

WOMEN IN SOCIAL SECURITY

Another controversial issue is the question of coverage for homemakers. There is currently much opposition to both the concept and substance of a proposal for Social Security credits for full-time unpaid workers in the home. Such activities are to be done "for love alone," so that the attempt to give homemaking a market value is seen as destructive of the affectional basis of family life, and also as provoking resentment among husbands. The mechanics for collecting such a levy are often ridiculed.

Most disadvantaged among older women are those called "displaced homemakers," the divorced or widowed nonemployed women who are too young (under age 62) to collect Social Security but whose children are too old (over 18) to qualify for dependent's allowances. These women frequently have few skills or training for jobs, and are overlooked by most poverty programs. To secure any income, they relinquish their assets and apply for welfare.

A great deal of confusion exists over the Social Security status of women, both those who have worked in paid employment for all or part of their adulthood, and those who have been exclusively homemakers. Much of this confusion arises from the regulations themselves, as various categories of individuals have become eligible for different types of benefits every time the Social Security Act is amended. This has led to many apparent inequities. Benefits vary not only according to when the worker was first covered and how much was contributed over the work life, but also age of retirement, ages of beneficiaries, degree of disability of beneficiaries, and care of dependent children. Thus, there are wide differences in the benefits received by retired women labor force participants, nonemployed wives of retired workers, and widows of beneficiaries.

Women Who Have Retired from Paid Employment. At age 62, women with the required quarter-years of covered employment may receive Social Security benefits. The average monthly payment of retired women is about four-fifths that of retired males. This is so because of the low-paying jobs held by most women and the likelihood of their having irregular employment histories, i.e., moving in and out of the labor force at various times in the life course. However, as a replacement for wages, women's benefits are closer to their earnings than is the case for most men.

Couples, Both Retired from Employment. The wife can receive her earned benefit plus a sum equivalent to the difference between that amount and the 50 percent of the husband's benefit to which a wife is entitled upon reaching age 65. It is a sad commentary on women's wages that many working wives do better to accept half of their husband's Social Security rather than their own entitlement.

Wives of Social Security Beneficiaries. As just noted, at age 65 the "dependent" wife of a retired worker receives an amount that is one half of the husband's benefit. This often raises the monthly benefits of a retired husband and his *nonworking wife* to a level higher than that of a retired couple in which *both* worked for the same income as the first couple with one wage earner. The contributions to Social Security of each couple was identical, but the nonworking wife gets more back from the system than the working wife. For example, if the husband of couple A earned $16,000 per year while each partner in Couple B earned $8,000, both families would be taxed the same amount. But the nonworking wife in Couple A would be entitled to a retirement benefit at half that of her husband.

Widows of Beneficiaries. The 1972 amendments to the Social Security Act raised the benefit level for widows from a bit over 80 percent of the deceased husband's amount to a possible 100 percent under certain circumstances (especially if disability and dependent children are involved). Although the original act and its amendments assumed that the survivor of a beneficiary would be female, a recent court case has extended these benefits to husbands of deceased female workers, who are caring for dependent children. The Supreme Court held that the regulations unjustifiably discriminated against the woman worker by affording her family less protection than did men's employment (*Weinberger* v. *Wiesenfeld*, no. 73–1892, March 19, 1975).

A task force appointed by the Senate Special Committee on Aging has submitted a *Working Paper on Women and Social Security*, which has been the basis for some revision of the benefit formulas, most notably the reduction from twenty to ten years for years married before a widow or divorced homemaker is eligible to receive partial benefits from the former husband's contributions. Most of the recommendations of the Task Force on Women and Social Security remain to be acted upon; and another Task Force has been appointed by the Secretary of Health, Education and Welfare to explore the issue further (U.S. Senate, 1977, p. 12).

A Look Ahead. Even though increasing proportions of women are entitled to Social Security benefits on their own earning record—almost 54 percent of all women beneficiaries in 1974, compared with 43 percent in 1960—these earnings remain very low compared with men's income. In fact, the ratio of women's earnings to those of men has *not* changed appreciably over the past twenty-five years and does not seem likely to do so in the foreseeable future. This means that even though young women today will work longer and earn more than older women in the labor force, their benefits in retirement will still not be greater than those of dependents and survivors of men (Mallan, 1976).

Social Security, it should be remembered, was devised at a time when working women and displaced homemakers were considered exceptions and certainly not representative of the true American family. Nor was the system originally designed to become the major instrument of income transfer over the life course, or to become the economic mainstay of millions of retirees. Many of the current problems of the system are related to this major shift in purpose. That Social Security is intended to be a retirement income, however, is embodied in its "test" requirement. In 1978, beneficiaries over 65 who earn over $4,000 annually have their benefits proportionately reduced, to age 72, after which benefits are paid to all those who are eligible regardless of other income. The new Social Security Act amendments raise this earnings ceiling by $500 increments through 1982, after which it will be pegged to wage increases. Also, beginning in 1982 there will be no limit on earnings of those age 70 and over.

Social Security Benefits. Although the average monthly Social Security payments in July, 1979 were about $285 for a retired worker and $250 for a widow or widower, the range is considerable, from a high of almost $500 to a low of less than $130. These differences are the result of different lifetime earnings and hence contributions into the system. The *replacement ratio* is the percentage of preretirement income (an average of the best five years) which one receives after leaving the labor force. Low earners receive a higher replacement ratio (63 percent) than do high lifetime earners (35 percent), but in most cases this simply brings the former *up* to the poverty line. Recent amendments to the Social Security Act have coupled the benefits to the cost of living; when the Consumer Price Index rises, so do the pension payments, in 6.5 percent increments.

Summary. The Social Security System has come under increasing scrutiny in recent years. There are a number of areas of concern including funding, dependency ratios, sex discrimination, added responsibilities for the Social Security administration, and confusion over the goals of the system. Nonetheless, Social Security is the basic means of income maintenance for most older Americans. The problems arise because old people are retiring earlier and living longer—how ironic that what should be a cause for celebration is defined as a "major social problem" when considered in its economic aspects only.

Social Security, as seen later in this chapter, is not the only source of income for many in retirement. For women and minority males, however, Social Security benefits are typically their sole financial support; these are also the groups with the lowest lifetime earnings and subsequently lowest retirement benefits. Their jobs will be among the most tedious and unsatisfying, but it is they who need most to continue employment. Yet the poor also have generally lower health status than the nonpoor, adding another "push" toward retirement.

Other Pensions. The decision to retire before the mandated age is influenced by the availability of additional retirement income through *private pensions,* or in the case of civil servants (who collect a government pension rather than Social Security) who have had other employment which makes them eligible for Social Security as well, a dual set of benefits. Individuals in employment not covered by private pension plans are able to make tax deductible contributions to their own retirement funds—up to $1,500 in an *Individual Retirement Account* in a savings bank, or up to $7,500 in a *Keogh plan* for the self-employed. Other high-wage earners (e.g., management personnel and executives of corporations) are often able to participate in deferred profit sharing as well as generous pension plans, a tax-free diversion of profits that works to the advantage of both employee and employer.

There are also private pension plans for nonmanagement employees, primarily in high-skilled occupations and in firms with very few women or minority employees. There are a number of problems with these plans, however. Typically, survivors are not covered, so if the worker dies or leaves before becoming eligible, the worker's spouse and other dependents receive nothing. Nor did the worker have a right to carry pension credits to another employment, a procedure known as *vesting.* Further, the pension funds derived from workers' contributions were left to the unregulated control of trustees to invest as they saw fit. In the case, for example, of the Central States Teamsters Fund, many of these investments took the form of loans to gambling casino operators; in other cases, loans were made to relatives and friends of the trustees.

In view of these problems, Congress passed the Employee Retirement Income Security Act (ERISA) in 1974, the main provisions of which were to give vesting rights to employees after a certain number of years; to make it necessary to *offer* annuity plans to married participants that would provide survivor benefits; and to set up procedures for the regulation of pension funds.

One unintended consequence of ERISA was to add to the administrative costs of such arrangements, so that many small businesses decided to terminate their plans. Congress is presently revising the regulations in order to make the paperwork less burdensome to employers.

Despite these difficulties, 20 million retirees received benefits from private pensions in 1978, and 48 million contributed to these plans. In spite of allegations of mismanagement and a federal investigation, the Teamsters have recently reelected their leadership. And the pension funds of New York City employees' unions were crucial to staving off bankruptcy in that city through the purchase of city bonds. The future of private pensions, however, is not at all clear. The movement toward expansion of such plans was at least temporarily stalled by ERISA, but many high-level and skilled workers may make private pensions a condition of employment in the future, and the contribution of employers to union pension funds is still a prime bargaining point, often replacing immediate wage demands.

Veteran's Benefits. Some servicemen (and they were almost all men), whose war experiences resulted in partial or full disability, have been eligible throughout their lives for monthly payments. In old age these benefits become a proportionately greater part of income. Typical pensions, however, are only $1,500–$2,000 per year.

Saving and Securities. A large number of Americans, whether covered by pension plans or not, seek old-age security through their own savings. This course is obviously easier for those who have earned a higher work life income, but many moderate income earners elect to save rather than spend. One form of savings that also generates income is investment in stocks, bonds, and savings certificates ("securities" in many senses of the word). In 1973, 63% of persons 65 + received some money income from this type of asset.

OAA, Public Assistance, and SSI. These are programs designed to give income support to those who are not eligible for Social Security (that covered only part of the labor force in 1937, with other groups "blanketed in" at various times since) or whose work history has been so erratic or minimal as to greatly reduce their benefits. As of 1974, SSI replaced the patchwork of federal, state, and local programs of public assistance for the aged, blind, and disabled. SSI is administered by the Social Security Administration and is a federal effort, financed from general revenue, although states may decide to add to SSI an amount that cannot be used to disqualify a recipient from the national program.

As of late 1978, over 4,200,000 individuals received SSI, 49 percent of whom were 65+ (the remainder being blind and disabled persons under 65). Roughly one fourth of the total disbursements for SSI are made by the states.

Lest the impression be given that SSI ensures against poverty, it should be noted that the average monthly federal payment in July 1978 was $189.40 for an individual and $284.10 for a couple—provided that the recipients live in their own dwelling; the benefits are reduced for those who reside elsewhere. If the recipients are fortunate enough to live in a state that supplements SSI, the additional payments in 1976 averaged $35 per month for a single person and $50 for a couple. Typical payments are still well below the income that the Bureau of the Census described in 1977 as the poverty line or "threshold." In other words, SSI does not provide an old-age income that is adequate for minimal subsistence.

Fortunately, over two-thirds of aged SSI recipients also receive Social Security benefits sufficient to reach the poverty level.

INCOME ADEQUACY

Since most old people are not in the labor force, their incomes tend to be considerably lower than when they were working. Among Social Security recipients, the *replacement ratio* is typically under 50 percent, and, in the aggregate, incomes reported for persons 65+ are less than half of those reported for younger workers. As a rough generalization, then, old people will have retirement incomes that are slightly under half of preretirement earnings. For example, in 1974, the *median* personal income for white males age 55–64 was $14,552, whereas that for white males 65+ was $7,314; comparable figures for black males were $9,500 and $5,074 (Statistical Abstract of the U.S., 1978, p. 448). Both white and black female income earners are less disadvantaged in retirement only because they were more disadvantaged in employment; never earning much, their replacement ratios tend to be quite high.

Retired persons, however, do not have many of the same expenses as do younger persons; few have children to support or to send through college, and most have been able to pay off their home mortgages. It is also thought that elderly consumers have lost the need to "keep up with the Joneses" or to engage in displays of fashion. There are certainly no costs relating to work such as travel, clothing, and lunches. Many of the leisure activities preferred by old people are not expensive: reading, watching television, handicrafts, and card playing, for example. But we do not know if these choices are determined by low incomes as much as by age.

On the other hand, expenses of the elderly for health care items rise, and Medicare does not cover some of the most basic health expenses of old age (see Chapter 8). Many old people, fearful of becoming totally dependent upon their adult children, attempt to retain as much savings as possible against the day when they can no longer maintain an independent residence. They will do without daily necessities in order to husband their resources.

The full effect of inflation on the elderly has been eased by the recent coupling of Social Security benefit levels to the Consumer Price Index. Many communities have cut-rate bus fares for senior citizens, and merchants offer special shopping days or discounts for the elderly. Admission prices to movies, ball games, or amusement areas are often lower for old people, especially if they come at hours when attendance is typically low.

What seems to be a very small income when looked at objectively may or may not be perceived as "small" by the recipient. We must ask the elderly themselves for a subjective answer to the question, "How adequate are retirement incomes?". Some clues emerge from the Harris survey: in a sample in which the median household income for those 65+ was $4,800 (in 1974), only 15 percent indicated that "not having enough money to live on" was a "very serious" problem, but an additional 25 percent stated that this was a "somewhat serious" problem (this is in contrast to the 62 percent of the total public who thought that not having enough money would be a "very serious" problem for those 65+). However, 12 percent of those 65+ were still employed and some of the elderly homemakers may have been married to men still in the labor force, so that the 40 percent who indicate some problem of income inadequacy probably underestimates income worries among the fully retired.

This finding is not unique. Survey research, especially the type that attempts to assess needs, more often than not reports a surprisingly low level of expressed "need" among elderly respondents. Such was the case for a probability sample of over 800 old people in Morris County, N. J., who were administered a standard Needs Assessment questionnaire in order to guide the county Office on Aging in planning services for the future (Biesty, Hess and DiComo, 1977). Respondents were extremely reluctant to admit to any need that required others to assist them (see also Moen, 1978). The findings could reflect objective and subjective reality, but are probably also related to the "self-sufficiency" values that were characteristic of the respondents' socialization, as well as an unwillingness of the respondents to display shortcomings to a stranger/interviewer. On the other hand, researchers and social agencies are under some pressure to find problems, and, ironically, are often disappointed when they do not. From a cohort perspective, however, it seems likely, as Moen (1978) also concluded, that incoming cohorts of old people will be much more experienced in receiving benefits and agitating for entitlements, and thus less likely to gloss over or understate felt deprivations.

POVERTY

Although a majority of older Americans have found their retirement incomes adequate to their needs (even if these are lowered to meet the reduced income), a large number experience poverty even with their full benefits. The "poverty level" for persons 65+ in 1977 was estimated to be $3,637 for a two-person family and $2,895 for an individual—yet one of every seven old people in America fell below even these bedrock thresholds! As the Senate Special Committee Report stated, "All in all, 3.3 million older Americans were classified as poor in a Nation with a gross national product averaging $1.7 trillion for 1976" (p. 4). The report goes on to note that that 3.3 million was actually a conservative estimate since it did not include the institutionalized or those on, or slightly above, the poverty threshold. "If the near poor are added to the official poverty figures and the hidden poor estimates (those in institutions or the homes of relatives), more than 7 *million* older Americans would have incomes below the poverty line or so very close to it that they would have difficulty appreciating the difference" (p. 5).

For those elderly who receive either SSI or Social Security without any other income source, the average monthly payments are at or below poverty thresholds for individuals, and only slightly above in the case of husbands and wives both receiving benefits. In New York City, in a state that also provides supplements for SSI recipients, over one fourth of these people do not have enough to live on, and another 20 percent found themselves worse off than under public assistance plus food stamps (Zander, 1978).

Nonetheless, the great majority of old people are *not* poverty stricken, by either objective or subjective measures. Indeed, if one looked only at the census data it would appear that the proportion of old people in poverty was only slightly greater than might be expected by chance if poverty were equally distributed among all age groups. In 1976 about 12 percent of the total population was officially regarded as living below the poverty level, as were 15 percent of persons 65+. But these aggregated figures hide glaring disparities between subgroups of the elderly.

Differences by Race and Sex. By age 65 most women and Blacks are no longer in the labor force, so that very few have income from earnings. Moreover, while they were employed, both groups earned approximately 60 percent of white male incomes, on the average. It is thus not surprising that in retirement both of these subgroups are relatively disadvantaged.

In interpreting Table 7–10 it must be noted that "family heads" comprise the majority of white males, whereas "unrelated individuals" refers to most older women and almost half of elderly Blacks. In other words,

Table 7–10. Per Cent Family Heads and Unrelated Individuals 65+ Below Poverty Level: 1974

Family Heads:	All Races	White	Black
Total	9.5	7.7	27.6
Male	8.9	7.7	23.9
Female	13.0	8.1	36.8
Unrelated Individuals:			
Total	31.8	28.9	60.5
Male	26.8	23.7	44.3
Female	33.2	30.3	68.8

Siegel, Jacob S., "Demographic Aspects of Aging and the Older Population in the United States," Current Population Reports, Special Studies, P–23, No. 59, May, 1976. United States Department of Commerce, Bureau of the Census, United States Printing Office, Washington, D.C. Adapted from Table 6–8, p. 58.

the impact of the distributions in Table 7–10 is greater than appears, especially since most older people *are* unrelated females, a proportion that increases with advancing age.

When we talk about poverty and aging, we are essentially referring to widowed women of both races, with unrelated black females the most disadvantaged subgroup—two thirds of whom have incomes below the poverty level, which comes to under $60 per week.

OLD PEOPLE AS CONSUMERS

We have written elsewhere (Hess, 1974) of the relative neglect of the aged in the commercial media, largely, we suggested, because old people are "poor copy" and poor sales prospects, since their disposable income is not very great when compared with even the teenage market. Those products that are targeted to the older consumer tend to reflect the negative stereotyping of old age: hair coloring, false teeth adhesives, laxatives, and so forth. These products are typically advertised on evening news programs that are watched by a large proportion of those 55+.

In the aggregate, as one Secretary of Health, Education and Welfare has frequently pointed out, old people receive a large share of all social welfare expenditures, about 24 percent of the federal budget for fiscal 1978 or 5 percent of the Gross National Product for 10 percent of the population (Califano, 1978). But at the individual level, as we have seen, most old people live at the edge of sufficiency. Since their futures are affected by forces largely out of their control, most of the elderly are very careful about their immediate expenditures, and some try to save as much as possible against the day when they may have to enter a nursing home.

The leisure home industry has been very successful in appealing to older persons, but only to that very small segment which has very high incomes. Other entrepreneurs who have benefited from a large number of old people are those who took advantage of the private profit aspects of Medicare to build and operate nursing homes, and the physicians who treat elderly patients (see Chapter 8).

In general, the impact of elderly consumers on the economy has been minimal. As seen in Table 7–11, most of the expenditures of elderly household heads are for basic necessities. This leaves very little left for discretionary consumer goods; indeed, even clothing accounts for only 5 percent of the total.

HOUSING

A home is both the major asset and expense for many old people. It is an asset, however, that cannot easily be turned into ready cash. Seventy per cent of dwelling units headed by persons 65+ are owner-occupied. Since

Table 7–11. Annual Consumer Expenditures by Age of Family Head, 1973

	55–64 Years		65+ Years	
Family income before taxes	$13,080.00		$6,841.00	
Average Annual Expenditures, total (current consumption expenses) [a]	$ 7,922.03		$4,888.01	
	Dollars	Per Cent	Dollars	Per Cent
Food, total	$1,607.99	12.3	$1,113.29	16.3
Alcoholic beverages	72.21	[b]	30.65	[b]
Tobacco products	138.61	1.0	61.39	1.0
Housing, total	2,143.26	16.4	1,600.05	23.0
Clothing, total	608.74	4.7	311.17	5.0
Transportation, total excluding trips	1,691.74	12.9	727.87	10.7
Health care, total	560.01	4.3	497.47	7.3
Personal care (selected expenses)	132.22	1.0	84.74	1.2
Recreation, total	674.53	5.2	353.23	5.2
Reading materials	47.79	[b]	31.37	[b]
Educational, total	118.59	1.0	9.76	[b]
Miscellaneous	126.36	1.0	67.03	1.0

[a] Excluding personal insurance, gifts, contributions.
[b] Less than 1%.
U.S. Department of Labor, "Average Annual Expenditures for Commodity and Service Groups Classified by Nine Family Characteristics, 1972 and 1973," *Consumer Expenditures Survey Series: Interview Survey, 1972 and 1973* (1976); *Fact Book on Aging,* NCoA (1978), p. 66.

most of these homes have been lived in by the same family for over twenty years, over 80 percent are now mortgage free. Although this should lower housing expenses in comparison with younger heads of household, there are many drawbacks to these residences. The remaining expenses—property taxes and utility rates—have increased greatly over the past decade, and at rates higher than that at which retirement income has increased. This is why older voters are likely to turn down local school budgets (which, in most communities, are still funded through property taxes).

A second housing problem for elderly owners is the structural soundness of their dwelling. About half of these houses were built before World War II, and although in some ways they are better constructed than many built since then, these homes are often in need of major repair, with plumbing and electrical installations that may also require attention.

Further, the neighborhood in which these homes are located has probably undergone major changes in the last twenty years, often perceived as threatening by the older resident (see Chapter 10).

Although the average size of a home owned by an older person is somewhat smaller than that owned by younger family heads, there are fewer occupants. This means a very low density (no overcrowding), an important measure of housing quality. But such houses are often too large to be cared for adequately. There are few alternatives available to the elderly homeowner, and most of these are too costly, so that the aged couple or individual often remains in inappropriate housing.

The other 30 per cent of elderly households are rental units, almost two thirds of which are occupied by a single person. Most of these are in urban areas where the elderly are frequently "blockbound" in the inner city. Ethnic and racial minority aged are particularly likely to be in this situation. Property tax relief measures rarely affect renters, whereas cost increases are directly passed on to them by landlords in the form of higher rents. Yet where rent control has been enacted, a frequent outcome is abandonment of the building by the landlord and subsequent deterioration of the building through neglect.

Rural renters fare no better; their dwellings are the most structurally unsound of all types of elderly housing—the majority are without even indoor plumbing. Rural renters are most likely to be black or, in the Southwest, Mexican-Americans. Since most federal housing programs (see Chapter 8) are targeted to the cities where a more concentrated effort can be made, there seems little relief in sight for the housing problems of the rural aged.

Actually, it is the *least* deprived who are able to seek out, purchase, or apply for special housing in any setting (Carp, 1976). The well off can move to retirement communities, and the less affluent but educated and competent elderly have the knowledge and motivation to deal with local housing authorities. Conversely, the worst housed are also apt to be rejected by public housing gatekeepers, or they do not know where and how to apply for consideration.

Public housing accounts for a very small segment of elderly households, perhaps 3 percent. Another 5 percent of old people are institutionalized, and some fraction of a per cent can be found in mobile home parks, boardinghouses, and the like. It is estimated that 20 percent, or 4 million, older Americans need rehousing (Carp, 1976); that is, by objective standards their current dwellings are unsatisfactory, either structurally or environmentally. There is reliable evidence that a move by older people to more appropriate housing leads to improvements in their physical and emotional and social functioning—although there is a selection process on the part of housing authorities and people who elect to move that could account for this finding: those likely to improve are the ones who are chosen for public housing or can afford to seek a dwelling in the private market.

Yet very few old people express a desire to change their residence. In spite of the high costs of their housing, the inadequate structures, and dangerous environments, most elderly respondents are quite satisfied with their homes or apartments. In the Harris survey, only 4 percent of those 65+ listed housing as a "very serious" problem (although this figure includes 18 percent of Black respondents and 12 percent of those at the lowest income level). A study by the Department of Housing and Urban Development in 1973 found that old people were not so different from younger household heads in the assessment of their living conditions and in their reluctance to move: about 73 percent of renters and owners, old and young, indicated "undesirable" street conditions, but about 95 percent of these "would not like to move" (1973 *Annual Housing Survey*). However, when older people do move they cite housing needs as the major reason for their decision.

Housing is the major single expense item for old people, both owners or renters. Elderly owners, compared to younger ones, pay proportionately more of their total income in property taxes and utility bills. In 1973, as shown in Table 7–9, about one fourth of the budget of an aged head of household was spent on housing. It is estimated today that closer to one third of an old person's expenditures are housing-related, a proportion that is somewhat higher than that of younger heads of household. Nor are elderly renters any better off: in 1973, 41 percent of renters 65+ (compared to 22.5 percent of the total population) paid at or over 35 per cent of their income on gross rent.

Prospects

Work and Retirement. The amendments to the Age Discrimination in Employment Act signed in 1978 raised the mandatory retirement age to 70 for most workers in private employment (those in firms with more than 70 employees), and removed age limits altogether for Civil Service personnel. The exceptions already noted, tenured professors (until 1982) and executives with retirement benefits in excess of $27,000 per year (not including Social Security), are designed to move top people out of positions that block the path for talented juniors. The net effect of all this, however, is not expected to be very great: the trend toward early retirement seems well established. The best estimate of the Social Security Administration is that no more than 12 percent of retirees would be able and willing to return to work if it were possible, although an equal proportion might need to return to work if their retirement incomes did not keep pace with rising costs (Motley, 1978). The great majority of those already retired, however, have health conditions that would make employment difficult or stressful, or have sufficient income to make retirement their most attractive option.

On the other hand, some 200,000 workers are expected to take advantage of the opportunity to remain employed (if they can do the jobs to which they are assigned) after age 65. In general, these are those who need earnings. One outcome will undoubtedly be an easing of the strain on the Social Security System as these employees will be contributing to the system rather than receiving pensions. But there may also be an increase of persons 65–69 collecting unemployment insurance because they would be considered "looking for employment" (at ages at which they are least likely to find new jobs). It remains to be seen whether or not the reluctance of some older employees to leave the labor force will cause resentment among younger workers whose upward mobility is being blocked by those with seniority rights.

The trend toward retirement before age 65 should continue as better educated and generally better paid cohorts of workers perceive retirement as a period when they can pursue a variety of lifetime interests. Less attached to the work ethic and more used to nonwork gratifications than their parents, the retirees of the future are likely to redefine the meaning of their retirement years—not so much in terms of "losing" the work role as of "gaining" a well-earned opportunity for other activities.

Income. To the extent that retirement income determines one's decision whether or not to retire, there is both good and bad news. The good news is the linking of Social Security to the cost of living, and the fact that most men and women will realize higher benefits from Social Security as their lifetime earnings increase. Knowing that retirement will be their lot, many will also save and plan for these years.

As to the availability of private pensions, the news is mixed: these plans may become a major aspect of collective bargaining, and vesting rights are now ensured. But the new regulations have caused a number of employers to withdraw their pension plans, and "multiemployer plans" (those negotiated by unions in an industry with a number of employing firms) are not sufficiently monitored. This area of economic life is still in great flux, but it appears that some nationwide system for ensuring the solvency of private pension plans will soon be established.

The bad news, or more problematic aspects of income maintenance, stems from the possibility that retirees will be living for twenty years or more on their pensions—in some cases they will be receiving benefits for almost as long a period as they paid into the system. This trend threatens the solvency of the Social Security System and is leading to pressures for reduced benefits, longer work lives, or some other way of financing the system. The whole question of lifetime income transfers has yet to be faced by our society.

In all respects—source of income, housing, consumption—the status of old people, though they are relatively poorer than younger persons, reflects the socioeconomic distribution of individuals at earlier life stages. The advantages that characterize the life course of white males continue through old age. They are more likely than other subgroups to receive earnings from work, to retire with higher Social Security benefits as well as additional pensions and other sources of income, to live as head of household with spouse, and to have appropriate housing. Retirement resources both reflect and reproduce the social stratification system (Henretta and Campbell, 1976).

Therefore, whatever public policies reduce income disparities in general, or ensure equal opportunities in employment and housing, will ultimately reduce the economic disadvantage of old people. It is easier, however, to isolate these issues as problems of the elderly than as the consequence of long-term and deeply embedded inequities in the economic system and society as a whole.

Research Exercises

1. Divide the class into debating groups to research and argue the case for and against mandatory retirement. Select a panel of judges from the faculty to rate the arguments.

2. *Observe* food markets and drugstores to study the consumer behavior of old people and compare it with the behavior of younger shoppers.

3. *Draw up* your *budget* as an average recipient of Social Security benefits of $270 per month.

Discussion Questions

1. Your parents have asked your opinion about selling their house as soon as the last child moves out. What would your advice to them be? If your parents are renters, would you advise them to stay or to move?

2. The President has asked you to help design a replacement for the Social Security System. What would you suggest?

8

The Politics of Aging

In Perspective

Political behavior relates to the maintenance of civil order, and political power is the ability to make decisions affecting the lives of others in terms of their rights and obligations as members of a social group. The distinguishing feature of simple societies is that political activities are often indistinguishable from economic, familial, or religious behaviors; often, all are organized along lines of kinship. But it is important to remember, as shown in Figure 2–5, that the strength of family-based political control has varied with the mode of subsistence in a curvilinear fashion. Hunting and gathering societies are considered to be relatively egalitarian because there is very little over which to exercise control. Husbands and wives are economically interdependent, as are members of hunting parties. Marriages rarely involve extensive gift exchange and are frequently freely contracted rather than arranged. And life is short—with high infant mortality, epidemic diseases, and high maternal death rates. What minimal *social stratification* (i.e., the unequal distribution of power and rank) exists is on the basis of sex and age and skill. Age is important for a number of reasons: the respect that attaches to ancestors in any kinship system, the accumulated wisdom and experience that comes with age, and the probability that the few individuals who live beyond age 50 can still perform valued services to the group. Yet the younger adult males will become the leaders of the group through their prowess in hunting.

As the small hunting bands give way to larger groups maintained by herding and horticulture, it becomes necessary to develop order-keeping roles that transcend specific family lines. This is the origin of political institutions. Over the course of history, as more efficient modes of subsistence permit denser populations and lead to greater division of labor, centralized political institutions emerge—first in limited areas and ultimately covering entire nation-states. Positions in these political systems are primarily ascribed, inherited offices. In agricultural societies this produces an aristocracy and monarchy claiming to rule by divine right.

Monarchies, like the hierarchical religions that typically emerge in the agricultural phase of history, are very supportive of the patriarchal family structures that also characterize these societies. The king, as God on Earth, rules over his subjects as does a father over his dependents, and the Lord over His flock. That royalty is family-based further reinforces the analogy between royal and paternal power. Age and sex thus become decisive as dimensions of power in agricultural societies. Ownership of land is crucial to control, and it makes a great difference who marries whom and inherits what. The eldest male of a family benefits from the example of the royal sovereign, just as the monarchy is bolstered by the habit of filial respect in the family.

With the development of trade and mercantile interests in the Fourteenth Century, followed by the Protestant challenge to the Church of Rome and its hierarchical religious authority, family-based controls weakened and political structures that represented other than royal or family interests emerged. That plain citizens should have rights against the king, and negotiate directly with God about their personal salvation, suggests that individuals may have similar rights against other rulers. At first, these political powers were restricted to those who held property, but gradually the right to vote was extended to others (including those without land or education, and, only a few decades ago in the most technologically advanced societies, women). When suffrage is universal, age differences between adults are obliterated; that is, parents and adult offspring are political equals. And when officeholders are elected, incumbents cannot claim rights to an office simply because they have occupied it for a number of years, nor can they directly bestow the office on relatives. Indeed, the virtue of bureaucratic organization of government tasks lies precisely in its substitution of merit for *nepotism* (the assigning of office to a relative), and of universal standards rather than favoritism toward kin.

On the other hand, *experience* in office is often a source of power (especially where seniority is the criteria for leadership), and in many societies wisdom is thought to reside in older rather than younger leaders—or at least maturity is preferred to potential rashness. In general, representative and democratic government is subversive of hierarchical power relationships in the religious and familial spheres, and, ultimately, even in the economic area. For those who exercise power on the basis of their age alone, the dominance of achievement criteria in modern societies means that age-based claims must also have some functional dimension, i.e. that greater age be associated with some public good. Although age *per se* is no longer an assured basis of individual power, the rise of the modern state is, paradoxically, associated with increased political activity on behalf of old people as a group. One of the hallmarks of mature industrial nations is the degree to which care of the very young and the very old, as well as other nonproducing persons, is assumed as a public responsibility. The politics of aging is thus also the description of legislation and programs designed for the elderly.

Current Scene

LEGISLATION AND GOVERNMENT PROGRAMS

Although the development of social welfare programs in the United States occurred later and has been less extensive than in other industrial societies, it is clear that care of the aged in America has been transposed from the family to the public sphere. Beginning with the limited coverage of Social Security in the late 1930s (several decades after its introduction in Western Europe), programs to benefit the aged have gradually found acceptance by the American public, more so than efforts to assist any other special group. Our society, it should be noted, has not yet placed its programs for the elderly within a broader concept of social welfare throughout the life course, which means that the aged are a special category and that what is done for old people is not articulated with developments earlier in life or with a full-spectrum social welfare delivery system.

Income maintenance programs—Social Security and SSI—are discussed in Chapter 7, where it is noted that the whole question of lifetime income flow has not been addressed. However, in the years ahead more workers may elect to leave the labor force before age 60, or automation may make their labor unnecessary, at the same time they are likely to live for two or more decades. Whether or not Social Security or any other pension scheme can continue to operate on the fiction of repaying for past productivity is questionable. This method personalizes retirement incomes in contrast with the European models that treat the elderly as worthy of care by virtue of their citizenship rather than their economic contribution. These are political and philosophical as well as economic considerations, and at the moment the United States is very different from other modern nations in this respect.

As a result of this particular value position, programs for old people in the United States are segmented in terms of the life course and also in their administrative apparatus. The two pieces of legislation to be discussed in detail—Medicare and the Older Americans Act—are both characterized by *not* being part of more comprehensive plans. Were there a national health insurance system, there would be no need for Medicare; and if there were community social service centers, much of the Older Americans Act would be unnecessary.

Health Insurance. The struggle for an old age health insurance plan in the United States began in earnest after World War II and ended two decades later with legislation that established Medicare. The twenty years of controversy were a tribute to the influence and tenacity of the medical establishment (physicians and hospitals) that spent millions of dollars in their campaign against the legislation, evoking fears of "socialized medicine" as the beginning of the end of the free enterprise system. Fee-for-service was portrayed as the American Way, and national health insurance was depicted as a foreign import comparable to the Trojan horse. The campaign against Medicare was successful until the mid-1960s, and even now, when overwhelming majorities in public opinion polls endorse the concept of national health insurance, comprehensive legislation in this area has yet to be enacted. Ironically, it now appears that physicians and hospitals are the prime beneficiaries of the peculiar health insurance system embodied in Medicare.

Nonetheless, Medicare represented a great victory for those who had fought for some way of reducing the risk of financial ruin for old people (and their families) as one's health worsens with age. The Medicare coalition was composed of organized labor, northern liberals, and large numbers of nonaffiliated old people and their offspring.

Medicare was enacted as Title XVIII of the Social Security Act Amendments of 1965, accompanied by Title XIX (Medicaid), which provided payments for certain types of medical services to the very poor of any age. Since many older people are also poor, or become so through extraordinary medical needs, a large number of Medicaid recipients are 65+.

Medicare. Available to almost all Americans over 65 (95 percent were eligible in 1976), Medicare is a federally administered program with two types of coverage. Part A is hospital insurance for inpatient, skilled nursing home, and home health services. This is financed in much the same fashion as Social Security, from contributions by employees, employers, and self-employed workers. Part B is voluntary—subscribers can enroll for coverage of other physician fees for a small monthly premium ($8.20 per month as of 1979). These fees cover part of the cost, the rest coming from general tax revenues.

Medicare, however, does not cover many other expenses for the ill old person including: the first $160 of a hospital stay, the first $60 of most doctor's bills, and daily charges for lengthy stays in hospitals or skilled nursing facilities. Moreover, Medicare does not cover prescriptions and *prosthetic* (adaptive) *devices* such as eyeglasses, canes, hearing aids, and false teeth. Thus, in 1977, old people paid about one third of their total medical expenses directly from personal income. Medicare covered roughly 44 percent of the total, with Medicaid accounting for the remainder. The average old person still spends several hundred dollars a year, often as much as 10 percent of disposable income, to secure only the most basic health care.

Other aspects of Medicare have caused additional hardship. The coverage for skilled nursing home care of Part A is limited: up to 100 days *following* hospitalization. It is not uncommon that a very ill or frail old person is routinely sent to the hospital after the 100 days have elapsed to be treated there for a short time and then released back to the nursing home for another 100 days. Care in a psychiatric hospital has a *lifetime* limit of 190 inpatient days!

Medicaid. Designed to pay for the health care of the very poor, this program is financed jointly by the states and the federal government but administered primarily by the various states. The states set eligibility rules, standards of care, and payment rates (of which the federal government pays a proportion, also fixed by the states). Unlike Medicare, Medicaid places no time limit on nursing home stays. It is in the manipulation of these funds that most abuses of the system, as well as most abuses of the patients, have taken place (Mendelson and Hapgood, 1974).

Since one of the conditions for eligibility for Medicaid is that the individual have no personal assets that could be used to pay for nursing home care, there have also been abuses among the recipients and their families. One fairly common tactic is for an elderly person to turn over all assets to adult offspring; in this fashion, members of relatively affluent families have qualified as indigents. At the other extreme, an extended nursing home stay can use up whatever limited assets an older person or couple does have before becoming eligible for Medicaid.

It might seem that there ought to be a more rational way for providing medical care to old people. Most reformers feel that the profit-making aspect of such care has been responsible for both the skyrocketing costs of Medicare/Medicaid and the shoddy behavior of many health care providers. However, conditions in state hospitals do not enhance confidence in government-run services. More could be done to encourage nonprofit organizations such as religious and fraternal associations to operate nursing homes, but these organizations are currently experiencing financial problems (while the sects enjoying new growth and wealth are not yet interested in retirement communities or nursing homes).

Reform of the Medicare/Medicaid systems is clearly called for. At the very least, supervising agencies could enforce existing regulations, but it appears that until the public demands action, the nursing home industry and physician associations will continue to influence legislators, especially at the state level (Mendelson and Hapgood, 1974). At the federal level, an office of inspector general has been created in the Department of Health and Human Services, which has jurisdiction over the Social Security Administration.

Older Americans Act.   For all the publicity being given to what Henry Pratt (1971) has called the "Gray Lobby" today, history may show that 1965 was the year of peak legislative activity on behalf of the aged. Along with Medicare, Congress passed an omnibus bill known as the Older Americans Act. This act funded for the next ten years a variety of programs and services for old people, and projects for researchers, educators, social service personnel, and administrators, among others. The original appropriation was for $6.5 million, a sum that has increased steadily with each year. When the act was extended for three more years in 1975, funding levels were increased dramatically, with over $400 million appropriated for 1977. Of the many sections, or titles, of this act the following deserve detailed attention:

Title IV provides grants for training, research, and the establishment of academic gerontology centers. In 1977, $26.5 million was appropriated for these purposes, over half for training programs. These funds are administered by the Administration on Aging (AoA). Almost all the *training grants* have been awarded to universities and colleges to upgrade their gerontology course offerings and to introduce gerontological content into the professional curriculum. Some money went to individual students to pursue gerontological training, and some went to the states for the training of administrative and social welfare personnel. Similarly, *research grants and contracts* (on specific topics chosen by AoA) were largely distributed to colleges and universities, although some independent research organizations and state agencies have been successful applicants. The *multidisciplinary centers of gerontology* are almost by definition university-based. These centers perform training, research, consultation, and information-gathering functions for the university community or other setting in which a variety of disciplines are represented.

Title IV has thus provided the impetus for expanding gerontological content in institutions of higher education (see Chapter 11). Further, by distributing grants to specific researchers and institutions, Title IV has enhanced the status and power of gerontologists within the university. These funds allow for the hiring of graduate assistants, pay some of the normal departmental overhead, and are an impressive sign of institutional recognition.

There may be some question regarding the degree to which the elderly themselves have profited from Title IV. Most gerontologists and those in Washington who support these programs claim that the state of knowledge of aging is still so rudimentary that research must be encouraged. Supporters of these programs also point to the effect of training and teaching in the reduction of stereotypes and negative attitudes toward aging and old people. The critics of such funding claim that the kind of information produced by most academic research has very little practical value, that the introduction of gerontological content could as easily be accomplished through normal academic channels, and that the control of the direction of the field is being concentrated among a select few who sit on AoA advisory boards and undertake peer review of grant proposals.

The other major sections of the Older Americans Act—Titles III, V, and VII—were merged in the 1978 amendments to the act. The intent of consolidating these sections was to make local program planning and delivery more efficient. Administratively, the 1978 amendments extend the Act through 1981, allowing State and Area Agencies to develop three-year plans rather than operate on a year by year basis. The amendments further encourage an advocacy role for the "aging network" of Federal, State, and Area offices.

Other amendments require a nursing home ombudsman (advocate for the public) program for each State; give Native American tribes the option of receiving funding directly from the Administration on Aging; and liberalize eligibility for community service employment to those with incomes 25 percent over the poverty threshhold.

Title III provides for state or regional Area Agencies on Aging (AAA) to be established in almost 600 planning and service sectors across the nation (each containing roughly 40,000 persons 60+). Today there are AAAs in all but a few such areas, three quarters of which are operated by local government bodies, although any nonprofit agency could develop and carry out the tasks of an area agency. The major function of the AAA is to coordinate and facilitate delivery of services for the elderly within their area, but *not* to provide these services. The original act required special emphasis on the needs of low-income and minority aged, but the new act singled out as priority services transportation, legal and other counseling, home repair/renovation programs, and home-based forms of care. Funding ceilings go from $300 million in 1979 to $480 million in 1981.

Additional money is available for model or demonstration projects under both federal and state auspices. Model projects are important ways to test and develop what might later become policies and programs nationwide; they also allow for flexibility and risk-taking. But the primary legacy of Title III will be the network of AAAs as an infrastructure for comprehensive services to the aged. There is already a National Association of State Units on Aging whose members exchange information, assess experiences, and perceive themselves as part of the Gray Lobby.

The old Title V provided for the establishment of multipurpose senior centers. Although this title was added in 1973 amendments to the Older Americans Act, it was not funded until 1976, when $5 million was distributed among the states on a one-fourth matching basis (the states must provide 25 percent of the cost). The appropriation for 1977 was $20 million. Applications originate at the state level and are reviewed by the AAAs before submission to the commissioner of AoA. These steps allow maximum local flexibility while maintaining some overall planning control with the ultimate aim of providing integrated services in each area.

Title V Senior Center funding is now encompassed under Title III B, with an emphasis on multi-purpose centers as focal points for the delivery of a variety of services. Operating costs and limited construction are allowed under the new authorization.

Title VII, on the other hand, is an extensive well-funded program for nutrition projects. In 1977 over $200 million was allotted to the states, depending on their 60+ population, for congregate meals at "nutrition sites" and for the meals-on-wheels program that brings one hot and one cold meal each weekday to the homebound elderly. By the end of 1978, over 9,732 sites served 470,000 meals a day, and 1,534,000 old people participated. No means test is required although the act does require special consideration of minority and poor populations, which should affect the location of sites. In 1978, Title VII nutrition programs were incorporated in the new Title III C, and a home-delivered meals component was added (III C–2), with the following authorized ceilings (in millions of dollars):

	1979	1980	1981
Nutrition Sites	350	375	400
Home-delivered Meals	80	100	120

Evaluations of Title III-C have become a secondary industry; indeed, 1 percent of the 1977 budget—or $2 million—has been allocated for studies of the program's appeal and effectiveness. The indications are that participants in the program do benefit in terms of health status and improved eating habits.

What does all this mean? Clearly, programs for older Americans have been extended and their administration made more efficient. As it happened, Congress authorized but did not appropriate the necessary funds for 1979, so that the Area agencies have been operating at 1978 levels and the new programs are not funded at all. A long term serious problem, however, is not the level of funding but the potential for various individual programs to lose their specific funding into one "bloc grant" for local authorities to apportion. On the one hand, local control is desirable so that programs meet local needs; on the other hand, local agencies might be placed under great political pressure to fund some programs and not others if the monies are not earmarked in advance. The politicization of Area Agencies is a real problem especially when the agency personnel are appointed by state and county office-holders. From the senior author's experience as a member of the Advisory Board and consultant to an Area Agency, however, there appears to be trend toward professionalization among agency personnel, abetted by the Association of Area Agencies, so that a commitment to their clientele affords some resistance to outside pressures.

OTHER LEGISLATION AFFECTING OLDER AMERICANS

Title XX for social services under the Social Security Act also provides incentives to the states to design special services to low-income families and individuals in order to make them self-sufficient and to avoid premature institutionalization. Some states are experiencing difficulty in coming up with their 25 percent matching money, and still other problems have developed in the use of a "means test" to determine eligibility. But, in general, the states and AAAs have made use of some of these funds to extend and maintain services for the poor elderly.

Revenue sharing and *community development* grants have often been used by communities to fund projects that are directly or indirectly beneficial to old people. Federal manpower and employment programs to offset the effects of recession have also been utilized by persons 55+, but old people make up only a small proportion of those served—for example, only 3.5 percent of CETA (Comprehensive Employment and Training Act) employees in 1976. An additional 20,000 older workers were employed in community service and development projects funded by the federal government under other legislation.

The Department of Transportation (DOT) and the Department of Housing and Urban Development (HUD) are charged with special programs for the aged, but neither of these bodies has as yet a broad national policy, either for dependable transportation or decent, affordable housing. DOT has issued regulations for making buses accessible to the elderly and the handicapped, but not until September 1979 were public transit buses purchased with DOT funds required to have ramps and "kneeling steps." By the time such vehicles are phased in, it will be close to the turn of the century.

HUD has had a program for many years, Section 202, authorizing loans to nonprofit sponsors of senior housing, but only in the last few years has the funding level for this program been adequate to carry projects to completion. One of the many problems with Section 202 is the reluctance of some communities to issue required zoning variances. Land that is ideal for tax-exempt housing for the elderly—centrally located, level, and near shops and churches—is also valuable for tax-paying commercial development. On the other hand, some communities are quite willing to build senior housing or to set aside spaces in public projects for older tenants, as a means of complying with their responsibility to provide housing for low-income families. The aged are often preferable to other types of poor.

Summary. In terms of income maintenance and health care, the elderly have been singled out for special programs that, whatever their failures and faults, are major accomplishments for a society that lacks an integrated social welfare policy. In addition, other legislation and departments of government have programs that aid old people directly or indirectly. Indeed, according to one Secretary of Health, Education and Welfare (DHEW), America's aged receive a disproportionate share of public funds and services (Califano, 1978).

ADMINISTRATIVE DEVELOPMENTS

The "special status" of the elderly has been acknowledged through the creation and survival of the Special Committee on Aging of the United States Senate, and a comparable entity in the House of Representatives. No special committee has been established for children, for women, or for minority groups, although there are special committees for veterans and for small business.

The vast Social Security Administration oversees the operation of the pension and health-care systems, conducts major research, and publishes a monthly *Bulletin*. Moreover, the Older Americans Act established an additional administrative unit within DHHS, the Administration on Aging, to oversee the operation of the various services and programs provided in its titles. The staff of AoA issues guidelines and evaluates applications for research, monitors the AAAs, approves grants to the states, and serves as a communications channel for the "aging network" that is composed of thousands of academics, social welfare workers, administrators, and others involved in the study or practice of serving the aged.

The most recent manifestation of this institutionalization of aging concerns is the establishment of a National Institute of Aging (NIA), within the National Institutes of Health, in late 1974. The major task of NIA is to support research on aging, especially in the biomedical field, but also in the social and behavioral areas. Some research projects are intramural (undertaken within NIA), and others are conducted through grants to researchers and institutions throughout the country. In 1978,

NIA will have about $37.7 million for this purpose (these funds are in addition to the grants under Title IV of the Older Americans Act, distributed through AoA).

Renewed interest in aging has also been shown at the National Institute for Mental Health (NIMH) where approximately 5 percent of the research budget for 1977 was in the area of aging, and where a Center for Studies of Mental Health of the Aging has been established to coordinate the research and training programs in NIMH and allied institutes.

Punctuating these legislative and administrative acknowledgments of Senior Power have been a series of highly publicized conferences on aging. The first of these was a National Conference on Aging in 1950, followed by White House Conferences in 1961 and 1971, and one in the planning stages for 1981. No other interest group has had this many White House conferences, which offer a national forum, media coverage, and access to the administration—a general heightening of interest in the topic. Pratt (1978) has suggested that these conferences have gradually moved from being purely symbolic to having some influence on legislation, often in ways unintended by the White House. Pratt believes that the conference scheduled for 1981 will be less effective than that of 1971 since most of the easier tasks proposed will already have been accomplished, and that there may be a return to rhetoric. There is in all such presidential gestures the possibility of the conference itself being substituted for substantive change, as is the case of many presidential commissions (e.g., on race relations, crime, civil disobedience, and so on).

The willingness of Congress to fund all these efforts, and to do so at levels higher than that requested by the administration in most cases, testifies to either an interest in aging among our lawmakers or to a perceived political power bloc of aged constituents, or perhaps both (since legislators will themselves be tomorrow's old people). Legislators must also be concerned with their middle-aged constituents who might otherwise have to provide for the care of their aged parents in an inflationary era.

POLITICAL BEHAVIOR OF OLD PEOPLE

Voting. One of the most consistent findings in political sociology is that participation in elections for national office is highest for voters aged 45–65 and only somewhat lower for those 65+. Given the probability of illness, disability, lack of transportation, and other impediments to getting to the polling place, the participation of older voters is even more remarkable than may appear. If participation rates were based on the number of persons physically able to vote rather than on the total population 65+, this age group would have the highest voting rate. Since political participation scores tend to be lower for women than for men at all ages, it was thought that the overpresentation of women at higher ages would depress the old age vote, but in the 1976 presidential election, even though a higher percentage of men than women cast ballots, the preponderance of women in the age strata 45+ meant that these women accounted for a higher percentage of the total vote (see Table 8–1). Voting trend data suggests that political participation of women will increase with educational level, native-birth, and lifetime experience as a voter.

In 1976, older people, representing 11 percent of the population, cast almost 16 percent of the votes. Obviously, this represents a political bloc of some consequence even though it is primarily female.

In local elections, the elderly are also more likely to vote than those aged 18–24. To some extent, the younger voters are disenfranchised through geographical mobility, and in part they lack a sense of concern for a community in which they may be temporarily located. This gives the older voters added power, which is often exercised in defeating school budgets, but is not yet systematically used to promote programs for the aged. It appears that the political presence of old people at the local level is as a "veto force" rather than one united around positive goals.

Other Forms of Participation.   Political activism (working for candidates, running for office, involvement in grass-roots organizing, lobbying and writing to officials, and the like) among the elderly tends to be less intense than for those in middle age. The falloff in participation scores recorded by some political scientists, however, may be less a function of age than of education and income, a cohort rather than aging effect, based on cross-sectional rather than longitudinal data. Many of today's old people have had less than a high school education and relatively low occupational status, both of which are associated with low political participation. On the other hand, most old people have been in one location for a decade or more which gives them a stake in community politics. Overall, older voters (55 and up) are very much involved in political life, if not to the degree of persons 45–54, at least much more so than the presumed "activist" young people (Verba and Nie, 1972).

Interest in Politics.   Again, in spite of educational and occupational characteristics and a sex ratio that should depress interest, old people demonstrate high levels of political concern and knowledge. For example, old people watch the evening news on television, read newspapers, and listen to the news on radio more frequently than most younger age groups. The elderly are also more likely to answer surveys on political questions with great intensity and firm beliefs. Much of this interest may be the result of simply having experienced more of history, or of having fewer other preoccupations. But there is no question that older voters are prime consumers of political messages and information.

Table 8.1. Participation in Presidential Elections, by Population Characteristics: 1968 to 1976

[As of November. Covers civilian noninstitutional population, 18 years old and over, except prior to 1972, 21 years old and over. Includes aliens. Figures are based on a population sample. Differences in percentages may also be due to overreporting of voting by persons in the sample.]

Characteristic	1968				1972				1976			
	Persons of voting age (mil.)	Persons reporting they voted Total (mil.)	Per Cent voting [1]	Percent reporting not voting [1]	Persons of voting age (mil.)	Persons reporting they voted Total (mil.)	Per Cent voting [1]	Percent reporting not voting [1]	Persons of voting age (mil.)	Persons reporting they voted Total (mil.)	Per Cent voting [1]	Percent reporting not voting [1]
Total	116.5	79.0	67.8	32.2	136.2	85.8	63.0	37.0	146.5	86.7	59.2	40.8
Male	54.5	38.0	69.8	30.2	63.8	40.9	64.1	35.9	69.0	41.1	59.6	40.4
Female	62.1	41.0	66.0	34.0	72.4	44.9	62.0	38.0	77.6	45.6	58.8	41.2
White	104.5	72.2	69.1	30.9	121.2	78.2	64.5	35.5	129.3	78.8	60.9	39.1
Black	10.9	6.3	57.6	42.4	13.5	7.0	52.1	47.9	14.9	7.3	48.7	51.3
Spanish origin [2]	(NA)	(NA)	(NA)	(NA)	5.6	2.1	37.4	62.6	6.6	2.1	31.8	68.2
18–20 years old	.4	.1	33.3	66.7	11.0	5.3	48.3	51.7	12.1	4.6	38.0	62.0
21–24 years old	11.2	5.7	51.1	48.9	13.6	6.9	50.7	49.3	14.8	6.8	45.6	54.4
25–34 years old	23.2	14.5	62.5	37.5	26.9	16.1	59.7	40.3	31.5	17.5	55.4	44.6
35–44 years old	22.9	16.2	70.8	29.2	22.2	14.7	66.3	33.7	22.8	14.4	63.3	36.7
45–64 years old	40.4	30.2	74.9	25.1	42.3	30.0	70.8	29.2	43.3	29.8	68.7	31.3
65 years and over	18.5	12.2	65.8	34.2	20.1	12.7	63.5	36.5	22.0	13.7	62.2	37.8
Median age (yr.)	45.2	46.7	(X)	(X)	42.4	44.9	(X)	(X)	41.5	45.1	(X)	(X)

Residence:												
Metropolitan	75.8	51.5	68.0	32.0	99.2	63.8	64.3	35.7	99.6	58.9	59.2	40.8
Nonmetropolitan	40.8	27.5	67.3	32.7	37.0	22.0	59.4	40.6	47.0	27.8	59.1	40.9
North and West	81.6	58.0	71.0	29.0	93.7	62.2	66.4	33.6	99.4	60.8	61.2	38.8
South⁴	34.9	21.0	60.1	39.9	42.6	23.6	55.4	44.6	47.1	25.9	54.9	45.1
School year completed:												
8 or less	30.4	16.6	54.5	45.5	28.1	13.3	47.4	52.6	24.9	11.0	44.1	55.9
9–11	20.4	12.5	61.3	38.7	22.3	11.6	52.0	48.0	22.2	10.5	47.2	52.8
12	39.7	28.8	72.5	27.5	50.7	33.2	65.4	34.6	55.7	33.1	59.4	40.6
More than 12	26.0	21.1	81.2	18.8	35.1	27.7	78.8	21.2	43.7	32.2	73.5	26.5
Employed	70.0	49.8	71.1	28.9	80.2	52.9	66.0	34.0	86.0	53.3	62.0	38.0
Unemployed	1.9	1.0	52.1	47.9	3.7	1.9	49.9	50.1	6.4	2.8	43.7	56.3
Not in labor force	44.7	28.2	63.2	36.8	52.3	31.0	59.3	40.7	54.1	30.6	56.5	43.5

NA Not available.
X Not applicable.
¹ Includes do not know and not reported.
² Persons of Spanish origin may be of any race.

Source: U.S. Bureau of the Census, *Current Population Reports*, series P–20, Nos. 192, 253, and forthcoming report.
Statistical Abstract of the United States, 1978, p. 508.

On all these measures—with the understandable exception of contributions of money—old people are politically active, perhaps because one can do a great deal without having to spend money. There are strong cohort effects on political behavior: the era in which one first develops an interest in civic affairs is crucial for a sense of political effectiveness. Those born at the turn of the last century, who came to adulthood during the 1920s would probably be less politically involved than those who first voted in the 1930s, a period of great political change and controversy. Moreover, the foreign-born who were caught up in the early trade union movement probably would be more politically aware than other age peers. Some of these speculations can be tested, such as the within-group comparison just mentioned, although trade union organizers in the 1930s may be different from other cohort members in some ways that independently affect political participation, such as religion, ethnicity, and education. The between-cohort comparisons are less easily tested: which of all the possible influences over fifty or more years is likely to account for attitudes toward politics in old age—including age itself? The question is too complex for easy answers.

Political Orientations. It is commonly thought that old people are both more conservative than younger voters or than when they themselves were young. Much survey data seems to support this thesis for the United States and other industrial societies. Older voters tend to identify with traditional parties and candidates, perhaps because they reflect the values of their own early socialization. Moreover, once identified with any party, the older the voter, the less likely he/she is to change preference, a conservative (in the sense of less flexible) behavior probably associated with the effects of "duration in the role" (Hudson and Binstock, 1976). That is, the longer one plays a role, the greater is the investment of self-image in that behavior, and hence, the greater is the reluctance to change. The third trend is for some individuals to move to more conservative stances in general as they age. The explanation for this tendency could be "duration in the social system", i.e., an enhanced stake in things as they are, the familiar and comfortable way of seeing the world.

But the more carefully the data are analyzed, the more dubious the "old age conservatism" thesis becomes. Some of this conservatism, especially in cross-sectional studies, may be an artifact of increased liberalism among incoming cohorts of voters, so that by comparison older voters seem less interested in change. Glenn (1974) noted that aging cohorts tend to move in the general direction of public opinion as a whole, but less dramatically than younger ones; thus, "according to almost any definition of conservatism, people have typically become less, rather than more, conservative as they have grown older, in conformity with general societal trends" (p. 185). However, relative to younger voters, old people will appear to be, and will define themselves as being, concerned with upholding traditional values.

On *specific issues* which are of immediate importance to older Americans, voters 65+ may appear to be quite liberal, but not necessarily more so than the general public. In the Harris survey, the great majority of respondents 65+ felt that government had the responsibility for income maintenance in old age, less than two fifths endorsed the traditional answer that one "should provide for oneself," and only 8 percent thought that children should provide for their parents. These figures differ only slightly from those for the general public. Nor are older Americans so worried about the advent of socialized medicine that they fail to give overwhelming support to federally financed health insurance (Riley, Johnson, and Foner, 1972; but see Clemente, 1975).

On other specific issues, with the exception of the Gray Panthers, older people find it difficult to approve such manifestations of the "new morality" as the legalization of marijuana, homosexual rights, the feminist movement, interracial marriage, or relaxed standards of dress in public. But the views of the elderly on these topics are probably less rigid today than they were several decades ago, more liberal than those of their parents, and more tolerant than many believe them to be (Nahemow and King, 1978).

Political Office. Old age is rarely perceived as a bar to high office; indeed, the "elder statesman" is a reassuring figure. Where political leadership is ascribed, a headman or monarch will rule till death. But since life expectancy before the twentieth century was somewhat problematic, and since many rulers were also military leaders, their reigns were often limited. Under modern conditions, the nearest equivalents are military dictators or civilian leaders of totalitarian states: one thinks of General Franco of Spain, Salazar of Portugal, the Politburo of the Soviet Union, and the leadership of the People's Republic of China. Even in democratic republics old men have been chosen to head the state, including Adenauer of Germany (nicknamed "Der Alte"), Eisenhower of the United States, DeGaulle of France, and a number of premiers of postwar Italy. These men represent stability and continuity in both unstable and established political systems.

In times of revolutionary change younger men (and possibly a few women) are sometimes able to come to power, but if the revolution is successful, these become the new establishment with a vested interest in maintaining their control. Democratic elections are a mechanism whereby old blood can be peacefully replaced by new, but here, too, duration in office is associated with enhancement of authority. The longer one has been in Congress, for example, the better assignments one gets in the committee system, and these committee posts carry great power in deciding which bills reach the floor for a vote, and how much money will be spent in which states for what purposes. The more power an official has through this seniority system, the more this official will be able to do for his/her constituents, and the more likely he/she is to be reelected.

Recent changes in the procedures for assigning committee posts in Congress have reduced the salience of seniority, but have not led to a drastic shift in the age composition of Congress. Rather, as Table 8–2 indicates, much depends upon the specific election, although the trend is toward younger ages for members of the House of Representatives.

Most of the very old congressmen are from the South, traditionally a conservative part of the country, and they are gradually being replaced by younger candidates who are politically moderate, reflecting attitudinal changes that have occurred in that region over the past decade. But it would be a mistake to equate youth with liberalism in American politics today, since many northern liberals are being replaced by more conservative juniors. However, to the degree that elected officials are no different from the general public, aging incumbents should share the conservatizing tendencies that have been noted for older voters.

Table 8–2. Members of Congress, by Sex and Age: 90th to 95th Congresses

[As of January 1 of the 1st year of each Congress. Figures for Representatives exclude vacancies]

Members of Congress and Year			Age (in years)					
	Male	Female	Under 40	40–49	50–59	60–69	70–79	80 and over
Representatives								
90th Congress, 1967	424	10	56	150	135	73	15	4
91st Congress, 1969	425	10	39	160	140	80	13	3
92d Congress, 1971	421	12	40	133	152	86	19	3
93d Congress, 1973	419	14	45	132	154	80	20	2
94th Congress, 1975	416	19	69	138	137	75	14	2
95th Congress, 1977	417	18	81	121	147	71	15	—
Senators								
90th Congress, 1967	99	1	5	20	30	30	14	1
91st Congress, 1969	99	1	5	25	28	29	13	—
92d Congress, 1971	99	1	4	24	32	23	16	1
93d Congress, 1973	100	—	3	25	37	23	11	1
94th Congress, 1975 [1]	100	—	5	21	35	24	15	—
95th Congress, 1977	100	—	6	26	35	21	10	2

— Represents zero.
[1] Includes Sen. Durkin, N.H., seated Sept. 1975.
Source: Compiled by U.S. Bureau of the Census from U.S. Congress, Joint Committee on Printing, *Biographical Directory of the American Congress, 1774–1961,* and *Congressional Directory.*
Statistical Abstract of the United States, 1978, p. 504.

Aging in Social Systems

The influx of younger (and nonwhite and female) officeholders is more obvious at the state and local levels; but here, too, age in office confers advantages in terms of having more time to give out favors and to construct alliances.

It would appear that two offsetting currents are at work in the political system today: the attractiveness of new faces promising instant solutions to old, intractable problems, as contrasted with a yearning for stability and known quantities in a period of rapid, often upsetting change. As public opinion seems to be shifting to the right of center, both these trends could eventuate in the election of young conservatives.

In general, age as an indicator of experience and seniority status is gradually becoming less important, and the link between age and ideological orientation is less certain than ever. In other words, age itself is losing political meaning, although it may remain a consideration as a personal attribute of a candidate.

POLITICAL ORGANIZATIONS OF THE ELDERLY

If old people are ten percent of the total popultion, they are over 15 percent of those eligible to vote, and probably close to 20 percent of the active voters in most elections. And if they also have felt needs for income maintenance, medical care, and other services, why is there no Senior Citizen Political party? Some of the reasons are unique to organizing old people, and others to the viability of special interest political movements in the United States.

The early attempts to create a mass organization of old people, in California during the Great Depression, came to naught: the Townsend movement and the Ham and Eggs movement both failed to create lasting organizations capable of keeping followers together over time. The basic proposal of Townsend and other Depression-spawned plans was for a federally administered monthly income for all old people provided that they retired from work and spent the money within each month—thus opening employment and increasing the "velocity" of money turnover. Personality clashes, power struggles, and lack of funding are common handicaps of splinter groups in American politics, so that without passionate attachment to a common set of goals, members break up into factions that are more interested in fighting one another than in pursuing their mutual interests. But these abortive movements also illustrate a problem peculiar to organizing the aged: there are very few specific programs that so diverse a group can agree to support, and there is no one overarching political orientation that could distinguish them; and above all, there is little consciousness of kind, i.e., a sense of belonging to one another.

Within these constraints, however, a number of age-based organizations have emerged since the failures of the 1930s and early 1940s. These organizations are of several types: some are mass membership organizations, whereas others represent the interests of those who work with or for the aged.[1]

Organizations of Retired Persons. The largest of the mass-based organizations of the elderly began as an association of retired educators in the late 1940s—the National Retired Teachers Association, founded by Ethel Percy Andrus. Later, in the 1950s, the organization received financial assistance from Leonard Davis, an insurance executive. So successful did NRTA become in providing its members with life insurance, an information network, travel and prescription discounts, and other items of material well-being, that a spinoff, the American Association of Retired Persons was founded in 1958 for nonteacher retirees. NRTA-AARP, which today has well over 10 million dues-paying members aged 55 and over, maintains a Washington, D.C. office that tracks legislation of interest to members. Because of its early close relationship with the insurance industry, NRTA-AARP maintained a basically conservative position in the Medicare crusade, but has recently taken relatively liberal stands on national health insurance and federally-sponsored senior volunteer programs. Despite its vast membership, NRTA-AARP remains a rather unlikely base for a mass movement with the aim of restructuring American institutions.

A less conservative but also less powerful organization is the National Council of Senior Citizens (NCSC), formed in 1961 with funds and encouragement from the AFL-CIO (American Federation of Labor-Congress of Industrial Organizations) to lobby for Medicare. Since then, an attempt has been made to develop local councils and clubs open to nonunion retirees. Membership in NCSC is over three million, but active participants are much fewer, and most of these are former activists in the labor union movement. It is possible that aging union members are more radical than the younger rank-and-file—a cohort effect of being a young union member in the period between the world wars.

The third, and smallest, organization of retired persons is the National Association of Retired Federal Employees (NARFE). Composed of former civil service personnel, who receive a federal employee pension rather than Social Security, this group serves as a monitor of congressional action on its pension system. There are fewer than 200,000 members, and the leadership has not been especially active on broad issues of concern to old people in general.

Pratt (1974) argues that these three mass membership groups have succeeded where the earlier movements failed because they have been able to organize effectively with national offices, local branches, and paid ad-

[1] The following discussion is based upon the detailed descriptions and analyses of Henry J. Pratt (1974, 1976).

ministrators. In order to attract and keep dues-paying members, these groups have had to offer something in return: services, lobbying success, and at the local level, activities and companionship. NRTA-AARP is a multimillion dollar operation, deriving income from the sale of insurance and its travel packages, and from advertising in its magazine by the Colonial Penn Insurance Companies. The NSCC is similarly beholden to the labor unions. NARFE offers some limited services to its members but has no source of outside income. Not only are the contemporary mass-membership groups well organized and financed but they exist in what Pratt calls "a more benign external environment" than did the earlier movements; that is, there is more general support for their objectives. Both Binstock (1972) and Pratt (1974) suggest that the age-based interest groups operate as part of the Establishment, lobbying in a fashion similar to that of other interest groups, within the rules of pluralistic competition. The two political scientists differ greatly in their evaluation of the outcome of age-based politics, with Pratt holding that the gray lobby's constant pursuit of moderate goals may over time produce far-reaching cumulative changes in national policy, as for example the enlargement of social security coverage over the past two decades. Binstock and others are less sanguine (see Binstock, p. 375).

There have indeed been major victories: Medicare and the Older Americans Act; White House Conferences in 1961 and 1971, and a third to be held in 1981; the establishment of a National Institute of Aging. But with the exception of Medicare, none of the other achievements has materially affected the status of poor and near-poor older Americans. Some would say that the mass membership organizations have been coopted, i.e., become part of the status quo, in return for symbolic gestures such as the White House Conferences and NIA, and that the beneficiaries of most programs have not always been the aged, much less those old people in greatest need.

Other Organizations with Age-Based Interests.   This category includes a range of special interest associations, from the American Association of Homes for the Aging to the National Caucus on the Black Aged (NCBA). The former, along with the American Nursing Home Association and similar groups, are called *trade associations*. Trade associations have a variety of functions—lobbying for beneficial legislation, avoiding what they perceive as excessive regulation, and gathering and disseminating useful information—but their essential purpose is to protect members' rights to realize profits from their trade.

Organizations of health and welfare agencies, such as the National Council of Health Care Services, the National Council on the Aging, and the National Association of State Units on Aging, do have the client (older) population as a major focus, but constituent members (typically middle-aged) are also concerned with the maintenance of their own agencies: securing grants, expanding services, funding programs, and the like.

A third type of group with age-based interests is represented by the Gerontological Society, the Association for Gerontology in Higher Education, the National Action Forum for Older Women, and the NCBA. The first two are largely composed of academic researchers, teachers, and those involved in training practitioners (see Chapter 10). It is important to note, again, that there is considerable tension between those who believe that learned societies should be devoted exclusively to the advancement of knowledge and expansion of academic programs, on the one hand, and those who feel that these societies must become *advocates* for the aged, especially since academic gerontologists are themselves profiting from the funding provisions of the Older Americans Act. The practitioners and academics who are especially concerned with the black aged and older women are also attempting to correct biases in research and theory that often limit studies conducted by white middle-class males. In the case of the aged, the early emphasis on work, retirement, and the need for meaningful activity, reflected the clear concerns of aging males. Conversely, topics such as displaced homemakers, poverty, race and sex discrimination, commitment procedures, and nursing home abuses have received less attention or funding.

The Gray Panthers.[2]   One of the high points of the 1976 Annual Meeting of the Gerontological Society was a debate between the society's officers and Maggie Kuhn, the convener of the Gray Panthers. The Panthers' perception of themselves as being in opposition, while the other age-based organizations operate with or within the Gerontological Society, exemplifies the tension between the aging establishment and the advocates of radical change in the society as a whole.

Although the Panthers have only five thousand dues-paying members (both young and old), the organization has received an enormous amount of media coverage, in part because of Kuhn's charismatic qualities, and in part because of the radical positions on social issues taken by an organization of old people. To some extent, the Panthers have become the conscience of gerontology, asking such questions as, Is the profession of gerontology a parasite feeding on the expanding population of older people? Does the Gerontological Society exist primarily to acquire research and training funds for universities and to advance the goals of its members?

The Gray Panthers have also offended other constituencies--the American Medical Association, insurance companies, and those who believe that old people, especially sweet old ladies, should not engage in militant action or street theater, or support the decriminalization of marijuana,

[2] This section is based on Jacobs and Hess (1978).

the Equal Rights Amendment, gay rights, and school busing. These positions have undoubtedly cost the Panthers much support from many old people, and signs of moderation have been evident in the public pronouncements and convention platforms at recent Panther meetings. If the Panthers are to broaden their membership it can only be among old people who are likely to be more conservative, or among young people likely to be more radical, than is public opinion in general. Other problems facing the Panthers include the need to establish an organizational framework—to keep membership lists, collect dues, and dispense information—which will be difficult for a group that prides itself on the absence of hierarchy, and one that is based on grass roots spontaneity (the same issue that has plagued the Women's movement in its attempt to avoid power/status structures).

The Panthers also exemplify the difficulties of social movements founded by charismatic figures, as was the Townsend movement; some leadership functions must be routinized, or bureaucratized, in the event of the leader's death. This is a particularly salient problem in organizations led by old people, which may explain why the Establishment age-based organizations typically have paid administrators who are not elderly.

In comparison with the 10 million members of the NRTA-AARP, the Gray Panthers appear quixotic indeed, tilting at windmills on behalf of disadvantaged and politically marginal minorities. Hopes of a coalition between activist youth and old people, that seemed so possible in the late 1960s, have diminished. There is the further possibility of a "backlash" against the demands of the aged, with the Gray Panthers isolated as left-wing "crackpots" and troublemakers.

The Panthers are now faced with a number of dilemmas: to gain membership perhaps at the cost of diluting principles, to raise money from a constituency that is impoverished, and to build a structure that may subvert local autonomy. But the many small victories of local Panther "packs" and the continued existence of a militant age-based movement serve the essential purposes of all radical groups—to hold out a vision of the best, and to raise consciousness by questioning sacred values. The Panthers' major contribution, however, may be simply the example they present of one form of successful aging: to care enough to struggle at the risk of being trivialized or ridiculed, and yet to remain committed to goals that are beyond immediate self-interest.

The New Gray Lobby. Age-based organizations are only one segment, though perhaps the largest, of the Gray Lobby. Legislation to improve the income level or health-care benefits of old people is often supported by their children, who might otherwise have to undertake these responsibilities. Many middle-aged voters are also thinking in terms of their own aging, having an *anticipatory stake* (Riley and Waring, 1976) in such programs. There are also the gerontologists, social welfare practitioners, nursing home operators, and others who derive their living from the study and care of the aged. Most recently, as a consequence of the Older Americans Act, a network of federal and state and local offices has become involved in planning and coordinating services to the aged.

The power of the Gray Lobby was demonstrated several times in the past few years: in amendments to the Social Security Act; the revision of the Age Discrimination in Employment Act; the extension and expansion of the Older Americans Act; and the fight to save the Special Committee on Aging, a special committee of the Senate that had become a major resource for the Gray Lobby. The committee was slated for extinction in a major reorganization of the Senate committee system. The committee staff had developed a highly professional expertise, and simply having a committee that was solely devoted to the particular interest of the elderly was in itself a source of power in Washington. Faced with the threat of extinction of the committee, age-based organizations put their lobbyists to work, gerontologists applied whatever political pressure they could, and other concerned parties wrote in support of the committee. When the vote came in the Senate, it was overwhelmingly decided that, with some modifications, the Special Committee on Aging would remain a separate entity.

These developments—raising Social Security taxes and benefits, extending the ages of mandatory retirement, and saving the Senate committee—led the media to herald the arrival of "senior power" as a new force in national politics (e.g., *New York Times*, October 24, 1977, p. 1).

Prospects

SENIOR POWER: PRO AND CON

Do the mass membership organizations, the "aging network" stretching from AoA through the Area Agencies to the local Senior Center, and the combined political influence of older voters and their children, those who provide and administer services to them and those who study and teach about aging, add up to senior power, or is the Gray Lobby a "paper panther," so to speak?

There are a number of reasons for contending that an old-age vote is real and is becoming more significant. The population as a whole is aging, which means that the interests and concerns of older people will be increasingly salient compared to those of children and youth (both of which groups have dominated the American scene since the end of World War II). As one example of this shift from young to old, some law enforcement experts believe that the current demand for harsh punishments and reenactment of the death penalty reflect the fears of older people in an aging society, whereas the earlier emphasis on rehabilitation and special treatment of the juvenile offender mirrored a general commitment to youth (*New York Times*, July 7, 1978).

There is also some evidence that jobs will become scarcer as more industrial tasks are automated. Should this occur, retirement ages would be lowered, thrusting many not-so-old persons into the position of being like the old in terms of their employment status and possibly with respect to income. Neugarten (1974) suggested that this development would fill the ranks of the aging with relatively well-educated, healthy, and politically active recruits. Moreover, younger old people can typically provide more vigorous and long-term leadership than many old-age movements have thus far been able to muster. This, however, presupposes that these "young-old" will identify themselves as old people, which is doubtful. It seems more likely that the young-old will be at least as motivated as those now-old to avoid such stigmatization (Rosow, 1967). On the other hand, if the young-old share the material deprivations of the very old—inadequate incomes, and needs for health care, transportation, and housing—they will also share their political concerns. Self-image will struggle with self-interest, which could lead to a redefinition of social welfare that covers the whole life course rather than being confined to an end stage based on age.

A third trend supporting the senior power thesis is the effects of current agitation. As aging and old age become part of our taken-for-granted world, consciousness of ourselves as aging individuals and of the aged as having real, unmet needs becomes widespread. Those who are not old can sympathize with, and support the legislative interest of, the aged. Also, most middle-aged Americans have at least one if not both parents still living, and if in-laws are considered, there are four old people for whom one might have some responsibility. The "aging constituency," therefore, is far broader than the Gray Lobby.

On the other hand, several compelling arguments lead to the conclusion that senior power peaked during the period 1965–77. For one, to the extent that current legislation removes the most serious barriers to independent and dignified old age for a majority of older Americans, the pressure needed to push for further gains will be dissipated. In many other areas of national life, the past several years have seen a retreat from the commitment to improve the lives of the very poor. As long as most have benefited and are "doing o.k." there is no reservoir of indignation to tap. Thus the paradox that success (of most programs for the aged) often brings defeat (of the impulse for a thoroughgoing restructuring of services). As Hudson and Binstock (1976) stated: "(since the) desirable policy goal (of) a radical redistribution of income to the aged . . . has not been realized . . . (we can) conclude that whatever the power of aging-based organizations, it has not redressed the economic problems of the severely disadvantaged aged (p. 390)."

Dale Vinyard (1976) has noted that most public programs do not radically change the status of the very poor, whose poverty in old age is a continuation of the disadvantages and social neglect of preceding decades. Programs targeted only to the poor have always had less public support (even when children are the recipients) than have programs for those felt to be somewhat more deserving, such as the aged. Vinyard reminds us that public assistance in the Great Depression was favorably perceived as old-age relief, but as the case load has shifted over time in favor of minority women and children, public assistance becomes controversial and stigmatized, and called "welfare" with a negative connotation.

The very respectability conferred by NIA, AoA, the Senate committee and White House conferences, and the legislative gains already accomplished gives credence to the belief that old people are adequately cared for and that for them to ask for more would be slightly greedy. The extent to which leaders of age-based movements have been coopted, brought into the establishment through consultation, also blunts the edge of a radical critique. Nor can academic gerontologists, as recipients of federal grants, be expected to bite the hand that feeds them. From this viewpoint, the Gray Lobby will be occupied in maintaining existing structures (with perhaps more funding), or, at the very least, in forestalling cutbacks (Hudson, 1978). And, in truth, it must be acknowledged that most old people are relatively well off and satisfied; there is no ground swell among the aged for important new initiatives. The 1974 Harris Survey reported that those 65+ and the general public agree that older people are in better financial shape than they were a decade ago.

There is the additional factor of a potential backlash against the aged (Ragan, 1976; Hudson, 1978). As programs single out the older population for special benefits, others receive smaller pieces of the "social service pie." Younger wage earners who must support many of these initiatives through their taxes might feel resentful, and age-based antagonisms between the young and old could become intensified. However, the alternative of supporting one's parents without federal programs is not very attractive and much more expensive (see Chapter 7). If the media persist in emphasizing the "burden" placed on the younger worker, negative attitudes toward the aged can only be aggravated. Again, a universal and life-long array of social services could reduce the sense of strain or relative deprivation of any one age group.

Another argument against the emergence of senior power takes note of the great diversity among the aged (Ragan and Davis, 1978) that has been alluded to throughout this book, and which may be the most distinguishing characteristic of today's old people. There is, for example, the range of income that separates white married males from unrelated Black females; or the subcultural variations in the last cohorts to contain large numbers of foreign-born. Since each old person is the product of six or more decades of unique personal experiences, it is no wonder that we find more within-group diversity among the old than among the young. There are few issues that can unite so heterogeneous a body of people, few needs that all can share, and no one philosophical position from which to speak for the aged.

This consideration leads to the final thesis of those who discount the possibility of an age-based political movement. Ours is an "interest group" polity (Binstock, 1972; Hudson and Binstock, 1976), in which contending power blocs limit the gains of any one, and pressures in one direction produce countervailing forces. Not only will an interest group based on old age encourage resistance among other age groups, but old people themselves will have loyalties built up over a lifetime to other special interests. An older voter has a long history of identification with a nationality group, a religious orientation, an economic interest, or an ideological position—none of which may coincide with age-based politics. The interests of old people, then, will conflict with those of other groups seeking public services, and the interests of old people are not consistent within the age group—indeed, precisely the opposite appears to be the case (Hudson, 1978). Only if the majority of old people were equally and severely disadvantaged by virtue of their age would we anticipiate their developing the consciousness of the kind that is essential to a mass movement.

To summarize, although the aged have been favored in political policy, largely because of widespread public acceptance of their claims, there are many reasons to believe that their power will be considerably diminished in the future. Senior Power will most likely be directed to maintaining current levels of support and service. Were age-based politics to be pursued to their logical conclusion, the question of poverty and the lifelong conditions leading to it would have to be addressed, and there is no evidence that this is the direction in which our nation is moving at this time. If old people follow the public trend, but at a more conservative level, we can hardly expect them to be the source of a radical shift in American values. This is what makes the Gray Panthers so newsworthy. It may also be the case that incoming cohorts of old people will be more politically cohesive and demanding, especially those whose political consciousness was forged in the 1960s, but they are a long way from being old and much may happen to their cohort in the meantime.

Research Exercises

1. The Gray Panthers, 3700 Chestnut Street, Philadelphia, Pa., 19104, will put you in touch with the "pack" in your area for *participant observation* of grass-roots political activity. From your experience with the Panthers write an essay on organizing the elderly.

2. Using *library sources,* especially historical records of the 1930s, reconstruct the origins of old-age movements in the United States.

3. *Interview* local political leaders regarding their views of the older voter's needs and interests, and on the question of age as a criterion for office holding.

4. *Review* the political science *literature* for evidence of age-based political movements in other industrial societies.

Discussion Questions

In a mock convention, debate the planks in the platform of the Senior Power party for 1982.

What are the advantages of a seniority system in allocating legislative positions?

Will the old people of 2000–2020 (who were reaching political maturity in the late 1960s) be less conservative than previous cohorts of older voters?

Are there potential dysfunctions to legislation that is targeted to particular age groups?

9

The Family in
Later Life

Perspectives

The family life of old people has been studied by a variety of researchers: demographers, anthropologists, social scientists in the field of marriage and the family, gerontologists in general, and most recently, historians. Because family life typically covers the life course and involves two or more generations, it is an important area for the study of historical change and of the interplay between personal biographies and social forces—all the elements of cohort analysis. As Riley (1976, 1978) has pointed out, the aggregate behavior of cohort members constitutes change. If there were no differences in the life course of successive generations, there would be no change. Yet cohort members are themselves influenced by events occurring in the world at large that impinge on their lives and affect the timing of role entry and exit. Marriage, fertility, migration, and mortality are primary demographic processes, and they are also the very stuff of family life.

In simple societies, in which kinship is the basis of most social relationships, family status and roles become tantamount to social status and roles. This has led many to contend that the position of the elderly in those societies was not problematic, but even somewhat exalted since the head of a family could command deference and care from juniors. However, "elders" were not necessarily ancient, and the period of caretaking would be relatively short. Nor is age-based authority without strain, especially if a son must wait for a father's death before achieving full adult status (as is the case in rural societies even today).

The past two hundred years of American and English history are referred to by many as the "good old days" when old people were well cared for by loving, extended families—Goode's (1963) "classical family of Western nostalgia." As we now know, the position of the elderly was far from assured, and the multigeneration family was a fleeting phenomenon (Demos, 1965). There is little reason to believe that old people were better cared for within the family than they are today, or that modern offspring are more uncaring of their parents than were those of the eighteenth or nineteenth centuries (but see Fischer, 1977). Once family size and average life expectancy are taken into account, the status of old people may not have deteriorated as much as popular belief would have it.

There is, however, a very great difference between family life in agricultural as contrasted with industrial societies, and the changes probably began well before the rise of factories (Shorter, 1975). In many respects, these shifts can be considered losses for the elderly, but there is also evidence that people of all ages are positively attached to the new patterns of courtship and marriage, and independent households. Although there is much controversy over the definition of "modernization," and over whether or not the concept refers to societal level phenomena or mental states or both, and how it relates to industrialization and urbanization, *ideal types*, or broadly characterized descriptions, of two contrasting family systems are used here: the traditional and the modern, roughly correlated with the transition from agricultural to industrial economies (but see P. Laslett [1976] for the argument against referring to a "before" and "after").

The ramifications of the Industrial Revolution for the family and household are extensive. Let us first distinguish *household*, the number of persons who share a residence, from the *family*, those who consider themselves to be economically and emotionally dependent upon one another by virtue of a consanguine (linked by blood) or conjugal (yoked by the artificial bond of marriage) relationships. The traditional family of agricultural societies is often pictured as one in which nuclear units remain embedded in a consanguine kinship group, frequently sharing a household or living near one another. The *modern* family, on the other hand, is ideally depicted as the conjugal pair with dependent children in an independent household, bound to kin by voluntary ties of affection.

There is increasing evidence from historians of the family that household structure in this country and some parts of Europe has not drastically changed over the past two hundred years. Rather, when adults other than the married pair were recorded as household members, these were not necessarily elder kinfolk, but were much more likely to be lodgers, servants, or apprentices (B. Laslett, 1973). If an older relative was in the household, this was not a long-term arrangement, given the typical life expectancies; that is, a widowed father or mother would join the house hold for a few years prior to his/her death.

In general, modernization is accompanied by a reduction of consanguinality, with a concomitant enhancement of conjugality (Goode, 1963). The nuclear family, which is relatively isolated from other families, also undergoes a qualitative change; it has turned inward, with the couple and their children seeking emotional gratification from one another. Other family members are cast outside this little world of privatized domesticity.

Crucial to this conjugal exclusiveness is the ability to choose a mate according to highly personal criteria—thus "romantic love" and relative freedom in the matter of mate selection. Arranged or family-based marriage choices as an element of parental power are no longer necessary: there is little family property to be concerned about, and alliance-making is not required for civil order.[1] Social placement is more achieved than ascribed, and the couple expect more from marriage than economic security, sexual access, or just getting along. Although parents attempt to control their children's exposure to potential marriage partners—by choosing schools, neighborhoods, and churches; instilling expectations and values; and exercising veto privilege in extreme cases—this is difficult to accomplish when young people enjoy as much physical mobility as they do today. One might say that the automobile not only changed the location of courting behavior but effectively diminished parental power in this crucial area. Today's parents are, however, tomorrow's old people, and today's young courters will be tomorrow's parents—the freedom we seek in young adulthood is not without its cost in later years.

In essence, then, the Industrial Revolution reduced the influence of kinship in many crucial respects. In the early stages of industrial development, the extended family was an important source of job information, child care, resource pooling, and selective mobility (Hareven, 1978). The extended household was also characteristic of many first- and second-generation immigrant families in America. Even though most immigrants had emigrated unmarried while still in their late adolescence and young adulthood, they retained expectations of consanguine obligations. Economic circumstances further reinforced the tendency to share households, while affording care of the young and ill, and providing an emotional

---

[1] An interesting exception that proves the rule is among the very wealthy, where considerations of property and prestige are still very important, and where marriage choices may be controlled by parents.

"home" to the recently uprooted and their offspring caught between two cultures. But this, too, was a temporary phenomenon, and by the third generation most of these families were indistinguishable from the historical norm of nuclear family life. The very poor, however, typically maintain multigeneration households for financial and emotional support.

The history of the family has thus far been discussed in most part in terms of intergenerational relationships—the links between parents and children at the end of the life course. This is what the general public usually refers to in assessing changes in the family of later life, often with reference to "abandonment" or even the "dumping" of elderly relatives. But there is another aspect to the family life of old people: an extended period of postparental togetherness. This is a relatively recent development, partly caused by increased life expectancy of both men and women, by generally earlier ages at first marriage (until very recently), and by lower fertility and closer child spacing, both of which are consequences of lowered infant mortality and improved contraception methods.

Taken together, these trends have resulted in a couple's having their two or three children in the first decade of marriage, so that child-rearing is completed while both are in their late forties or early fifties, with at least a decade of joint survival ahead of them. In the earlier part of this century, it was highly unlikely that both parents would survive the departure of the last child. Today, even allowing for the large families of the Baby Boom (1947–1957), the youngest child will have left home when the parents are under age 55. At ages 60–64, the great majority of men and women are still married and living alone together. This is truly a revolutionary change, with consequences that are discussed later in this chapter. The important point is that the family life of old people is much more a matter of their independent marriage relationship than it is of their dealing with other kin, including adult offspring, and this intergenerational autonomy persists even when the marriage is terminated through death.

Current Scene

THE AGED FAMILY

In this section we examine the marital status and living arrangements of old people. The older population is composed of married couples, the never-married, and the divorced and widowed. Where one lives and the relationship to others in the household both vary by marital status. Being old seems to exaggerate the effects of being married or not, and marital status appears to intensify the effects of aging. By this is meant that in

Table 9–1. Marital Status by Age and Sex: 1950–1990, in Per Cents

	Male		Female	
	55–64	*65+*	*55–64*	*65+*
		1950		
Single	8.9	8.0	7.2	8.0
Married				
(spouse present)	79.2	63.3	62.8	34.3
Widowed	7.1	23.6	25.5	55.3
Divorced	2.1	2.2	2.2	0.7
		1975		
Single	6.5	4.7	5.1	5.8
Married				
(spouse present)	81.8	77.3	66.7	37.6
Widowed ⎫	4.0	13.6	20.3	52.5
Divorced ⎭	4.5	2.5	5.3	2.6
		1990		
Single	4.4	5.9	4.5	6.3
Married				
(spouse present)	85.1	73.0	70.4	35.1
Widowed	10.5	21.1	25.1	58.6
Divorced				

Adapted from Table 6–1, p. 46, in Siegel, Jacob S., "Demographic Aspects of Aging and the Older Population in the United States," Current Population Reports, Special Studies, Series P–23, No. 59, May, 1976. United States Department of Commerce. Bureau of the Census, United States Printing Office, Washington, D.C.

old age it makes a great difference whether one is married or not, perhaps more so than at any other stage. Let us look at the data and suggest some of the implications.

Marital Status. Table 9–1 compares marital status by sex and age for 1950 and 1975, and provides similar data predicted for 1990.

The differences by sex in Table 9–1 are striking. The great majority of older men are married, and most old women are widowed. Although the proportions married for both sexes increased between 1950 and 1975, by about 3–4 per cent in the age group 55–64, the change after age 65 was dramatically different: an increase of 14 per cent in married men compared with an increase of only 3 per cent for women. Projections to 1990 show a decline in the proportions still married at age 65 +, possibly reflecting the high divorce rates for those marriage cohorts.

The sex difference in marital status increases with age. Examining the data for 1975, for example, the totals for those 65 + are averages of two very different subgroups:

Table 9–2.

	65–74	75+
Males:		
Married	83.9	70.0
Widowed	8.8	23.3
Females:		
Married	49.0	23.4
Widowed	41.9	69.4

Adapted from Table 6–1, p. 46, in Siegel, Jacob S., "Demographic Aspects of Aging and the Older Population in the United States," Current Population Reports, Special Studies, Series P–23, No. 59, May, 1976. United States Department of Commerce, Bureau of the Census, United States Government Printing Office, Washington, D.C.

These figures reflect three more basic demographic realities: the longer life expectancy of women, the tendency for husbands to be several years older than their wives, and differential rates of remarriage. More females survive to older ages, and most will have been married to men two to five years their senior. The consequences of this are that most old men will have a living spouse, and that most old women will not. To add to the marital imbalance, in 1971, for example, remarriage rates for men 65 + were seven times those of comparably aged women. Older men are a scarce commodity on the marriage market, and have the advantage, as do men of any age, of being able to marry women considerably younger than themselves. Old women, like young ones, are more constrained in the choice of partner. A woman's value on the marriage market is typically determined by her physical attractiveness (especially youthful beauty), a quality that tends to diminish with age. A male's value, however, is more closely related to his ability to provide, which often increases with age. Even in old age, when their income may be halved, men are still desirable mates.

In Chapter 4 the possibility was raised that female death rates might become more similar to those of males, which would decrease somewhat the excess of older women. Age differences between men and women at first marriage have also narrowed (Presser, 1976). But the 1990 Census Bureau projections in Table 9–2 do not indicate a major change in the almost diametrically opposite proportions of married compared to widowed men and women 65 +

Old people who are married differ from those who are not along a number of other dimensions. Persons with poorer health, lower income, and lesser resources of all kinds have lower life expectancies than the more affluent, and their marriages, on the average, are less stable or satisfying. Older divorced and widowed persons are more likely to have financial and health problems as well as the experience of loneliness. As noted in Chapter 7, the median income for unrelated individuals 65 + in 1976 was less than half of those married, and unrelated individuals are two to three times more likely than family heads to have incomes below the poverty line. Many of these are women whose husbands were never fully covered by Social Security, or who receive partial benefits as survivors of workers with low lifetime earnings.

Conversely, those still married are younger, healthier, and wealthier, with higher levels of morale and life satisfaction than the nonmarrieds. This frequent finding of a relationship between marital status and well-being, as with so many facts of older life, requires closer examination. Not all widowed people are unhappy, for example; much depends on the quality and length of the marriage, and how soon after the death of a spouse the person is questioned. It is also possible that it is not marriage itself but younger age, better health, and higher income of the married that account for their well-being. When these variables were controlled statistically, morale differences between married and widowed older white women disappeared (Morgan, 1976).

Marital Interaction. Recognizing that older couples will be a highly selected group of people whose marriages have not dissolved, and that most have been married to the same person for four or more decades, how do older couples compare with both younger couples or themselves at earlier periods of the life course? An extensive literature describes variations in marital happiness according to the stage of the family life cycle (indeed, there is a sizable literature simply defining these stages). By most accounts, couples in the "empty nest" display levels of marital satisfaction that are comparable to that of newlyweds. Stated differently, couples with children at home, especially preschoolers and teenagers, appear less satisfied with life and their marriage than do those without children at home. Children place a strain on resources, on energies, and on communication between husband and wife (Miller, 1976). If the parents survive the twenty-plus years of child rearing, it is possible that their relationship has been strengthened by the challenges and shared experiences. The positive feelings of postparental couples could also be a product of duration in the role: that is, the more of one's life experience an individual shares with another, the greater is the investment in maintaining the relationship and in perceiving it as successful or pleasurable—to admit otherwise would bring into question all the prior commitments to the role (Spanier, Lewis, and Cole, 1975).

We must be careful in assessing most of these studies since the data are cross-sectional—people at different life stages are interviewed at one time—rather than longitudinal—the same individuals reinterviewed at different time periods. We do not really know whether or not a contemporary young couple will, in their old age, resemble the elderly of today. Each cohort experiences a different slice of history at particular moments in the life course. Expectations of marriage and of the roles within it have undergone secular change, so that the young couple are entering a relationship that they may define in terms different from those who married in the early part of this century. Then, too, it is possible that within a marriage, roles and values are renegotiated at various points; we should not assume that the relationship continues for fifty years without change. Among the changes noted by researchers are a greater tolerance of the partner, enhanced ability to cope with problems, and an increased commitment to the partnership—another example of the effects of duration in the role and dissonance reduction. It is also true, statistically, that the longer a marriage has lasted, the lower is the probability of divorce.

As parenting responsibilities terminate, companionate activities increase. In the period between the leaving of the last child and the onset of retirement, most couples are under less financial and emotional strain than they were in the preceding decades, which probably accounts for their enhanced feelings of satisfaction in life and in their marriage. A growing body of research reports a "coming together in the middle years" (Livson, 1976), which extends through the remainder of marriage. What this refers to is a convergence of psychological traits between older men and women in general, but especially within the marriage. Freed from the requirements of parenthood and occupational advancement, wives and husbands can relax the more rigid sex-role prescriptions of their earlier life together and respond to the other impulses of self that had been defined as inappropriate to those major life tasks. Wives and husbands come to share a similar set of personality characteristics, wives expressing greater assertiveness, and husbands expressing greater nurturance (Neugarten, 1968; Lowenthal et al., 1975; Gutmann, 1976). Such a convergence —often referred to as *androgyny*, or the expression of both masculine and feminine traits—has been found to be associated with adaptability and mental health in later life (as well as at earlier stages). If the current reexamination of sex-role stereotypes leads to a looser definition of sex-appropriate behaviors at all ages, perhaps more individuals will come to old age with higher levels of satisfaction in their marriage and life as a whole. The earlier time in life at which the major tasks of mothers and fathers is completed could have profound implications for theories of psychosocial development through the life course.

Sexuality. Another aspect of intimate relationships in later life (not necessarily limited to the married), which has received little consideration until very recently, is sexuality. That older people are interested in sex often comes as a surprise to those who have been socialized to perceive sexuality in the context of youthful beauty and energy. In general, sexual activity declines gradually over the course of a marriage, but most people with partners can remain active and interested into their seventh and eighth decades (Rubin, 1972). The need for physical closeness, caressing, and other display of intimacy may even become elevated in old age; the capacity, however, frequently declines. The greater barrier is a shortage of male partners at older ages.

Since current cohorts of old women contain many who were socialized to a fairly restrictive model of sexual behavior, sexual deprivation may not be a major problem. Incoming cohorts, however, will have had an entirely different experience of sexuality throughout their lives, leading some experts (Otto, 1969) to predict increased homosexuality among older women, or some form of polygyny (one man with several female partners). On the other hand, Cleveland (1977) sensibly notes that a model of sexuality based on the behavior of young people could be inappropriate for elderly lovers, and that the publicity given to sexuality in later life may be setting up impossible standards, which further inhibits old people.

In summary, the lives of those still married in old age can be emotionally and sexually satisfying, and, for many, the best time of their lives. For the nonmarried—the divorced and widowed and single—old age often brings additional deprivations, many of which are illustrated in the following sections.

Family Status. Family status is a census classification referring to the relationship of respondents to those with whom they live. In 1976, over 83 percent of older men and almost 58 percent of women 65+ were "in families" as head, spouse of head, or as another relative. Almost 16 percent of the men and slightly over 41 percent of women were *primary individuals,* in a household of their own. Fewer than 1 percent of either men or women were *secondary individuals* in a household with nonkin. Approximately 5 percent—higher for women, lower for men—of all persons 65+ were inmates of institutions in 1976 (see Chapter 6 for the probabilities of being institutionalized at some time in old age).

Family status has undergone a marked shift in the last fifteen years.

Table 9–3 shows significant changes in family status for both men and women. For the men the major change has been a decrease of those living with other relatives (typically an adult daughter) and a comparable increase in those living as head of family. The shifts for females are more extensive and varied; the proportion in families decreased, mostly in the category of "living with others" (a 6 percent drop, as was true of men), and the percentage of "primary individuals" increased (7 percent as compared to 1 percent for the men). In other words, the family status of men as heads of households has been enhanced over time, and that of women as

Table 9–3. Family Status of Persons 65+, in 1965 and 1975, by Sex (in per cents)

	1965		1975	
	Male	*Female*	*Male*	*Female*
In families:	80.3	62.9	79.8	56.1
Head	71.3	10.7	76.1	8.5
Wife of head	—	33.3	—	35.0
Other relative	9.0	18.9	3.7	12.7
Primary individual	13.9	30.6	14.8	37.3
Secondary individual	2.3	2.2	1.2	1.2
Inmate of an institution	3.5	4.3	4.2	5.3

Adapted from Table 6–3, p. 48, Siegel, Jacob S., "Demographic Aspects of Aging and the Older Population in the United States," Current Population Reports, Special Studies, Series P–23, No. 59, May, 1976. United States Department of Commerce, Bureau of the Census, United States Printing Office, Washington, D.C.

"primary individuals" has increased. Neither are to be found in the household of adult offspring in the proportions of only fifteen years ago. These trends are better understood when placed in conjunction with the data on living arrangements.

Living Arrangements. As shown in Table 9–4, the major change is in the proportions of older women living alone. Although some people may see this development as a sign of loosened family bonds (if not outright rejection), the evidence is quite clear that these living arrangements are preferred by both the older women and their children. In 1977, the percentage of women 65+ living alone increased to almost 40 percent, and the proportion living with someone else declined by almost 2 per cent.

Most of the elderly who live alone are female "unrelated individuals," a category whose median annual income in 1977 was $3,412. This means that half of these women receive less than that amount. Housing choices will be somewhat limited even for those with incomes up to $8,000. It is the oldest, poorest, and often frailest women who eventually make a home with a relative; and they will present certain difficulties for those who assume their care. The wonder is not that so few aged parents share a home with an adult child, but that so many do not. The resilience of old widows is remarkable. Where so much research has demonstrated the link between morale/life satisfaction and income, health, and marital status, many of these widowed, ill, and impoverished women survive, and do so with great dignity.

It is nonetheless better, by all the indices of well-being, to be married and living with spouse as head of house. The nonmarried who remain as

Table 9–4. Living Arrangements of the Population 55+ by Age and Sex: 1965 and 1975 (in per cent)

	Male			Female		
	55–64	65–74	75+	55–64	65–74	75+
1965						
In Households	97.5	97.5	93.6	98.4	97.4	92.0
Living alone	7.0	11.7	15.7	15.5	27.9	29.9
Spouse present	80.3	75.3	54.0	63.8	43.3	19.0
Living with						
someone else	10.2	10.5	23.9	19.1	26.1	43.1
Not in Households	2.5	2.5	6.4	1.6	2.6	8.0
1975						
In Households	98.1	97.1	92.6	98.8	97.5	90.0
Living alone	7.6	12.1	18.2	17.4	32.9	40.6
Spouse present	80.7	79.6	63.3	66.1	46.2	20.1
Living with						
someone else	9.7	5.4	11.2	15.3	18.4	29.3
Not in Households	1.9	2.9	7.4	1.2	2.5	10.0

Adapted from Table 6–2, p. 48, in Siegel, Jacob S., "Demographic Aspects of Aging and the Older Population in the United States," Current Population Reports, Special Studies, Series P–23, No. 59, May, 1976. United States Department of Commerce, Bureau of the Census, United States Printing Office, Washington, D.C.

heads of household are somewhat better off than those who are "other relatives," at least in terms of mortality (Kobrin and Hendershot, 1977).

To the degree that happiness in marriage is related to general satisfaction or morale in later life, the widowed and divorced will score low. This affects the woman more than the man, since the marriage has probably occupied a greater part of her life span (Lee, 1978). Moreover, the generally lower incomes of widows, even those who have worked, places them at a disadvantage relative to widowers (Atchley, 1975). Thus, even though the lonely widower is an object of sympathy and compassion, he has greater material resources upon which to draw than does the widow.

It is in this context that the data on living arrangements are to be interpreted; not as a loosening of intergenerational ties but as a strengthening of the independence of the older women.

INTERGENERATIONAL RELATIONSHIPS

One of the effects of longer life expectancy is an increase in the prevalence of three- and even four-generation families. An individual in her/his early fifties is almost as likely as not to have at least one surviving parent and one married child (with the possibility of at least one grandchild). The force of kinship may have declined in terms of obligations to share resources, but the sheer number and variety of intergenerational relationships that must be juggled simultaneously over extended periods has probably increased.

There has also been an historical shift in the life stage at which these family responsibilities are concentrated: from early to late middle age. The aging parents of adult children are themselves the offspring of ancient parents, one of whom could survive well into an eighth decade. Although the proportion of older Americans in general has expanded, the greatest rate of increase is at the oldest age levels: the percentage 85+ is growing at a faster rate than the older population as a whole. Although only 12 percent of those age 62–63 in a national sample (Social Security Administration, 1969) had a living parent, this percentage is expected to increase. Census Bureau projections of a *family dependency ratio*, i.e., the number of persons 80+ relative to those 60–64 shows a somewhat erratic pattern: From 49:100 in 1975 to 73:100 in 2000, dropping to 45:100 in 2020 before jumping to 70:100 in 2030. These ratios are simply the reverse of birthrates—parents per children rather than children per couple, but they are all very much higher than the 21–28:100 ratio that prevailed up to 1950 (Siegel, 1976, p. 56).

One implication of these data is that kinship ties may be as complex as ever, though in different ways. Children today might not have an elderly relative in the household, but they will probably have known all four of their grandparents and several great grandparents, and for a longer part of their lives than previously. The children's parents will also have to play the role of "child" for a considerable span of adulthood. And more old people will be able to observe the growth of grandchildren and great-grandchildren. In a very important sense, kinship ties are far from dead in the contemporary family; changed in quality, perhaps, but greater in quantity.

The study of intergenerational relationships in later life is, therefore, far more complicated than is often assumed. There are aged offspring with ancient parents, middle-aged children of aging parents, young adults with two sets of older relatives, and children dealing with three senior generations. Furthermore, there are important cohort differences in the composition of each family generation (for example, fewer foreign born) and in life course experience (education, mobility, and health status), which make generalizations extremely hazardous. But there are some clear trends and other reasonable predictions that can be made about intrafamily relationships.

Aged Offspring and Ancient Parents. The growing population of octogenarians will be composed primarily of widowed women. At ages 75+ there are now only 56 men for every 100 women, and census predictions are for a continued decline in this sex ratio into the next century. For this reason many gerontologists see the problems of aging as important issues for the Women's Movement; or, more precisely, that problems of older women should be a major focus of gerontology. In addition, responsibility for the care of an aging parent has typically been placed upon daughters and daughters-in-law as part of their kin-keeping tasks in the division of family labor. Not only are women felt to be "naturally" more adept at interpersonal relationships and nurturance, and to have more time, but to be closer to their parents, especially their mothers, than are sons. Because of the constancy of the wife/mother role, there probably has been less variation in life experience between adjacent generations of women than of men, so that it is logical to expect women to share the basic orientations and concerns that make coexistence comfortable.

Thus, a retired or widowed daughter caring for her very old mother (or father) will not be uncommon in the future; a far cry, however, from the youngest daughter of Victorian fiction who renounced marriage and a life of her own to care for a widowed father. It is possible that the doubly widowed household affords greater financial security and companionship to the two women. Although many mothers and daughters will have enjoyed the kind of relationship that makes it possible to share a household in old age, others will not, but will do so out of a sense of duty or lack of alternatives. We cannot infer from this, or any other living arrangement of the aged, any conclusions regarding the quality of relationships.

Short of the shared household are a variety of other helping relationships and living options. Most old people, as has been noted, live independently, alone or with a spouse, and continue to do so until it becomes impossible, for either physical or financial reasons, to maintain an independent residence. But the probability of illness and accidents increases with age. Most offspring of very old parents are aware of the need to keep in frequent contact with their parents, and are prepared to interrupt their own activities in case of an emergency. There is evidence that children of the very old do everything possible to *delay* the entry of a failing parent into a nursing home; all alternatives are tried before institutionalization (Riley and Foner, 1968). It is usually only after some dramatic change in the health of the old person or in the children's ability to care for the parent that a long-term care facility is considered. The absence of less drastic and more affordable alternatives may prevent further delay in institutionalization.

Caring for a frail, often incontinent, or emotionally unstable parent is extremely trying; the wonder is that so many offspring, themselves elderly, attempt to do so for so long. And many do *not* make the attempt. Hospital personnel who must find suitable living places for discharged elderly patients often complain of neglect and abuse in the home of relatives, who nonetheless resist other types of placement (see also Steinmetz,

1978). That the average age of nursing home residents is over 80 and that their health status is so precarious is testimony to the attempts that are made to maintain old people in the community. Unfortunately, not all of this effort stems from filial affection. Financial considerations, such as the cost of nursing homes or hopes of receiving an inheritance in return for care will influence the choice of where the older person is placed, and the children's home may *not* be the best choice. Ironically, the nursing home from which offspring claim they are saving their parents might actually provide a higher level of care in some cases.

Middle-Aged Children and Aging Parents. A different set of circumstances guide the relationships between those at midlife (late forties and early fifties) and their young-old parents, many of whom are still living with a spouse and most of whom are in relatively good health.

Much attention has recently been focused on the middle aged. Described by one gerontologist as the "caught generation" (Vincent, 1972), those at midlife are portrayed as being pressured from all sides: from within by the first intimations of their growing old, from above through increased concern over their parents, and from below with the expense of educating and the emotions of launching their children. To some extent the midlife crisis of the middle-class male can be seen as peculiar to the cohort born in the 1920s. It is no wonder that fathers of relatively large families, sons and grandsons of surviving elders, at the peak of career commitment, and aware of their need to prepare for retirement, feel overburdened!

Middle-aged women today, on the other hand, often feel underburdened. Their child-rearing tasks completed, with the expectation of living three or more decades, many of these women are taking advantage of the opportunities generated by the Women's Movement to move into the world of work or school. As they eagerly step out to "do their own thing" at last, they may find their freedom severely curtailed by claims on their attention from an ailing or recently widowed parent or from an adult child returned to the nest following some personal setback.

Much evidence from survey research indicates that the middle aged are, on the whole, less happy or satisfied with their lives than people at other ages, and more likely to complain that they lack the time to do things they would like to (Campbell, Converse, and Rodgers, 1976). However, once they are retired, with their children gone, many will complain of not having enough to do. Role strain and slack are built into the age structure of work, earnings, leisure, and family responsibilities, all of which vary by sex and social class.

An imbalance and potential conflict between the demands placed on the worker and the resources available, results in a *life cycle squeeze* (Oppenheimer, 1974; Estes and Wilensky, 1978). This occurs earlier for blue-collar workers, since they reach occupational peaks sooner than those in white-collar jobs, and is often an inducement for working-class wives to enter the labor force.

Whether one is over- or underdemanded in terms of earnings and energies is often related to measures of morale. The periods of greatest stress occur when there are preschoolers in the family (which is also when earnings are low, especially if the wife had worked before leaving her job to care for the children) and, again, when teenagers are about to be launched. For most couples, as noted earlier, the departure of the children brings a dramatic increase in parental satisfaction and revitalization of the marital relationship. One exception to this pattern is the middle-aged mother who has invested all of her emotional energies in the maternal role and becomes severely depressed (Bart, 1970). Postparental depression in women, often taken as symptomatic of menopausal malfunction, will probably decline as more women have alternative bases of self-esteem and as the timing of physiological menopause ceases to coincide with the departure of children. Most women today survive their children's leaving quite well, and many report enhanced well-being (Glenn, 1975; Clausen, 1972).

The postparental couple will, however, find themselves increasingly involved with their aging parents, but the context in which this occurs today is very different from what it was even a few decades ago. Today's middle aged are the first cohort of offspring who are fully released from an obligation to provide at least a minimum level of income maintenance and health care to their parents. Conversely, the aged parents are aware that they need not depend upon their children for their basic subsistence. Hess and Waring (1978) contend that intergenerational relationships are in the process of redefinition from obligatory to voluntary, and that what may look to some as a collapse of family bonds could more accurately be considered a strengthening. When ties of affection and caring are maintained out of a mutual wish to do so, these ties should be deeper and more satisfying than when they are sustained only out of duty or necessity that so often leads to resentment. But this is not to say that parent-child relationships in later life will be free of controversy or sacrifice. Nor, clearly, does it mean that each generation lives in semi-isolation from the other.

CONTACTS AND EXCHANGES BETWEEN GENERATIONS

There is an extensive two-way flow of visits and assistance between generations, but we must avoid overstating the consequences of this process. Some writers have hailed the intergenerational exchange network as a confirmation that extended kinship is alive and well in modern societies (Sussman and Burchinal, 1962). Others point to the increasing proportions of people at all ages who live in independent households and interpret within-family exchanges as the least binding of possible kin ties (Hess and Waring, 1978; Gibson, 1972). The volume of visiting and helping is truly impressive, especially since it takes place among family members who typically do not live together, and is essentially voluntary.

Data from various surveys is strikingly similar: over 80 percent of those 65+ have living children or grandchildren, and about 80 percent of these see one of their children at least once a week. The same proportion live within a day's drive from a descendant. We do not, unfortunately, have full information on contacts of parents with *all* offspring, and it is possible that a large number of parent-child pairs do *not* see one another frequently. A small proportion of old people, especially those still in their sixties, have an adult child living in their household, and others, mostly older widowed females, live with an adult child. Both of these cases inflate the data on parent-child contacts when included in overall statistics.

Helping patterns and the exchange of services and goods vary, as might be expected, by the needs and resources of generation members. Among the inner-city elderly of New York, for example, over three fourths of the old people report giving help to their children, and 87 percent report receiving assistance such as gifts, crisis intervention, and help from their children with the chores of daily living (Cantor, 1976). In this sample, the lower the social status, the greater was the reliance on children; and the more disabled the older person, the greater was the aid from children. Black and white percentages were very similar, and the Hispanic aged were most likely to see, telephone, and help their children and to receive help in return. Also, almost half of the Hispanic aged depended solely on kin for their support network, compared to less than two fifths of the elderly whites and blacks.

More typical of the general pattern are the findings from the Harris survey (1975).

The generally high level of assistance from parents to children is supported by evidence from other, more limited studies reviewed by Riley and Foner (1968). Transfers of goods and money from the old to the young are not uncommon, but this varies considerably by age and marital status: married males in their early sixties are often still supporting one or more children who are in the early stages of work and family life. It is difficult to estimate how much money is transferred within the family; gifts may flow from the old to the young in order to avoid estate taxes. On the other hand, older widowed females are very likely to be receiving rather than giving gifts of money. The rule in these exchanges appears to be from the less to the more needy family members. When in need, the majority of old people would call upon kin rather than friends, neighbors, or social agencies. In immediate emergencies, when offspring are not at hand, friends and neighbors are an important resource.

Table 9–5. Ways in Which Public 65+ Say They Help Their Children or Grandchildren (Base: those with children or grandchildren). (In Per Cent)

	White %	Black %
Give gifts	91	75
Help out when someone is ill	68	73
Take care of grandchildren	54	49
Help out with money	45	41
Give general advice on how to deal with some of life's problems	37	62
Shop or run errands	34	33
Fix things around their house, or keep house for them	26	31
Give advice on bringing up children	20	52
Give advice on running a home	19	41
Give advice on jobs/business matters	18	32
Take grandchildren, nieces, or nephews into your home to live with you	15	26

Louis Harris and Associates, *The Myth and Reality of Aging in America*, Washington, D.C.: National Council on the Aging, 1975, p. 77.

The flow of support within a three-generation lineage is likely to be from the middle generation to *both* aged parents and young adult children. Although it is possible, as Sussman, Cates, and Cole (1976) have suggested, that many adult offspring provide care for the aging parent in return for eventual inheritance, accumulated assets can also be depleted through the years of retirement, particularly if skilled nursing is required, leaving little to be inherited. On the other hand, Rosenfeld (1978) reports increasing numbers of elderly leaving money to friends they have made after moving away from their children.

Expectations of support *from* adult children will also vary by such background characteristics as ethnicity and religion. Many contemporary elderly have *extended expectations* (Seelbach and Sauer, 1976) based on their own traditional socialization abroad or in America at the turn of the century. White ethnic elderly have been found to feel resentful at being "abandoned" by their upwardly mobile children (Lopata, 1976), but also unhappy when they are taken into a child's household and treated like a guest (Cosneck, 1970). Among black families, however, extended households are a means of conserving resources for both generations, and appear also to generate less resentment.

Parental caretaking is often perceived as costly on the part of adult children—in terms of time and energy and emotional reserves. Some sacrifice will be required, especially if the aging parent is taken into the household. It is not surprising that members of both generations often express low levels of morale under these circumstances. The prospect of reviving the original dependency relationship, or of reversing it, are probably equally abhorrent, which accounts for the low proportions of middle-aged offspring who express a willingness to take on the primary care of an ailing parent. Nor can the old person be unmoved by the experience of relative helplessness, which could explain the greater reluctance of old men as compared to old women to seek support from children.

Summary. The preferred pattern of intergenerational relationships is "intimacy at a distance" (Shanas, 1973), and by choice. Both parents and offspring are apt to be dissatisfied when they are in forced contact with one another (especially in the same household), and to have higher morale scores when intergenerational exchanges are freely chosen.

Grandparent and Grandchild. The role of grandparent in modern societies has been referred to as a "peculiar noninstitution," an amorphous set of possibilities, varying by race, ethnicity, social class, and age (Clavan, 1978). There are few set norms for the role, and fewer sanctions—if one does not know what a grandparent should do, it is difficult to define a poor performance. Moreover, what might please the child could infuriate the parent. Perhaps even more than the parent/child relationship in later life, the relationship between grandchild and grandparent is voluntaristic and open to idiosyncratic role negotiation. As Troll (1971) has put it: grandparent is becoming an achieved rather than an ascribed status, as role incumbents seek to establish a favored position with the grandchildren, or refuse to perform in any but the most surface manner.

The differentiation between the roles of grandmother and grandfather is hazy. For example, as a class exercise, a group of students in a gerontology course was asked to list their images of the role of grandfather and grandmother. As indicated on the next page, there was little distinction between them. Once one becomes a grandparent, sex-linked expectations for behavior seem to drop away, perhaps partially because of the asexuality that is erroneously generally accorded the old.

These results suggest that although some sex-stereotypical behavior is expected by grandparents, the major perceived differences between grandfathers and grandmothers have largely disappeared.

One reason why normative prescriptions seem to be lacking today is related to the demographic trends that affect so much else in family life. Grandparents of small children are as likely as not to be middle aged, healthy, independent, married, and working, hardly the stereotypical Gramps or Granny. It is the great-grandparent who most closely resembles the traditional image, yet by the time the actual grandparent

Adjectives Used to Characterize the Roles

Grandfather	Grandmother
Same Adjectives	
Proud	Proud
Loving	Loving
Family historian	Family historian
Supportive	Supportive
Loveable	Loveable
Teacher	Teacher
Generous	Generous
Lonely	Lonely
Respected	Respected
Different Adjectives	
Impatient	Stronghold of family
Chauvinistic	Fragile
Eager to please	Most understanding
Considerate	Concerned

reaches that stage, the grandchildren will be much older and more difficult to relate to for many old people (Neugarten and Weinstein, 1964).

There are, however, class and race differences particularly in the role of grandmother. Among blacks and many ethnic groups, a widowed grandmother is an extremely functional family member. In the working class, grandmothers frequently run the household and care for children while other adults in the family are at work. In cases in which the child's mother is a single parent, the role of the grandmother may be crucial. As an unused resource for unmet needs, grandparents could become a major source of child-care assistance and home management to many middle- as well as working-class families (Clavan, 1978).

Although the increasing number of working mothers and single-parent families should create a bull market for grandparents (whose supply has been increasing through early retirements), this resource has been underutilized for a number of reasons. First, many grandparents, particularly those of infants, are very much still engaged in their own family and social life. For another, the generational differences between young women and their aging mothers may lead to conflict over child-rearing practices, or jealousy over the child's attentions. Nor can it be assumed that mothers and daughters are less in conflict than fathers and sons; in the realm of the home, mothers and daughters may find their rivalry deepened. For their part, many grandparents resent being used as captive baby-sitters (Lopata, 1973). Their enjoyment in the role is greater when it is assumed voluntarily than when it is taken for granted. One ambitious scheme that has been proposed would have groups of grandparents providing cooperative nursery care, so that children could have the benefits of peer interaction, and old people without nearby grandchildren could become a major component of the child-care system (Hess, Clavan, and Vatter, 1977). The Foster Grandparent program has shown an encouraging degree of success on its limited one-to-one basis (Saltz, 1971).[2]

A common observation is that grandparents and grandchildren seem to get along better together than either does with the middle generation. Anthropologists have remarked on similar behavior in other societies: in the *avoidance taboos* between adult offspring and in-laws, and in the *joking relationship* between grandchildren and grandparents in situations in which the elders do not reside in the same household or remain as heads of family. It seems that when authority relations must be maintained, the equality implicit in joking is disruptive. Modern grandparents can relax with their grandchildren because they are not in positions of superordination and subordination within a family system. Another related reason why relations are smoother when the middle generation is skipped is suggested by Homans (1961): interaction between members of adjacent statuses (or age strata, in our case) often magnifies the awareness of inequality, whereas that between members of alternate strata is relatively free of acute consciousness of status differences.

It is ironic that at a time when what might be called the "grandparent ratio"—the number of surviving grandparents per child—is at its highest, the role of grandparent remains unstructured and often unfilled. If this is true of grandmothers, it is even more so of grandfathers. Little has been said, or studied, of the grandfather, largely because he does not yet appear to be an important role player in his offspring's family. Most males at older ages are still married and have their own households to oversee, and most men in our society are still brought up to perceive care giving as women's work. One of the very few studies of grandfathers concluded that family relationships are not very important to the morale of old men (Watson and Kivett, 1976).

SPECIAL PROBLEMS OF MINORITY FAMILIES

The difficulties experienced by members of minority groups—especially Blacks and Hispanics—are related to their higher incidence of poverty rather than to special subcultural factors. The relative deprivation of minority aged, as detailed in Chapter 7, is a continuation of earlier patterns of discrimination in employment, housing, and education. Low lifetime earnings, irregular employment, and fewer years in jobs covered by

---

[2] This is a volunteer program in which old people visit, tutor, and play with relatively deprived youngsters.

Social Security all mean lower-than-average benefits in retirement for Blacks and Hispanics. As a consequence, twice the proportion of elderly Blacks and Hispanics, compared to whites 65+, live at or below the poverty line. For unrelated individuals, over half the Black and Hispanic aged are poor, in contrast to less than one third of whites. The mortality rates for nonwhites are such that many minority males do not live long enough to collect their minimal Social Security benefits, but a disproportionately high number of Black men receive disability payments and leave children young enough to collect survivor benefits. Compared with younger members of minority groups, the elderly are much more likely to be poor, and as discussed in Chapter 4, also more apt to be ill, disabled, and homebound than comparably aged whites.

It is possible, however, that discrepancies between white and nonwhite populations become less extreme in old age, i.e., that old age is a great leveler of rank and privilege (Kent, 1971). In contrast, others see the aging Black or Hispanic as a person in "double jeopardy" (Jackson, 1971). These hypotheses were tested by Dowd and Bengtson (1978) on a multiethnic sample. They found that in terms of income and self-reported health, Blacks and Mexican-Americans were doubly disadvantaged, but on variables measuring social contact, increasing age lessened the differences among the ethnic groups. Indeed, Mexican-Americans scored highest on measures of contact with children, grandchildren, and other relatives. Although ethnic differences diminish with age, it is quite possible that the heightened deprivation of the minority elderly in income and health status becomes the impetus for high levels of family contact, as compensatory, adaptive behavior.

The plight of minority elderly is further obscured by the fact that aged Blacks and Hispanics make up a much smaller segment of their populations than do aged whites: about 7 percent of all Blacks, and 4 percent of Hispanics, compared to 11 percent for whites. These figures reflect the higher fertility rates and lower life expectancies of minority group members. Perhaps old age levels some status differences between white and nonwhite, but the deprivations are still more extreme for Blacks and Hispanics, even when all are "in the same boat" of the inner city, as the following comparisons of elderly poor in New York City demonstrate.

The high proportion of the elderly living with others (not spouse) are probably sharing a home with an adult child, a not uncommon arrangement for the poor of any racial or ethnic group. When these multigeneration families are looked at from the standpoint of the junior members, commentators often perceive a "tangle of pathology" by stressing the absence of young male breadwinners and role models. The grandmother who cares for her daughter and grandchildren is portrayed as a matriarch, with the implication that male children are being somehow castrated (or ill equipped for achievement). Yet these same observers often deplore

Table 9–6. Major Demographic Characteristics of Inner City Elderly Respondents, 1970

	Total	White	Black	Spanish
	(N = 1551)	(N = 766)	(N = 580)	(N = 205)
Socioeconomic Status				
Working and lower class	74.7	63.8	85.3	85.3
Income: under $2,500/yr. (est. per capita)	63.8	55.6	71.3	73.6
Occupation: Manual	67.6	57.3	79.4	72.4
Education: 8th grade or less	59.9	50.1	65.3	80.4
Marital Status				
Married	34.3	35.9	29.3	42.6
Widowed	42.0	39.9	45.2	41.1
Never married	13.4	17.3	10.8	6.1
Separated or divorced	10.3	6.8	14.8	10.3
Living Arrangements				
Live alone	39.2	47.4	33.1	26.2
Live with spouse	33.4	34.7	29.0	41.0
Live with others (not spouse)	27.4	17.9	37.9	32.8
Health				
Have health problem(s)	67.3	62.8	72.1	70.6
Self-perceived health as poor	23.8	20.6	25.2	31.4
Incapacity-Index: severely impaired or incapacitated	15.4	13.6	15.5	22.2

Cantor, Marjorie H., "The Configuration and Intensity of the Informal Support System in a New York City Elderly Population: Is Ethnicity a Determining Factor?", paper presented at the 29th Annual Scientific Meetings of the Gerontological Society, New York City, October 14, 1976.

the isolation of the middle-class grandparent and of nuclear families in general.

If we consider the multigeneration family as an adaptation to the reality of poverty and underemployment, it is neither to be deplored nor romanticized. For many, the arrangement will permit a higher standard of living than with separate households, as well as continuity of child care and companionship for the elderly. Indeed, it is often the home of the grandmother to which her daughters and their young children return; females are 30 percent of the total heads of household 65+ among Blacks, as compared with 12 percent for elderly whites.

The more common course for the Hispanic aged is to become a member of the household of a son or daughter (the preference for daughters is not as evident among Hispanics as it is for whites and Blacks). Much has been written and surmised about the respect for elders and family cohesiveness in the Hispanic tradition, but poverty and generational differences in acculturation have taken their toll, and some studies have found the Hispanic elderly isolated and unhappy (even while they are in the household of relatives). It is also important to make a number of distinctions within the Spanish-speaking population: the Mexican-Americans of the Southwest are very different, culturally and in terms of their Americanization experiences, from the Puerto Ricans of the industrial urban Northeast, and both differ from the Cubans in the Southeast and the South American minorities who are scattered throughout the East Coast. There is a stratification system within this population, much of which was learned after immigration, based upon skin color, education, land of origin, and so forth. The experience of aging in these communities will vary accordingly. Similar to white ethnic groups, however, the poor and uneducated among them, clinging to traditional expectations for care that cannot always be fulfilled, will have the lowest morale in old age. Following the lead of the National Council on Black Aged, an Asociacion Nacional Pro Personas Mayores was formed in 1975 to coordinate efforts on behalf of the Spanish-speaking aged. The Asociacion has received AoA support for research and model projects.

Other racial minorities, Native Americans and Asian-Americans, have problems that are peculiar to their history in this country. The extremely low life expectancy of Native Americans, and the generally poor health status of tribal members both young and old, has led to an emphasis on improved medical care and health services for them. This was the primary recommendation of the First National Indian Conference on Aging in 1976 (funded by AoA) and its follow-up, the National Indian Council on Aging. As with so many attempts to alleviate the conditions of Native Americans, the health care program has foundered over definitions of who is an Indian and whether or not the funds should be administered through the tribes or state governments. Thus, only a few provisions of the Health Care Improvement Act (beginning in 1978) will, as things stand, benefit the aging. There is also pressure to see that provisions of the Older Americans Act are fully realized for older Indians, but the states that have large Indian populations also have high proportions of other aged to care for with limited funds.

The Asian-Americans, many of whom have been in this country for several generations, have the same cultural-barrier problem as many Hispanics, especially if they remain within the protective environment of the ethnic enclave in urban centers (Wu, 1975). For the aged, there is the additional impact of social mobility among their children. Although Chinese-American and Japanese-American families in general have higher than median incomes, the elderly among them are often found among the worst-housed and most impoverished inhabitants of the inner city (Carp, 1976). When one realizes the importance of filial piety and ancestor reverence of these cultures, the plight of the aging Asian-American becomes especially poignant. There is, however, some evidence of strong interpersonal dependencies among Japanese-Americans, even in the third generation, while, at the same time, generational economic self-sufficiency is encouraged (Osako, 1976; Leahy, 1977). This combination of emotional and physical closeness with independence in financial matters might account for the notable upward mobility of Japanese-American families.

The poor, and racial minorities in general, are underenumerated in the census and most other survey research designs. Many old people live alone in relatively inaccessible locations. In addition, they are fearful of intruders, do not speak the language of interviewers, and are therefore rarely found on official records. Other poor and minorities are hidden away, as it were, in the homes of relatives whose households often contain a variety of members at different times, so that no firm count of them can be made. If, as is the case for old women especially, one has never worked in a job covered by Social Security, or applied for welfare entitlements, or voted, there may be no record of one's existence.

Prospects: The Future of the Family of Later Life

Demographically, a continuation of secular trends would indicate more postparental couples jointly surviving young old-age. The onset of widowhood will occur later in time, although there will eventually be an increase of widows in the aged population as a whole. But incoming cohorts of old women will have higher educational attainment, longer work lives, and probably higher incomes than women currently 65+; all of these variables are associated with a preference for living alone rather than with a son or daughter. As Senior housing becomes increasingly available, many will choose to live with others of their age in independently maintained apartments. If, in addition, intermediate care facilities are developed and home health services are augmented, most of the elderly will be able to remain in the community until they reach extreme old age. This may require that adult children be ready to assist them, to supervise and select the appropriate setting, and to provide companionship, but in a manner that also permits a measure of independence for both generations.

A number of forces are at work that would lead us to predict a loosening of intergenerational bonds in later life: geographic and social mobility; the differences in cohort experience, life stage, and other shared conditions that evoke a sense of shared fate; the psychological barriers that will always separate those who have been parent and child; and the multiple transitions of later life that each generation experiences at different times, straining the ability to help one another. Above all, Social Security and Medicare, by transferring the responsibility for aged relatives from the family to the wider society, have reduced the need for old people to bargain for care with their offspring. With the services mandated by the Older Americans Act, most old people will be able to secure for themselves what they might have had to ask from their children a few decades ago. While diminishing the necessity for exchanges of goods and services between generations, these trends obviously do not preclude families from enjoying high levels of interaction, if they choose.

Some people believe that the American family is disintegrating because family members are no longer obligated to provide care, except to the very young (and even in this case, day-care centers are perceived as destructive of the middle-class family). We have argued that removing care of the elderly from the emotion-laden uncertainties of family politics could strengthen family bonds. A popular concept among social work professionals is *filial maturity* (Blenkner, 1965)—the ability to become a "dependable resource" for an aged parent without falling into the pattern of reversed roles, thus permitting the old person graciously to accept the dependency relationship. As with so many prescriptions for mental health and development, filial maturity is easier to describe than to attain. But the independence allowed through public programs for income maintenance and health care should promote rather than inhibit this kind of parent/child relationship.

Other social forces that enhance generational ties are built into the socialization process itself: not only being taught to honor thy mother and father but also having the actual experience of learning from them and having them as the first role models of adulthood. Moreover, we have noted the volume of visiting, caring, and exchange that characterize the great majority of American families. There appears to be a very strong sense of shared interests as well as values among members of a family. Few old people with family have been abandoned, although some choose not to have contact with offspring. It is, rather, those without family who are most isolated, impoverished, and likely to be institutionalized. Old men without family ties are more vulnerable to suicide, motor vehicle and pedestrian death, and other accidents than are similarly deprived old women (Gove, 1973). It is certainly possible that the proportion of isolated elderly will increase, because of lessened dependence upon kin and the fact that there will be fewer children per couple. As a potential corrective, many public programs are being vigorously directed at the elderly who live alone in the hopes of preventing their isolation.

Old people with living children typically have higher morale scores than those without, but health and income are even more crucial to happiness in later life. Moreover, much evidence suggests that it is when contact with offspring can be regulated to suit the needs of the older person that satisfaction with the relationship is highest. These are precisely the conditions that will increasingly characterize old age. For those lacking income or good health, the existence of children can be crucial to well-being, but for most old people today, and probably more so in the future, the ability to maintain independent living, both physically and financially, will be the best predictor of satisfaction and morale in later life.

A new set of tasks confronts the middle-aged offspring of aged parents: to act as guides and protectors in dealing with the bureaucracy that now surrounds family life and aging. The children can intervene on behalf of parents, ensure their entitlements, and deal with red tape (Shanas and Sussman, 1977). It is also their lot to manage the terminal illness of a parent. Given the development of heroic efforts to sustain life, and the later ages at which old people face death, decisions must be made by the middle-aged offspring whether to continue or cease such efforts. There is an ironic symmetry here as the child supervises the parent's death in much the same setting as the parent gave life to the child. Although these decisions can bring renewed closeness to family members, they can also become occasions for displays of guilt and grief.

For the minority elderly, problems of life and death are often less philosophical than those facing the white and well-off aged. Above all, the reduction of poverty and isolation must become a primary goal of programs for the aged. But this process should begin much earlier in the family cycle. Any program that enhances the resources of Blacks, Hispanics, Native Americans, and Asian-Americans will be of some help to those now old, but, more importantly, it will increase the possibility of a comfortable old age for incoming cohorts. Unfortunately, there does not now appear to be strong public sentiment for this type of effort; to the contrary, antipoverty programs are being dismantled or reduced in scope. The few minimal initiatives of AoA are simply inadequate for dealing with the root problems of the minority aged, particularly those trapped in the inner cities. For these old people, family networks remain vital to their survival, although younger family members are beset with their own problems and needs.

But where economic necessity does not require familistic orientations, the pattern of intergenerational relationships will increasingly move from an obligatory model to one of voluntary interaction. Trends toward democratization within the modern family, that is, greater equality between husband and wife and between parents and children, based on respect for the individual (of whatever age and sex), suggest that genuine affection will replace duty as the basis for continued contact and exchanges in later life. In this sense, intrafamily bonds should be strengthened for being freely chosen and maintained.

Research Exercises

1. The new field of family history has produced data leading to a revision of commonly accepted ideas of the family life of old people. Review the material on intergenerational relationships and the transfer of property.

2. Interview students who grew up with an older relative in the household. Describe the positive and negative aspects of this arrangement.

3. One extensive sociological study of widowhood is Helena Znaniecki Lopata's *Widowhood in an American City*. Select some key questions from this study to replicate on a sample of widows in your community. How do your findings support or qualify the data from Chicago in the early 1970s as described in Lopata's book?

Discussion Questions

Is intergenerational conflict inevitable?

What are the responsibilities of adult children toward their aged parents?

Is polygyny a viable alternative for old people?

What changes do you foresee for family life in the future? How will you bring up your children and what do you expect from them?

10

Involvement
and
Isolation

———◆———

The family is only one of a number of social networks into which an older person can be integrated. Sociologists use the term *primary group* to describe face-to-face relationships involving regular interaction between participants who are able to display a range of personality traits. Primary groups are contrasted to *secondary groups*, with social systems that are more impersonal, temporary, and narrowed to a limited set of transactions. Behavior in primary groups is typically *expressive*, ie.., engaged in for the satsisfactions of doing so, with no other end in mind. Secondary group interaction is considered *instrumental*, i.e., used as a means to some more distant goal.

It is often thought that old age brings a respite from instrumental role playing. Certainly, retirement represents the loss of a secondary group attachment, but since the work place was also a source of comradeship (which many retirees miss as much as their paycheck), there may actually be no great change in the balance between primary and secondary group involvement. Many activities do not decline with age: political and religious engagement show little reduction until advanced old age. The daily transactions of shopping and dealing with providers of services continue as before. Indeed, being old can increase the number of instrumental contacts with bureauccracies and their personnel. What does change with retirement and the empty nest is the amount of time available for either instrumental or expressive activities of one's own choice. We explore these possibilities in this chapter and the next.

In Perspective

Because primary groups are ideally characterized by intimacy and acceptance, they are felt to be essential to well-being and similar variables (happiness, satisfaction, mental health, and morale). As noted in the case of the family, which is *the* basic primary group, contact with children and grandchildren is an important ingredient of life satisfaction for old people but not an essential one. Income and health status are, in most studies, better predictors of positive feelings in old age. An additional factor in sustaining high levels of morale is the existence of what are called "informal support systems," sources of companionship and care in addition to family, such as the neighborhood, friendship networks, and *voluntary associations.*

Throughout human history, as the model of sociocultural development in Chapter 2 illustrates, most people's lives unfolded in bands, extended kinship groups, or villages. The integration of old people into the broader community was probably no more problematic than that of other family members; indeed, the line between private life and public participation was minimal (B. Laslett, 1973). The web of kinship was reinforced by the exchange of marriage partners and gifts, which bound families together in alliances of friendship and support. Thus, whether by virtue of their ascribed family status, or by the obligations of reciprocity from others, older people were usually firmly embedded in community relationships. But, again, we must remember that relatively few people lived to advanced old age, and that their treatment varied by the subsistence base of the group.

In historical times, village life—often idealized—was generally conducted in view of others, with little age segregation, and was based on extensive patterns of mutual aid. Within the large cities of early industrial societies, people from the same village would cluster in a neighborhood; and in the contemporary metropolis we find ethnic areas or "urban villages" (Gans, 1962) in which traditional relationships are preserved to some degree. As with so much of the past, however, these arrangements are often inaccurately romanticized: immigrants from abroad and rural migrants were not always able to provide for their aged relatives or to command care from their own offspring. Zimmerman (1976) reported on the numbers of aged in New York's poorhouses in the nineteenth century. And we need only look at the rolls of welfare recipients today to realize that ethnic and religious obligations to care for one's own are not always honored at either the family or community level, and perhaps never were, even in the "good old days" before industrialization. The breakup of the medieval order of Western Europe created a large enough class of vagrant aged to make them the primary objects of the first Poor Laws, and what subsequently became known as poorhouses were largely populated by old people. The movement of peasants off the land, lack of employment, and family breakdown, all left old people penniless and isolated in the sixteenth century as surely as in the nineteenth or twentieth centuries.

We really know very little about the nonfamily primary group activities of old people in the past. It is difficult enough to reconstruct family relationships (P. Laslett, 1976); other records are more perishable. Religious organizations, workers' guilds, and close friendships must have offered our forebears additional social supports, but we do not know how these affiliations varied by age or what meanings were attached to them. It is likely that guilds and religiously based charities originated in part to care for their own, including widows and other needy aged. But, if care of old people was legally a family responsibility, non-kin had no great obligation to assist. In any event, there is no compelling evidence that old people today are more bereft of social services than in the past. What has changed is the auspices of support from private charity to public programs. Nor is the city a more isolating environment than rural areas; for all of their impersonality and crowding, urban centers are at least full of other people, shops, and a variety of media.

Current Scene

The availability of social networks and their utilization depend upon a host of other factors. Where one lives, as well as one's health and mobility, living arrangements, financial standing, and family contacts are the most obvious social variables. Personality characteristics also come into play: some people are more gregarious than others, make friends more or less easily, or adapt to losses in particular ways. The amazing diversity of old people makes generalizations extremely tentative in assessing the importance and consequences to them of nonfamily social integration.

In this chapter, moreover, we must rely upon data derived from a large number of small studies that used different samples and different measures of subjective states. Although Larson (1978) argued that a global variable "subjective well-being" underlies research on "morale," "happiness," and "satisfaction," all of which are associated in much the same way with the social conditions previously enumerated, findings are often contradictory, confusing, and noncumulative (Seltzer, 1975). In some part, this is a result of the phenomena under study—feelings related to expectations that are variable in terms of social location and history. But partly, also, the proliferation of small-scale studies is the result of the organization of academic rewards: original research and publications are required for the doctorate, promotion, and tenure. The grant system is typically geared to studies with limited objectives and immediate data payoffs. And discovering the key to happiness in later life is the modern equivalent of finding the fountain of youth.

PLACE OF RESIDENCE

Before turning to the material on support systems, it is important to take note of where old people are currently most likely to reside in the United States. The census data shown in Table 10–1 indicates that the elderly live mostly in urban areas and especially in the inner city.

Not only do almost three fourths of all old people live in cities, but the proportions of Black and Hispanic aged in the central cities is far higher than for whites. Indeed, almost half of all minority elderly live in the largest urban centers. However, old people are found in about the same proportion in urban areas as in the population as a whole, i.e., about 10 per cent of the total.

The remaining one fourth of persons 65+ live in rural areas, almost all in places with populations under one thousand (farms, villages, and hamlets). Interestingly, the rural/urban distribution had not changed much in the decade between 1960 and 1970, and there is little reason to believe that it will be much different in the 1980 census. It is the young people who move, and the old who are left behind. For example, although only 4.5 percent of the rural aged live in places having populations of between 1,000 and 2,500, they compose a higher proportion of the population of these towns than in any other settings—almost 14 percent. This is because of the heavy out-migration of young people from small rural places, a trend that accelerated in the postwar years. Where old people are *not* found in any sizable proportion are the suburbs and medium-sized towns, precisely the places populated by those young couples who left both the farm and the city. At the turn of the twenty-first century, however, these couples will be 65+ so that many suburbs will "gray" over time. It remains to be seen if these suburban aged will remain or migrate to either more urban or more rural settings.

The effect of current migration patterns has been to concentrate the aged and their problems in two locales: the inner city and rural/farm areas. In the cities, poverty and high prices, poor health care, and fear of crime are prevalent and well publicized. But there is also much poverty, poor health, and lack of facilities for the aged in rural America.

Rural Elderly.   Being old down on the farm is not as idyllic as portrayed on television or folklore. Since farm people are primarily white Anglo-Saxon

Table 10–1. Distribution of the White, Black, and Spanish-Heritage Population 65 Years Old and over by Urban and Rural Residence and by Size of Place: 1970

Race	1970 Total	Urban — Total	Urbanized areas — Total	Urbanized areas — Central cities	Urbanized areas — Urban fringe	Other places of — 10,000 or more	Other places of — 2,500 to 10,000	Rural — Total	Rural — Places of 1,000 to 2,500	Rural — Other rural	1960 Total	1960 Urban	1960 Rural
Per Cent of All Ages													
Total	9.9	9.8	9.4	10.7	7.8	10.8	12.2	10.1	13.6	9.6	9.2	9.2	9.3
White	10.3	10.3	10.0	12.0	8.0	11.1	12.5	10.3	13.9	9.7	9.6	9.7	9.6
Negro and other races	6.8	6.4	6.0	6.2	5.3	8.3	9.3	8.4	9.9	8.2	6.1	5.8	7.1
Black	6.9	6.5	6.0	6.2	5.4	8.7	9.7	8.7	10.4	8.5	(NA)	(NA)	(NA)
Spanish heritage [1]	4.1	4.0	3.9	4.2	3.4	4.3	5.0	4.6	(NA)	(NA)	(NA)	(NA)	(NA)
Per Cent of All Areas													
Total	100.0	72.9	55.3	34.1	21.2	8.9	8.7	27.1	4.5	22.6	100.0	69.6	30.4
White	100.0	72.6	54.8	32.5	22.4	9.0	8.8	27.4	4.6	22.7	100.0	69.7	30.3
Negro and other races	100.0	76.2	60.9	51.4	9.5	8.5	6.8	23.8	2.9	20.9	100.0	68.0	32.0
Black	100.0	76.5	60.9	52.1	8.8	8.7	6.9	23.5	2.8	20.7	(NA)	(NA)	(NA)
Spanish heritage [1]	100.0	86.3	70.9	50.8	20.2	7.7	7.7	13.7	(NA)	(NA)	(NA)	(NA)	(NA)

NA Not available.

[1] For New York, New Jersey, and Pennsylvania, persons of Puerto Rican birth and parentage only; for five Southwestern States, persons of Spanish language or Spanish surname; for remaining States, persons of Spanish language. Note that persons of Spanish origin may be of any race.

Census of Population: 1970, General Population Characteristics, Final Report, PC(1)–B1, United States Summary, table 52, and PC(1)–C1, United States Summary, table 118.

From: Siegel, Jacob S., "Demographic Aspects of Aging and the Older Population in the United States," Current Population Reports, Special Studies, Series P–23, No. 59, May, 1976. United States Department of Commerce, Bureau of the Census, United States Printing Office, Washington, D.C., p. 24.

Protestants they may have become the repository of our faith in the enduring American values of self-reliance, hard work, and closeknit families. It is important symbolically that the rural elderly be perceived as independent, God-fearing, and surrounded by loving kin. The great popularity of *The Waltons* television series tells us more about the longings of viewers than the lives of country people during the Depression.

Appalachian families do indeed display great family cohesiveness, with elder males retaining patriarchial powers despite poverty and unemployment—but at some material and psychic cost to their wives and children (Coles, 1968; Lozier and Althouse, 1974). And contrary to popular myth, these rural families have been the recipients of social welfare programs, although cultural isolation and antigovernment sentiments have impeded the full utilization of the limited services available. Many Americans perceive Appalachian whites as folk heroes, shunning welfare and trusting in the Lord. The reality, of course, is much more complex, and the virtues of independence can conflict with other worthy goals. The status of the elderly who have offspring remaining in "the Hollows" is fairly secure, supported by the mores of the community. But most studies of Appalachian life have concentrated on the roles of men as traditional family heads. Elderly widows face a more uncertain future and are often dependent upon the goodwill of their sons and daughters-in-law.

Far more typical of rural elderly are the old people of the Midwest Farm Belt and Rocky Mountain states. Though relatively important as a proportion of total population in these states, the aged are few in number and widely separated, which creates a major problem in the delivery of services to them. Physicians are few and far between throughout rural America, hospitals serve enormous geographical areas, and care is extremely expensive to provide. Providing meals-on-wheels to the elderly is almost impossible if the wheels have to cover hundreds of miles a day. Transportation is costly and time-consuming, either to bring services to the elderly or to take old people to clinics and social centers. A common complaint of officials from these states is that even though they receive funding on the basis of population 65+, as do all states, it costs much more to provide the services to rural elderly than to those in more densely populated areas. Further, these states have difficulty raising the matching funds required for many federal-state joint programs. As a consequence, proposals have been made in Congress for changes in the Older Americans Act that would acknowledge the special difficulties of serving the rural aged. For instance, the recent Rural Health Service Clinics Act allows for Medicare and Medicaid reimbursements for nurse practitioners and physician assistants—although neither is reimbursed for services to old people in areas where medical doctors are relatively abundant.

Poverty is not only a city problem. One third of rural elderly have incomes below the poverty level, as compared to 25 percent in the central cities and 17 percent in the suburbs. Included here are migrant workers and southern rural Blacks, as well as unemployed miners of Appalachia—people who are often outside the welfare/special service system altogether.

The extreme poverty of certain rural subgroups is reflected in data on housing. Over half of all substandard dwellings in the United States are in rural areas, a figure that includes the majority of nonwhite residences. Actually, the rural elderly are more likely than the urban elderly to own their home—79 percent compared to 55 percent in 1973. But the rural dwelling is very often structurally deficient, i.e., lacks plumbing or needs major repair. In 1970, for example, over 80 percent of rental units occupied by rural Blacks lacked plumbing facilities, in contrast to about 25 percent for comparable whites (HUD, 1973).

To the extent that low educational attainment, poverty, and lack of transportation are associated with failure to utilize services for physical and social well-being, and with isolation and withdrawal, the rural aged suffer manifold handicaps. Moreover, where public programs are in effect, the technical problems and cost of providing service have limited the number of elderly recipients and the range of services offered. In the South and Southwest, nonwhite rural aged represent especially deprived and politically powerless subpopulations. In Appalachia, a fatalist philosophy further inhibits service utilization.

The rural elderly, no less than other old people, are a heterogeneous group: sharecroppers, migrant laborers, mountaineers, "good ole boys," and the country folk of *Saturday Evening Post* covers. What they share are low incomes, inappropriate or inadequate housing, and difficulties in transportation.

Urban Elderly. Many of the same problems affect old people who live in cities. Poverty is endemic among inner-city dwellers of any age, but more so for the elderly. Prices are high and almost everything *must* be purchased in the cities. Poor people, and especially those with limited physical mobility, cannot hunt for bargains or comparison shop—as a consequence, they pay more. People who are dependent upon monthly checks may need credit from shop owners, which is another reason why they shop at relatively expensive neighborhood stores rather than in supermarkets.

Urban transportation is not a major problem for the elderly in terms of availability, but fares are expensive, platforms are difficult to negotiate, and subway stairs are a formidable obstacle to many. Some cities have instituted reduced fares for the elderly, and others are using federal funds to equip buses with platforms that can be lowered. Moreover, most city residents are within walking distance of shops, churches, and other amenities, including parks and resting places.

Health care, also, is less problematic for city dwellers; physicians and hospitals are concentrated in urban areas. However, the quality of such services, especially for the urban poor, is open to question. Many old people are served in clinics, some of which have been dubbed "Medicaid mills" because of their high volume of billing for the treatment of the indigent. On the other hand, these facilities *are* located where the poor live. They are open long hours and do provide necessary services, which is more than can be said of most physicians in private practice.

CRIME AND THE ELDERLY

The housing problems of the urban elderly are less structural than the environmental, and the urban elderly often live in fear of crime in deteriorating neighborhoods. Data on crime against the elderly for 1974–75 show quite clearly that, for all crimes, except personal larceny with contact, old people are the *least* likely of any age group to be victimized:

Although infrequently victimized, the elderly are profoundly affected by such attacks. In a very practical sense, whatever is stolen from an old person will represent more of a loss than the same amount taken from someone who can earn it back immediately (Cook et al., 1978). These crimes offend our sensibility: old people are "unfair" objects, who are rendered especially vulnerable by failing eyesight, poor hearing, and an inability to run away (U.S. Senate, 1977, p. 198).

The most important effect of crime against the aged is the high level of fear engendered among old people. In the Harris survey (1975), "danger of being robbed or attacked on the street" was the most frequently cited obstacle to getting where they wanted to go. Fear of crime as a "very serious" personal problem, however, was experienced by only 24 percent of older respondents, although close to 50 percent of the general public thought that it would be. When those old people who answered that fear of crime was a "somewhat serious" problem are added to those for whom it is a "very serious" problem, almost half—47 percent—of respondents 65+ expressed a sense of danger.

Fear of crime, therefore, is not a characteristic of all or even most old people, but is far in excess of the actual probability of being victimized. Since those who are most likely to become the victims of crime against the elderly are female, poor, and live alone in the inner city, those who are most fearful of crime are, accordingly, female, black, and metropolitan area residents (Clemente and Kleiman, 1976), especially those without social support systems (Sundeen and Mathieu, 1976). This is clearly a very realistic perception.

Old people are especially vulnerable to confidence games. Since they are often unsophisticated and lonely, many old women are prime targets of younger women who promise them easy rewards for a few minute's investment of money. At the beginning of the month, when Social Secu-

Table 10–2. Personal Victimization Rates, 1975 (By Type of Crime and Age of Victim) Rate per 1,000 Persons in Each Group

Sex and Age	Number of Persons in the Group	Crimes of Violence	Rape	Robbery Total	Robbery With Injury	Robbery Without Injury	Assault Total	Assault Aggra-vated	Assault Simple	Crimes of Theft	Personal Larceny With Contact	Personal Larceny Without Contact
Both sexes	166,732,000	32.7	0.9	6.7	2.1	4.6	25.1	9.5	15.5	95.8	3.1	92.7
12–15	16,443,000	54.6	0.8	11.4	2.6	8.7	42.4	12.1	30.3	158.3	3.0	155.4
16–19	15,944,000	64.2	2.4	10.6	3.5	7.2	51.1	21.4	29.7	162.1	3.3	158.8
20–24	18,005,000	59.2	2.6	10.8	3.2	7.6	45.8	18.8	27.1	146.6	4.3	142.2
25–34	30,268,000	39.2	1.2	6.3	2.2	4.0	31.7	11.7	20.0	109.8	2.9	106.9
35–49	33,688,000	20.5	0.3	4.6	1.5	3.1	15.6	6.6	9.0	80.2	2.8	77.5
50–64	31,076,000	13.5	0.2	4.3	1.7	2.6	8.9	3.3	5.6	51.3	2.7	48.6
65 and over	21,309,000	7.8	0.1	4.3	1.2	3.1	3.4	1.5	2.0	24.5	3.3	21.2

U.S. Department of Justice, Law Enforcement Assistance Administration, *Criminal Victimization in the United States: A Comparison of 1974 and 1975 Findings* (Washington, D.C., February 1977), p. 13.

rity checks arrive, con artists are very active, and old people are then in greatest danger of being robbed or bilked.

Even if one has not been personally attacked or experienced danger, an old person could feel very uncomfortable when a known and trusted neighborhood fills up with "strangers," people whose language is unfamiliar and whose customs offend them. The old shops give way to new types, and the ethnic community dissolves through attrition. The great advantage of cities, namely their variety of people, places, housing options, and life-styles, is experienced by many old people as profoundly upsetting. But for others, adapting to these changes, making new friends and discoveries, and remaining in the center of activity have given zest to their later years. Senior centers in central cities have become important resources for both types of old people. Some will come to the center to meet others like themselves, while remaining aloof from those of different backgrounds. Senior centers have also been a place for old people to meet across race and ethnic and religious divisions.

Thus both rural and urban elderly experience constraints in maintaining social networks and in taking advantage of social services. Both will have some, if not most, of their children living at great distances from them. And since both the rural and inner-city aged have spent their lives in the same location, major changes will have taken place around them: the exodus of jobs and young people for the former, and neighborhood debilitation and an influx of strangers for the latter. Yet we cannot assume that many of these elderly would like to move. The familiar is often preferred to the unknown, and there are still old friends, sharers of a mutual past, with whom they can spend their futures.

INFORMAL SUPPORT SYSTEMS

Friendship. In old age the role of friend becomes particularly salient. Friends both augment and supplement social networks based on kinship, and are at least as crucial to the well-being of old people as are their relatives (Blau, 1973). Many studies have found that contact with friends is *more* conducive to morale or life satisfaction than, for example, contact with one's children (Arling, 1976) or grandchildren (Robertson and Wood, 1978). The finding that best expresses the critical importance of an intimate friend is that of Lowenthal and Haven (1968), in which having a "confidant" was associated with mental health, whereas the absence of intimacy signified difficulties in adapting to the losses of old age. Although some old people will designate a relative as their "close friend," and men are especially likely to cite their wives (who rarely name their husbands), the great majority report having at least one non-family friend on whom they can rely for assistance and companionship.

In general, sex differences in friendship in old age parallel those throughout the life course: males have a wider circle of friends and often higher levels of overall interaction, but females have more diverse and intense relationships (Hess, 1977; Powers and Bultena, 1976). Women are more likely than men to have an intimate friend, to have close friends outside the family, and to be able to replace lost contacts with new ones. In old age, this interpersonal versatility of women is frequently cited as a major determinant of their ability to cope with material deprivation. The death of a spouse can be devastating, particularly to the woman who devoted herself to her husband (Lopata, 1973), but it is even more lethal for men. Men who describe their wives as their best friends will be desolate when they are widowed, at a high risk of mental illness and suicide (Bock, 1972; Bock and Webber, 1973). Ironically, older men, particularly those in the working class, who were brought up to fear females and feminine behavior, such as intimacy, and who, therefore, did *not* treat their wives as confidantes, will be similarly isolated in widowhood (Lowenthal and Haven, 1968). However, Atchley (1977) argued that the superior material resources and marriageability of widowed men can account for a morale advantage over widowed women.

Since most men are married and remain so until death, they are not always handicapped by an inability to sustain intimate relationships. The married couple do, after all, have one another. The marriage that was so important for women in earlier stages of the life course is particularly preservative of men in old age. In widowhood, the woman's lifelong training in role discontinuity and in self-disclosure and intimacy allow her to turn to friends and her children for social support and to establish new bonds of closeness with others. As for the men, Powers and Bultena (1976) found that widowed and poor men were more likely to have an intimate friend than the married and more affluent males. Nor, incidentally, were the socially isolated old people characterized by low morale in this sample of midwesterners.

Many old people are apparently quite content in their social isolation, including "shopping bag ladies," who roam the city with no permanent dwelling place (Hand, 1977), occupants of single-room occupancy (SRO's) hotels (Stephans, 1977), and others who live alone in boardinghouses. For many, this pattern is a continuation of a lifetime spent as a "loner"; for others, it is a welcome opportunity to disengage in old age from relationships that are overdemanding. For most old people, however, there is survival value in having someone with whom to share one's world—to construct meaning and to provide material and emotional support. Two thirds of a skid row sample reported having friends, many living outside the area (Rooney, 1976); these proportions, however, declined with length of residence on the street (which was also associated with advanced age).

Friends are generally drawn from a pool of similars; that is, we tend to select friends from those who are like us in some crucial respect (*homophily* as defined by Lazarsfeld and Merton, 1956; Hess, 1972). For one thing, status similars are equals, and friendship is basically an egalitarian relationship. For another, those who share our social world verify attitudes, beliefs, and behaviors, and are rewarding to be with on that account. Additionally, the effect of proximity on friendship—that we are likely to interact with those near us, which reduces the investment of time and effort needed to sustain the relationship—is reinforced by the tendency to live in an area with others like ourselves. The residential distribution of old people cited earlier in this chapter suggests that *age-segregation* has been one consequence of migration patterns in the mid-twentieth century (Cowgill, 1978).

It follows that *age-homogeneous* settings where there are many age-peers will be more conducive to friendship formation than *age-heterogeneous* living arrangements. Although large numbers of old people, a majority in the Harris survey (1975), say that they prefer living with persons of all ages, there is much evidence to indicate that age-segregated environments are associated with greater interaction and satisfaction (Rosow, 1967). Simply having a larger pool of status similars from which to select a compatible friend must confer an advantage.

Age-peers are likely to be chosen as friends at all life course stages, not only because they are probably status equals in other respects but because they will have shared the same slice of history, have been socialized in the same period, and undergone key experiences at the same times in their lives. In old age the shared past is longer and the future is more problematic than at earlier stages, dual inducements to consciousness of kind. However, large numbers of old people resist moving to retirement communities or to senior housing precisely because they wish to avoid age-homogeneity. Carp (1976) points out many methodological flaws in the studies that report increased satisfaction with age-segregated settings; these findings could as well be the result of other attributes of the housing such as safety, cleanliness, modern appliances, and convenience.

There are also environmental constraints to consider: the very old, like the very young, are limited in their ability to travel. This lack of mobility may result from physical decrements, low income, or fear of leaving the neighborhood. Some old friends will have moved away or died or themselves become homebound. These conditions heighten the effect of proximity; if other old people are nearby, they provide the pool of eligibles for new friendships. In nursing homes, for example, friends are often chosen from those in nearby rooms, although not necessarily from those actually sharing a ward (sometimes close is too close). Neighborhoods with same-aged residents should, therefore, provide fertile ground for friendship formation, whereas the ability to respond to one another's needs will determine the duration of the relationship.

Involvement and Isolation

Neighbors. The configuration of relatives, friends, and neighbors (not always mutually exclusive categories) with whom the old person interacts is called an "informal" support system to distinguish it from the formalized, bureaucratic supports that are available through social agencies and government programs. With very few exceptions—even the bag ladies and SRO residents can count on peers in an emergency—old people have such a support network, and much research is aimed at finding systematic variations among subgroups of the aged. Table 10–3 presents the findings for a multiethnic sample of low-income elderly New York City residents in 1970.

As shown in Table 10–3 Hispanic aged were more likely than Blacks or whites to have spouses and children as the major component of their "functioning" network. "Functional" in this research was defined as someone with whom the respondent interacted and who was, therefore, available for social support. On the other hand, Blacks have the highest proportion of networks consisting of friends and neighbors. When asked a series of attitude questions, Hispanics consistently gave more family-centered responses compared to both whites and Blacks. But two thirds of the total sample, with no significant differences by ethnicity, agreed with the statement "Friends and neighbors are frequently more help to an older person than his own family" (Wilker, 1976). Although these inner-city elderly had extensive contact with their children, receiving gifts and services and crisis assistance, friends and neighbors were their day-to-day sources of intimacy and concern. Cantor (1975) has claimed that the density of central cities encourages extensive interaction with neighbors (contrary to so many theories of urban anomie and anonymity). Since most inner-city old people live in age-heterogeneous housing, friends will

Table 10–3. Proportion of Respondents with Each Type of Functioning Social Network Component By Ethnicity

Functional Component	White (N = 766) Per Cent	Black (N = 580) Per Cent	Spanish (N = 205) Per Cent	Total (N = 1551) Per Cent
Spouse	34.7	29.0	41.0	33.3
Child	54.0	53.2	72.5	56.1
Sibling or Relative	56.2	57.6	43.8	55.1
Friends and/or Neighbors	54.2	59.1	47.5	55.1
None	6.6	4.3	4.6	5.4

Cantor, Marjorie H., "The Configuration and Intensity of the Informal Support System in a New York City Elderly Population: Is Ethnicity a Determining Factor?" Paper presented at the 29th Annual Scientific Meetings of the Gerontological Society, New York City, October 14, 1976.

often be younger than the elderly respondents. This is another reversal of expected patterns.

In a study of San Antonio aged, Carp (1975) also found that centrality of residence was associated with involvement in social life, number of friends, and satisfaction with social network. Living at the periphery of the city reduced activity, autonomy, and satisfaction. Low density of peers, and dependence on public transportation or the assistance of others, limits all types of contact, although some will prefer the greater safety of life at the fringe to living at the center.

Lopata (1975), however, has contended that social engagement is more a matter of personal than residential resources. In Chicago at least, and perhaps wherever concentrations of foreign- and farm-born elderly are found, poverty, lack of education, and reliance on primary kin (who fall away over time) leave the old person extremely vulnerable to isolation. Black and white ethnic widows in central Chicago did not have the multi-faceted support systems found by other researchers, and they did not have the knowledge or interpersonal skills to seek out alternatives to family members.

Nonetheless, for the 20–30 percent of all old people who do not have a living child or who do not have contact with their offspring, friends and neighbors are the primary source of social support, especially if they are also bereft of spouse. Yet there is no clear evidence that these elderly increase their interaction with nonrelatives in order to compensate for low levels of family contact. Some studies have found that old respondents living alone or without strong family ties were more likely to participate in community activities than were those with high levels of family inter-action (e.g., Trela and Jackson, 1976). Other researchers found no rela-tionship between integration into social activities and the quantity or quality of family contacts (e.g., Spakes, 1976).

The pattern of dependency on friends in contrast to that on relatives is illustrated in a study of Kansas City elderly by Berghorn et al. (1978): if relatives lived nearby, they were called upon when needed, but when no children or other kin were in the area, the elderly depended upon friends and neighbors. Since the urban area in which this sample lived was so run-down that few younger adults lived there, dependency on kin was minimal, although reliance on friends and neighbors was not related to age concentration. The researchers explained this pattern in terms of the relative "costs" of various actions. Given the cultural level aversion to dependency of any sort in our society, claims on children can at least be justified by evoking the norms of reciprocity and filial piety that are also culturally valued.

A third set of studies indicated that people tend to maintain in old age the patterns of social involvement to which they were habituated earlier. Some old people are either high or low interacters with *both* family and others, which suggests the effect of personality types (e.g., Croog, Lipson, and Levine, 1972). But many other variables affect opportunity and desire for interaction, such as health, mobility, education, income, concentration of age peers, and other aspects of the environment. In fact, the balance between friends and kin as social supports varies by so many factors that generalizations are almost impossible (Sherman, 1975a, 1975b; Bild and Havighurst, 1976, p. 63–69).

It is also difficult to separate characteristics of a setting from the traits of people who are likely to be found there. That is, certain types of housing will appeal to certain kinds of individuals with either reserved or outgoing personalities, accustomed to certain levels of social interaction. Housing alternatives also attract people at different income and educational levels with their class-linked interpersonal and material resources.

Obviously, informal support systems will be as varied as the older population itself. There is no "best" pattern, only opportunities from which each old person constructs a set of supportive relationships. Income and health/mobility, as ever, are major determinants of the range of choices, and of satisfaction with the outcome. Cognitive processes may also be at work, so that the individual adjusts expectations to the reality of what is possible.

In addition to friends and neighbors, companions are to be found in the more structured settings of clubs and churches and other membership groups to which a person belongs by choice.

VOLUNTARY ASSOCIATIONS

Two centuries ago, the French traveler Alexis de Tocqueville was struck by the vitality of associational life in the United States. The number and variety of voluntary groups remain very high—over 13,000 national non-profit associations in 1976 and innumerable local organizations. There are religious bodies, fraternal societies, labor unions, trade associations, political and charitable organizations, veteran's groups, social clubs, athletic teams, and neighborhood associations—almost any interest that can be shared can also be organized. Americans are "joiners," with many having two or more affiliations through most of their adult life.

There is an age-related pattern to participation in voluntary associations: low in young adulthood, peaking in middle age, with a gradual decline in old age (Riley and Foner, 1968). At any life stage, membership is tied to other roles: the parent of an elementary school child, for instance, is likely to be involved in PTA, Cub Scouts, and Little League, and to have a church affiliation. Other memberships are related to social class: unions, country clubs, alumni associations, service organizations (Jaycees, Kiwanis, Elks), or bowling teams. There are also very clear sex divisions: men belong to men's clubs (often to avoid being with women), and women belong to "ladies auxiliaries," altar guilds, and the like.

The curvilinear pattern of voluntary association membership—low in early and late adult life and high in the middle years—illustrates the problem of interpreting data on aging. People may lose interest or the ability to sustain membership in old age, which would be an *aging effect*. The clustering of roles through the life course may reduce the opportunities for the young and old to affiliate, a *life course effect*. The current data on old people may be peculiar to persons born before World War I, or to the sex/race/ethnic composition of these cohorts, clearly *cohort effects*. Or, the loss of income and other deprivations of old age today could inhibit organizational involvement, a *period effect*. Data would be needed from different cohorts, over time, to test these possibilities. There is some evidence, when the same respondents were questioned before and after retirement, that there was little dropoff in associational participation until age 70 (Cutler, 1977).

Membership and participation are two different measures of organizational involvement. Membership could remain high while participation declines, or the aging individual could limit memberships while increasing activity in the few remaining associations, such as the church (see Chapter 11).

It is often assumed that voluntary association activity, as an indicator of social integration, is important to psychological well-being. And there is some evidence of the positive effects of social participation on happiness (Graney, 1975). But most research has found very little statistical relationship between associational membership and psychological outcomes, once physical health and socioeconomic status are taken into account (Cutler, 1976). That is, the link between participation/membership and measures of well-being is often an artifact of their both being associated with better health and income. Even church-related activities, the one area with independent effects on well-being in one national probability sample, may operate indirectly: through concentration of age peers or as a reflection of a generalized "religiosity" that is frequently correlated with morale and satisfaction (Cutler, 1976).

Another confounding variable is race/ethnicity. In general, research indicates that Blacks, and in some cases other minority groups as well, have higher levels of voluntary association membership and participation than do whites, presumably to compensate for exclusion from the mainstream. In this case, lower income and poorer health operate *within* the minority group to distinguish high participants from low. Two recent researches have verified these relationships for Blacks, although not for Mexican-Americans (Antunes and Gaitz, 1975), or white ethnics (Clemente et al., 1975). Much of the Black participation was church related, whereas whites were more active in fraternal, senior citizen, and ethnic-identity organizations (Clemente et al., 1975). In both studies, there also appears to be very little change in participation by age: that is, old age did not overcome race/ethnicity differences.

One important response to the increasing proportions of the aged in the society as a whole, but particularly in urban centers, has been the growth of voluntary associations of and for the aged, beginning with the Golden Age Clubs founded by churches and charitable organizations. The senior center movement received a major boost from the Older Americans Act. Since the centers are clearly limited areas of activity, they have thus been much studied by gerontologists. But since each senior center is unique in terms of clientele, auspices, and range of services, the findings from these studies have been similarly varied.

One persistent topic of research has been, who uses senior centers? There are theoretical arguments and research evidence to support two very different conclusions. On the one hand, since participation and social class are positively related in middle age, the relationship between them should persist in old age, such that relatively affluent people will have the knowledge and means to utilize these facilities and to derive benefits from their participation. Being more skilled in interpersonal relationships, the affluent elderly will make friends readily and be able to exercise leadership (Tissue, 1971). On the other hand, these individuals are least dependent upon the centers for socializing, and are most likely to resent being thought "old fogies." Data from the Harris survey (1975) found very few old people reporting attendance at a senior center or golden age club during the past year—only 18 percent of those 65+ and 8 percent of those 55–64. But it was those in the *lowest* income group who were most likely to have attended senior centers and did so more frequently. Women were more likely to participate in centers than men, and Blacks more so than whites. Moreover, of the 87 percent over age 55 who had not been to a center in the last year, less than one fourth indicated any interest in doing so—these, typically, were Blacks, women, and those with annual incomes under $7,000. When asked what was keeping them from attending, lack of convenient facilities, transportation problems, and poor health were mentioned by a little under half of all respondents, and "no time, too busy" was mentioned by one third.

For those who join and use the senior centers, the experience has most often been beneficial to them; however, those with unhappy experiences have dropped out, so that findings from participants will usually be very biased. The small percentage reported in the Harris survey (1975) still represents 5 million old people. And if these centers appeal largely to women, Blacks, and those with low incomes, or people who are all three, then the benefits of membership will have accrued to those who are most in need. It is unfortunate that so many more are denied the experience through a lack of facilities and transportation.

Friendships, informal support networks, and voluntary associations are important integrative mechanisms. For those without active family ties, such involvements may be crucial to their well-being. Old age has so often been characterized as "roleless" in terms of the valued statuses of our society—work, child rearing, and civic leadership—that we often overlook the more mundane opportunities for social interaction and relationships. But not all old people are involved in even these systems. At least 20 percent do not have active kin networks, and another large minority remain outside the informal support systems, often by choice.

SOCIAL ISOLATION IN OLD AGE

It is perhaps indicative of a value bias in our society that volumes have been written on the conditions for social integration of the elderly, and very little about the antecedents or functions of social isolation. Disengagement theory evoked a storm of protest, not only because the thesis ran counter to our beliefs about the therapeutic value of activity and interaction, but also because it was felt that if isolation were thought to be the natural or preferred state of things in old age, public efforts to improve the condition of old people would lose their urgency. It is less upsetting to perceive isolates as "exotics"—skid row derelicts and bag ladies—than as examples of successful aging.

Social integration occurs along a continuum from isolation to total involvement, and both happy and unhappy individuals will be found at any point. Although most research strongly supports the beneficial outcome of social network supports, it must also be recognized that social demands could be perceived as stressful. For example, those who have been relative loners throughout adulthood and who have attained successful patterns of adaptation—socially and psychologically—are threatened by interventions for their own good. Aged wanderers in our central cities might be eyesores, but they offend only our sensibilities; indeed, they may represent the ultimate expression of such deeply held American values as free enterprise and personal independence. Many of these individuals have led socially and economically marginal existences for decades —in the world of traveling circuses, fairs, and other entertainments. Without children or having lost touch with any they may have, never having married or being survivors of dissolved unions, and with unstable work histories, they have somehow always scraped along and would prefer to do so in the future.

The important variable is probably not isolation per se but the fit between what one has become used to and what is available in the environment. The recently widowed, for example, will have high or low morale depending upon their ability to find companionship in the immediate setting. The impact of isolation can be devastating for those accustomed to companionship, whereas being thrust into contact with others will upset isolates.

At least three sets of factors should be considered when assessing the effects of isolation: lifelong patterns of adaptation; the current resources and needs for affiliation of the old person; and the social supports at hand. Exchange theorists would note the costs of various actions compared to potential benefits. To admit loneliness or to walk to a senior center, for example, are "investments" for which one expects a comparable return; when interaction fails to meet expectations, one feels "cheated" and often withdraws from further contact. In this case, isolation is actually more comfortable than involvement. Many old people find the demands of others for attention, time, and energy more than they can easily give, which becomes another impetus for their withdrawal. Role strain and slack are functions of the balance between demand and supply of role-playing capacities. The slackness brought on by retirement or the death of friends and family will be experienced as discomfort by those with reserves of energy (i.e., both willing and able), and as relief by those with limitations on ability and willingness to make the effort.

Income and health status once more enter the equation. The very poor and very ill are trapped in their immediate environment, so that what is offered there becomes crucial to their well-being. The more mobile and affluent can range further for satisfying activities, reducing their dependency on the environment but raising their expectations of outcomes. Abrupt changes in physical and financial conditions not only have a direct impact on one's sense of well-being but also an indirect effect by changing the structure of costs and benefits of various types of involvement.

Nor is high involvement with kin and others always associated with positive feelings. In many studies, frequency of kin contact has been found to bear a curvilinear relationship to measures of well-being—what we call the "Goldilocks Effect" (Hess and Waring, 1978), whereby both too many and too few visits generate feelings of resentment, but a "just right" number allows the older parent to feel cared for without being overrun by kin. Moreover, the elderly who live with offspring and grandchildren are often among the most unhappy old people. It is important to distinguish between the number of contacts and their meaning; *quantity* cannot be automatically translated into judgments of *quality* of the relationship (Lowenthal, 1976).

In essence, the study of social integration is more complex than that suggested by simplistic assumptions of the value of involvement. Yet, the quest for community, our human need for others with whom to define and share our experiences, and the saving graces of intimacy make it most likely that the old, as well as the young, reach out to one another in their mutual search for meaning.

SELF-HELP AMONG THE AGED

Between the polar types of isolation and full engagement in work, family life, and voluntary associations, the great majority of old people proceed through the final stages of the life course with variable degrees of integration into social networks, contingent on their physical capacities, material resources, and the nature of their residential settings.

A recurring theme in sociology is the contrast between what Ferdinand Toënnies called *Gemeinschaft*, or "community," and *Gesellschaft*, or "society"; the former relating to primary group interactions and the latter to the distant, formalized relationships of modern life. Our historical model (Chapter 2) suggests a progressive increase in secondary group relationships with societal complexity. Max Weber spoke of the "demystification of the world" as rationalized and bureaucratized formal organizations increasingly regulate social life. At the same time, individuals are thought to be less bound to primary relationships, no longer embedded in kinship groups or stable neighborhoods. Thus atomized, modern people become David Riesman's (1950) "lonely crowd." Although much of this formulation is overstatement, it is probably safe to say that many Americans feel a loss of community and experience a sense of being controlled by distant, unaccountable leaders. Hence the widespread popularity of encounter groups, religious revivals, and the search for roots (as well as of anti-government attitudes).

Another aspect of the quest for community is the development of *self-help groups*, an important phenomenon of the last decade, which attempts to fill the gap between individual problems and the bureaucratic service delivery system. Members of self-help groups organize voluntarily to provide mutual aid for their shared condition, whether an illness, an incapacity, a habit they desire to break, consciousness of victimization or discrimination, or plain loneliness. In the case of the aged, old age cannot be "cured" through mutual aid, but isolation and stigmatization can certainly be lessened. Self-help efforts among the aged are difficult to categorize since many groups have formed only to provide companionship (expressive) and others to initiate change in public policy (instrumental); some are unstructured (helping relationships) and others have definite meeting times and places (voluntary small groups). But these descriptions are "ideal types"; in reality most self-help efforts are a mixture of expressive and instrumental behaviors. Hess (1976) offered the following schema for classifying these possibilities.

| Structure: | Function: | |
	Expressive	Instrumental
Emergent	A. Spontaneous helping	B. Senior power
Crystalized	C. Voluntary small groups	D. Interest groups

Spontaneous helping refers to the mutual-support systems generated in the natural community—the helping and socializing patterns with friends and neighbors described earlier in this chapter. Although Lopata (1976) found much loneliness and lack of support, others have reported extensive helping networks, often enhanced by concentrations of old-age peers or status similars. Two observational studies illustrate how these mutual aid relationships arise spontaneously from the daily interactions of those living separately but together in a limited area. Johnson (1971) studied working-class retirees in a mobile-home community, and Hochschild (1973) observed middle-class widows in an apartment house. In both cases an intricate social system based on the exchange of services and goods (primarily of the baked variety) emerged over time, shaped also by a recognition of boundaries. The participants created a world of shared meanings and reciprocal roles in much the same fashion as any face-to-face group will under conditions of relative anomie. For old people living in a common place, the structure of interpersonal relations is often modeled on that which they knew as family members. The healthier persons take on a parental role vis-à-vis the more dependent, or a siblinglike interaction arises between equals.

In contrast to these instances of unintentional community, there appear to be few intentional communes of the aged. Communal living in America is associated with the young, and is largely limited to one (or two, with infants) generation. Streib and Streib (1976), however, noted the possibility of urban communes for the aged, or arrangements whereby a number of elderly could jointly own a residence and employ a manager. Perhaps the generation that came to adulthood in the 1960s will, in their old age, be more disposed to communal living than those now old. The compelling advantages of sharing expenses and gaining companionship without losing privacy may yet make communards out of very unlikely candidates.

When helping patterns do not arise spontaneously in the natural community, social workers have often tried to manufacture "neighborhood communities" or "good neighbors," with mixed results (e.g., Ross, 1975; Faulkner, 1976). Within nursing homes and retirement communities, similar efforts have been attempted (Seguin, 1973). Peer group counseling and volunteer programs for services to the elderly by other old people, such as RSVP, are more formalized and properly belong in the cell *voluntary small groups* as gerontological equivalents of Alcoholics Anonymous. The other two cells have been examined in Chapter 8, on political organization of the elderly.

When old people unite for direct political action, especially at the local level—for lower utility rates or more senior housing, for example—they gain consciousness of kind, a sense of efficacy (if successful), and also the opportunity to be with one another in goal-directed activity. All this could lead to continued social interaction among newly found comrades. Conversely, social clubs that bring old people together for essentially expressive activity could become staging areas for political behavior. And as the self-help movement itself continues to grow—there is now a Self-Help Clearinghouse and Newsletter—efforts by the elderly, and on their behalf, should also gain favor and funding.

Major problems are faced by self-help groups of old people. Much depends on large numbers of the elderly defining themselves as old, as having interests in common with the most disadvantaged aged, and being able to transcend other loyalties. Crucial, too, is the ability to provide sustained leadership in a subpopulation characterized by shortened life expectancy, prone to chronic illness, and declines in energy and attention. Lastly, there is the built-in danger to the self-help movement as a whole: to the degree that the problems being dealt with by group members are generated at the societal level (poverty, deficiencies in public services, inequities in health care, and so on), asking people to help themselves is comparable to blaming the victim and displacing the burden for change.

Prospects

This section could well be titled "The Clouded Crystal Ball" since predictions regarding the social networks of old people must take into account changes at the individual level, in the environment, and the interaction between the two. Trends can suggest contradictory possibilities.

For example, to the extent that isolation in the inner city is related to being foreign born, poorly educated, and ill adapted to urban life, there should be less isolation in the decades ahead. But the proportion of old people living alone will probably continue to increase, especially as women possess the material and inner resources for independent living. Also, as more couples jointly survive the early decades of old age, fewer individuals (particularly men) will feel the need to establish extensive nonfamily support systems.

If residential areas are becoming more age-homogeneous, old people will have enhanced opportunities for socializing and friendship formation, but this same trend could isolate the elderly as a category. Much of the stereotyping and negative images of aging, which result from an absence of old people in the daily lives of younger persons, will go unchallenged, perhaps distancing the elderly psychologically as well as physically. The countertrends in this respect are the increasing visibility of the elderly as a political force, the new awareness generated in the media and through gerontology courses, and the extended survival of family members. However, most new housing, both public and private, appears to be age segregated, unlike the experimental communities in Scandinavia and Israel that provide for a mixture of age groups. Indeed, those elderly with high incomes and presumably greatest freedom of choice tend to move to retirement communities that exclude young people. But it is not that clear that lower-income elderly prefer age-segregated housing; just being the same age does not necessarily provide a common base of experience if major ethnic, religious, racial, and social class distinctions inhibit socializing. Ideally, a range of housing options should be available: for those who seek age peers, or who prefer to be alone, or who seek the companionship of juniors. The economic realities of housing construction in the United States at this time suggest strongly that old people are priced out of the market, making them increasingly dependent upon public housing. Senior housing will probably appeal to many, particularly when age-integrated public housing is likely to contain a number of "problem families" with juveniles.

Since voluntary association membership and participation are linked to physical mobility, interest in public affairs, and socioeconomic status, the prospects are for continued activity in the affiliations of midlife as well as those centered on aging. Our guess, however, is that the "young-old" will make *value-stretches* downward rather than upwards, that is, to define their behaviors as an extension of middle-age patterns rather than a variation on old age, and thus remain aloof from age-based voluntary associations.

What the future may bring, in all the spheres of activity we have discussed, is a pushing back of the entire process of social aging. The characteristics that new cohorts of the elderly will increasingly share are precisely those associated with social integration: more education, assured income, delayed onset of debilitation, and organizational involvement. But it will be an integration into the structures of midlife maintained into one's seventies. The transition to "real" old age will occur in the midseventies rather than the midsixties. With the exception of income, very few other resources will decline abruptly with retirement, and it is not impossible to devise a system of income flow over the life course that will be much smoother than at present. Thus, the social integration of the young-old will become less problematic while that of the old-old becomes more so, but it is the latter who seem to prefer and benefit from age-homogeneous environments. Friendships may become more important to the young-old than at present simply because they will have fewer children and more age peers, while informal neighborhood support systems will be most crucial to the old-old remaining in the community.

These speculations underscore the need to think of diverse groups of old people and very different types of social networks. There is no "best" and perhaps not even a "better" outcome. Some will prefer to depend upon their offspring, others on friends, and still others on no one, and all can be quite satisfied. If we are to plan safe and satisfying environments for the elderly, we should begin by recognizing this diversity.

Research Exercises

1. If *sample survey* data are available, compare the answers of old people in age-integrated environments to those of old people in age-segregated residential settings. Also, those old people with a large number of friends in the immediate area may differ from those with few or no close friends.

2. If the survey data are not useful or usable, draw a *convenience sample* of old people in senior housing, their own households, and in household of a relative, to question on measures of well-being, feelings of usefulness, friendship (number and closeness), and so on.

3. Differences between old people who visit senior centers and those who do not are also worth exploring, although it will be difficult to assess cause and effect on some variables.

4. *Observation* at a site where old people interact regularly could yield *sociometric* data: mapping and counting who sits with whom, initiates conversation, chooses to be with, and so on. Some old people will be sociometric "stars" and others will be "isolates." Follow-up interviews of these types should focus on attitude variables.

Discussion Questions

At this point in your life what type of residential setting do you think you would prefer in old age, and why?

You have been awarded a federal grant to redesign senior centers to attract more participants. What would you suggest?

How can contact between old people and young ones be enhanced?

Why do so few old people do volunteer work, even among other elderly?

11

Religion, Education, and Leisure

Although the economic, family, and political aspects of aging have received the bulk of research attention, largely because of their centrality in the life space of old people (if not people of all ages), activities in other spheres of social life are also important to the well-being of the elderly. Although the roles of old people in religious institutions are both extensive and historically consistent, their educational and leisure activities are fairly recent phenomena. The patterns developed by current cohorts, the first to realize many years of retirement from major productive roles, will become tomorrow's norms.

Religion

PERSPECTIVES

The involvement of elders in religious functions—as leaders and participants—has always been preeminent. In preliterate societies, where ritual depends upon an oral tradition, older members of the group are valued repositories of knowledge, and may also benefit from being thought nearer to the gods by virtue of their advanced years. Formalized religions generally select spiritual leaders from among the most experienced, and hence wiser, but who are also persons presumed to be removed from worldly temptations. Since tenure in priestly office depends upon holiness, a quality that does not deteriorate over time, religious hierarchies tend to become populated by the longest lived. In contrast, faiths that are based on revelation and *charisma* can, initially at least, have youthful leaders, but the process that Max Weber called "routinization of charisma" typically leads to a formal structure in which age gradually becomes a positive attribute. In general, religion, education, and politics are areas in which wisdom is valued. Whereas this wisdom was once thought to require a lifetime of training and commitment, today, in political and economic life, it is often associated with the most recent learning experience. Religious knowledge, however, remains unchanging—that is its very virtue; and the old have had longer to "know" the truth.

The previously mentioned supportive role of most religions in reinforcing family based hierarchies of power and prestige remains the case today. However, revolutionary secular ideologies, as functional equivalents of religious belief systems, often aim to destroy kin-based authority structures so that a new, transcendent loyalty can be attached to political leaders. This was the aim of the Communist regimes in the Soviet Union and Eastern Europe, and in the People's Republic of China. Both traditional religions and family structures had to be delegitimized, often ruthlessly and not altogether successfully. In modern America, we find *civil religion*, a secularization of authority that substitutes symbols of the civil community (national anthem, pledge of allegiance, secular holidays) for purely religious ones (hymns, prayers, crosses). This trend often serves to confuse the two realms (In God We Trust and One Nation Under God), so that in worshiping America many citizens believe that they are also doing the will of the Lord. Parents and political leaders claim to be doing the Lord's work when they make decisions.

But religions also support the family power structure directly. A cardinal teaching of the major world religions is the honor and respect owed to an elder, especially a father or mother, and parents are enjoined to produce offspring and raise them in the one true way. Religious institutions offer many supports to families—religious school instruction, socializing facilities, and pastoral counseling. Families support religions through attendance, contributions, and enrollment of children. The church or synagogue is thus a primary agent of socialization to filial responsibility.

Social scientists have noted the special functions of religious rituals for allaying anxiety over the unknown and in reinforcing the solidarity of the group after the death of a member. Old people, facing their own death and coping with that of spouses and friends, should be in great need of solace. Thus, elders have been consistently portrayed as both more superstitious and religious than younger people, who tend to keep "wandering from the path" of true belief.

For all these reasons, historical and eternal, the religious role of old people has been strong and enduring.

CURRENT SCENE

Although we know a great deal about the religious behavior of contemporary old people, there is still uncertainty concerning the meaning of this behavior. Evaluating the data up to 1968, Riley and Foner (1968) found that young and old alike report a religious identification, that attendance at services rises through adulthood and does not taper off until very old age, and that old people usually score slightly higher on measures of "religiosity" than do younger adults. Private devotions also seem to be more characteristic of old people, perhaps because the elderly have difficulty getting to a public place of worship.

Interpreting these findings, which have been supported by more recent research, is not so simple. Modern societies are considered to be increasingly secularized; the beliefs of old people then might reflect only their historical condition, having always been socialized at a more religious time than later cohorts. Illness, thoughts of one's own death, and the actual death of friends and relatives, could also reinforce a need in the elderly to find a transcendent meaning to life and death. Another possibility is that each generation begins more skeptical than their own parents, but that the need for psychic reassurance accompanies the progress through marriage, birth of children, aging, and abrupt transitions in the life course.

Yet another explanatory process focuses on selective survival: religious people may have qualities (faith being one of them) that are associated with long life. There is, for example, evidence that religiousness is correlated with life satisfaction and other measures of well-being (Edwards and Klemmack, 1973; Spreitzer and Snyder, 1974), although the direction of influence is not clear. Socioeconomic status is also related to church attendance and to well-being. A second type of selective survival argument considers change over time in the composition of the older strata: throughout the life course women are more likely to go to church and be devout than are men; therefore, the evidence of high religious involvement in old age might simply reflect the shifting sex ratio.

For whatever reason, the link between religiosity and aging continues to be very strong, as typified by the Harris survey (1975) data on page 295.

In spite of its theoretical interest, the religious activity of old people is not among the most frequently studied phenomena of later life. The research findings have been so consistent that this aspect of older life may have become taken for granted. In one of the few relevant reports to appear recently, the longitudinal data presented again supported previous research: religious attitudes remain high throughout old age, activity levels

Table 11–1. Importance of Religion in Your Life

	Total Public		Total Public						
	18–64 %	65 and Over %	18–24 %	25–39 %	40–54 %	55–64 %	65–69 %	70–79 %	80 and Over %
Very important	49	71	34	45	58	65	69	71	73
Somewhat important	33	21	40	35	29	25	22	21	19
Hardly important at all	17	7	25	20	12	10	8	8	6
Not sure	1	1	1	*	1	*	1	*	2

* Less than 0.5 per cent.

drop with advanced age, and females consistently had higher activity levels than males although the declines were parallel (Blazer and Palmore, 1976). In a small sample of southern Protestants originally tested in 1957 and again in 1974, religious activities were more important than religious attitudes for measures of happiness, adjustment, and usefulness, but neither was directly related to longer life. The researchers concluded that although there was no increase in religious interest, and even a decline in church attendance, "religion plays a significant and increasingly

Table 11–2. Attendance at a Church or Synagogue in Last Year or So

		When Attended Last				
	Attended in Last Year %	Within Last Week or Two %	A Month Ago %	2–3 Months Ago %	More Than 3 Months Ago %	Not Sure %
Total Public	75	71	13	7	9	*
18 to 64	74	70	14	7	9	*
65 and over	77	79	9	5	7	*
18 to 24	67	60	18	8	14	*
25 to 39	73	72	11	7	10	*
40 to 54	78	70	15	8	7	—
55 to 64	81	79	11	4	6	—
65 to 69	80	79	9	5	6	1
70 to 79	78	79	10	4	7	*
80 and over	68	76	10	6	8	*

* Less than 0.5 per cent.
Source: Louis Harris and Associates, *The Myth and Reality of Aging in America,* Washington, D.C.: National Council on the Aging, 1975, p. 181.

Religion, Education, and Leisure

important role in the personal adjustment of many older persons" (p. 85). One implication of these and related findings drawn by Blazer and Palmore is that religious organizations should consider ways to enhance and build upon the positive contributions of religious activity to well-being in later life. But religious activity may be measured too narrowly as church or synagogue attendance. Mindel and Vaughan (1978) argued for more subjective definitions of religious engagement, including private devotions. Radio and television are also important sources of spiritual engagement; indeed, religious programming and the number of religious stations have greatly increased in the past few years.

The issue of ministries to the aged has received little systematic study, even though the data given indicate that old people make up a large proportion of parishioners. Longino and Kitson (1976), noting that stereotypes had flourished in the absence of research, undertook the reanalysis of a national sample of American Baptist parish ministers from 1965 (before the wave of interest in aging). For these ministers, at least, ministry to the aged was apparently neither the most nor the least enjoyable of their pastoral responsibilities, but a majority preferred their work with young people and adults. Ministers who felt most comfortable with expressive contact, talking, and visiting were more likely to enjoy their work with the elderly than were ministers whose focus was social activism.

Hammond (1972) remarked upon an apparent change in old age by parishioners from an interest in instrumental (or goal-oriented) to expressive needs, which implies that older members seek comfort, reassurance, and anchorage from their religious affiliations. A "strategy" for parish churches, according to Hammond, must stress the neighborhood network, providing a location for senior activities, visiting the homebound, and counseling the dying person and her/his family. These basic pastoral functions were not the most popular, especially for younger ministers, in the period of civil rights activism when most of the studies cited by Hammond were conducted. Churches have since drawn back from social activism in favor of an emphasis on personal salvation—an emphasis that is more congenial to both aging parishioners and young people in search of stability.

On the other hand, where social activism is still an important religious responsibility, we also find continued organizing around age-related political goals, as, for example, the church-sponsored North Jersey Federation, described in Hess (1976). Concerns of old people are now probably more attractive rallying points for religious activism than the rights of homosexuals, the ordination of women, antinuclear demonstrations, and other contemporary social causes. The elderly should, therefore, profit from activist impulses within religious establishments combined with the dearth of competing attractions in the 1970s.

Another area in which religious bodies have been active on behalf of the aged is in the nonprofit sponsorship of homes for the aged, retirement communities, housing projects, and senior centers. Unfortunately, the high costs of construction and of health care, as well as inflation in general and increased life expectancy, have created major financial problems, leading to the closing of some of these facilities. The television program, "60 Minutes," reported recently on the dilemma facing elderly Methodists who had signed contracts for lifetime care many years ago, but whose current and future needs could not be met by the religious guarantors—a problem not unlike that of inadequately funded pension plans (Chapter 7).

At the local level, the costs of religious sponsorship of senior centers are considerably eased by the provisions of the Older Americans Act, but are somewhat complicated by the requirements for record keeping and adherence to state standards. The social and recreational needs of aging congregants has, in many cases, outweighed drawbacks such as removing the separation of church and state or providing for persons of all religions. But, in general, religious bodies have not become major sponsors of nonprofit facilities for old people.

PROSPECTS

Religion is the institutional sphere that shows the least change over time, and there is no reason to expect any dramatic shift in either the religious behavior of old people or in pastoral concern for the well-being of the elderly. Any changes that may occur will be in the direction of an increase in these factors. Although the secular trend has been toward reduced commitment to religious observance, we are now in a period of profound challenge to secularism, rationality, and intellectualism. The surge of evangelism, attempts to reassert fundamentalist control over schoolbook material, renewed interest in faith healing, and the like, all suggest that we are experiencing a revival in expressive religiosity. For as long as this movement lasts, the elderly should find the religious atmosphere of our society very congenial, reinforcing their beliefs and encouraging their participation. At the same time, our unsystematic impression is that whereas the elderly are active participants at prayer meetings, the main thrust of the new evangelism is directed toward young people and middle-aged adults, who are in a better position to contribute financially, and organizationally as proselytizers. The building plans of many newly established and enriched religious entrepreneurs include universities, medical centers, and extremely elaborate houses of worship, but not nursing homes and retirement communities. These latter remain the province of mainline religions, and, as noted, have not been especially successful undertakings.

As part of the development and dissemination of gerontological knowledge, we expect that some special training in ministering to the aged will be incorporated into the curriculum of seminaries. Since pastoral counseling has become increasingly sophisticated, and many younger clergy have been well trained in the social sciences, it would be most surprising if the special needs of older congregants did not receive attention. Yet we doubt that interest of organized religion in the aged will approach that for the needs of youth (who must be kept in the faith for religious organizations to survive) and for mature adults (the major financial support of the congregation).

There are conflicting trends regarding the ages of religious leaders. In denominations that stress tradition, hierarchy, and orthodoxy, age will continue to confer added authority. Popes, Anglican archbishops, Greek Orthodox patriarchs, and Grand Rabbis today typically do not reach their high office until after a slow lifetime movement up the ladder of power. Charismatic leaders, as noted, can be much younger—13-year-old gurus, infant Dalai Lamas, and prepubertal faith healers are extreme contemporary cases. For added credibility, though, young religious leaders often acquire a veneer of maturity. Much depends on the characteristics of followers; there is a tendency to trust spiritual guides who share one's experience and outlook. But older males remain steeped in the aura of authority, a quality as essential to leading a flock as a family, evoking the obedience to the father of childhood.

Education

PERSPECTIVES

Education was the last sphere of social activity to be removed from the family. In preliterate societies, the learning of adult roles involved a combination of observation of elders and on-the-job training. Until the Industrial Revolution was fairly complete, many jobs could be handed on from parent to child, and apprenticeships could be arranged. Even today, entry into a skilled trade controlled by apprentice training is often along family lines. When elders had the requisite knowledge, and where there are no alternative sources, their experience becomes the wisdom of the group.

The direct transmission of job skills and placement is more difficult today. Modern industrial economies require high levels of literacy and large numbers of specialists with diverse skills. Therefore, a variety of educations must be offered, and young people must be motivated to learn the requisite skills. Further, if children and youths are unnecessary for the economy, another set of activities must be provided. As a result of all these forces, modern societies have become characterized by universal education covering increasingly longer periods of time.

One outcome is that birth cohorts are successively better educated, or, more precisely, have had more years of schooling than previous ones. Whatever authority the elders may hold by virtue of their greater knowledge is obviously minimized when juniors are likely to know more and to have learned it more recently than their parents.

Partly because of their educational advantages, many young persons entering the labor force frequently begin at a level as high or higher than their parents have achieved in a lifetime. Much of this apparent upward mobility, however, has resulted from the changing structure of occupations, with more places opening up at the white-collar, managerial, and service fields, and commensurately fewer places becoming available in the laborer categories.

There is an underlying irony here, and possibly a great deal of intergenerational tension, in the realization of the American Dream. That one's children should do better, reach higher, and achieve more was the immigrants' goal; most parents still expect their offspring to move upward in the stratification system. But this leads to a growing gap between the generations, and to an undermining of parental authority.

The perception of education as *the* mechanism for selection by merit obscures the crucial continuing effects of ascription. The quality of schools, the facilities for learning available in the community, encouragement in the home, and the ability to pay for postsecondary education are still related to family social-class placement. To this extent, the elders can control the educational outcomes for juniors, although the goal remains the preparation of the child to outstrip the achievements of the parents.

Traditionally, teachers, like priests and statesmen, are thought to improve with age. The gray-bearded professor, complete with a case of absentmindedness, was until recently, a figure of instant credibility. The system of tenure, intended to insulate teachers from public pressures, in the normal course of events will operate to increase the average age of faculty. Parsons and Platt (1972) maintained that a clear age difference is essential to the socialization process, so that faculty (analogous to parents in the family) derive their power to transmit knowledge, in part, from their superior age. This characteristic of academic authority is being challenged today in the same fashion as is age-based authority in the political, economic, and family systems.

CURRENT SCENE

Educational Attainment. As Table 11–3 (Uhlenberg, 1977) demonstrates, the years of schooling completed by each successive cohort are consistently higher. By the turn of the next century, over 70 percent of white men and women age 60–64 will have had full high school educations, with a

Table 11–3. Percentage Distribution of White Population Aged 60–64 by Years of School Completed: USA, 1930–2000

Year	White Males				White Females			
	0–7	8–H.S. 3	H.S. 4	Some College	0–7	8–H.S. 3	H.S. 4	Some College
1900								
1910			NA				NA	
1920								
1930 [a]	45.6	41.8	6.1	6.5	39.1	45.9	9.5	5.5
1940	41.3	43.0	7.8	8.0	35.6	45.8	11.5	7.1
1950	40.4	39.5	10.1	10.0	35.5	41.7	13.2	9.5
1960	32.8	43.4	11.2	12.6	28.7	43.5	15.3	12.5
1970	21.4	41.7	19.1	17.7	17.6	40.8	24.0	17.6
1980 [b]	12.5	35.1	30.5	21.8	10.2	34.9	37.4	17.5
1990 [b]	9.7	30.3	30.9	29.1	7.2	28.9	43.4	20.5
2000 [b]	6.4	22.3	37.7	33.6	5.3	23.4	46.9	24.4

[a] Distribution of the population aged 70–74 in 1940 (the same cohort, but 10 years later).

[b] The distribution of this cohort at age 60–64 is assumed to be the same as its distribution in 1970, when it was younger.

Sources: U.S. Censuses of Population: 1940, Vol. IV, Part 1, Table 18; 1950, Vol. II, Part I, Table 115; 1960, PC(1)–1D, Table 173; 1970, PC(1)–1D, Table 199.

From Uhlenberg, Peter, "Changing Structure of the Older Population of the USA During the Twentieth Century," *The Gerontologist*, Vol. 17, No. 3, 1977, p. 201.

large proportion having had some college experience. However, this table does not reflect the trend of the past decade for women to enter institutions of higher education *after* marriage and childbearing.

Many gerontologists have taken these data as signifying that each successive cohort of old people is potentially more sophisticated in dealing with the contingencies of modern life. Predictions of senior power are partly based on the existence of a pool of educated older people, although it is just as likely that enhanced coping ability will serve to protect these individuals from the negative effects of aging. It is probably not education as much as the economic advantages that go with college degrees that account for the relationship between education and well-being in old age.

Nor do years of education necessarily indicate better; there is some reason to believe that school curricula have been progressively watered down and stretched out. But whatever it means in terms of quality, the educational attainment of incoming cohorts of elderly will be comparable to that of the population as a whole.

Older People in Educational Settings. Schools are the most age-graded institutions in our society. Differences of a single chronological year determine educational identity and the entire status system of students. At the college level, however, age lines have become increasingly less precise since 1945 when returning veterans under the GI Bill "aged" the campuses. Today we are seeing another wave of returnees, primarily women. See Table 11–4 on page 302.

These 1.6 million older students are working toward degrees or certificates. Additional millions are engaged in other forms of adult education: to refresh skills, learn new leisure-time pursuits, or follow personal interests.

Many postsecondary institutions, beginning to feel the effects of the end of the Baby Boom cohort, are actively encouraging older students. The need to find new sources of students is heightened also by a drop in the proportion of high school graduates going directly to college. As the traditionally appropriate age group declines, college places are increasingly occupied by people over the age of 30.

Enrollments have increased most at two-year colleges, where the proportion of students 35+ is higher than at four-year institutions. Since most older students are also in the labor force, urban campuses and community colleges are particularly convenient, relatively inexpensive, and accommodating to part-time study. Yet the "graying" of the campus is widespread in prestige institutions as well: as a means of maintaining enrollment from a hitherto untapped clientele.

Older students are a varied lot, not only in their age distribution but in their goals: some are acquiring skills, others are retraining, still others are resuming educational careers after interruption, and some are pursuing old or new interests. The influence of the Women's Movement has been crucial to creating a climate in which women can return to school even while raising children, to enable them to prepare for eventual labor force participation or simply to pursue an interrupted education.

In addition to welcoming older students in general, many colleges and universities have developed programs specifically for the elderly, defined variously from age 50 on up. These programs take the form of summer weeks at residential colleges, weekend courses, single-course offerings, and many innovative programs such as the Institute for Retirement Studies at Case Western Reserve University in Cleveland and the Institute for Retired Professionals of the New School for Social Research in New York City. As with most such programs, tuitions are subsidized or substantially reduced for retired persons. Not only do the elderly perform well as students but their presence is a learning experience for their younger classmates. Other colleges, such as the College of Notre Dame in Maryland, have established special courses designed for the elderly.

The difference in task performance between the old and young in cross-sectional studies does not necessarily reflect a decline in intelligence of students age 60+. As noted in Chapter 5 many noncognitive factors in-

Table 11–4. Type of School Attended by Persons 35 and Older, by Sex, Marital Status of Women, and Race, October 1976

[Per cent distribution]

Item	Total		Elementary and high school	College					Trade or vocational [2]
	Number (in thousands)	Per Cent		Total	Full time	Part time	Under-graduate [1]	Grad-uate	
Both sexes	1,604	100.0	4.1	74.0	13.1	60.9	56.0	18.0	21.9
Men	646	100.0	3.4	75.4	15.1	60.3	52.8	22.6	21.2
Women	958	100.0	4.6	73.0	11.7	61.3	58.1	14.9	22.4
Married, husband present	622	100.0	3.2	75.1	10.6	64.5	60.0	15.1	21.7
Other marital status	336	100.0	7.1	69.1	13.6	55.5	54.6	14.5	23.7
White	1,399	100.0	3.6	73.8	12.3	61.5	55.0	18.8	22.6
Black and other	205	100.0	7.8	75.0	18.1	56.9	62.3	12.7	17.2

[1] Includes both full-time and part-time students.
[2] In the Current Population Survey, these schools are called "special schools."
Monthly Labor Review (July 1977), p. 44.

fluence test scores: educational attainment, test anxiety, experience in test taking, self-image, and motivation (Barton et al., 1975; Woodruff and Walsh, 1975). What had at first been interpreted as a decline in learning capacity with old age is now more accurately interpreted as cohort differences in test-taking abilities. Life-span psychologists are in the process of determining to what degree certain cognitive capacities, if any, do decline with age. Today's aged, though, have certain difficulties in learning that can be greatly improved by changes in teaching techniques. For example, time limits and other anxiety-arousing situations often impair the performance of older test takers compared to younger, more experienced subjects. Clearly, much can be done to improve old people's test performance by reducing stressful aspects of the situation.

Old people in higher education, however, are more typically found among the faculty than in the student body. Faculty are also age-graded: full professors are usually older than associates, and assistants are commonly older than instructors. The stereotype of the gray-beard professor is still quite accurate, in terms of both age and sex. Young faculty, who are graduate student teaching assistants or instructors, bridge the gap between students and professors. With the increasing age heterogeneity of the student body, many teachers will be younger than their students, but this does not seem to have disturbed the socialization process, despite Parsons and Platt's (1972) predictions.

A different age-related problem in academe is the tendency over time for departments to become older. In a period of nongrowth in faculty such as exists today, this means fewer opportunities for entry and advancement to younger faculty, and especially for women (some of whom are reentering postponed careers) and minority group members for whom affirmative action programs have recently been formulated. The changes that were recently enacted in mandatory retirement rules in universities specifically acknowledge this problem, but delay the imposition of involuntary retirement provisions for several years (See Chapter 8).

Academic fields vary greatly in the extent to which age is a factor in the ability to make important contributions. In mathematics and the sciences, new models and experiments can supplant older ones quite quickly, and breakthrough insights by young researchers are very common (Zuckerman and Merton, 1972). Other disciplines rely on the slow accretion of bits and pieces of knowledge, so that the longer one is at it, the more valuable that store of knowledge becomes, as in the study of history or language or literature. In the practice of law, medicine, or psychiatry, the sheer number of cases handled often leads to greater expertise, so that age-related capacities expand rather than contract. Sigmund Freud, for instance, began his major achievements after age 40.

Another aspect of both academic life and professional activity that makes longevity in the role possible is greater flexibility in scheduling. For academics, there are limited hours (and the longer one has been teaching the *fewer* hours), and compressed work schedules, with long periods for reflection and relaxation. At the other extreme, attorneys, physicians, and similar professionals are noted for their long hours of work. Although they are not constrained by the 9 to 5 routine of most businesses, professionals have considerable freedom in setting their office hours and often have the possibility of tapering off gradually with age. For these reasons, among others, postgraduate education is associated with long work lives.

Gerontology in Higher Education. The need for information on America's growing population of old people, coupled with increased funding from the federal and state governments, has produced a tenfold increase over the past five years in the number of academic institutions that offer gerontological courses or entire programs. The first annual meeting of the Association for Gerontology in Higher Education (AGHE) in 1975, had about 100 participants; fittingly, the theme of this meeting was "Gerontology as a New Frontier in Higher Education" (Hess, 1975). By 1976, an AGHE survey revealed over 1,200 postsecondary schools with gerontology offerings, which were designed to stimulate research, teach gerontology, and prepare trained personnel for age-related programs in the society. Obviously, the variety of such offerings is enormous, depending on the resources of each institution, the goals of program developers, funding, and the personnel available. Predictably, the most recent meetings of AGHE have been devoted to program development, persistent issues, and the dilemmas of growth and diversity.

As a reader of this book, you are part of the surge of interest in gerontology and the proliferation of courses. As with Black studies in the late 1960s and women's studies more recently, the emergence of a social issue promotes both the desire to know more about the issue and an ideological commitment to redress past neglect or discrimination. Race, sex, and age are all ascribed characteristics that have been used as bases of social stratification, as discussed in Chapter 3. To the extent that accurate information is gathered and disseminated, false foundations of discrimination can be discredited. The knowledge that combats stereotypes and destroys myths liberates both the knower and the object of such studies. But as the experience of Black and women's studies has shown, research, teaching, and mass media campaigns are not effective against the biases built into our minds and our social structures about people's abilities and capacities on the basis of race, sex, and age. Nonetheless, courses such as the one in which you are now enrolled can bring the elderly back into the consciousness of younger members of the society, and also prepare students for their own inevitable aging.

There is, however, an emerging problem of premature specialization in gerontology, as in Black studies, Jewish studies, and women's studies—where substantive knowledge in that specific field is emphasized at the cost of integrating the information into liberal arts curricula in general.

PROSPECTS

The increasingly high educational attainment of elderly cohorts has profound implications for the future of aging and the lives of old people. It is possible that many declines in functioning that have been assumed to be age induced will be shown to be cohort related. Cognitive skills, morale, self-image, maintenance of independent residence, and ability to deal with complex bureaucracies all could be enhanced in the future through the effects of longer exposure to schooling not only in the pre-adult years but throughout the life course. If both the original quantity and quality of schooling and the opportunity to upgrade skills at later ages are increased, many disadvantages of the elderly vis-à-vis younger students and workers will be eliminated or narrowed. Indeed, when "state of the art" training is equalized among age groups, experience could again become the crucial variable in occupational worth.

Dependency on kin, especially offspring, should be lessened or at least delayed to advanced old age. Although it is not always possible to separate the effects of education from the income and health statuses associated with levels of schooling, the ability to manipulate symbols and to understand the social structure should serve to reduce powerlessness—both real and apparent. A sense of control over one's life would be reflected in the wish to live independently and to construct voluntary networks for mutual support.

The enhancement of cognitive skills and coping strategies that will become available to future elderly could, as already suggested, produce an age-based political movement, led by an articulate and energetic cadre of young-old activists. Yet the same characteristics will allow many to maintain the activities of middle age through additional decades, inhibiting identification with the interest of the infirm and/or very old. The one conclusion that can be made with assurance is that educational attainment enlarges the range of possible life-styles in old age.[1]

This expansion of options is both the cause and consequence of the renewed interest of many old people in continuing their education. The concept of lifelong education is being taken very seriously today by edu-

[1] We must not lose sight, however, of the inherent elitism in education—some colleges are more equal than others—or of the overriding effect of socioeconomic status. Nelson Rockefeller, for example, never finished college, and even as he reached 70 at the time of his death was rarely perceived as an "old man." Many other wealthy and powerful men also had relatively low levels of educational attainment. Also, at each level of education, the returns in wages and promotions to Blacks and women are far lower than those to white males.

cators and administrators, not only out of necessity to fill classrooms but out of recognition that the rate of change in our knowledge base is so rapid that many workers will need refresher or retraining courses several times during a career.

Postsecondary institutions are gradually accommodating themselves to the fact that many women will have discontinuous educational careers, returning on part- or full-time bases at any point in adulthood. For colleges and universities to recognize this trend is a matter of good business, not sheer altruism. All these changes argue for flexibility in educational structures, for the removal of barriers to part-time study, and for the revision of admissions standards. To encourage older people to continue their educations should be more than the gesture it so often is today, but a desired goal in its own right. The classroom of men and women at all stages of adulthood, of varied occupations, marital statuses, and socioeconomic background is a learning environment by itself. Special programs for old people should have self-destruction as a goal, although they may be required in the short run. The long-term best interest of colleges and universities strongly argues for increased programming for students of all ages.

Leisure

PERSPECTIVE

A third strand of activity in later life is the use of leisure time. In the past, too few old people survived family and/or work responsibilities to spend even a few years, much less several decades, with time that was not obligated to these responsibilities. For many who are currently retired, the use of time presents a major problem. The universality of mandatory retirement (until the federal legislation of 1978) in conjunction with increased life expectancy makes current cohorts of old people major pioneers in the use of leisure. As recently as four decades ago it was not unlikely that a man would die before his last child left home, or that a woman in her fifties could be caring for a minor child. Then, too, the proportion of self-owned businesses and farms, enterprises in which the older couple would remain active until physically incapable, was greater only a generation ago.

Now that years without productive or reproductive tasks are possible, there remain psychological barriers to their enjoyment. The Puritan work ethic, which is so much a part of the American value system, has instilled a deep mistrust of nonproductive uses of time. To activate the commitment to work, people must also be convinced that nonwork is sinful: "the devil finds work for idle hands" (which, incidentally, should help us understand American attitudes toward welfare recipients). The discomfort of many retirees today can be traced to their lingering fear that their leisure leaves them open to temptation, and, therefore, cannot be contemplated, much less enjoyed.

Any unease over what to do in retirement may be less a consequence of lingering Puritanism than lack of practice in satisfying or sustained use of leisure at earlier stages. For, contrary to popular belief, there has been *no* appreciable reduction since 1948 in hours worked per week by nonstudent males (Owen, 1976):

Table 11–5. Hours Worked per Week by Nonstudent Males

Year	Unadjusted	Adjusted for Growth in Vacations and Holidays
1948	42.7	41.6
1950	42.2	41.0
1953	42.5	41.4
1956	43.0	41.8
1959	42.0	40.7
1962	43.1	41.7
1966	43.5	42.1
1969	43.5	42.0
1972	42.9	41.4
1975	42.5	40.9

Monthly Labor Review (August 1976), p. 1.

Between 1901 and 1948, there *was* a marked decline from 58.4 to 42.0 hours a week among men, and for *all* workers the average was 38.1 hours in 1975, but this was a result of the influx of students and married women who typically work less than 40 hours per week. The nonstudent male has as long a workweek today as he did thirty years ago. This is so because most workers have chosen to use their higher earnings for consumption purposes rather than for leisure—these are the fathers of the Baby Boom children. Future cohorts of workers, with fewer children to raise and educate, may resume the secular trend to a shorter work week.

Actually, given these data, plus the great increase in labor force participation of married women and students, Owen (1976) argued that the overall amount of leisure time of American adults has *declined*, even allowing for added vacation days and holidays. Therefore, although the work life may be shortened today through later entry and earlier exit than before 1945, the amount of leisure time during that work life has not increased by more than a few days a year. Nonetheless, a major goal of the American labor movement remains the reduction of the workweek (which may only free some for moonlighting).

Recreation has become a major industry—special vehicles, equipment, resorts, air travel, private pools, and tourism—accounting for an increasing proportion of consumer expenditures over the past twenty-five years (*Statistical Abstract*, 1978, p. 431). Total spending on recreation has increased sixfold since 1950 (p. 235). Apparently, Americans *are* able to enjoy their leisure. Days off, vacations, and even retirement can be defined as "well-earned" respites from work. Indeed, it could even be said that the pursuit of pleasure has taken on characteristics of the work ethic: don't waste time, improve your skills, try hard to enjoy. There is also a thread of conspicuous consumption running through the advertisements, a peculiar American variation on the Puritan ethic that would shock our dour forebears. Each incoming cohort of retirees will have been exposed to this new definition of leisure for a longer period than the preceding one.

CURRENT SCENE

How *do* those 65+ spend their time? A small proportion will have remained in the labor force, and married women will continue to be engaged in homemaking, but most old people will have many unobligated hours to allocate as they choose. Such choices, though, are not altogether "free." There are many limiting conditions present in old age, some the result of physical incapacity, others a matter of cohort experience or of changes in the environment. Among these variables are ability for self-care and mobility, disposable income, convenience of facilities, one's sense of propriety, and fear of crime. Thus, what an old person might wish to do with leisure time is restricted by what one *can* do. Data on preferences are likely to be biased by this realization of limitations and the tendency toward cognitive consistency; that is, respondents attempt to bring desires and capacities into line and to find satisfaction in the activities that are available to them.

A decade ago, Riley and Foner (1968) looked for evidence of an "institutionalization of the leisure role" among the many retired persons with days and hours at their disposal. The research data at that time suggested that if such a role were to crystallize it would involve more solitary and sedentary activities than those chosen by younger people. Yet, even if consistent patterns emerge for the currently retired, can we assume that norms and customs developed by those now old would hold for successive entrants whose use of leisure at earlier stages will be very different? Further, given the diversity of old people, the concept of a leisure role seems unduly restrictive, unless it is at the same level of generality as work role—that which the individual does with her/his leisure time or work time—*and* as socially accepted (if not quite as highly valued).

In general, most research (though of the cross-sectional variety) shows that older respondents are less likely than younger ones to participate in sports or in recreational activities, and more likely to watch television or to be "doing nothing". This pattern may be changing as participation in such sports as tennis and running has increased among adults in general. Also, programs of exercises for the elderly are being presented on non-commercial television and at senior centers. Visiting friends and gardening have been found to increase in retirement in some samples, but not in others. Data from the Harris survey (1975) are fairly representative of current findings from cross-sectional studies:

Table 11–6. "A Lot of Time" Personally Spent Doing Various Activities by Public 65+ Compared with Public 18–64 (in Per Cents)

	18–64 %	65+ %	Net Difference
Socializing with friends	55	47	− 8
Caring for older or younger members of the family	53	27	−26
Working part-time or full	51	10	−41
Reading	38	36	− 2
Sitting and thinking	37	31	− 6
Gardening and raising plants	34	39	+ 5
Participating in recreational activities and hobbies	34	26	− 8
Watching television	23	36	+13
Going for walks	22	25	+ 3
Participating in sports, like golf, tennis, swimming	22	3	−19
Sleeping	15	16	+ 1
Participating in fraternal or community organizations	13	17	+ 4
Just doing nothing	9	15	+ 6
Doing volunteer work	8	8	—
Participating in political activities	5	6	+ 1

Louis Harris and Associates, *The Myth and Reality of Aging in America,* Washington, D.C.: National Council on the Aging, 1975, p. 57.

This overall lowered level of activity is a typical finding (Gordon, Gaitz, and Scott, 1976), although there is some evidence that *variety* of activities may increase with retirement (Peppers, 1976). In other words, an older person is a gadfly who may do more different things than before but not spend a lot of time at any one. Peppers (1976) found that those who increased their range of interests had higher life satisfaction scores than did respondents whose activity levels remained constant or declined. Although many of the activities reported in this research were sedentary

Table 11–7. Median Number of Hours Spent Yesterday with Media

	Total	Under $7,000	$7,000–$14,999	$15,000 and Over	Total Public			White	Black
					Some High School or Less	High School Grad/ Some College	College Grad		
Watching television	1.8	2.1	1.8	1.5	2.1	1.8	1.2	1.8	2.1
Listening to radio	1.2	1.2	1.2	1.2	1.2	1.2	1.1	1.2	1.3
Reading newspapers	.9	.8	.9	1.0	.9	.9	1.0	.9	.8
Reading magazines	.4	.4	.4	.4	.3	.4	.5	.4	.4
Reading books	.4	.3	.4	.4	.3	.4	.5	.4	.4

	Total Public							
	Total	18–24	25–39	40–54	55–64	65–69	70–79	80 and Over
Watching television	1.8	1.8	1.6	1.8	1.8	2.4	2.2	2.0
Listening to radio	1.2	1.8	1.3	1.1	1.0	1.0	.9	.9
Reading newspapers	.9	.8	.9	1.0	1.0	1.0	.9	.9
Reading books	.4	.4	.4	.4	.3	.3	.3	.3
Reading magazines	.4	.4	.4	.4	.4	.4	.4	.4

Louis Harris and Associates, The Myth and Reality of Aging in America, Washington, D.C.: National Council on the Aging, 1975, p. 208.

and solitary, Peppers noted that these were also the preferred activities of respondents *before* retirement. Respondents who were able to continue engagement in sociable and physically active pursuits also scored high on life satisfaction and adjustment to retirement, even with income and health taken into account. However, the male retirees in this study were selected from the membership lists of groups of retired persons, so that the sample was biased in favor of joiners.

Atchley (1971) reported that many retirees find a great deal of positive value in their leisure activities, especially when continuity can be maintained with a preretirement identity. Taking issue with those who hold that the work role is so imperative and all-important a basis of self-worth that retirement must lead to negative outcomes (exemplified by Miller, 1965) Atchley found that respondents varied in their attachment to the work role, that most had multiple identities, and that leisure was a valued attribute of retirement. Having enough money and retired friends with whom to share the nonwork status were prime predictors of retirement adjustment, suggesting that it is the loss of income rather than the work role that accounts for the negative effects of retirement. Moreover, persons whose work roles emphasized social relations skills (see also Simpson, Back, and McKinney, 1966) were able to adjust most readily to retirement, since these are precisely the qualities required for many leisure pursuits. Conversely, professionals (who learn to manipulate symbols) and manual workers (who are oriented to things) will have a harder time adjusting to retirement activities that are centered on socializing, although the former may do more reading and the latter may do more hobby work than before retirement. The common theme is that activities that build upon skills and interest of preretirement will probably lead to satisfaction and adjustment in leisure.

Atchley's work points to a set of common misconceptions about old people: that they feel useless without work, haven't enough to do, and just sit around vegetating. In the Harris (1975) survey, people in general were asked what they thought "most people over 65 (spent) a lot of time doing?"; when these responses were compared to the actual percentages of old people who said they spent a lot of time doing various activities (see Table 11–6), the general public had *overestimated* by 20–30 percentage points the proportions 65+ who watched television, sat and thought, just did nothing, or slept! In fact, many respondents 65+ thought that other old people were more sedentary than they themselves were, but overall the elderly respondents were more accurate than those below age 65. Possibly, these expectations operate as self-fulfilling prophecies, so that some old people, having internalized the rocking-chair image, feel that other behavior would be inappropriate, which is probably an effect that is limited to the cohorts now old. The data suggest rather the situation of *pluralistic ignorance*, in which each individual feels that she or he is an exception whereas others fit the stereotype, not knowing that these others are also "deviant" (see Chapter 3).

These myths of aging further serve to support the work ethic by reinforcing the idea that absence of work is *the* problem of aging (about which little can be done except to raise the age of mandatory retirement), rather than income, health, safety, and companionship—about which a great deal could be done, but at considerable expense. Most of the research reviewed in this book suggests that income adequacy and health status are prime determinants of the decision to retire, rather than an attachment to work. Leisure is not an especially frightening spector to the large number of workers with positive attitudes about early retirement. That those approaching retirement express more misgivings than younger workers need not represent an identity crisis because of the loss of the work role as much as a realistic assessment of a decline in one's standard of living and an apprehension over a major change in life-style.

Nor is it necessarily the case that old people want something called meaningful roles, which are defined in terms that emphasize instrumental worklike aspects. Very few retirees seek out opportunities to perform service to others or to become politically active on behalf of old people, although those who become involved in RSVP, Foster Grandparents, and other programs find the experience extremely rewarding (but those who did not, of course, will have dropped out). The proportions enrolled in various educational settings, as noted earlier in this chapter, are extremely small, despite the growing attempts by younger people to create what they consider activities, programs, and jobs that are appropriate for old people.

Many decrements in leisure participation are not unique to old age. Gordon, Gaitz, and Scott (1976) found consistent declines by age in the proportions of respondents with high leisure participation. From a peak at ages 20–29, participation rates declined steadily for most activities, dramatically for those taking place outside the home or requiring exertion and less obviously for sedentary ones. There was one reversal: *solitary* activities were more frequently engaged in by older rather than younger respondents. Although male scores were typically higher than females, with the expected variation by sex-role appropriateness of the activity, both male and female scores declined steadily on the overall participation measure. These findings suggest that the low participation rates of old people might well be a continuation of lifelong trends, if we can make a life-course observation from cross-sectional data. As people's interests crystallize, they may become more selective in what they chose to invest their time and energy.

Since most of our information on age differences in the uses of leisure are from cross-sectional studies, we cannot assume that today's young people will make later life leisure choices that are similar to the ones made by today's old people. Although it is logical to expect participation in sports and outdoor activities to decline with age, many other activities are related not to energy levels but to past experience and current income.

If a "leisure role" does exist for old people today it is largely sedentary, solitary, and home-based, although visiting, gardening, walking, and religious participation are also popular uses of leisure time. Worklike interests, such as crafts and hobbies, are not pursued intensively by more than a small fraction of old people. Activities requiring outlays of money on transportation are severely reduced in retirement and widowhood. Inexpensive pursuits, such as watching television, socializing with friends, and working around the home are maintained at roughly preretirement levels, if not increased. Solitary relaxation is a very common activity.

To some extent, the more "withdrawn" activities could be a result of not having the physical, emotional, or material resources to remain fully engaged, or of a lack of supportive services and convenient facilities. We know, for instance, that these activities are more characteristic of the "old old" than the "young old." By the same evidence, however, it could be argued that many elderly (like younger people) adjust their activities to their energies, and are quite content doing so. Perhaps the explanatory variable is this "fit" between role-playing opportunities and capacities. If we remember the majority of old people who do not go to senior centers, even when available, or decline to engage in political, educational, and voluntary association activities, we must assume that this is a rational choice for many. This is not to say that old people should not be encouraged in all these activities, and their participation made as easy as possible, but that we should also respect the decision not to participate, when that choice has been made from real alternatives.

We have emphasized the problems of *retired* persons, both men and women, because for them the availability of leisure time is in clear contrast to the obligated hours of employment. Yet the "unobligated" older woman may experience as much difficulty in adjusting to the loss of major instrumental roles as does the retired individual. For many women, the increase in discretionary time is gradual, beginning when her children are in school full time. Some have chosen to return to school themselves, or to go to work, or to increase volunteer commitments. These women will also be spending, on the average, over fifty hours a week at homemaking tasks, which leaves them with less leisure time than adult male workers. At the other extreme are women whose time is *underdemanded*. There is much speculation, though little evidence, that middle-class, middle-age homemakers who do not find satisfying leisure activities consume great quantities of alcohol and prescription drugs. There is more evidence to support the thesis that boredom with housework and/or loss of the parent role will lead to mental illness among women without alternative uses of time (Bart, 1970; Gove and Tudor, 1973). The great majority of older women however, do find ways to minimize role slack, and could be considered pioneers of a "new life-style" in aging (see Conclusion). A second category of older women are not so fortunate in their options or resources: the "displaced homemaker." Most "unemployed nurturers" with children over age 18 (and thus no longer eligible for Aid to Dependent Children payments) must enter the unskilled labor force, or, if they can prove themselves physically or mentally unable to sustain employment, apply for SSI benefits.

PROSPECTS

Future cohorts of old people, just as current and past ones, will carry into old age the habits and customs developed over the years and which are part of their peculiar slice of history. Many trends are observable among those now in young adulthood that may affect their use of leisure in old age: widespread travel, activities outside the home for women, and the popularity of individual sports such as running, tennis, and golf. We can only guess at the effect of higher educational attainment on reading habits and cultural interests.

The income, health, and physical mobility resources of the young-old, especially those choosing early retirement, argue for high levels of leisure participation of the active variety, whereas the growing numbers of very old will undoubtedly add to the proportion of elderly who prefer passive and sedentary activities. Research designs that have only one category of old people, everyone over 65+, run the risk of averaging out these two patterns into a statistic that describes neither.

The world around the aged will also have changed greatly. Public support of senior centers, outreach programs, educational opportunities designed for older students, and an awareness of their needs and interests by religious institutions—are all environmental factors that could increase the range of choices for those entering old age in the decades ahead.

Another change of some importance is the proliferation of preretirement counseling and educational programs. Some are sponsored by employers and unions, others emanate from educational or community organizations, and still others are free-lance operations. Since participation in these programs is on a voluntary basis, it is difficult to assess the degree to which adjustment to retirement is enhanced; "good retirees" may have selected themselves for the preretirement experience. Nonetheless, these programs can be seen as visible efforts to demystify retirement. Less obvious, but extremely helpful in "regularizing" the experience of retirement, is the fact that workmates will probably leave at the same time, what Atchley (1972) referred to as a "retirement cohort." When retirement is a common fate, expected and planned for, leisure can become another shared experience, also anticipated and planned for.

There are a number of reasons for expecting that the use of leisure will not be a major problem for old people in the future. At the level of values, a deemphasis of the work role as a source of identity and concomitant concern with personal fulfillment could lead to a positive attitude toward the opportunities presented by the expansion of leisure time. When retirement expectations are built into the individual's life plan, anticipatory socialization and the companionship of others remove fear of the unknown and a sense of isolation. The changing composition of cohorts further suggests greater competence and resources for finding satisfying activities *before* as well as during retirement. A gradual withdrawal from active participation will undoubtedly take place, but at later ages. The many efforts undertaken today to provide the supports required for maintaining old people in the community—senior centers, transportation arrangements, housing options, and health care delivery—will enhance opportunities for socializing and "being in the world." Roles for old people are being developed and expanded in education, politics, religion, and volunteer programs.

Models for the satisfying use of leisure time that are evolving today could become the norm tomorrow—and not only for old people. We envisage the time when the life course will no longer be composed of relatively exclusive activity segments as is the typical pattern today:

leisure/	education/	work	/leisure
0–4	5–21	21–65	65+

Rather, as was probably the case of our hunting and gathering forebears, we foresee a multistrand life course in which leisure, work, education, and family life are intertwined at most stages, with one activity or the other becoming most salient at certain ages but rarely to the degree of concentration that we experience in modern societies:

Leisure
Education
Family
Work

Karl Marx spoke of a world in which one could hunt before noon, fish in the afternoon, and enjoy the companionship of friends in the evening. Utopian, perhaps, but there is a growing population of persons who are attempting to combine two or more major activities at one time: working mothers; students in the labor force; those who "drop out" of school or work for a period of trying alternatives; high school students allowed release time for employment; men who take paternity leave; and older people who reduce their work time in order to travel or be with family and friends. Retirement would certainly be less a difficult transition than a simple shift of emphasis, and so also for other points of radical change in the role cluster. A certain richness to the texture of life would make old age less discontinuous to all that has come before, while many of the effects of aging that are so obvious today will be muted.

Research Exercises

1. *Interview* ministers, priests, and rabbis concerning their perception of older congregants, learn whether or not there are programs for the elderly in the church or synagogue, the content of pastoral counseling to the aged, and how well prepared the clergy were to deal with these problems.

2. *Examine* information from the *sample survey* on religious behavior and the uses of leisure time.

3. *Inventory* the educational opportunities for old people in your community. What is available? Are there special courses? What are the inducements or drawbacks to participation by the elderly.

4. Ask a number of old people (as varied as possible) to keep *time budgets* for one week. If a different group is contacted for each week of the course, you should have several dozen budgets for comparison.

5. If your college or university has older students, conduct *interviews* to find out how their decision to return to school was made, what supports were available to them, how they feel in a classroom with young students, and so forth.

Discussion Questions

Students who have been in classes with older people should report on the experience—their impressions, reactions of classmates, and the demeanor of the senior student.

How would you explain the link between age and religiosity?

If you were allowed to schedule one day a week of television for the elderly, what type of programs would you select?

Conclusion

———••———

It is the function of an introductory textbook to present an overview of a field of study, touching however briefly on the major areas of research interest. Because the study of aging and old age encompasses biological, psychological, and social variables, and has an historical dimension, an Introduction to Social Gerontology covers an enormous range of topics with as much depth as possible in a few hundred pages written for beginning students. Authors of introductory textbooks must make decisions about what to include and how much detail to offer on a given theme. Readers will no doubt have found some points relatively neglected in our presentation, and other issues perhaps overstressed; it is both the challenge and burden of social gerontology that there is so much to study. Moreover, almost all findings in this field are by nature tentative. What pertains to those who are old today may not apply in the future. Even biological aging is subject to intervention and modification. Nor are psychological processes as universal as is often claimed. Attitudes, even consciousness itself—the interpretation of self and one's place in the world—have changed through time and vary from one culture to another.

In these concluding pages we recapitulate the major themes of the preceding chapters, integrate these themes into a coherent statement on the condition of old people today, and indicate how aging and the life course might change in the decades ahead.

We begin with the observation that social gerontology evolved out of a desire to know more about aging and old age at a time when large numbers of Americans outlived valued roles and when their medical and social needs became defined as public issues rather than personal problems. Gathering data, however, is an empty exercise unless the process is guided by adequate theory and suitable methods. Much of our early understanding of growing old was marred by value judgment (conscious and unconscious) and faulty research designs. But as discrepancies and contradictions accumulated, other social scientists were drawn to the problem of conceptual clarification, and out of the ferment of the past decade has come a more sophisticated insight into the complexities of aging. Where, for example, we had once naively assumed from cross-sectional data that growing older led to attitude change, we must now pay attention to the period in which early socialization took place, or to the impact of history on persons of different ages, as well as to possible age-related effects.

Although considered primarily as an attribute of individuals, age is an element in social structure. To be of a given age is to be placed in the social order, eligible for certain roles, given access to positions of power, be deemed worthy of respect, and so forth. Age and sex together produce some form of stratification system in any society, but there is enormous cross-cultural and cross-temporal variation in the status of elders. Within the same society, there are differences on the basis of sex, race, and social class, all of which are often more powerful indicators of well-being than is age alone.

Nor does aging take place in a cultural vacuum. There are ideals and images and meanings that are attached to age. Cultural beliefs and values determine the way in which childhood or adulthood or old age are perceived at any one time and place. Just as children have been variously seen as essentially evil or innocent, or like primitives or as miniature adults, so have old people been revered or reviled, or deemed essential or expendable. The secular beliefs regarding old age in our society today have been assailed as constituting "agism," and old people are thought to have internalized negative self-images because of this denigration. But the data suggest that although many elderly feel that others have written them off, they themselves are managing quite nicely. The old people who are not managing so well are most often suffering from low incomes rather than from age discrimination.

In general, however, it is clear that old people in modern industrial societies lack many of the bases of power, prestige, and property that bolstered their status in other times. Yet we must bear in mind that the position of older family members has always been somewhat problematic and that it may be no worse today than in many a less complex society and earlier historical epoch.

Turning to the contemporary United States, we discussed the biological and psychological processes associated with growing old, and the institutionalization of those whose bodies and minds require constant care.

Aging brings many changes in an organism, but the rate of decline, the efficacy of adaptations, and the differential onset of these processes lead us also to examine social characteristics—race, sex roles, and socioeconomic status. If poverty is a major factor in low health status and morale in old age, Medicaid is a minimal solution. Loneliness and sensory deprivation have roots much earlier in life, and institutionalization is probably more a matter of personal and social resources than of one's mental condition. That is, many of the negative outcomes of old age are neither general nor inevitable.

It is also possible that medical investigations will lead to interventions that can maintain functioning for longer periods than at present, just as psychologists have devised techniques for reducing the effects of aging on the task ability of old people. In other words, the process of physical aging could be very different in the future, rendering unnecessary many of the long-term health programs recently devised for the care of the aged. The new emphasis on prevention and health maintenance could greatly reduce or delay the onset of chronic conditions. On the other hand, increased exposure to cancer-causing agents could offset other gains.

Whereas an extension of the period of good health remains a distant goal, the more immediate task is to reduce inequalities in health status by race and income, a goal well within the abilities of a society that has sent men to the moon.

With regard to psychological changes, many previously "inevitable decrements" have been shown to be greatly influenced by environment and education. Indeed, "senility" turns out to be a catchall category for symptoms derived from a number of treatable conditions that are unrelated to organic brain damage in many cases. The causal direction of the link between madness and deprived social statuses is often assumed by mental health professionals to be from the mental incapacity to the social deprivation. Sociologists, however, might suggest the reverse: that deprivation leads to depression, loss of motivation, and even pathological adaptations.

To what extent the personality shifts of later life are part of a universal developmental schema is not yet clear. For example, in the future we can expect the expression of cross-sex-linked traits to characterize many individuals throughout their life course rather than appearing as a form of sex-role relaxation in midlife. It is probably safe to say that the organization of self-concepts undergoes continual change as crucial roles are added or subtracted from one's life space. This process, however, may be less abrupt if education, work, and leisure are interwoven throughout life rather than occupying exclusive segments of the life course.

Institutionalization is an emotion-laden topic. There is no question that many old people require continual care that is more skilled than that which can be provided by the family. And, unlike the case of criminal institutionalization, it cannot be shown that community-based care for the elderly is less expensive than that provided by congregate-care facilities. Contrary to popular belief, institutionalization may be the most effective way to deal with the very ill elderly. The problem lies in the quality of care we are willing, as a society, to provide: nursing homes can be nurturing environments, and even state institutions can be humanely operated—but not as either is currently financed.

In Part Three we reviewed the social aspects of aging. How are old people integrated into the institutional spheres of the economy, polity, religious and educational activities, and family life? The facts are of the "good news/bad news" variety. On the one hand, most old people maintain (and some even increase) their political and religious involvement, and succeed in constructing viable support systems of relatives, friends, and neighbors. Ties with adult children are generally described as satisfying, and a majority of old people consider themselves at least as well off as "most people your age." But lowered income, physical constraints, and the death or incapacity of age peers combine to narrow the life space of many elderly. There are fewer people and places to visit, less money for necessities let alone a few luxuries, and not many valued roles to play.

The picture becomes clearer when we distinguish the "young-old" from "the old-old." Those between the ages of 55–70 could, in the future, be best described as in "late maturity": their health and income status, and high probability of being married, are predictive of positive outcomes—a sense of well-being, enjoyment of leisure, and reinvolvement through volunteer activity. Rather than feeling "cooled out," they may see themselves as having earned a respite from obligatory roles. If it is the case that American values are undergoing change—a dilution of the Puritan work ethic by an emphasis on personal growth and pleasure—then the loss of the work role and child-rearing responsibility may be welcomed while guilt over "doing nothing" diminishes. As we have remarked often, the next cohort of old people will, for the most part, be native-born, with at least a high school education. Most will have shared in the affluence of the 1950s, have full entitlement to Social Security and Medicare benefits, and expect only limited assistance from their children.

What we think of as problems of old age will increasingly describe the lives of the very old, the frail, and the poor. Many of these are minority aged, and the great majority will be female: categories with traditionally minimal claims to power, prestige, or property. Those in greatest need will be those least able to influence policy. This is why many gerontologists feel that senior power has peaked—the easy goals have been obtained: an end to mandatory retirement, introduction of Medicare, increases in Social Security benefits, and the creation of an Administration on Aging. The harder goals—full and universal health care, community-based home services, decent low-cost housing, humane long-term care facilities, and income adequacy for all old people—are thought to be too costly and to affect only a few.

All these factors have led to a dilemma in the study of old age: does one "accentuate the positive" by dispelling negative images and presenting the upbeat aspects of aging, the optimism and expressed satisfactions of most old people in our country today? Or, at the risk of reinforcing stereotypes, should we continue to emphasize the plight of those who live out their years in wretched health and abject poverty, often abused by those charged with their custody? Obviously, both portrayals must be presented; either alone distorts the reality of growing old in America. The decision whether or not to devote additional societal resources to programs for the most deprived and vulnerable aged is a *political* one, but others will have to do the lobbying for the powerless, and convince Americans that a decent and dignified old age is a legitimate claim in a society that prides itself on a devotion to human rights. Yet resources expended in one place cannot be spent in another; priorities must be set. At the moment we leave these decisions to the give-and-take of political interest groups. Who speaks for the aged? The mass membership age-based organizations, gerontologists, and service providers often speak for their particular interests—holding the line against any cutback in funding, urging a bit more for pensions, research, and nursing home construction. We can probably agree that these activities are all to the good, but "the good is the enemy of the best" when partial measures reduce the pressure for more extensive gains. On the other hand, some will argue that the "best is the enemy of the good" if, in holding out for thoroughgoing change, advocates refuse to support partial solutions. To provide the very best for our old people, current programs would have to be extended and new initiatives undertaken in the areas of health care and income maintenance *throughout the life course*. This is not the path that our lawmakers have chosen—yet.

As students of social gerontology and as individuals facing your own aging and that of your parents, you have a stake in these matters. We hope that this volume has broadened and deepened your understanding of aging and the position of old people in our society.

Glossary

Achieved Status. Achieved status is a defined position in the social structure of a society that is acquired by an individual through her or his own efforts. Achieved status is generally accomplished by use of ability, skills, or knowledge and implies competition in order to attain it. The major criterion for such status is personal accomplishment rather than ascribed status characteristics such as race, sex, or family. Achieved status is sometimes known as *assumed status*. (See *Ascribed Status.*)

Activity Theory. Activity theory emphasizes the positive aspects of remaining engaged in the social world and finding substitute roles for those that are lost through widowhood or retirement. Old age is thus not viewed as qualitatively different from middle age.

Age Categories. Age categories are culturally defined divisions of the life course and are based on the differences associated with one period of life as opposed to another, including variations in behavior, physiological capacity, psychological functioning, and access to social roles. Childhood, adolescence, young adulthood, midlife, and old age are commonly used age categories in American society today.

Age Grading. Age grading refers to the stratification of a society or social system into different statuses, based on age groupings. In each age group, the members are expected to conform to culturally prescribed and proscribed behavior patterns, or age norms, and to play certain roles. In simple societies, age grading was extensively used to assign social status, including power, rights, and obligations. Membership in a given age group has different meanings through time; for example, teenagers in the Depression were expected to work and contribute to the family; today they are expected to remain in school. Adulthood in the first case is conferred early; in the latter, it is delayed.

Age Heteronomous. This term denotes dissimilarity in ages. For example, the population of the United States is age heteronomous; the average movie theater audience is also age heteronomous.

A marriage between a 92-year-old man and a 60-year-old woman or between a 20-year-old woman and a 52-year-old man would both be examples of age heterogamy, or marriage between two people widely different in age.

Age Homogenous. Age homogeneity denotes people similar to one another with respect to chronological age. For example, a group of men and women aged 65 would be described as age homogeneous. Societies are never age homogenous, but rather are age heteronomous, containing people at all stages of the life course.

Age Norms. These are prescriptions and proscriptions for behavior, expectations shared by members of a society concerning what people of a given age should do and how they should comfort themselves. For example, "big boys don't cry" and "old women shouldn't wear bikinis" are both age norms.

Age Segregation. Age segregation denotes the voluntary or involuntary separation of people on the basis of age. Residential areas, human services, or other facilities may be age segregated. For example, retirement communities, nursing homes, and senior citizens' centers are all age-segregated facilities, as are some "young singles" clubs, college dormitories, and so on.

Age Strata. Age strata are dimensions of society in which people are categorized on the basis of age, and in which age becomes a basis for control over resources and entry into or exit from social statuses.

Altruistic Gene. A term coined by sociobiologists, the altruistic gene refers to the assumption that evolutionary forces operate to preserve the gene-carrying organism, even when self-sacrifice is required to do so. Thus men are willing to die in battle to preserve their genetic endowment, which lives on in their offspring and, to some extent, brothers and sisters.

Androgyny. The expression in one person of both stereotypically "masculine" and "feminine" traits, found to be associated with adaptability, flexibility, and life satisfaction, is known as androgyny. A recent test, utilizing adjectives describing various gender-typed traits, has been developed by Sandra Bem to measure androgyny.

Anomie. Anomie is a state of confusion, insecurity, "normlessness." As originally defined by Emile Durkheim, anomie referred to a property of the social and cultural structure of society, rather than to a property of individuals. Anomie occurs when there is a disjunction between cultural norms and goals and the socially possible capacities of members of the group to act in accord with them. [For further details, see Merton (1957)].

Anticipatory Stake. A process by which one thinks beyond one's own immediate welfare and benefits and envisages probable future needs is an anticipatory stake. In the care of the aging, middle-aged people may look ahead to their own old age and see that they have an anticipatory stake in programs that benefit the elderly.

Ascribed Status. Ascribed status is status that is based on automatic acquisition or inherited position in the social structure, rather than on effort or accomplishment. Examples of ascribed status include race, age, and sex. (See *Achieved Status.*)

Attitude. An attitude is a tendency to act in a consistent fashion toward related objects, persons (including oneself), and situations. Attitudes are learned and may be positive or negative. All attitudes may form a cluster, that is, be highly related to one another but distinct from other attitudes held by the individual; for example, attitudes to old people may form a consistent cluster that is unrelated to other attitudes, such as political conservatism or liberalism.

Authority. Authority is power that is recognized, legitimized, and institutionalized in a society and that is normally based on *status* rather than on personal qualities of the leader.

Avoidance Taboos. This denotes a restriction on behavior that functions to prohibit or limit the degree of involvement of people in a social relationship and to maintain formality. An avoidance taboo found in some societies is the mother-in-law taboo, where interaction between a husband and his wife's mother is limited by custom.

Behavior Modification. A psychotherapeutic technique based on learning theory, or the premise that learning is based on a stimulus-response relationship, behavior modification attempts to alter patterns of responding by altering the individual's reactions to a particular factor or event in the internal or external environment.

Belief. A belief is a statement about the perceived reality that is accepted by an individual as true and factual and that may be based either on faith (e.g., religious beliefs) or on empirical observations, traditions, or group consensus. It may be true or false and may or may not be subject to empirical testing of its truth or falsity. For example, the belief that thunder precedes lightning is subject to test; the belief that there are angels is not.

Bureaucracy. A bureaucracy is a formal organization characterized by formal rules, highly trained experts with technical skills, division of labor, hierarchical chain of command and centralization of authority, and emphasis on rationality and impersonality. It is an *ideal type*; actual formal organizations approach this definition to varying degrees.

Charisma. This is a term that was used initially by sociologist Max Weber to denote a quality of personality making a person appear to possess extraordinary, almost superhuman, abilities of leadership. Literally, the term means "gift of grace" and derives from the concept of special power inherent in the priesthood. A charismatic leader may or may not hold a position of official leadership; rather, leadership is based on special personal qualities. Jesus, Mohammed, and Joan of Arc are examples of charismatic leaders.

Chronological Aging. Chronological aging refers to the biological changes occurring within an individual, such as increased strength in adolescence and early adulthood and decreased physical strength in old age. Chronological aging is not, however, synonymous with psychosocial aging (see *Psychosocial Development.*)

Civil Religion. A secularization of authority that substitutes symbols of the civil community (national anthem, pledge of allegiance, secular holidays) for purely religious symbols (hymns, prayers, church holidays or saints' days), civil religion is common on the current American scene. In civil religion, patriotism and nationalism often become confused with "God's work"; for example, in World War II, many felt "God is on our side."

Cognitive Consistency. This term refers to relative congruence of ideas, attitudes, beliefs, and perceptions, so that one's system of knowledge and ways of viewing the world contain a minimum of contradictions.

Cognitive Dissonance. A term introduced by the social psychologist Leon Festinger, cognitive dissonance occurs when contradictory beliefs, attitudes, or perceptions are held by an individual. When cognitive dissonance occurs, the individual generally feels uncomfortable and thus attempts to reduce conflict between opposing beliefs or attitudes by modifying one or more aspects to restore cognitive consonance.

Cohort. A cohort is a number of people having a common characteristic; for example, all people born in 1910–1915 form a *birth cohort*. No two birth cohorts age in the same way, for each undergoes a particular history and reaches old age with unique experiences.

Cohort Analysis. The study of a number of people with some common characteristic over a relatively long period of time is called cohort analysis. For example, all people born in 1945 could form an age cohort that is followed over time and then compared with the life course of those born in 1905 or 1925.

Comparative Analysis. A study of different types of groups or societies to ascertain similarities and differences in patterns of behavior is the method employed in comparative analysis. Examples include comparisons of people in the United States who were born in the Great Depression to people born during World War II, in order to ascertain the impact of history on behavior, or comparisons between the United States and India with respect to patterns of industrialization.

Conceptual Model. A conceptual model is comprised of interrelated concepts, that is, generalizations about what is common to a class of things. Conceptual models are not concerned with mathematical quantification but rather with logical interrelationships.

Conjugal Family. The term *conjugal family* is often used synonymously with *nuclear* family and refers to a form of social organization where relationships center around the marital ties between husband and wife. Consisting of husband, wife, and unmarried children, it is the most common form of the family in contemporary industrialized societies.

Consanguine. The term *consanguine* denotes relationship by common ancestry. A consanguine family is a type of organization where emphasis is placed on the blood relationships of its members rather than on the marital relationship between husband and wife. An example is the clan organization of old Scotland.

Cross-Cultural. Cross-cultural methods encompass the gathering of comparable data from different societies to test hypotheses about behavior. For example, in gerontology, cross-cultural studies have indicated that the status of the aged varies according to the social structure of the society studied.

Cross-Disciplinary. The gathering of data from different disciplines or fields of study that cuts across classic boundaries of inquiry.

Cross-Sectional. Cross-sectional studies involve comparison of two or more groups observed or questioned at one time only. Much work comparing old to young people has been cross-sectional, where a group of young adults may be compared to, say, attendees at a senior citizens' center. A cross-sectional design in gerontology does not take into consideration the impact of cohort experiences, cultural variations, and other sources of difference.

Dependency Ratio.   The dependency ratio describes the proportion of income earners to those not producing income; for example, the number of dependent children, nonworking spouses, and retired persons. The dependency ratio of those 65 and over to those in the prime work years was 0.26 in 1975.

Depth Interview.   A depth interview is detailed and intensive, designed to permit exploration of variables and to yield new insights on a problem. Depth interviews may be structured or unstructured.

Disengagement Theory.   Developed by Cumming and Henry from data gathered in Kansas City, disengagement theory postulates that successful aging involves a *mutual* withdrawal of the old person from obligatory social roles hitherto occupied. Old age is thus seen as qualitatively different from other life stages, and there is greater concern with the self.

Ethology.   Ethology is the scientific study of animal behavior. Many of the generalizations to human behavior made by *sociobiologists* are based on ethological studies of various species.

Exchange Theory.   The basic assumption of exchange theory is that people seek to maximize benefits from an interaction while incurring the least costs in terms of prestige, self-esteem, and other personal variables.

Expressive Behavior.   Expressive behavior, as opposed to instrumental or task-oriented behavior, is concerned with socio-emotional aspects of conduct. According to sociologist Talcott Parsons and other members of the functionalist school, women are trained in expressive behavior, men in task-oriented behavior. In the modern American family, according to Talcott Parsons, the wife is an expressive leader who manages emotional tensions within the family, and the husband is an instrumental leader, whose responsibilities are to be the achiever of goals, including being the breadwinner.

Extended Expectations.   Extended expectations are based on traditional socialization that may no longer fit the pattern of usual contemporary expectations for behavior. Many contemporary elderly have extended expectations for care, based on their own socialization, and may feel resentful when these expectations are not met by their upwardly mobile children.

Extended Family.   An extended family includes three or more generations and is usually *consanguine* rather than conjugal. For example, an extended family might include grandparents, their married children and spouses, and grandchildren, as well as other relatives related by blood to the grandparents. It has never been a common family form in industrial society.

Familism.   Familism is characterized by a strong sense of family, rather than individual, interests or values as paramount. Individual personalities of family members are subordinate to the interests and welfare of the family as a unit.

Family Dependency Ratio.   The number of parents per children—the flip side of birth rates—is the family dependency ratio. For example, in 2030, the estimated ratio of surviving parents to surviving children is 70:100.

Family Status. Family status is a United States census classification, denoting the relationship of respondents to those with whom they live. Family status may be subdivided into 1) in families; 2) *primary individual;* 3) *secondary individual;* (4) institutional inmate.

Filial Maturity. A concept employed by social worker Margaret Blenkner, filial maturity describes the ability of an adult child to become a dependable resource for an aged parent without falling into a pattern of reversal roles. While highly desirable, as it permits the aged parent to maintain self-respect while being dependent, it is difficult to attain.

Filial Piety. The respect and deference owed to a father or uncle is known as filial piety. Filial piety reflects the patriarchal social order of a traditional society and the high status of older males within that society; it reinforces the traditions of the society.

Focused Interview. This type of interview is centered on a specific topic or set of topics. While questions need not be specified in advance, the area in which information is sought is pre-determined.

Gemeinschaft. *Gemeinschaft* is a term used by the sociologist Ferdinand Tönnies to describe an ideal type of society, characterized by predominance of primary-group relationships, kinship ties, tradition, and consensus. In German, the word *Gemeinschaft* means "community." (See *Gesellschaft*, the other ideal type used by Tönnies.)

Gesellschaft. The term *Gesellschaft* refers to a type of society in which secondary relationships dominate, that is, social relationships are formal, contractual, impersonal, and specialized. In German, *Gesellschaft* means "society" and is a term used by the sociologist Ferdinand Tönnies to denote the opposite of *Gemeinschaft* community, or informal, relatively unspecialized, and personal relationships. Both gesellschaft and gemeinschaft are *ideal types*. (See *Ideal Type*.)

Gray Lobby. A term coined by Pratt, the Gray Lobby is comprised not only of age-based organizations, such as the AARP, Gray Panthers, and so on, but also of middle-aged voters, people concerned with the care of their aged parents, professionals who earn their living from study and care of the aged, and other diverse groups concerned with social legislation that will benefit the elderly.

Ideal Type. An ideal type is a tentative model of reality that provides a strategy to compare, describe, and test hypotheses about the social world. Developed by Max Weber, an ideal type is not a true picture, but a model of reality that is subject to test and refinement. "Traditional family," "bureaucracy" and "marginal man" are examples of ideal types.

Individual Retirement Accounts. Individuals in employment not covered by other private retirement pension schemes are able to make tax-deductible contributions of up to $1500 per year in an Individual Retirement Account (IRA) at a savings bank.

Institutional Sphere. Different institutional spheres include political, educational, economic, and religious areas that are separate from the family. In a society with little *social-structural differentiation*, institutional spheres are not separate; an example is the clans of old Scotland, where all institutional functions were performed within the clan. In the United States today, there are diverse institutional spheres, interdependently related to one another.

Institutions. Institutions are interrelated systems of social roles and norms organized around satisfaction of a basic human need. Usually familial, economic, political, religious, and educational institutions are considered the basic social institutions.

Instrumental Behavior. As opposed to expressive or socio-emotional behavior, instrumental behavior is centered on task performance and work-oriented aspects of conduct. (See *Expressive Behavior*.)

Interview. An interview is a "conversation with a purpose," that is, it takes place between an investigator and a respondent, for the purpose of gathering information. Interviews are of several kinds: *depth, focused*, and *structured*. (See glossary headings for definitions.)

Interview schedule. Used in structured interviews, the interview schedule consists of a list of prepared questions used by an interviewer to structure and guide his or her interviewing of a respondent. It is useful, in that a standard set of questions is asked in a carefully prearranged order, thus reducing the likelihood that the interviewer will bias responses.

Joking Relationship. A joking relationship is a socially approved pattern of interaction that allows certain relatives or other people with specified social statuses to joke with one another without impropriety or anger. It is least likely to occur when authority relationships must be maintained.

Keogh Plan. The Keogh Plan permits self-employed individuals in employment not covered by other retirement income programs to make tax-deductible contributions of up to $7500 per year to their own retirement funds.

Life-Cycle Squeeze. A life-cycle squeeze occurs when there is an imbalance between the demands for earnings and energies and the available resources; upon reaching an occupational peak, in midlife one may be squeezed by demands and ability to meet them. Examples are the blue-collar worker with an aged parent requiring care or a child in college, and no prospects for advancement.

Life Expectancy. The term *life expectancy* refers to the average number of years an individual could expect to live at various ages, for example, at birth, age 20, age 45, and so on. Life expectancy has increased dramatically in the United States since 1900; however, there are dramatic differences associated with race, sex, and socioeconomic status.

Life Span Development. Life span development denotes the emotional and cognitive changes within an individual that are associated with various stages of life. Changes in social roles are key in initiating positive or negative developmental changes throughout the life span; the individual's responses to role losses or additions thus are the catalysts for development throughout the life span.

Life Stages. The succession of age-based clusters of social roles is commonly viewed as comprising a set of life stages. Stages of life are longitudinally linked to one another, where each stage is an outgrowth of the preceding stage.

Longitudinal. The adjective *longitudinal* literally means "over time"; in longitudinal studies, the same set of people is observed or interviewed as they grow, develop, and age.

Looking-Glass Self. A concept introduced by sociologist Charles Cooley, the looking-glass or reflected self denotes the conception of self that one forms as a consequence of the views others hold of him. It is a concept employed in *symbolic interactionist* analyses of behavior.

Mandatory Retirement. Mandatory retirement refers to the provision in labor contracts or regulations of an employing institution that, at a given age, an employee *must* retire. Mandatory retirement provisions in the United States have recently been reevaluated, and the age ceiling has been raised from 65 to 70 for most workers.

Master Status. A master status trait is one that provides a key basis for identity of the individual as having a particular status in society. Examples of master status traits include age, sex, or physical handicap; the master status trait provides the basis for interaction and role expectations. Concretely, the person who is physically handicapped, a Ph.D, and a poet may be "placed" by other people on the basis of his or her most visible trait—physical handicap—and treated accordingly.

Matriarchal. The matriarchal family is one in which the mother is the dominant power and formal head of the family; power is not shared with other family members. (See *Patriarchal*.)

Matrilineal. Matrilineal refers to the custom of tracing ancestry and sometimes inheritance only through the mother and her female family line; such tracing of lineage is unilateral, that is, only relatives of one parent are considered. (See *Patrilineal*.)

Matrilocal. The adjective *matrilocal* refers to the custom in some societies for a married couple to reside in the same geographic locale, sometimes the same household, as the wife's mother. In the United States, married couples tend to establish neolocal, that is, their own chosen places of residence, according to personal preference rather than to familial relationships dictated by custom.

Mode. The mode is a statistical measure that denotes the most commonly occurring value. For example, in a graph, it is the bar or point with the greatest number of cases or observations.

Mean. The mean is the arithmetic average of a series of numerical values. The mean and *median* are identical in a so-called normal, or bell-shaped, curve distribution. If, however, there are a few extreme values, the mean will not be equal to the median. Because a few extreme values can throw off the mean and make it misleading, the median is often used instead. For example, in describing income, the mean may provide misleading data; if a few people are making $20,000 but most are making $10,000 or less, the mean does not present as accurate a picture as does the median.

Median. The median is a statistical measure that denotes the numerical value that is the middle point in a series of values. For example, if the median age of a population is 35, one knows that half the population is under 35 years of age and half is over 35. See *Mean* for a comparison of median and mean.

Modernization. The term *modernization* is often used to denote societal changes occurring as a result of the industrialization of society. Modernization refers to an increasing complexity of social organization in which the majority of social relationships are formal and contractual; where there is a division of labor; and where talent, education, and other achieved characteristics are stressed as determinants of status.

Multidisciplinary. The adjective *multidisciplinary* denotes several disciplines or fields of inquiry employed to approach a particular area of interest. For example, gerontology is a multidisciplinary science, in which sociologists, anthropologists, psychologists, biologists, chemists, physicians, and so on are all involved in contributing to the knowledge base on human aging.

Necrophobia. Necrophobia (*necro* is Greek for "death") refers to fear of and aversion to death and dying.

Nepotism. Originally denoting the favoritism of nephews by sixteenth-century prelates of the church, nepotism now has a broader meaning—favoritism shown or positions given to relatives or close friends. Sometimes the term *nepotism* has been invoked to prohibit husband and wife working for the same employer, even when no idea of favoritism is implied.

Norm. A norm is a rule for behavior and denotes the right and proper way of behaving, speaking, dressing, and other everyday parts of our social lives. Norms are learned through socialization, and one generally takes norms for granted, precisely because they are "the norm." Norms may be either proscriptive (thou shalt not) or prescriptive (thou shalt). Many norms are informal, that is, they do not have the force of statutory law.

Observation Studies. Observation studies are undertaken by a trained observer who systematically records the behavior of all participants in a setting and then categorizes and analyzes these observations. The limitation of observation studies is an obvious one—not very many people can be accurately observed at a time. Yet observation studies may yield rich data on everyday behavior.

Participant Observation. Participant observation studies are undertaken by a trained observer who both participates in and systematically records the behavior of all participants in a setting.

Patriarchal. The patriarchal family is a form of family organization in which the father is the formal head and dominant power figure. In some societies, such as ancient Rome, the patriarch of the family had the power of life or death over all other family members. (See *Matriarchal*.)

Patrilineal. The adjective *patrilineal* refers to the tracing of ancestry, and sometimes inheritance only, through the father and his male ancestors in a family. Both patrilineal and matrilineal descent are unilateral; that is, only one parental lineage is considered. In the United States and most industrial societies, descent is traced bilaterally, that is, through both parents.

Patrilocal. The adjective *patrilocal* refers to the custom in some societies for a married couple to reside in the husband's father's geographic locale or home, rather than in the mother's home or according to their own choice.

Peer Group. The term *peer group* denotes people of the same age or approximately equal status.

Period Influences. Period influences denote the impact of extraneous events on the measurement of variables. For example, a survey of attitudes toward smoking could be influenced by the recent publication of a Surgeon General's report. It is possible that period influences do not affect all age cohorts similarly, which only adds to the difficulties of pinpointing cohort differences.

Pluralistic Ignorance. A term introduced by Floyd Allport in 1933, pluralistic ignorance denotes a situation in which individuals believe incorrectly that each of them is alone in believing in (or rejecting) certain values when, in fact, many other people feel just as they do.

Primary Group. A term coined by sociologist Charles Cooley, the primary group is intimate; interaction is spontaneous and involves the "whole person." Common values are shared, and direct personal contact among members occurs. The family is an example of a primary group. Primary groups are distinguished from *secondary groups*, where interaction involves only a segment of people's lives.

Primary Individual. A United States Census classification, a primary individual is defined as a person who lives in a household of his or her own but not in a family.

Prosthetic Device. A prosthetic device (sometimes called a prosthesis) is an artificial replacement of a limb, tooth, or other part of the body. Artificial limbs, false teeth, canes, hearing aids, and walkers are examples of prostheses, all of which augment or replace lost functions of the body.

Psychosocial Development. Psychosocial development refers to the series of developmental tasks that provide opportunities for personality changes throughout the life course. For example, the psychoanalyst Erik Erikson has suggested that each stage of life has its own developmental tasks for the individual; the way in which one resolves these tasks has profound personality implications for the self.

Research Method. A strategy by which a theory may be tested, research methods should be (but not always are) chosen to fit the particular theoretical model to be tested. Research methods in the social sciences include *interviews*, *observation* and *participant observation*, analysis of available statistical data (births, deaths, migration, and the like), laboratory experiments, questionnaires, and so forth.

Rites of Passage. Originally used by Van Gennap in 1909, rites of passage are ceremonies that mark a significant transition in an individual's life from one phase of the life course to another. Such rites give emotional support to the individual entering a new status and also provide official indication that the individual now has new rights and obligations. For example, in American society religious ceremonies, such as confirmation and Bar Mitzvah, mark the end of childhood and the entry into adolescence.

Role. The term *role* encompasses a pattern of behavior that is structured around specific rights and obligations and associated with a particular status position. Role is thus the dynamic aspect of status; that is, it is the totality of behavior associated with a particular status.

Role Partner. The role partner plays a reciprocal role to a specific role player; reciprocal roles are related and inseparable. For example, husband-wife, parent-child, teacher-student are role partners playing reciprocal roles.

Role Players. The term *role player* is used to denote a person who occupies specific roles and acts in a manner that conforms to the social norms appropriate for that role.

Role Slack. Role slack occurs when an individual's capacities to play one or more roles is underutilized. It has been suggested that role slack may account for the storminess of adolescence and the discomforts of old age—role capacities, while present, are not channeled into legitimate roles.

Role Strain. Role strain denotes difficulty or stress in fulfilling expected role obligations, often because the demands on the energies required to play the role are too great or are perceived as inappropriate by the *role player*.

Secondary Group. Introduced by sociologist Charles Cooley, the term *secondary group* is characterized by common interests but relatively segmented relationships in comparison to the *primary group*. Face-to-face interaction may occur, although it is not necessary. Examples of secondary groups include members of the National Association of Retired Professionals (where there are common interests but where no face-to-face interaction necessarily occurs) and a group of people attending a senior citizens' center. Interests are shared but are specialized in nature.

Secondary Individual. A term employed by the United States Census in describing living arrangements of the population, a secondary individual is a man or woman who lives in a household with non-kin. It should be distinguished from *primary individual*, that is, one who lives in one's own household but not in a family.

Secular. The term *secular* designates that which is not sacred or tradition-bound; it is associated with pragmatism and rationality. Modern industrial societies are predominantly secular in orientation, where ideas and objects are subject to critical evaluation rather than taken entirely on faith, and where power is assigned more on the basis of achievement (through education and the like) than on "divine calling" or tradition.

Secular Beliefs. These are beliefs characterized by a lack of concern with the sacred, the supernatural, or with values associated with traditionalism or conservatism. Instead, the secular emphasizes utilitarian, pragmatic, and rational values; change and innovation may be valued. Modern American society is usually considered as one that stresses secular beliefs and values. The concept of the secular versus the sacred was developed by sociologist Howard Becker.

Self-Fulfilling Prophecy. A concept developed by Robert Merton, self-fulfilling prophecy describes the process by which a belief held about a social situation or group actually becomes true because one believes and acts as if it were true and thus alters the reality. For example, the old are considered to have little social worth, and if people act as if the old have little value, the old themselves are likely to regard this last stage of life (and perhaps themselves) as not socially worthy.

Self-Help Groups. Self-help groups attempt to fill the gap between individual problems and the bureaucratic service delivery system. Organizing voluntarily, self-help groups attempt to provide mutual aid for their shared concerns or problems. Recent examples include single-parent groups, home-birth groups, people who have had cancer, and so on. Most groups have a mixture of *instrumental* and *expressive* behaviors.

Social Construction. That which is socially constructed is a product of social interaction within a social system; that is, it is not "natural" or inevitable. For example, life stages in the life course are social constructions rather than immutably and biologically defined; thus, one may be an "old man" at 40 in societies where life is short and nutrition is poor.

Social Control. Social control encompasses social and cultural means by which conformity to social and behavioral norms is obtained. Social control may be either formal (through laws, rules, and regulations) or informal (praise, ridicule, public opinion). Social control may also be negative—depending on punishment or ridicule; or positive—depending on the promise of tangible social rewards, such as money or diplomas; or intangible rewards, such as approval.

Social Stratification. The concept of social stratification describes a relatively permanent ranking of status and role in a society or social system, whereby people are arranged into categories, or *strata,* based on how much power, prestige, or wealth they command.

Social-Structural Differentiation. The extent to which arrangements for fulfilling necessary social tasks have been separated out of the family as a locus for their completion is known as social-structural differentiation. In very simple societies, there may be little such differentiation, and necessary tasks are carried out within the kinship network.

Sociobiology. Sociobiology is a relatively new area of inquiry. At its basis is the premise that evolutionary forces act to preserve the gene-carrying organisms most beneficial for group survival.

Status. This term refers to a location in a system of social relationships. Each status is characterized by rights and obligations that relate to it and distinguish it from other statuses in the social structure. For example, *wife, mother, student, lawyer, child,* and *pianist* are all statuses. Often status is used to convey position in a hierarchy (as in status in the socioeconomic structure). The dynamic or behavioral aspect of status, according to anthropologist Ralph Linton, is a *role.* (See Ralph Linton, *The Study of Man,* Appleton-Century-Crofts, 1936.)

Stem Family. Two types of stem family are recognized: 1) a family composed of one nuclear group (husband, wife and child(ren)) plus one or more other relatives who do *not* form a second nuclear family; 2) a small extended family that includes two nuclear families of adjacent generations. An illustration of the first is husband, wife, child, and grandmother. An illustration of the second is the two-generation family—husband, wife, child, husband's mother, and husband's father.

Strata. (singular: stratum) A stratum designates any division of people into subdivisions, including social classes, sex, age, or other socially relevant characteristics.

Structured Interview. A structured interview essentially consists of a series of questions prepared in advance and asked the respondent; the interviewer records responses and may probe for explanation but does not seek information not required by the interview schedule.

Subculture of Aging. A concept proposed by the sociologist Arnold Rose, the subculture of aging encompasses the premise that the aged have developed their own norms, customs, and consciousness.

Symbolic Interaction. A school of thought in sociology and social psychology, symbolic interaction stresses the importance of language and communication in formation of the self and in determining patterns of social relationships. George Herbert Mead and Charles Cooley were influential in developing this approach to the study of behavior.

Traditional Family. The traditional family is an *ideal type* of family system, generally depicted as one in which nuclear, that is, husband-wife-children units, remain embedded in a blood-linked kinship group, sharing the same household or living near one another. The traditional family is most closely identified with agricultural, nonindustrial societies and should be distinguished from another *ideal type*, the modern or nuclear family.

Value. Value denotes a desired object or goal or an abstract principle of behavior to which members of a group feel strong attraction. Examples of values are *success, freedom, justice,* and *romantic love*.

Voluntary Associations. Voluntary associations are quasi-formal or formal organizations that are formed to meet commonly perceived needs or to deal with specific problems. Services are provided largely by unpaid volunteers. Examples include RSVP, League of Women Voters, and Alcoholics Anonymous.

WASP. This is an acronym commonly used to describe a category of people who are White, Anglo-Saxon, and Protestant, that is, of British descent. The term is often used loosely to denote people of Northern European descent; in any case, it is something of a misnomer, as nobody today is of "pure" Anglo-Saxon origin.

Bibliography

ALLEN, P. "A Consumer's View of California's Mental Health Care System." *Psychiatric Quarterly*, 48, No. 1, 1974, 1–13.

ANDERSON, T. W., et al., "Vitamin C and the Common Cold: A Double Blind Trial," *Canadian Medical Association Journal*, 107, 1972, 503–508.

ANSELLO, EDWARD F. "Broadcast Images: The Older Woman in Television (Part 1)." Paper presented at the Annual Meeting of the Gerontological Society. Dallas, Tex., November 1978.

—— (ed). "Old Age and Literature: A Developmental Analysis." *Educational Gerontology*, 2, No. 3, 1977, 211–366.

ANTUNES, GEORGE, and CHARLES M. GAITZ. "Ethnicity and Participation: A Study of Mexican-Americans, Blacks, and Whites." *American Journal of Sociology*, 80 No. 5, 1975, 1192–1211.

ANTONOVSKY, ANTON. "Social Class, Life Expectancy, and Overall Mortality." In E. Gartley Jaco (ed.), *Patients, Physicians, and Illness*. New York: The Free Press, 1972, 5–31.

ARENSBERG, DAVID. "Cognition and Aging: Verbal Learning, Memory Problem Solving, and Aging." In Carl Eisdorfer and M. Powell Lawton (eds.), *The Psychology of Adult Development and Aging*. Washington, D.C.: American Psychological Association, 1973, 74–97.

ARIES, PHILIPPE. *Centuries of Childhood. A Social History of Family Life*. New York: Alfred A. Knopf, Inc., 1962.

ARLING, GREG. "The Elderly Widow and Her Family, Neighbors, and Friends." *Journal of Marriage and the Family*, 38, No. 4, 1976, 757–768.

ARMS, SUZANNE. *Immaculate Deception: A New Look at Women and Child-birth in America*. Boston: Houghton Mifflin Company, 1975.

ARNHOFF, C. "Old Age in Prime Time." *Journal of Communication*, 26, No. 4, 1974, 86–87.

ATCHLEY, ROBERT C. "Retirement and Leisure Participation: Continuity or Crisis?" *The Gerontologist*, 11, No. 1, 1971, 13–17.

——. "Dimensions of Widowhood in Later Life." *The Gerontologist*, 15, No. 2, 1975, 176–178.

———. "Selected Social and Psychological Differences Between Men and Women in Late Life." *Journal of Gerontology*, **31**, No. 2, 1976, 204–211.

———. *The Sociology of Retirement.* Cambridge, MA.: Schenkman Publishing Co., Inc., 1976.

———. *Social Forces in Later Life.* Belmont, Cal.: Wadsworth Publishing Co., Inc., 1977.

BACHRACH, LEONA. *Deinstitutionalization: An Analytical Review and Sociological Perspective.* National Institute of Mental Health, Series D, No. 4. Washington, D.C.: U.S. Government Printing Office, 1976.

BALTES, PAUL B., and GISELA V. LABOUVIE. "Adult Development of Intellectual Performance: Description, Explanation, and Modification." In Carl Eisdorfer and M. Powell Lawton (eds.), *The Psychology of Adult Development.* Washington, D.C.: American Psychological Association, 1973, 157–219.

BARFIELD, RICHARD E., and JAMES N. MORGAN. "Trends in Planned Early Retirement." *The Gerontologist*, **18**, No. 1, 1978, 13–18.

———. "Trends in Satisfaction with Retirement." *The Gerontologist*, **18**, No. 1, 1978, 19–22.

BART, PAULINE. "Mother Portnoy's Complaint." *Transaction*, **8**, 1970, 69–74.

BARTON, ELIZABETH M., JUDY K. PLEMONS, SHERRY L. WILLIS, and PAUL B. BALTES. "Recent Findings on Adult and Gerontological Intelligence." *American Behavioral Scientist*, **19**, No. 2, 1975, 224–236.

BASCUE, L. O., and R. E. LAWRENCE. "A Study of Subjective Death Anxiety in the Elderly." *Omega*, **8**, No. 1, 1977, 81–90.

BEATTIE, WALTER. "Aging and the Social Services." In Robert Binstock and Ethel Shanas (eds.), *Handbook of Aging and the Social Sciences.* New York: Van Nostrand Reinhold Company, 1976.

BEKKER, L. DeMOYNE, and CHARLES TAYLOR. "Attitudes Toward the Aged in a Multigenerational Sample." *Journal of Gerontology*, **21**, No. 1, 1966, 115–118.

BENNETT, RUTH, and LUCILLE NAHEMOW. "Institutional Totality and Criteria of Social Adjustment in Residences for the Aged." *Journal of Social Issues*, **21**, No. 4, 1965, 44–79.

BERGER, BRIGITTE. *Societies in Change.* New York: Basic Books, Inc., Publishers, 1971.

BERGHORN, FORREST S., DONNA E. SCHAFER, GEOFFREY H. STEERE, and ROBERT F. WISEMAN. *The Urban Elderly: A Study of Life Satisfaction.* Montclair, N.J.: Allanheld, Osmun & Co., Publishers, Inc., 1978.

BIESTY, PATRICK, BETH B. HESS, and WILLIAM DI COMO. "The Elderly of Morris County, N.J.: A SCAN Survey of the Elderly of Morris County, New Jersey." Morris County Office on Aging, mimeo, 1977.

BIGNALL, J. C., "Coronary Heart Disease and Blood Cholesterol." *Lancet*, No. 1, 1975, 1074.

BILD, BERNICE R., and ROBERT J. HAVIGHURST. "Senior Citizens in Great Cities: The Case of Chicago." *The Gerontologist*, **16**, No. 1, 1976, 4–88.

BINSTOCK, ROBERT H. "Interest Group Liberalism and the Politics of Aging." *The Gerontologist,* 12, 1972, 265–280.

BINSTOCK, ROBERT H., and ETHEL SHANAS (eds.). *Handbook of Aging and the Social Sciences.* New York: Van Nostrand Reinhold Company, 1976.

BIRREN, JAMES E. (ed.). *Handbook of Aging and the Individual: Psychological and Biological Aspects.* Chicago: University of Chicago Press, 1959.

——. "Toward an Experimental Psychology of Aging." *American Psychologist,* 25, 1970, 124–135.

——, and K. WARNER SCHAIE (eds.). *Handbook of the Psychology of Aging.* New York: Van Nostrand Reinhold Company, 1976.

BLAU, ZENA S. "Changes in Status and Age Identification." *American Sociological Review,* 21, No. 2, 1956, 198–203.

——. *Old Age in a Changing Society.* New York: New Viewpoints, 1973.

BLAZER, DAN, and ERDMAN PALMORE. "Religion and Aging in a Longitudinal Panel." *The Gerontologist,* 16, No. 1, 1976, 82–85.

BLENKNER, MARGARET. "Social Work and Family Relationships in Later Life with Some Thoughts on Filial Maturity." In Ethel Shanas and Gordon Streib (eds.), *Social Structure and the Family: Generational Relations.* Englewood Cliffs, N.J.: Prentice-Hall, Inc., 1965.

——, "Environmental Change and the Aging Individual," *The Gerontologist,* 7, No. 2, part 2, 1967, 101–106.

BLUM, RICHARD H. "Case Identification in Psychiatric Epidemiology: Methods and Problems." *Milbank Memorial Fund Quarterly,* 40, No. 3, 1962, 253–88.

BOCK, E. WILBUR, and IRVING L. WEBBER. "Suicide Among the Elderly: Isolating Widowhood and Mitigating Alternatives." *Journal of Marriage and the Family,* 34, 1972, 24–31.

BONDAREFF, W. "Morphology of the Aging Nervous System." In James E. Birren (ed.), *Handbook of Aging and the Individual: Psychological and Biological Aspects.* Chicago: University of Chicago Press, 1959, 36–72.

BOTWINICK, JACK. *Aging and Behavior.* New York: Springer Publishing Co., Inc., 1973.

——, and LARRY W. THOMPSON. "Components of Reaction Time in Relation to Age and Sex." *Journal of Genetic Psychology,* 108, 1966, 175–183.

—— et al. "Predicting Death from Behavioral Test Performance." *Journal of Gerontology,* 33, No .5, 1978, 755–762.

BOURESTOM, NORMAN, and SANDRA TARS. "Alterations in Life Patterns Following Nursing Home Relocation." *The Gerontologist,* 14, No. 6, 1974, 506–510.

BOYLIN, WILLIAM, SUSAN K. GORDON, and MILTON NEHRKE. "Reminiscing and Ego Integrity in Institutionalized Elderly Males." *The Gerontologist,* 16, No. 2, 1976, 118–124.

BRIM, ORVILLE G., JR. "Male Mid-Life Crisis: A Comparative Analysis." In Beth B. Hess (ed.), *Growing Old in America.* New Brunswick, N.J.: Transaction Books, 1976, 163–179.

BRIZZEE, KENNETH R. "Qualitative Histological Studies on Aging Changes in

Cerebral Cortex of Young, Adult and Aged Long-Evans Rats." In D. H. Ford (ed.) *Progress in Brain Research,* **40.** New York: Elsevier North-Holland, Inc., 1973.

BRODY, ELAINE M. "A Million Procrustean Beds." In Beth B. Hess (ed.), *Growing Old in America.* New Brunswick, N.J.: Transaction Books, 1976, 259–272.

―――― et al. "A Longitudinal Look at Excess Disabilities in the Mentally Impaired Aged." *Journal of Gerontology,* **29,** No. 1, 1974, 79–84.

BROMLEY, D. B. *The Psychology of Human Aging.* Baltimore: Penguin Books, 1966.

BULTENA, GORDON L., and EDWARD A. POWERS. "Denial of Aging: Age Identification and Reference Group Orientations." *Journal of Gerontology,* **33,** No. 5, 1978, 754–768.

BURGESS, ERNEST W. "Aging in Western Culture." In Ernest W. Burgess (ed.), *Aging in Western Societies.* Chicago: University of Chicago Press, 1960, 3–28.

BUSSE, EWALD W. "Findings from the Duke University Geriatrics Research Project on the Effects of Aging Upon the Nervous System." In H. T. Blumenthal (ed.), *Medical and Clinical Aspects of Aging: Aging Around the World.* New York: Columbia University Press, 1962, 115–124.

―――― et al. "Psychoneurotic Reactions of the Aged." In Erdman Palmore (ed.), *Normal Aging.* Durham, N.C.: Duke University Press, 1970, 75–83.

BUTLER, ROBERT N. *Why Survive? Being Old in America.* New York: Harper & Row Publishers, Inc., 1975.

BUTLER, ROBERT N., and MYRNA LEWIS. *Aging and Mental Health.* St. Louis: The C. V. Mosby Company, 1977.

CALIFANO, JOSEPH A., JR. "The Aging of America: Questions for the Four-Generation Society." *Annals of the American Academy of Political and Social Science,* **438,** 1978, 96–107.

CAMPBELL, ANGUS, PHILIP E. CONVERSE, and WILLARD L. RODGERS. *The Quality of American Life: Perceptions, Evaluation, and Satisfaction.* New York: Russell Sage Foundation, 1976.

CANTOR, MARJORIE. "Life Space and the Social Support System of the Inner City Elderly of New York." *The Gerontologist,* **15,** No. 1, 1975, 23–27.

CANTOR, MARJORIE H. "The Configuration and Intensity of the Informal Support System in a New York City Elderly Population." Paper presented at the annual meeting of the Gerontological Society. New York City, October, 1976.

CARP, FRANCES M. "Effects of Improved Housing on the Lives of Older People." In Bernice L. Neugarten (ed.), *Middle Age and Aging.* Chicago: University of Chicago Press, 1968, 409–416.

―――― . "Life Style and Location Within the City," *The Gerontologist,* **15,** No. 1, 1975, 27–34.

―――― . "Housing and Living Environments of Older People." In Robert H. Binstock and Ethel Shanas (eds.), *Handbook of Aging and the Social Sciences.* New York: Van Nostrand Reinhold Company, 1976.

———, and EUNICE KATAOKA. "Health Care Problems of the Elderly of San Francisco's Chinatown." *The Gerontologist*, 16, No. 1, 1976, 30–38.

CATH, STANLEY. "Psychoanalytic Viewpoints on Aging—An Historical Survey." In Donald P. Kent, Robert Kastenbaum, and Sylvia Sherwood (eds.), *Research Planning and Action for the Elderly*. New York: Behavioral Publications, 1972, 279–314.

CAVAN, RUTH, ROBERT J. HAVIGHURST, and ERNEST BURGESS. *Personal Adjustment in Old Age*. Chicago: Science Research Associates, Inc., 1949.

CLARK, MARGARET, and MONIQUE MENDELSON. "Mexican-American Aged in San Francisco: A Case Description." *The Gerontologist*, 9, No. 2, 1969, 90–95.

CLAUSEN, JOHN A. "The Life Course of Individuals." In Matilda White Riley, Marilyn E. Johnson and Anne Foner, *Aging and Society, vol. 3: A Sociology of Age Stratification*. New York: Russell Sage Foundation, 1972, 457–514.

CLAY, VIDAL S. *Women: Menopause and Middle Age*. Know, Inc., 1977.

CLAVAN, SYLVIA. "The Impact of Social Class and Social Trends on the Role of Grandparent." *The Family Coordinator*, 27, No. 4, October 1978, 351–358.

CLEMENTE, FRANK. "Age Differences in Perception of National Priorities." *The Gerontologist*, 15, No. 1, part 1, 1975, 61–63.

———, and MICHAEL B. KLEIMAN. "Fear of Crime Among the Aged." *The Gerontologist*, 16, No. 3, 1976, 207–210.

——— et al. "Participation of the Black Aged in Voluntary Associations." *Journal of Gerontology*, 30, No. 4, 1975, 469–472.

CLEVELAND, MARTHA. "Sex in Marriage: At 40 and Beyond." *Family Coordinator*, 25, No. 3, 1976, 233–240.

COHEN, SANFORD I., ALBERT J. SILVERMAN, and BARRY M. SHMAVONIAN. "Influence of Psychoanalytic Factors on Central Nervous System Functioning in Young and Aged Subjects." In ERDMAN PALMORE (ed.), *Normal Aging: Reports from the Duke Longitudinal Study, 1955–1969*. Durham, N.C.: Duke University Press, 1970, 250–265.

COLES, ROBERT. "Life in Appalachia—The Case of Hugh McCaslin." *Transaction*, 5, No. 7, 1968, 23–33.

COLLINS, MARJORIE. "Ageism in the Medical Profession." Paper presented at Women's Caucus, annual meeting of the American Public Health Association, Miami, Florida, 1976.

COMFORT, ALEXANDER. "Age Prejudice in America." *Social Policy*, 7, No. 3, 1976, 3–8.

COOK, FAY LOMOX, WESLEY G. SKOGAN, THOMAS D. COOK, and GEORGE E. ANTUNES. "Criminal Victimization of the Elderly: The Physical and Economic Consequences." *The Gerontologist*, 18, No. 4, 1978, 338–350.

COOPER, W. "A Woman's View of the Menopause." In S. CAMPBELL (ed.), *The Management of the Menopause and Postmenopausal Years*. Baltimore: University Park Press, 1975.

CORSELLIS, J. A. N. "Distribution of Neuro-pathological Changes in Mental

Hospital Patients with Particular Reference to Age at Death." In H. T. Blumenthal (ed.), *Medical and Clinical Aspects of Aging: Aging Around the World*. New York: Columbia University Press, 1962, 58–62.

CORSO, JOHN G. "Sensory Processes and Age Effects in Normal Adults." *Journal of Gerontology*, 26, No. 1, 1971, 90–105.

COSIN, L. Z. "Experimental Treatment of Persistent Senile Confusion." *International Journal of Social Psychology*, 4, No. 1, 1958, 24–42.

COSNECK, BERNARD J. "Family Patterns of Older Widowed Jewish People." *Family Coordinator*, 19, 1970, 368–373.

COSTA, PAUL, and ROBERT KASTENBAUM. "Some Aspects of Memories and Ambitions in Centenarians." *Journal of Genetic Psychology*, 110, No. 1, 1967, 3–16.

COULEHAN, JOHN L., et al. "Vitamin C Prophylaxis in a Boarding School." *New England Journal of Medicine*, 290, No. 1, 1974, 6–10.

COWGILL, DONALD O. "Residential Segregation by Age in American Metropolitan Areas." *Journal of Gerontology*, 33, No. 3, 1978, 446–453.

———, and LOWELL D. HOLMES. *Aging and Modernization*. New York: Appleton-Century-Crofts, 1972.

CROOG, SYDNEY H., ALBERTA LIPSON, and SOL LEVINE. "Help Patterns in Severe Illness: The Roles of Kin Network, Non-Family Resources and Institutions." *Journal of Marriage and the Family*, 34, 1972, 32–41.

CUMMING, ELAINE, and WILLIAM HENRY. *Growing Old: The Process of Disengagement*. New York: Basic Books, 1961.

———. "Engagement with an Old Theory." *International Journal of Aging and Human Development*, 6, No. 3, 1976, 187–191.

———. "Further Thoughts on the Theory of Disengagement." *International Social Science Journal*, 15, 1963, 377–393.

CURTIN, SHARON R. *Nobody Ever Died of Old Age: In Praise of Old People*. New York: Little, Brown & Company, 1972.

CUTLER, STEPHEN J. "Transportation and Changes in Life Satisfaction." *The Gerontologist*, 15, No. 2, 1975, 155–159.

———, and ROBERT L. KAUFMAN. "Cohort Changes in Political Attitudes: Tolerance of Ideological Nonconformity." *Public Opinion Quarterly*, 39, No. 1, 1975, 63–81.

———. "Membership in Different Types of Voluntary Associations and Psychological Well-Being." *The Gerontologist*, 16, No. 4, 1976, 335–339.

———. "Aging and Voluntary Association Participation." *Journal of Gerontology*, 32, No. 4, 1977, 470–479.

DAVIS, KAREN. "Equal Treatment and Unequal Benefits: The Medicare Program." *The Milbank Memorial Fund Quarterly (Health and Society)*, 53, No. 4, 1975, 449–488.

DELAY, JEAN. *Les Maladies de la Mémoire*. Paris: Presses Universitaires de France, 1970.

DEMOS, JOHN. "The American Family in Past Time." In Arlene S. Skolnick and Jerome H. Skolnick (eds.), *Family in Transition*, 2nd Ed. Boston: Little, Brown & Company, 1977, 59–77.

DIAMOND, MARIAN CLEEVES. "The Aging Brain: Some Enlightening and Optimistic Results." *American Scientist,* 66, No. 1, 1978, 66–71.

DICKEN, CHARLES. "Sex Roles, Smoking, and Smoking Cessation." *Journal of Health and Social Behavior,* 19, No. 3, 1978, 324–334.

DINGMAN, PAUL. "The Alternative Care is Not There." In Paul I. Ahmed and Stanley C. Plog (eds.), *State Mental Hospitals: What Happens when They Close.* New York: Plenum Publishing Corporation, 1976, 45–61.

DONAHUE, WILMA, W. W. HUNTER, D. COONS, and H. MAURICE. "Rehabilitation of Geriatric Patients in County Hospitals: A Preliminary Report." *Geriatrics,* 15, 1960, 263–274.

DOHRENWEND, BARBARA, and BRUCE DOHRENWEND. *Stressful Life Events.* New York: John Wiley & Sons, Inc., 1974.

DOWD, JAMES J., and VERN L. BENGTSON. "An Examination of the Double Jeopardy Hypothesis." *Journal of Gerontology,* 33, No. 3, 1978, 427–436.

DUBLIN, LÒUIS, ALFRED J. LOTKA, and MORTIMER SPIEGALMAN. *Length of Life.* New York: Ronald Press, 1949.

DUFF, RAYMOND S., and AUGUST B. HOLLINGSHEAD. *Sickness and Society.* New York: Harper and Row, Publishers, Inc., 1968.

EDWARDS, J. N., and D. L. KLEMMACK. "Correlates of Life Satisfaction: A Reexamination." *Journal of Gerontology,* 28, 1973, 497–502.

EISENSTADT, S. N. *From Generation to Generation,* 2nd Ed. New York: The Free Press, 1971.

EISDORFER, CARL, and M. POWELL LAWTON (eds.). *The Psychology of Adult Development and Aging.* Washington, D.C.: American Psychological Association, 1973.

ELDER, GLENN H., JR. *Children of the Great Depression: Social Change in Life Experience.* Chicago: University of Chicago Press, 1974.

EPSTEIN, LEON, and ALEXANDER SIMON. "Alternatives to State Hospitalization for the Geriatric Mentally Ill." *American Journal of Psychiatry,* 124, No. 7, 1968, 955–961.

ERIKSON, ERIK H. *Childhood and Society.* New York: W. W. Norton & Co., Inc., 1963.

ESPANSHADE, THOMAS S. "The Value and Cost of Children." *Population Bulletin,* 32, No. 1, 1977. Washington, D.C.: Population Reference Bureau, Inc.

ESTES, CARROLL L., and HOWARD E. FREEMAN. "Strategies of Design and Research for Intervention." In Robert H. Binstock and Ethel Shanas (eds.), *Handbook of Aging and the Social Sciences.* New York: Van Nostrand Reinhold Company, 1976, 536–560.

FESTINGER, LEON. *A Theory of Cognitive Dissonance.* Evanston, Ill.: Row, Peterson, 1957.

FINCH, CALEB E. "The Physiology of Aging." In Richard H. Davis (ed.), *Aging: Prospects and Issues.* Los Angeles: University of Southern California Press, 1976, 58–69.

———, and LEONARD HAYFLICK (eds.). *Handbook of the Biology of Aging.* New York: Van Nostrand Reinhold Company, 1976.

FINK, HOWARD H. *The Relationship of Time Perspective to Age, Institutionalization, and Activity*. Michigan State University Doctoral Dissertation, 1953.

FISCHER, DAVID HACKETT. *Growing Old in America*. New York: Oxford University Press, Inc., 1977.

FONER, ANNE. "The Polity." In Matilda White Riley, Marilyn E. Johnson and Anne Foner, *Aging and Society, Vol. 3: A Theory of Age Stratification*. New York: Russell Sage Foundation, 1972, 115–159.

———, and DAVID KERTZER. "Transitions Over the Life Course: Lessons from Age Set Societies." *American Journal of Sociology*, 83, No. 5, 1978, 1081–1104.

FOX, JUDITH HUFF. "Effects of Retirement and Former Work Life on Women's Adaption in Old Age." *Journal of Gerontology*, 32, No. 2, 1977, 196–202.

FRANKLIN, BENJAMIN. *Some Account of the Pennsylvania Hospital*. Baltimore: The Johns Hopkins University Press, 1754.

FREUD, SIGMUND. "On Psychotherapy." In Sigmund Freud, *Collected Papers*, Vol. 1. London: Hogarth Press, 1959.

———. "Sexuality and Aetiology." In Sigmund Freud, *Collected Papers*, Vol. 1. London: Hogarth Press, 1959.

FRIEDMAN, MEYER, and RAY H. ROSENMAN. *Type A Behavior and Your Heart*. New York: Alfred A. Knopf, Inc., 1974.

FUCHS, VICTOR. *Who Shall Live?* New York: Basic Books, Inc., Publishers, 1974.

GANS, HERBERT J. *The Urban Villagers*. New York: The Free Press, 1962.

GIBSON, GEOFFREY. "Kin Family Network: Overheralded Structure in Past Conceptualizations of Family Functioning." *Journal of Marriage and the Family*, 34, 1972, 13–23.

GINSBERG, ARLENE B., and STEVEN G. GOLDSTEIN. "Age Bias in Referral for Psychological Consultation." *Journal of Gerontology*, 29, No. 4, 1974, 410–415.

GLASER, BARNEY G. "The Social Loss of Aged Dying Patients." *The Gerontologist*, 6, No. 1, 1966, 77–80.

———, and ANSELM L. STRAUSS "The Social Loss of Dying Patients." *American Journal of Nursing*, 64, 1964, 119–121.

———, ———. *Awareness of Dying*. Chicago: Aldine Publishing Company, 1965.

———, ———. "Temporal Aspects of Dying as a Non-scheduled Status Passage." *American Journal of Sociology*, 71, No. 1, 1965, 48–49.

———, ———. *Time for Dying*. Chicago: Aldine Publishing Company, 1968.

GLENN, NORVAL D. "Aging and Conservatism." *Annals of the American Academy of Political and Social Science*, 415, September 1974, 176–186.

———. "Psychological Well-Being in the Post-Parental Stage: Some Evidence from National Surveys." *Journal of Marriage and the Family*, 37, 1975, 105–110.

———. "Aging and Attitudinal Stability." Paper distributed at Roundtable, American Sociological Association Meetings. San Francisco, 1978.

GLICK, IRA, ROBERT S. WEISS, and C. MURRAY PARKES. *The First Year of Bereavement.* New York: John Wiley & Sons, Inc., 1974.

GOFFMAN, ERVING. *Asylums.* New York: Anchor Books, 1961.

GOLDE, PEGGY, and NATHAN KOGAN. "A Sentence Completion Procedure for Assessing Attitudes toward Old People." *Journal of Gerontology,* 14, No. 3, 1959, 355–363.

GOLD, JOAN. "Comparison of Protective Service Projects." *The Gerontologist,* 12, No. 3, Part 2, 1974, 85.

GOLDFARB, ALVIN. "Mental Health in the Institution." *The Gerontologist,* 1, No. 4, 1961, 178–184.

GOODE, WILLIAM J. "A Theory of Role Strain." *American Sociological Review,* 25, 1960, 483–496.

———. *The Family.* Englewood Cliffs, N.J.: Prentice-Hall, Inc., 1964.

GORDON, CHAD, CHARLES M. GAITZ, and JUDITH SCOTT. "Leisure and Lives: Personal Expressivity Across the Life Span." In Robert H. Binstock and Ethel Shanas (eds.), *Handbook of Aging and the Social Sciences.* New York: Van Nostrand Reinhold Company, 1976, 310–341.

GORDON, JUDITH BOGRAD. "A Disengaged Look at Disengagement Theory." *International Journal of Aging and Human Development,* 6, No. 3, 1975, 215–227.

GOTTESMAN, L. W., and P. T. SCHNEIDER. "The Interactions of Opportunity, Mental Status and Attitudes in the Adjustment of Geriatric Mental Patients." Paper presented at Social Science Research Seminar. Markarya, Sweden, 1963.

GOTTESMAN, LEONARD, and NORMAN BOURESTOM. "Why Nursing Homes Do What They Do." *The Gerontologist,* 14, No. 6, Dec. 1974, 501–506.

GOVE, WALTER R. "Sex, Marital Status, and Mortality." *American Journal of Sociology,* 79, No. 1, 1973, 45–67.

———, and JEANETTE F. TUDOR. "Adult Sex Roles and Mental Illness." *American Journal of Sociology,* 78, No. 4, 1973, 812–835.

GRAHAM, DAVID T., et al. "Physiological Response to the Suggestion of Attitudes Specific for Hives and Hypertension." *Psychosomatic Medicine.* 24, 1962, 159–169.

GRANEY, MARSHALL S. "Happiness and Social Participation in Aging." *Journal of Gerontology,* 30, No. 6, 1975, 701–706.

GREEN, BRENT. "The Politics of Psychoactive Drug Use in Old Age." *The Gerontologist,* 18, No. 6, 1978, 525–530.

GRUENBERG, ERNEST M. "The Failures of Success." *Milbank Memorial Quarterly (Health and Society),* 55, No. 1, 1977, 3–24.

GUBRIUM, JABER. *Living and Dying at Murray Manor.* New York: St. Martin's Press, Inc., 1975.

GUNTHER, JOHN. *Death Be Not Proud: A Memoir.* New York: Harper & Row, Publishers, Inc., 1963.

GURIN, GERALD, JOSEPH VEROFF, and SHEILA FELD. *Americans View Their Mental Health.* New York: Basic Books, Inc., Publishers, 1960.

GURLAND, BARRY J. "A Broad Clinical Assessment of Psychotherapy in the Aged." In Carl Eisdorfer and M. Powell Lawton (eds.), *The Psychology of*

Adult Development and Aging. Washington, D.C.: American Psychological Association, 343–427.

GUTMANN, DAVID. "The Hunger of Old Men." In Beth B. Hess (ed.), *Growing Old in America.* New Brunswick, N.J.: Transaction Books, 1976, 55–80.

——. "The Cross-Cultural Perspective: Notes toward a Comparative Psychoolgy of Aging." In James E. Birren and K. Warner Schaie (eds.). *Handbook of the Psychology of Aging.* New York: Van Nostrand Rienhold Company, 1976.

HAMMOND, PHILIP E. "Aging and the Ministry." In Matilda White Riley, John W. Riley, Jr., and Marilyn E. Johnson (eds.), *Aging and Society, Vol. 2: Aging and the Professions.* New York: Russell Sage Foundation, 1969, 293–323.

HAND, JENNIFER. "Shopping Bag Ladies in Urban Areas." New School for Social Research, mimeo, 1977.

HARENSTEIN, LOUISE S., STANISLAV KASL, and ERNEST HARBERG. "Work Status, Work Satisfaction, and Blood Pressure Among Married Black and White Women." *Psychology of Women,* **1,** (Summer), 1977, 334–349.

HAREVEN, TAMARA K. "The Dynamics of Kin in an Industrial Community." In John Demos and Sarane Spence Boocock (eds.), *Turning Points.* Chicago: University of Chicago Press, 1978, S152–182.

HARRIS, ADELLA J., and JONATHAN FEINBERG. "Television and Aging: Is What You See What You Get?" *The Gerontologist,* **18,** No. 5, 1978.

HARRIS, LOUIS, and ASSOCIATES. *The Myth and Reality of Aging in America: A Study for the National Council on the Aging.* Washington, D.C.: National Council on the Aging, 1975.

——. *1979 Study of American Attitudes toward Pensions and Retirement.* Prepared for Johnson & Higgins, New York, 1979.

HAVIGHURST, ROBERT, et al. "Disengagement, Personality and Life Satisfaction in Later Years." In P. F. Hansen (ed.), *Age with a Future.* Copenhagen: Munksgaard, 1964, 419–425.

——. "Personality and Patterns of Aging." *The Gerontologist,* **8,** No. 1, 1968, 20–23.

—— et al. "Disengagement and Patterns of Aging." In Bernice L. Neugarten (ed.), *Middle Age and Aging.* Chicago: The University of Chicago Press, 1975, 161–172.

HEANEY, ROBERT P., EUGENE EISENBERG, and C. CONRAD JOHNSTON. "Postmenopausal Osteoporosis." In Kenneth J. Ryan and Don C. Gibson (eds.), *Menopause and Aging,* DHEW No. 73–319, Washington, D.C.: U.S. Government Printing Office, 1973.

HEBB, DONALD O. "On Watching Myself Get Old." *Psychology Today,* **12,** No. 6, 1978, 15–23.

HENRETTA, JOHN C., and RICHARD T. CAMPBELL. "Status Attainment and Status Maintenance: A Study of Stratification in Old Age." *American Sociological Review,* **41,** No. 6, 1976, 981–992.

HERON, WOODBURN. "The Pathology of Boredom." *Scientific American,* **196,** No. 1, 1957, 52–56.

HESS, BETH B. "Friendship." In Matilda White Riley, Marilyn E. Johnson, and Anne Foner, *Aging and Society, vol. 3: A Theory of Age Stratification.* New York: Russell Sage Foundation, 1972, 357–393.

———. "Stereotypes of the Aged." *Journal of Communication,* **24,** No. 4, 1974, 76–85.

———. "Gerontology as a New Frontier in Higher Education." *Proceedings* of the First Annual Meeting, Association for Gerontology in Higher Education. Madison, Wis.: 1975, 1–26.

———. *Growing Old in America.* New Brunswick, N. J.: Transaction Books, 1976.

——— et al. "Dimension of the Grandparent Role." Paper presented at the Groves Conference on Marriage and the Family. Grossinger's, New York, 1976.

———. "Self Help Among the Aged." *Social Policy,* Nov.-Dec. 1976, 55–62.

———. "Sex Roles, Life Course, and Friendship." Paper presented at Miami University. Oxford, Ohio: June 20, 1977.

———. "A Sociology of Age: What Would It Look Like?" In Mildred M. Seltzer, Harvey Sterns, and Tom Hickey (eds.), *Gerontology in Higher Education: Perspectives and Issues.* Belmont, Cal.: Wadsworth Publishing Company, 1978, 204–213.

HESS, BETH B., and JOAN M. WARING. "Parent and Child in Later Life: Rethinking the Relationship." In Richard M. Lerner and Graham B. Spanier (eds.), *Child Influences on Marital and Family Interaction: A Life Span Perspective.* New York: Academic Press, 1978, 241–273.

HOCHSCHILD, ARLIE R. *The Unexpected Community.* Englewood Cliffs, N.J.: Prentice-Hall, Inc., 1973.

———. "Diengagement Theory: A Critique and Proposal." *American Sociological Review,* **40,** No. 5, 1975, pp. 553–69.

HOMANS, GEORGE C. *Social Behavior: Its Elementary Forms.* New York: Harcourt Brace Jovanovich, 1961.

HOLMBERG, R. H., and N. ANDERSON. "Implications of Ownership for Nursing Home Care." *Medical Care,* 7, 1968, 300–307.

HOLMES, THOMAS H., and MINORU MASUDA. "Life Change and Illness Susceptibility." In Barbara S. Dohrenwend and Bruce P. Dohrenwend, *Stressful Life Events.* New York: John Wiley & Sons, Inc., 1974, 45–72.

HUDSON, ROBERT, and ROBERT H. BINSTOCK. "Political Systems and Aging." In Robert H. Binstock and Ethel Shanas (eds.), *Handbook of Aging and the Social Sciences.* New York: Van Nostrand Reinhold Company, 1976.

HUXLEY, LAURA ARCHERA. *This Timeless Moment.* New York: Ballantine Books, 1968.

International Journal of Aging and Human Development (special issue on disengagement), 6, No. 3, 1975, 183–228.

ISTOMINA, Z. M., et al. "Memory Characteristics of Elderly Individuals Engaged in High Level Intellectual Work." *Voprosky Psikhologii,* **13,** No. 1, 1967, 55–64.

JACKSON, JACQUELYNE J. "Negro Aged: Toward Needed Research in Social Gerontology." *The Gerontologist,* **11,** 1971, 52–57.

———. "Really, There Are Existing Alternatives for Aged Blacks." In Eric

Pfeiffer (ed.), *Alternatives to Institutional Care for Older Americans: Practice and Planning*. Durham, N.C.: Center for the Study of Aging and Human Development, 1973.

JACKSON, HOBART. "Planning for the Specially Disadvantaged." In Eric Pfeiffer (ed.), *Alternatives to Institutional Care for Older Americans: Practice and Planning*. Durham, N. C.: Center for the Study of Aging and Human Development, 1973.

JACOBS, RUTH, and BETH B. HESS. "Panther Power: Symbol and Substance." *Long Term Care and Health Services Administration Quarterly*, Fall, 1978.

JAFFE, A. J. "Pension Systems—How Much Myth? How Much Reality?" Paper presented at the 10th International Congress of Gerontology, Jerusalem, Israel: 1975.

JARVIK, LISSY F., and DONNA COHEN, "A Biobehavioral Approach to Intellectual Changes with Aging." In Carl Eisdorfer and M. Powell Lawton (eds.), *The Psychology of Adult Development and Aging*. Washington, D.C.: American Psychological Association, 1973, 220–280.

JASLOW, PHILIP. "Employment, Retirement, and Morale Among Older Women." *Journal of Gerontology*, **31**, No. 2, 1976, 212–218.

JOHNSON, COLLEEN LEAHY. "Interdependence, Reciprocity, and Indebtedness: An Analysis of Japanese-American Kinship Relations." *Journal of Marriage and the Family*, **39**, No. 2, 1977, 351–363.

JONES, HOWARD W., EUGENE J. COHEN, and ROBERT B. WILSON. "Clinical Aspects of the Menopause." In Kenneth J. Ryan and Don C. Gibson (eds.), *Menopause and Aging*. DHEW No. 73–319. Washington, D.C.: U.S. Government Printing Office, 1973.

KALISH, RICHARD A. "The Aged and the Dying Process: The Inevitable Decisions." *Journal of Social Issues*, **21**, No. 1, 1965, 87–96.

———. "A Continuum of Subjectively Perceived Death." *The Gerontologist*, **6**, No. 2, 1966, 73–76.

———. "The Effects of Death Upon the Family." In Leonard Pearson (ed.), *Death and Dying*. Cleveland: Case Western Reserve University Press, 1969.

KALLMAN, FRANZ J. "Genetic Factors in Aging: Comparative and Longitudinal Observations on a Senescent Twin Population." In Paul H. Hoch and Joseph Zubin (eds.), *Psychotherapy of Aging*. New York: Grune and Stratton, 1961, 227–247.

KAMERMAN, SHEILA B. "Community Services for the Aged: The View from Eight Countries." *The Gerontologist*, **16**, No. 6, 1976, 529–537.

KART, CARY S., and BARBARA BECKHAM. "Black-White Differentials in the Institutionalization of the Elderly." *Social Forces*, **54**, 1976, 901–910.

KASTENBAUM, ROBERT J. "Psychological Death." In Leonard Pearson (ed.), *Death and Dying*. Cleveland: Case Western Reserve University Press, 1969.

———, and SANDRA CANDY. "The 4% Fallacy: A Methodological and Empirical Critique of Extended Care Facility Population Statistics." *International Journal of Aging and Human Development*, **4**, No. 1, 1973, 15–21.

———. *Death, Society, and Human Experience*. St. Louis: The C. V. Mosby Company, 1977.

KATZ, SOLOMON H. "Anthropological Perspectives on Aging." *Annals of the American Academy of Political and Social Science*, **438**, 1978, 1–12.

KEENAN, BRIAN. "The Modesto State Hospital Closing: A Case Study of the Impacted Employees and the Community." In *Where Is My Home? Proceedings of a Conference on the Closing of State Mental Hospitals*. Menlo Park: Stanford Research Institute, 1974, 125–140.

KEMPLER, HYMAN L. "Extended Kinship Ties and Some Modern Alternatives." *Family Coordinator*, **25**, No. 2, 1976, 143–149.

KENT, DONALD P. "The Negro Aged." *The Gerontologist*, **11**, 1971, pp. 48–51.

KOBRIN, FRANCES E., and GERRY E. HENDERSHOT. "Do Family Ties Reduce Mortality? Evidence from the United States 1966–1968." *Journal of Marriage and the Family*, **39**, No. 4, 1977, 737–746.

KREPS, JUANITA M. "Social Security in the Coming Decade: Questions for a Mature System." *Social Security Bulletin*, 1976, 21–29.

KÜBLER-ROSS, ELISABETH. *On Death and Dying*. New York: Macmillan Publishing Co., Inc., 1969.

KUCHARSKI, L. THOMAS, ROYCE M. WHITE, and MARJORIE SCHRATZ. "Age Bias, Referral for Psychological Assistance, and the Private Physician." *Journal of Gerontology*, **34**, No. 3, 1979, 423–428.

LAFAVE, HUGH. "Reducing Admissions and Increasing Discharges." *Canada's Mental Health*, **14**, 1966, 7–11.

LARSON, REED. "Thirty Years of Research on the Subjective Well-Being of Older Americans." *Journal of Gerontology*, **33**, No. 1, 1978, 109–125.

LASAGNA, LOUIS. "Physicians' Behavior Toward the Dying Patient." In Orville G. Brim, Jr., Howard E. Freeman, Sol Levine, and Norman A. Scotch (eds.), *The Dying Patient*. New York: Russell Sage Foundation, 1970, 83–101.

LASLETT, BARBARA. "The Family as a Public and Private Institution." *Journal of Marriage and the Family*, **35**, 1973, 480–494.

LASLETT, PETER. "Societal Development and Aging." In Robert H. Binstock and Ethel Shanas (eds.), *Handbook of Aging and the Social Sciences*. New York: Van Nostrand Reinhold Company, 1976, 87–116.

LAZARSFELD, PAUL, and ROBERT K. MERTON. "Friendship as Social Process: A Substantive and Methodological Inquiry." In Morroe Berger, Theodore Abel, and Charles H. Page (eds.), *Freedom and Control in Modern Society*. Princeton, N.J.: D. Van Nostrand, 1954.

LEAF, ALEXANDER. "Getting Old." *Scientific American*, **229**, No. 3, 1973, 44–52.

LEE, GARY R. "Marriage and Morale in Later Life." *Journal of Marriage and the Family*, **40**, No. 1, 1978, 131–139.

LEMON, BRUCE W., VERN L. BENGTSON, and JAMES A. PETERSON. "An Exploration of the Activity Theory of Aging: Activity Types and Life Satisfaction among In-Movers to a Retirement Community." *Journal of Gerontology*, **27**, No. 4, 1972, 511–523.

LERNER, MONROE. "When, Why, and Where People Die." In Orville G. Brim, Jr., Howard E. Freeman, Sol Levine, and Norman A. Scotch (eds.), *The Dying Patient*. New York: Russell Sage Foundation, 1970, 5–29.

LEVEY, SAMUEL, et al. "An Appraisal of Nursing Home Care." *Journal of Gerontology*, **28**, No. 2, 1973, 222–228.

LEVINSON, DANIEL, CHARLOTTE N. DARROW, EDWARD B. KLEIN, MARIA H. LEVINSON, and BRAXTON MCKEE. *The Seasons of a Man's Life*. New York: Alfred A. Knopf, Inc., 1978.

LE VINE, ROBERT. "Intergenerational Tensions and Extended Family Structure." In Ethel Shanas and Gordon F. Streib (eds.), *Social Structure and the Family*. Englewood Cliffs, N.J.: Prentice-Hall, Inc., 1965.

LINTON, RALPH. "Age and Sex Categories." *American Sociological Review*, **7**, 1942, 589–603.

LIVSON, FLORINE B. "Coming Together in the Middle Years: A Longitudinal Study of Sex Role Convergence." Paper presented at Annual Meeting of the Gerontological Society. New York: 1976.

———. "Cultural Faces of Eve." Paper Presented at Annual Meeting of the American Psychological Association, San Francisco, 1977.

LONGINO, CHARLES F., JR., and GAY C. KITSON. "Parish Clergy and The Aged." *Journal of Gerontology*, **31**, No. 3, 1976, 340–345.

LOPATA, HELENA ZNANIECKI. *Widowhood in an American City*. Cambridge, Mass.: Schenckman Publishing Co., Inc., 1973.

———. "Support Systems of Elderly Urbanites: Chicago of the 1970s." *The Gerontologist*, **15**, No. 1, 1975, 35–41.

———. *Polish-Americans*. Englewood Cliffs, N.J.: Prentice-Hall, Inc., 1976.

LOUGHAN, CELESTE. "Novels of Senescence: A New Naturalism." *The Gerontologist*, **17**, No. 1, 1977, 79–84.

LOWENTHAL, MARJORIE FISKE, and PAUL L. BERKMAN. *Lives in Distress: The Paths of the Elderly into the Psychiatric Ward*. New York: Basic Book, 1964.

———, ———. *Aging and Mental Disorder in San Francisco*. San Francisco: Jossey-Bass, Inc., Publishers, 1967.

———, and CLAYTON HAVEN. "Interaction and Adaptation: Intimacy as a Critical Variable." *American Sociological Review*, **33**, 1968, 20–30.

LOZIER, JOHN, and RONALD ALTHOUSE. "Social Enforcement of Behavior Toward Elders in an Appalachian Mountain Settlement." *The Gerontologist*, **14**, 1974, 69–80.

MAAS, HENRY S., and JOSEPH A. KUYPERS. *From Thirty to Seventy*. San Francisco: Jossey-Bass, Inc., Publishers, 1974.

MACDONALD, A. D., and W. C. MARTIN. "The Legitimacy of Public Intervention on Behalf of Older Persons: A Three Generation Study." *The Gerontologist*, **12**, No. 3, Part 2, 1972, 65.

MCKEOWN, THOMAS, et al. "An Interpretation of the Decline of Mortality in England and Wales during the Twentieth Century." *Population Studies*, **29**, No. 3, 1975, 391–422.

———. *The Role of Medicine: Dream, Mirage or Nemesis?* London: The Nuffield Provincial Hospitals Trust, 1976.

———. "Determinants of Health." *Human Nature*, **1**, No. 4, 1978, 60–67.

MCKINLEY, JOHN B., and SONJA M. MCKINLAY. "The Questionable Contribution of Medical Measures to the Decline of Mortality in the United States in the Twentieth Century." *Millbank Memorial Quarterly (Health and Society)*, **55**, No. 3, 1977, 405–428.

McTAVISH, DONALD G., "Perceptions of Old People: A Review of Research Methodologies and Findings." *The Gerontologist*, 11, No. 4, Part 2, 1971, 90–101.

MADIGAN, FRANCIS C. "Are Sex Mortality Differences Biologically Caused?" *Milbank Memorial Fund Quarterly*, 35, No. 2, 1957, 202–223.

———, and R. B. VANCE. "Differential Sex Mortality: A Research Design." *Social Forces*, 35, 1957, 193–199.

MALLAN, LUCY B. "Women's Worklives and Future Social Security Benefits." *Social Security Bulletin*, April 1976, 3 ff.

MANARD, BARBARA, CARY S. KART, and DIRK W. L. VAN GILS. *Old Age Institutions*. Lexington, Mass.: Lexington Books, 1975.

MARKSON, ELIZABETH W., and JENNIFER HAND. "Referral for Death: Low Status of the Aged and Referral for Psychiactric Hospitalization." *International Journal of Aging and Human Development*, 1, No. 3, 1970, 261–272.

——— et al. "Alternatives to Psychiatric Hospitalization for Psychiatrically Ill Geriatric Patients." *American Journal of Psychiatry*, 127, No. 8, 1971, 1055–1062.

———. "A Hiding Place to Die." *Transaction/Society*, 9, No. 1/2, 1971, 48–54.

———, and PRISCILLA GREVERT. "Circe's Terrible Island of Change: Self Perceptions of Incapacity." *International Journal of Aging and Human Development*, 3, No. 3, 1972, 261–271.

———. "Guest Editor's Note: Disengagement Theory Revisited." *International Journal of Aging and Human Development*, 6, No. 3, 1975, 183–186.

———, and JOHN H. CUMMING. "The Post-Transfer Fate of Relocated Patients." In Paul C. Ahmed and Stanley C. Plog (eds.), *State Mental Hospitals: What Happens When They Close*. New York: Plenum Publishing Corporation, 1976, 97–110.

———. "Massachusetts: Comparisons and Contrasts: A Review of Deinstitutionalization Outcomes." Paper presented at the American Orthopsychiatric Association. Atlanta, Ga.: March 5, 1976.

———. "Factors in Institutionalization of the Ethnic Aged." In Donald E. Gelfand and Alfred J. Kutzik (eds.), *Ethnicity and Aging*. New York: Springer Publishing Co., Inc., 1979.

MARLOWE, ROBERTA. "When They Closed the Doors at Modesto." In Paul I. Ahmed and Stanley C. Plog (eds.), *State Mental Hospitals: What Happens when They Close*. New York: Plenum Publishing Corporation, 1976, 83–96.

MARSHALL, C., and E. WALLENSTEIN. "Beyond Marcus Welby, Cable TV for the Health of the Elderly." *Geriatrics*, 28, 1973, 182–186.

MASTERS, WILLIAM H., and VIRGINIA JOHNSON. *Human Sexual Response*. Boston: Little, Brown & Company, 1966.

MAZESS, RICHARD B., and SYLVIA H. FORMAN. "Longevity and Age Exaggeration in Vilcamba, Ecuador." *Journal of Gerontology*, 34, No. 1, 1979, 94–98.

MEDNICK, ROBERT A. "Death Anxiety and Sexual Fantasy," *Omega*, 8, No. 2, 1977–78, 117–127.

MEDVEDEV, ZHORES A. "Caucasus and Altay Longevity: A Biological or Social Problem?" *The Gerontologist*, 14, No. 5, 1974, 381–387.

MENDEL, WERNER M. "The Case for Closing of the Hospitals." In Paul I. Ahmed and Stanley C. Plog (eds.), *State Mental Hospitals: What Happens*

When They Close. New York: Plenum Publishing Corporation, 1976, 21–29.

MENDELSON, MARY ADELAIDE. *Tender Loving Greed.* New York: Vintage Books, 1975.

——, and DAVID HAPGOOD. "The Political Economy of Nursing Homes." *Annals of the American Academy of Political and Social Science,* 415, 1974, 95–105.

MERRIAM, IDA C. "Social Security and Social Welfare Indicators." *Annals of the American Academy of Political and Social Science,* 435, 1978, 117–139.

MERTON, ROBERT K. *Social Theory and Social Structure.* Glencoe, Ill.: The Free Press, 1957.

MEYER, NESSA G. "Changes in the Age, Sex, and Diagnostic Composition of First Admissions to State and County Mental Hospitals, U.S. 1962–72." U.S. Dept. of Health, Education, and Welfare, National Institute of Mental Health, Division of Biometry, Statistical Note no. 97, 1973.

MILLER, BRENT C. "A Multivariate Developmental Model of Marital Satisfaction." *Journal of Marriage and the Family,* 38, 1976, 643–657.

MILLER, STEPHEN J. "The Social Dilemma of the Aging Leisure Participant." In Arnold M. Rose and Warren A. Peterson (eds.), *Older People and Their Social Worlds.* Philadelphia, Pa.: F. A. Davis, 1965, 77–92.

MILLS, C. WRIGHT. *The Sociological Imagination.* New York: Oxford University Press, 1959.

MINDEL, CHARLES H., and EDWIN C. VAUGHAN. "A Multidimensional Approach to Religiosity and Disengagement." *Journal of Gerontology,* 33, No. 1, 1978, 103–108.

MISHARA, B. L. "Effects of a Rehabilitation Program for Chronic Elderly Mental Patients." Paper presented at 79th Annual Meeting of the American Psychological Association, 1971.

MOEN, ELIZABETH. "The Reluctance of the Elderly to Accept Help." *Social Problems,* 25, No. 3, 1978, 293–303.

MORGAN, LESLIE A. "A Reexamination of Widowhood and Morale." *Journal of Gerontology,* 31, 1976, 687–695.

MOTLEY, DENA K. "Availability of Retired Persons for Work." Retirement History Survey No. 12, *Social Security Bulletin,* April 1978, 1–12.

MOULTON, RUTH. "Some Effects of the New Feminism." *American Journal of Psychiatry,* 134, No. 1, 1977, 1–6.

MUSGROVE, F. *Youth and the Social Order.* Bloomington, Ind.: Indiana University Press, 1964.

NAHEMOW, NINA, and DAVID R. KING. "Political Conservatism: Myth or Reality." Paper presented at the Annual Meeting of the Gerontological Society. Dallas, Tex.: November 1978.

National Council on the Aging, Inc. *Factbook on Aging,* Washington, D.C., 1978.

NEUGARTEN, BERNICE L., and KAROL WEINSTEIN. "The Changing American Grandparent." *Journal of Marriage and the Family,* 26, 1964, 199–204.

—— et al. "Age Norms, Age Constraints, and Adult Socialization." *American Journal of Sociology,* 70, No. 6, 1965, 710–717.

———. "Age Groups in American Society and the Rise of the Young-Old," *Annals of the American Academy of Political and Social Science*, **415**, 1974, 187–198.

———. "Adult Personality: Toward a Psychology of the Life Cycle." In Bernice L. Neugarten (ed.), *Middle Age and Aging*. Chicago: University of Chicago Press, 1975.

———. "The Awareness of Middle Age." In Bernice L. Neugarten (ed.), *Middle Age and Aging*. Chicago: University of Chicago Press, 1975.

———, and GUNHILD O. HAGESTAD. "Age and the Life Course." In Robert H. Binstock and Ethel Shanas (eds.), *Handbook of Aging and The Social Sciences*. New York: Van Nostrand Reinhold Company, 1976, 35–52.

———. "Middle Age and Aging." In Beth B. Hess (ed.), *Growing Old in America*. New Brunswick, N.J.: Transaction Books, 1976, 180–197.

———. "Personality and Aging." In James E. Birren and K. Warner Schaie (eds.), *Handbook of the Psychology of Aging*. New York: Van Nostrand Reinhold Company, 1976.

NORRIS, VERA. *Mental Illness in London*. New York: Oxford University Press, 1959.

NOVICK, L. J. "Easing the Stress of Moving Day." *Hospitals*, **41**, No. 1, 1967, 64.

NUNN, CLYDE Z., HARRY J. CROCKETT, JR., and WILLIAM J. ALLEN, JR. *Tolerance for Nonconformity*. San Francisco: Jossey-Bass, Inc., Publishers, 1978.

OAKLEY, ANN. *Woman's Work: The Housewife—Past, Present, and Future*. New York: Vintage Books, 1974.

OPPENHEIMER, VALERIE K. "Life Cycle Squeeze: The Interaction of Men's Occupational and Family Life Cycles." *Demography*, **11**, 1974, 227–245.

ORNSTEIN, PHILLIP. *The Perception of Time*. New York: Penguin Books, 1970.

OSAKO, MASAKO M. "Intergenerational Relations as an Aspect of Assimilation: The Case of Japanese-Americans." *Sociological Inquiry*, **46**, No. 1, 1976, 67–72.

OTTO, HERBERT A. *The Family in Search of a Future*. New York: Appleton-Century-Crofts, 1969.

OWEN, JOHN D. "Work Weeks and Leisure: An Analysis of Trends: 1948–75." *Monthly Labor Review*, August 1976.

PALMER, STUART. *Prevention of Crime*. New York: Behavioral Publications, 1973.

PALMORE, ERDMAN (ed.). *Normal Aging: Reports from the Duke Longitudinal Study, 1955–69*. Durham, N.C.: Duke University Press.

———. *Normal Aging 2*. Durham, N.C.: Duke University Press, 1974.

———. "Total Chance of Institutionalization among the Aged." *The Gerontologist*, **16**, No. 6, 1976, 504–507.

PARSONS, TALCOTT. "Age and Sex in the Social Structure of the United States." *American Sociological Review*, **7**, 1942, 604–616.

———. "Definitions of Health and Illness in the Light of American Values and Social Structure." In E. Gartly Jaco (ed.), *Patients, Physicians, and Illness*. Glencoe, Ill.: The Free Press, 1958, 167–187.

———. "Toward a Healthy Maturity." *Journal of Health and Human Behavior,* **1,** 1960, 163–173.

———, and GERALD PLATT. "Higher Education and Changing Socialization." In Matilda White Riley, Marilyn Johnson and Anne Foner, *Aging and Society, vol. 3: A Sociology of Age Stratification.* New York: Russell Sage Foundation, 1972, 236–291.

PEPPERS, LARRY G. "Patterns of Leisure and Adjustment to Retirement." *The Gerontologist,* **16,** No. 5, 1976, 441–446.

PETERS, G. R. "Self-conceptions of the Aged, Age Identification, and Aging." *The Gerontologist,* **11,** No. 4, 1971, 69–73.

PETERSON, DAVID A., and ELIZABETH L. KARNES. "Older People in Adolescent Literature," *The Gerontologist,* **16,** No. 3, 1976, 225–231.

PHILLIPS, BERNARD. "A Role Theory Approach to Adjustment in Old Age." *American Sociological Review,* **22,** 1956, 212–217.

POWERS, EDWARD A., and GORDON L. BULTENA. "Sex Differences in Intimate Friendships in Old Age." *Journal of Marriage and the Family,* **38,** No. 4, 1976, 739–746.

PRESSER, HARRIET. "Age Differences Between Spouses." *American Behavioral Scientist,* **19,** No. 2, 1975, 190–205.

PRATT, HENRY J. "Old Age Associations in National Politics." *Annals of the American Academy of Political and Social Science,* **415,** 1974, 106–119.

———. *The Politics of Old Age.* Chicago: University Chicago Press, 1976.

———. "Symbolic Politics and White House Conferences on Aging." *Society,* **15,** No. 5, 1978, 67–72.

QUINT, JEANNE C. *The Nurse and the Dying Patient.* New York: The Macmillan Company, 1967.

RADER, VICTORIA N. "The Social Construction of Ages and the Ideology of Stages." Paper presented at the Annual Meeting of the Eastern Sociological Society, Philadelphia, Pa., March 1978.

RAGAN, PAULINE K. "Another Look at the Politicizing of Old Age: Can We Expect a Backlash Effect?" Paper presented at the Annual Meeting of the Society for the Study of Social Problems, New York City, August 1976.

———, and WILLIAM J. DAVIS. "The Diversity of Older Voters." *Society,* **15,** No. 5, 1978, 50–53.

REICH, ROBERT, and L. SIEGAL. "Psychiatry under Siege: The Chronically Mentally Ill Shuffle to Oblivion." *Psychiatric Annals,* **3,** No. 11, 1973, 35–55.

REICHARD, SUZANNE, FLORINE LIVSON, and PAUL G. PETERSON. *Aging and Personality.* New York: John Wiley & Sons, Inc., 1962.

REITZ, ROSETTA. *Menopause: A Positive Approach.* Radnor, Pa.: Chilton Book Company, 1977.

RICHMAN, JOSEPH. "The Foolishness and Wisdom of Age: Attitudes toward the Elderly as Reflected in Jokes." *The Gerontologist,* **17,** No. 3, 1977, 210–219.

RIESMAN, DAVID. *The Lonely Crowd.* New Haven: Yale University Press, 1950.

———, and DONALD HORTON. "Notes on the Deprived Institution." *Sociology Quarterly,* **6,** No. 1, 1965, 3–20.

RILEY, MATILDA WHITE, et al. "Socialization for the Middle and Later Years." In David A. Goslin (ed.), *Handbook of Socialization Theory and Research.* Chicago: Rand McNally & Company, 1968, 951–982.

——, and ANNE FONER. *Aging and Society, vol. 1: An Inventory of Research Findings.* New York: Russell Sage Foundation, 1968.

—— et al. *Aging and Society, vol. 2: Aging and the Professions.* New York: Russell Sage Foundation, 1969.

—— et al. *Aging and Society, vol. 3: A Sociology of Age Stratification.* New York: Russell Sage Foundation, 1972.

——, and JOAN M. WARING. "Age and Aging." In Robert K. Merton and Robert Nisbet (eds.). *Contemporary Social Problems,* 4th Ed. New York: Harcourt Brace Jovanovich, Inc., 1976, pp. 355–410.

——. "Aging, Social Change and the Power of Ideas." *Daedelus,* 1978.

ROBERTSON, JOAN. "Grandmotherhood: A Study of Role Conception." *Journal of Marriage and the Family,* 39, No. 1, 1977, 165–174.

ROONEY, JAMES F. "Friendship and Disaffiliation Among the Skid Row Population." *Journal of Gerontology,* 31, No. 1, 1976, 82–88.

ROSE, ARNOLD M. "The Subculture of the Aging: A Framework for Research in Social Gerontology." In Arnold M. Rose and Warren A. Peterson (eds.), *Older People and Their Social Worlds.* Philadelphia: F. A. Davis Company, 1965, 3–16.

——. "Group Consciousness among the Aging." In Arnold M. Rose and Warren A. Peterson (eds.), *Older People and Their Social Worlds.* Philadelphia: F. A. Davis Company, 1965, 19–36.

ROSENFELD, JEFFREY P. *The Legacy of Aging.* Norwood, N.J.: Ablex Publishing Corporation, 1979.

ROSENHAN, DAVID L. "On Being Sane in Insane Places." *Science,* 179, No. 4070, 1973, 250–258.

ROSOW, IRVING. "Old Age: One Moral Dilemma of an Affluent Society." *The Gerontologist,* 2, No. 4, 1962, 182–191.

——. *Social Integration of the Aged.* New York: The Free Press, 1967.

ROTH, JULIUS A., and ELIZABETH EDDY. *Rehabilitation for the Unwanted.* New York: Atherton, 1967.

RUBIN, ISADORE. "The 'Sexless Older Years': A Socially Harmful Stereotype." *Annals of the American Academy of Political and Social Science,* 376, 1968, 86–95.

RYDER, NORMAN B. "The Cohort as a Concept in the Study of Social Change." *American Sociological Review,* 30, 1965, 843–861.

SALTER, CHARLES A., and CARLOTA DELERMA SALTER. "Attitudes Toward Aging and Behaviors Toward the Elderly Among Young People as a Function of Death Anxiety." *The Gerontologist,* 16, No. 3, 1976, 232–236.

SALTZ, ROSALYN. "Aging Persons as Child Care Workers in a Foster Grandparent Program," *Aging and Human Development,* 2, 1971, 314–340.

SCHAIE, K. WARNER. "A General Model for the Study of Developmental Problems." *Psychological Bulletin,* 64, 1965, 92–107.

——. "Methodological Problems in Descriptive Developmental Research on Adulthood and Aging." In J. R. Nesselroade and H. W. Reese (eds.), *Life-*

Span Developmental Psychology: Methodology. New York: Academic Press, 1972.

SCHNEIDMAN, EDWIN S. *Deaths of Man.* New York: Quadrangle-The New York Times Book Co., Inc., 1973.

———. "Suicide in the Aged." In *Dealing with Death.* Los Angeles: Ethel Percy Andrus Gerontology Monograph Series, University of Southern California, 1973, 25–32.

SCHONFIELD, DAVID. "Memory Changes with Age." *Nature,* **208,** No. 5013, 1965, 918.

SCOTT, FRANCES G. "Factors in the Personal Adjustment of Institutionalized and Non-Institutionalized Aged." *American Sociological Review,* **20,** No. 5, 1955, 538–546.

SCULLY, DIANE, and PAULINE BART. "A Funny Thing Happened on the Way to the Oriface: Women in Gynecology Textbooks." *American Journal of Sociology,* **78,** 1973, 1045–49.

SEELBACH, WAYNE, and WILLIAM SAUER. "Filial Responsibility Expectations and Morale Among Aged Parents." Paper presented at the Annual Meeting of the Gerontological Society. New York: 1976.

SELTZER, MILDRED M. "The Quality of Research is Strained." *The Gerontologist,* **15,** No. 6, 1975, 503–507.

SELYE, HANS. *The Stress of Life.* New York: The McGraw-Hill Company, 1956.

SHANAS, ETHEL, et al. *The Health of Older People:* A Social Survey. Cambridge: Harvard University Press, 1962.

———. *Old People in Three Industrial Societies.* New York: Atherton Press, 1968.

———. "Family Kin Network and Aging: A Cross Cultural Perspective." *Journal of Marriage and the Family,* **35,** 1973, 505–511.

———, and MARVIN B. SUSSMAN (eds.). *Family, Bureaucracy, and the Elderly.* Durham, N.C.: Duke University Press, 1977.

SHEEHAN, TOM. "Senior Esteem as a Factor of Socioeconomic Complexity." *The Gerontologist,* **16,** No. 5, 1976, 433–440.

SHEEHY, GAIL. *Passages.* New York: E. P. Dutton and Company, 1976.

SHELTON, AUSTIN J. "The Aging and Eldership: Notes for Gerontologists and Others." *The Gerontologist,* **5,** No. 1, 1965, 20–23 and 48.

SHEPARD, HAROLD L. "Work and Retirement." In Robert H. Binstock and Ethel Shanas (eds.), *Handbook of Aging and the Social Sciences.* New York: Van Nostrand Reinhold Company, 1976, 286–309.

SHERIZEN, SANFORD, and LESTER PAUL. "Dying in a Hospital Intensive Care Unit: The Social Significance for the Family of the Patient." *Omega,* **8,** No. 1, 1977, 29–40.

SHIRK, J. K. *Female Hygiene and Female Disease.* Lancaster, Pa.: Lancaster Publishing Co., 1884.

SHOCK, NATHAN. "Systems Integration." In Caleb E. Finch and Leonard Hayflick (eds.), *Handbook of the Biology of Aging.* New York: Van Nostrand Reinhold Company, 1976.

SHORTER, EDWARD. *The Making of the Modern Family.* New York: Basic Books, Inc., Publishers, 1975.

SHULMAN, DAVID, and RUTH GALANTER. "Reorganizing the Nursing Home Industry: A Proposal." *Milbank Memorial Fund Quarterly (Health and Society)*, 54, No. 2, 1976, 129–143.

SIEGEL, JACOB S. "Demographic Aspects of Aging and the Older Population in the United States." Special Studies Series P-23, No. 59, May 1976. U.S. Department of Commerce, Bureau of the Census, U.S. Government Printing Office, Washington, D.C.

SIMOS, BERTHA G. "Relations of Adults with Aging Parents." *The Gerontologist*, 10, 1970, 135–139.

SIMON, ALEXANDER, MARJORIE F. LOWENTHAL, and LEON EPSTEIN. *Crisis and Intervention*. San Francisco: Jossey-Bass, 1970.

SIMPSON, IDA H., and JOHN C. McKINNEY (eds.). *Social Aspects of Aging* Durham, N.C.: Duke University Press, 1966.

SLATER, PHILIP. *The Pursuit of Loneliness*. Boston: Beacon Books, 1976.

SLOCUMB, JOHN C., and STEPHEN J. KUNITZ. "Factors Affecting Maternal Mortality and Morbidity Among American Indians." *Public Health Reports*, 92, No. 4, 1977, 349–356.

SOHNGEN, MARY. "The Experience of Old Age as Depicted in Contemporary Novels." *The Gerontologist*, 17, No. 1, 1977, 70–78.

SOLDO, BETH J., and GEORGE C. MYERS. "The Effects of Total Fertility on Living Arrangements Among Elderly Women." Paper presented at the Annual Meeting of the Gerontological Society. New York: 1976.

SONTAG, SUSAN. "The Double Standard of Aging." *The Saturday Review*, September 23, 1972, 29–38.

———. *Illness as Metaphor*. New York: Farrar, Straus & Giroux, 1978.

SPAKES, P. "Social Integration, Age, and Family Participation", Paper presented at the Annual Meeting of the Gerontological Society. New York: 1976.

SPANIER, GRAHAM B., ROBERT A. LEWIS, and CHARLES L. COLE. "Marital Adjustment Over the Family Life Cycle: The Issue of Curvilinearity." *Journal of Marriage and the Family*, 37, 1975, 263–275.

SPARK, MURIEL. *Memento Mori*. New York: Avon Books, 1967.

SPREITZER, ELMER, and ELDON E. SNYDER. "Correlates of Life Satisfaction Among the Aged." *Journal of Gerontology*, 29, 1974, 454–458.

SROLE, LEO, THOMAS S. LANGNER, STANLEY T. MICHAEL, MARVIN K. OPLER, and THOMAS A. C. RENNIE. *Mental Health in the Metropolis: The Midtown Manhattan Study*. New York: The McGraw-Hill Company, 1962.

———, and ANITA KASSEN FISCHER, "The Midtown Manhattan Study: Longitudinal Focus on Aging, Genders, and Life Transition," paper presented to the Gerontological Society. Dallas, Texas: November, 1978.

STANNARD, CHARLES I. "Old Folks and Dirty Work: The Social Conditions for Patient Abuse in a Nursing Home." *Social Problems*, 20, No. 3, 1973, 329–342.

STEINMETZ, SUZANNE K. "Battered Parents." *Society*, 15, No. 5, 1978, 54–55.

STEPHANS, JOYCE. *Loners, Losers and Lovers: A Sociological Study of the Aged Tenants of a Slum Hotel*. Seattle: University of Washington Press, 1977.

STEWART, FRANK HENDERSON. *Fundamentals of Age-Group Systems*. New York: Academic Press, 1977.

STREIB, GORDON F., and HAROLD ORBACH. "Aging." In Paul Lazarsfeld, William Sewell and Harold Wilensky (eds.), *The Uses of Sociology.* New York: Basic Books, Inc., Publishers, 1967.

——. "Old Age in Ireland: Demographic and Sociological Aspects." *The Gerontologist,* 8, No. 4, 1968, 227–235.

STRUYK, RAYMOND J. "The Housing Situation of Elderly Americans." *The Gerontologist,* 17, No. 2, 1977, 130–139.

SUCHMAN, EDWARD A., BERNARD S. PHILLIPS, and GORDON STREIB. "An Analysis of the Validity of Health Questionnaires." *Social Forces,* 36, 1958, 223–232.

SUDNOW, DAVID. *Passing On.* Englewood Cliffs, N.J.: Prentice-Hall, Inc., 1967.

SUNDEEN, RICHARD A., and JAMES T. MATHIEU. "The Fear of Crime and Its Consequences Among Elderly in Three Urban Communities." *The Gerontologist,* 16, No. 3, 1976, 211–219.

SUSSMAN, MARVIN, and LEE BURCHINAL. "Kin Family Networks: Unheralded Structure in Current Conceptualization of Family Functioning." *Marriage and Family Living,* 24, 1962, 231–240.

——, JUDITH N. CATES, and DAVID SMITH. *The Family and Inheritance.* New York: Russell Sage Foundation, 1970.

SUTTON, JEANNINE FOX. *Utilization of Nursing Homes, United States: National Nursing Home Survey, August 1973–April 1974.* Department of Health, Education and Welfare No. 77–1779. Washington, D.C.: U.S. Government Printing Office, 1977.

SZASZ, THOMAS S. *The Manufacture of Madness.* New York: Harper and Row, Publishers, Inc., 1970.

THEWLISS, M. *The Care of the Aged.* St. Louis: The C. V. Mosby Company, 1946.

THOMPSON, LARRY W., and GAIL R. MARSH. "Psychophysiological Studies of Aging." In Carl Eisdorfer and M. Powell Lawton (eds.), *The Psychology of Adult Development and Aging.* Washington, D.C.: American Psychological Association, 1973, 112–148.

THURNER, MAJDA. "Becoming Old: Perspectives on Women and Marriage." Paper presented at annual meeting of the American Psychological Association, San Francisco, 1977.

THUROW, LESTER C. "Not Making It in America: The Economic Progress of Minority Groups." *Social Policy,* 6, No. 5, 1976, 5–11.

TIBBITTS, CLARK (ed.). *Handbook of Social Gerontology.* Chicago: University of Chicago Press, 1960.

——. and WILMA DONAHUE (eds.). *Social and Psychological Aspects of Aging.* New York: Columbia University Press, 1962.

TITCHNER, J., et al. "Psychological Reactions of the Aged in Surgery: The Reactions of Renewal and Depression." *American Medical Association Archives of Neurology and Psychiatry,* 79, No. 1, 1958, 63–73.

TOBIN, SHELDON S., and MORTON LIEBERMAN. *The Last Home for the Aged.* San Francisco: Jossey-Bass, Inc., Publishers. 1976.

——. "The Mystique of Deinstitutionalization." *Society,* 15, No. 5, 1978, 73–75.

TOWNSEND, PETER. *The Last Refuge*. London: Routledge and Kegan-Paul, 1962.

TRELA, JAMES E. "Social Class and Association Membership: An Analysis of Age-Graded and Non-Age-Graded Voluntary Participation." *Journal of Gerontology*, **31**, No. 2, 1976, 198–203.

———, and D. JACKSON. "Family Life and Substitutes in Old Age." Paper presented at the Annual Meeting of the Gerontological Society. New York: 1976.

TROLL, LILLIAN E. "The Family of Later Life: A Decade Review." *Journal of Marriage and the Family*, **33**, 1971, 263–290.

TUCKMAN, JACOB, and IRVING LORGE. "Attitudes Toward Old Workers." *Journal of Applied Psychology*, **35**, No. 3, 1952, 149–153.

———, ———. "Attitudes Toward Old People." *Journal of Social Psychology*, **37**, 1953, 249–260.

———, ———. "When Aging Begins," and "Stereotypes About Aging." *Journal of Gerontology*, **8**, No. 4, 1953, 489–492.

TURNER, BARBARA F., "The Self Concepts of Older Women." In M. Seltzer (chair) and L. E. Troll (organizer), *Socialization to Become an Old Woman*. Symposium presented at the 85th Annual Convention of the American Psychological Association. San Francisco, 1977.

TURNER, HELEN, et al. "Programs for the Mentally Impaired in Homes for the Aged: Preliminary Report of a Survey." *The Gerontologist*, **7**, No. 3; 1967, 161–163.

UHLENBERG, PETER. "Changing Structure of the Older Population of the USA During the Twentieth Century." *The Gerontologist*, **17**, No. 3, 1977, 197–202.

U.S. Dept. of Commerce. *Statistical Abstract of the United States*. Washington, D.C.: U.S. Government Printing Office, various years.

U.S. Dept. of Health, Education, and Welfare; National Center for Health Statistics. *Vital Statistics of the United States, Vol. 2, Mortality*. Washington, D.C.: U.S. Government Printing Office, selected years.

U.S. Dept. of Health, Education, and Welfare. "Indian Poverty and Indian Health." *Indicators*, March 1964.

U.S. Dept. of Health, Education, and Welfare. *Public Health Service Publication 1000*, Series 22, No. 9, 1969. Washington, D.C.: U.S. Government Printing Office.

U.S. Dept. of Health, Education, and Welfare; Health Research Administration; National Center for Health Statistics. *Nursing Homes: A County and Metropolitan Data Book, 1973*. Washington, D.C.: U.S. Government Printing Office.

U.S. Dept. of Health, Education, and Welfare; National Center for Health Statistics. *Facts of Life and Death*. Rockville, Md.: Health Resources Administration, 1974.

U.S. Dept. of Health, Education, and Welfare; National Center for Health Statistics. *Health—United States—1975*, HRA No. 76-1232. Washington, D.C.: U.S. Government Printing Office, 1976.

U.S. Dept. of Health, Education, and Welfare; Health Resources Administration, *Health—United States—1976–77.* Washington, D.C.: U.S. Government Printing Office, 1978.

U.S. Dept. of Health, Education, and Welfare; National Center for Health Statistics. *Advance Data from Vital and Health Statistics,* No. 27, April 14, 1978. Washington, D.C.: U.S. Government Printing Office.

U.S. Dept. of Health, Education, and Welfare; Public Health Service. *Advance Report, Final Mortality Statistics, 1976,* DHEW, No. PHS 78–1120, **26,** 12, supplement 2. U.S. Government Printing Office, 1978.

U.S. House of Representatives, Select Committee on Aging. *National Crisis in Adult Care Homes, June 8, 1977,* Committee Publication 95–98. Washington, D.C.: U.S. Government Printing Office, 1977.

U.S. Dept. of Labor, Special Labor Force Report. "Work Experience of the Population in 1974." Washington, D.C.: U.S. Government Printing Office, June 1975.

U.S. Senate Special Committee on Aging, "Developments in Aging, 1977," Report No. 95–771. Washington, D.C.: U.S. Government Printing Office.

VAN BUSKIRK, C. "The Seventh Nerve Complex." *Journal of Comparative Neurology,* **82,** 1945, 303–30.

VERBA, SIDNEY, and N. NIE. *Participation in America: Political Democracy and Social Equality.* New York: Harper & Row, Publishers, Inc., 1972.

VERBRUGGE, LOIS M. "Females and Illness: Recent Trends in Sex Differences in the United States." *Journal of Health and Social Behavior,* **17,** No. 4, 1976, 387–403.

VERMEULEN, A., R. RUBENS, and L. VERDONCK. "Testosterone Secretion and Metabolism in Male Senescence." *Journal of Clinical Endocrinology and Metabolism,* **34,** No. 4, 1972, 730–735.

VINCENT, CLARK. "An Open Letter to the 'Caught Generation.'" *Family Coordinator,* **21,** 1972, 143–50.

VINYARD, DALE. "Rediscovery of the Aged: Senior Power and Public Policy." Paper presented at the Annual Meeting of the American Political Science Association. Chicago: 1976.

WARD, RUSSELL A. "The Impact of Subjective Age and Stigma of Older Persons." *Journal of Gerontology,* **32,** No. 2, 1977, 227–232.

WARING, JOAN M. "Social Replenishment and Social Change." *American Behavioral Scientist,* **19,** No. 2, 1975, 237–256.

WATSON, J. ALLEN, and VIRA R. KIVETT. "Influences on the Life Satisfaction of Older Fathers." *Family Coordinator,* **25,** 1976, 482–488.

WEINBERGER, LINDA E., and JIM MILLHAM. "A Multidimensional Multiple Method Analysis of Attitudes Toward The Elderly." *Journal of Gerontology,* **30,** No. 3, 1975, 343–348.

WEG, RUTH B. "The Changing Physiology of Aging." In Richard H. Davis (ed.), *Aging: Prospects and Issues.* Los Angeles: University of Southern California Press, 1976, 70–89.

WERTENBAKER, LAEL. *Death of a Man.* Boston: Beacon Press, 1974.

WILDAVSKY, AARON. "Doing Better and Feeling Worse: The Political Pathology of Health Policy." In John H. Knowles (ed.), *Doing Better and Feeling*

Worse: Health in the United States. New York: W. W. Norton, 1977, 105–123.

WILENSKY, HAROLD L. "Life Cycle, Work Situation and Social Participation." In Clark Tibbitts and Wilma Donahue (eds.), *Social and Psychological Aspects of Aging.* New York: Columbia University Press, 1962.

WILSON, C. W. M., and H. S. LOH. "Common Cold and Vitamin C." *Lancet,* No. 1, 1973, 638.

WILSON, ROBERT N. *The Sociology of Health: An Introduction.* New York: Random House, Inc., 1970.

WIMMERS, M. F., and F. MOL. "Psychosocial Factors: A Matter of Life or Death." *Nederlands Tijdschrift Voor Gerontologie,* 63, No. 3, 1975, 149–157.

WINCH, ROBERT F., and RAE LESSER BLUMBERG. "Societal Complexity and Familial Organization." In R. F. Winch and L. W. Goodman (ed.), *Selected Studies in Marriage and the Family,* 3rd Ed. New York: Holt, Rinehart & Winston, 1968.

WINSBOROUGH, HALLIMAN H. "Statistical Histories of the Life Cycle of Birth Cohorts: The Transition from Schoolboy to Adult Male." Center for Demography and Ecology. Madison, Wis.: University of Wisconsin, 1975.

WOOD, VIVIAN. "Age Appropriate Behavior for Older People." *The Gerontologist,* 11, (Winter, Part 2), 1971, 74–78.

———, and JOAN F. ROBERTSON. "Friendship and Interaction: Differential Effect on the Morale of the Elderly." *Journal of Marriage and the Family,* 40, No. 2, 1978, 367–375.

WOODRUFF, DIANA S., and DAVID A. WALSH. "Research in Adult Learning: The Individual." *The Gerontologist,* 15, No. 5, 1975, 424–430.

WU, FRANCES Y. T., "Mandarin-Speaking Aged Chinese in the Los Angeles Area." *The Gerontologist,* 15, No. 3, 1975, 271–275.

YANKELOVICH, SKELLY, and WHITE, INC. *Raising Children in a Changing Society.* Minneapolis, Minn.: General Mills, Inc., 1977.

YOUNG, ANNE McD. "Going Back to School at 35 and Over." *Monthly Labor Review.* United States Department of Labor, December 1975.

YUDKIN, JOHN. *The Nutrition Business.* New York: St. Martin's Press, 1978.

ZANDER, MARY. "Welfare Reform and the Urban Aged." *Society,* 15, No. 5, 1978, 59–66.

ZIMMERMAN, MICHAEL. "The Elderly Indigent in Preindustrial New York City." In Beth B. Hess (ed.), *Growing Old in America.* New Brunswick: Transaction Books, 1976.

ZUCKERMAN, HARRIET, and ROBERT K. MERTON. "Age, Aging, and Age Structure in Science." In Matilda White Riley, Marilyn Johnson and Anne Foner, *Aging and Society, vol. 3: A Sociology of Age Stratification.* New York: Russell Sage Foundation, 1972.

Index of Names

Allen, P., 168
Allen, William J., Jr., 351
Althouse, Ronald, 273
Anderson, N., 164
Anderson, T. W., 83
Andrus, Ethel Percy, 232
Ansello, Edward F., 72, 73
Antonovsky, Anton, 91, 152
Antunes, George, 283
Arensberg, David, 144
Ariès, Philippe, 49n., 50, 59
Arling, Greg, 277
Arms, Suzanne, 111
Arnoff, C., 72
Atchley, Robert C., 148, 191, 251, 278, 311, 314

Bachrach, Leona, 168
Baltes, Paul B., 122
Barfield, Richard E., 189
Bart, Pauline, 90, 130, 255, 313
Barton, Elizabeth M., 303
Bascue, L. O., 145
Beattie, Walter, 175
Beckham, Barbara, 159
Bekker, L. DeMoyne, 65
Bellow, Saul, 74
Bengtson, Vern L., 120, 261
Bennett, Ruth, 171
Berger, Brigitte, 153
Berghorn, Forrest S., 281
Berkman, Paul L., 165
Biesty, Patrick, 206
Bignall, J. C., 83
Bild, Bernice R., 282
Binstock, Robert H., 13, 228, 233, 237, 239
Birren, James E., 13, 120, 121, 125
Blau, Zena S., 68, 97, 132, 133, 277
Blazer, Dan, 295, 296
Blenkner, Margaret, 97, 166, 167, 265

Blum, Richard H., 142
Blumberg, Rae Lesser, 43
Bock, E. Wilbur, 278
Bondareff, W., 142
Botwinick, Jack, 121, 122, 124
Bourestom, Norman, 166, 171
Boylin, William, 145
Brim, Orville G., Jr., 41
Brizzee, Kenneth R., 124
Brody, Elaine M., 154, 174
Bromley, D. B., 122, 123
Bultena, Gordon L., 69, 278
Burchinal, Lee, 255
Burger, Isabel, 146
Burgess, Ernest W., 13, 56, 57, 62, 119, 132
Busse, Ewald W., 131, 142
Butler, Robert N., 56, 135, 142

Califano, Joseph A., Jr., 208, 223
Campbell, Angus, 126, 213, 254
Campbell, Richard T., 344
Candy, Sandra, 152
Cantor, Marjorie, 256, 262t., 280
Carp, Frances M., 166, 210, 279, 281
Cates, Judith N., 257
Cath, Stanley, 139
Cavan, Ruth, 119, 132
Clark, Margaret, 339
Clausen, John A., 255
Clavan, Sylvia, 258, 259, 260
Clay, Vidal S., 89, 90
Clemente, Frank, 229, 275, 283, 284
Cleveland, Martha, 249
Cohen, Donna, 121, 124, 142
Cohen, Eugene J., 88
Cohen, Sanford, 145
Cole, Charles L., 247, 257
Coles, Robert, 273
Collins, Marjorie, 89, 90
Comfort, Alexander, 158, 161

Converse, Philip E., 254
Cook, Fay Lomox, 275
Cook, Thomas D., 339
Cooley, Charles Horton, 66–67
Coons, D., 340
Cooper, W., 89
Corsellis, J. A. N., 142
Corso, John G., 82
Cosin, L. Z., 174
Cosneck, Bernard J., 257
Costa, Paul, 145
Coulehan, John L., 83
Cowgill, Donald O., 57, 279
Crockett, Harry J., Jr., 351
Croog, Sydney H., 282
Cumming, Elaine, 19, 95, 120, 132, 133, 134–35, 165, 171n.
Cumming, John H., 167, 168
Curtin, Sharon R., 154, 168
Cutler, Stephen J., 283

Darrow, Charlotte N., 347
Davis, Karen, 159
Davis, Leonard, 232
Davis, William J., 52, 238
Delay, Jean, 143
Demos, John, 242
Diamond, Marian Cleeves, 124, 143
Dicken, Charles, 103
Dickens, Charles, 152
DiComo, William, 206
Dingman, Paul, 155
Dohrenwend, Barbara, 86
Dohrenwend, Bruce, 86
Donahue, Wilma, 13, 174
Dowd, James J., 261
Dublin, L., 100
Duff, Raymond S., 114
Durkheim, Émile, 46, 103

Eddy, Elizabeth, 353
Edwards, J. N., 294
Eisdorfer, Carl, 125
Eisenberg, Eugene, 90
Eisenstadt, S. D., 44
Elder, Glenn H., Jr., 26
Epstein, Leon, 155, 172
Erikson, Erik H., 23, 96, 135, 139, 148
Espanshade, Thomas S., 341
Estes, Carroll L., 17, 254

Fefferman, Charles, 122
Feinberg, Jonathan, 72
Feld, Sheila, 343
Festinger, Leon, 68

Finch, Caleb E., 13, 88, 89
Fink, Howard, 145
Fischer, Anita Kassen, 28, 29
Fischer, David Hackett, 46, 242
Foner, Anne, 27, 33, 34, 37n., 41, 45, 50, 68, 70, 81, 121, 125, 126, 127, 131, 229, 253, 256, 282, 294, 308
Forman, Sylvia H., 101
Fox, Judith Huff, 191
Franklin, Benjamin, 152–53, 154
Freeman, Howard E., 17
Freud, Sigmund, 23, 25, 138, 144, 183, 303
Friedman, Meyer, 103
Fuchs, Victor, 342

Gaitz, Charles M., 283, 309, 312
Galanter, Ruth, 157, 164
Gans, Herbert J., 269
Gibson, Geoffrey, 256
Ginsberg, Arlene B., 97
Glaser, Barney G., 111, 113, 114, 115
Glenn, Norval D., 70, 71, 228,255
Glick, Ira, 104
Goffman, Erving, 169, 170
Gold, Joan, 175
Golde, Peggy, 65
Goldfarb, Alvin, 155
Goldstein, Steven G., 97
Goode, William J., 41, 242, 243
Goodman, L. W., 43
Goodman, Sara, 136n.
Gordon, Chad, 309, 312
Gordon, Judith Bograd, 133
Gordon, Susan K., 145
Gottesman, L. W., 171, 174
Gove, Walter R., 104, 265, 313
Graham, David T., 87
Graney, Marshall S., 283
Green, Brent, 98, 139
Grevert, Priscilla, 80
Gruenberg, Ernest M., 109, 112, 147
Gubrium, Jaber, 168
Gunther, John, 115
Gurin, Gerald, 174
Gurland, Barry J., 139, 142
Gutmann, David, 58, 248

Hagestad, Gunhild O., 53
Hammond, Philip E., 296
Hand, Jennifer, 159, 278
Hapgood, David, 218, 219
Harberg, Ernest, 88
Harenstein, Louise S., 88
Hareven, Tamara K., 12, 243
Harris, Adella J., 72

Harris, Louis, 66, 67t., 68t., 72, 127–29, 187, 188, 189t., 194, 195, 206, 211, 229, 238, 256, 257t., 275, 279, 284, 294, 295t., 309, 311
Haven, Clayton, 277, 278
Havighurst, Robert, 119, 120, 132, 134, 282
Hayflick, Leonard, 13
Heaney, Robert P., 90
Hebb, Donald O., 120, 124
Hendershot, Gerry E., 251
Henretta, John C., 213
Henry, William, 19, 95, 120, 132, 133
Heron, Woodburn, 148
Hess, Beth B., 41, 42, 47t., 72, 206, 208, 255, 256, 260, 278, 279, 286, 287, 296, 304
Hickey, Tom, 42, 47t.
Hochschild, Arlie R., 24, 133, 288
Hollingshead, August B., 114
Holmberg, R. H., 164
Holmes, Thomas H., 86
Homans, George C., 260
Horton, Donald, 159
Hudson, Robert, 228, 237, 238, 239
Hunter, W. W., 340
Huxley, Aldous, 113

Istomina, Z. M., 145

Jackson, D., 281
Jackson, Hobart, 159
Jackson, Jacquelyne J., 159, 199, 261
Jacobs, Ruth, 345
Jaffe, A. J., 194, 195, 199
Jarvik, Lissy F., 121, 124, 142
Jaslow, Philip, 345
Johnson, C. Conrad, 90
Johnson, Colleen Leahy, 346
Johnson, Marilyn E., 27, 33, 34, 50, 229
Johnson, Virginia, 88
Jones, Howard W., 88

Kalish, Richard A., 109, 111, 112, 113
Kallmann, Franz J., 124
Kamerman, Sheila B., 346
Karnes, Elizabeth L., 73
Kart, Cary S., 159, 160
Kasl, Stanislav, 88
Kastenbaum, Robert J., 111, 115, 145, 152
Katz, Solomon H., 20
Kaufman, Robert L., 340
Keenan, Brian, 155
Kempler, Hyman L., 346

Kent, Donald P., 261
Kertzer, David, 37n., 45, 341
King, David R., 229
Kitson, Gay C., 296
Kivett, Vira R., 260
Kleiman, Michael B., 275
Klein, Edward B., 347
Klemmack, D. L., 294
Kobrin, Frances E., 251
Kogan, Nathan, 65, 342
Kreps, Juanita M., 346
Kübler-Ross, Elisabeth, 111, 115
Kunitz, Stephen J., 101
Kuypers, Joseph A., 125, 130

Labouvie, Gisela V., 122
Lafave, Hugh, 347
Langner, Thomas S., 355
Larson, Reed, 270
Lasagna, Louis, 112, 114
Laslett, Barbara, 269, 270
Laslett, Peter, 45, 242, 243
Lawrence, R. E., 145, 336
Lawton, M. Powell, 125
Lazarsfeld, Paul, 279
Leaf, Alexander, 81
Lee, Gary R., 251
Lemon, Bruce W., 120
Lerner, Monroe, 110
Levey, Samuel, 164
LeVine, Robert, 45
Levine, Sol, 340
Levinson, Daniel, 27
Levinson, Maria H., 347
Lewis, Myrna, 142
Lewis, Robert A., 247
Lieberman, Morton, 165, 170
Linton, Ralph, 347
Lipson, Alberta, 340
Livson, Florine B., 58, 90, 134, 248
Loh, H. S., 83
Longino, Charles F., Jr., 296
Lopata, Helena Znaniecki, 257, 259, 267, 278, 281, 288
Lorge, Irving, 65
Lotka, Alfred J., 341
Loughan, Celeste, 73, 74
Lowe, J. C., 41, 62, 63t.
Lowenthal, Marjorie Fiske, 155, 165, 172, 248, 277, 278, 286
Lozier, John, 273

Maas, Henry S., 125, 130
MacDonald, A. D., 175
Madigan, Francis C., 10, 93–94
Mallan, Lucy B., 201

Manard, Barbara, 159, 160
Markson, Elizabeth W., 80, 114, 154, 155, 157, 159, 160, 161, 165, 167, 168, 171n.
Marlowe, Roberta, 168
Marsh, Gail R., 124
Marshall, C., 72
Martin, W. C., 175
Marx, Karl, 25, 46, 315
Masters, William H., 88
Masuda, Minoru, 86
Mathieu, James T., 275
Maurice, H., 340
Mazess, Richard B., 101
McCaffrey, Isabel, 171n.
McKee, Braxton, 347
McKeon, Thomas, 7, 108
McKinley, John B., 108, 109
McKinley, Sonja M., 108, 109
McKinney, John C., 311
McTavish, Donald G., 65, 66, 66t.
Mead, George Herbert, 67
Mead, Margaret, 110
Mednick, Robert A., 110
Medvedev, Zhores A., 101
Meier, Elizabeth, 188t.
Mendel, Werner M., 157
Mendelson, Mary Adelaide, 164, 168, 218, 219
Mendelson, Monique, 339
Merriam, Ida C., 349
Merton, Robert K., 61, 279, 303
Meyer, Nessa G., 156
Michael, Stanley T., 355
Miller, Brent C., 41, 247
Miller, Stephen J., 311
Millham, Jim, 65
Mills, C. Wright, 6
Mindel, Charles H., 296
Mishara, B. L., 174
Moen, Elizabeth, 206
Mol, F., 96
Moore, J. W., 41, 62, 63t.
Morgan, James N., 189
Morgan, Leslie A., 247
Motley, Dena K., 211
Moulton, Ruth, 350
Musgrove, F., 50
Myers, George C., 355

Nahemow, Nina, 171, 229
Nehrke, Milton, 145
Neugarten, Beatrice L., 39, 48n., 52, 53, 62, 63t., 120, 130, 131, 134, 135, 237, 248, 259
Nie, N., 225
Nixon, Richard, 109

Norris, Vera, 142
Novick, L. J., 166
Nunn, Clyde Z., 351

Oakley, Ann, 104
Opler, Marvin K., 355
Oppenheimer, Valerie K., 254
Orbach, Harold, 13
Ornstein, Phillip, 144
Osako, Masako M., 264
Otto, Herbert A., 249
Owen, John D., 307

Palmer, Stuart, 153
Palmore, Erdman, 120, 126, 152, 295, 296
Parkes, C. Murray, 104
Parsons, Talcott, 50, 57, 96, 299, 303
Paul, Lester, 111
Pauling, Linus, 83
Pepper, Claude, 192
Peppers, Larry G., 309
Peters, G. R., 69
Peterson, David A., 73
Peterson, James A., 120
Peterson, Paul G., 134
Phillips, Bernard, 96, 132
Platt, Gerald, 50, 299, 303
Plemons, Judy K., 336
Powers, Edward A., 69, 278
Pratt, Henry J., 219, 224, 232, 233
Presser, Harriet, 39

Quint, Jeanne C., 111, 113

Rader, Victoria N., 48
Ragan, Pauline K., 52, 238
Reich, Robert, 168
Reichard, Suzanne, 134
Reitz, Rosetta, 90
Rennie, Thomas A. C., 355
Richman, Joseph, 58
Riesman, David, 159, 287
Riley, Matilda White, 14, 27, 33, 34, 37, 41, 50, 51, 68, 70, 81, 121, 125, 126, 127, 131, 229, 235, 241, 253, 256, 282, 294, 308
Rilke, Rainer Maria, 113
Robertson, Joan, 277
Rockefeller, Nelson, 305n.
Rodgers, Willard L., 254
Rooney, James F., 278
Rose, Arnold M., 51, 56
Rosenfeld, Jeffrey P., 257

Waring, Joan M., 37, 255, 256, 286
Watson, J. Allen, 260
Webber, Irving L., 278
Weber, Max, 46, 287, 293
Weg, Ruth B., 81, 82
Weinberger, Linda E., 65
Weinstein, Karol, 259
Weiss, Robert S., 104
Wertenbaker, Lael, 115
White, Royce M., 97
Wildavsky, Aaron, 159
Wilensky, Harold L., 41, 254
Willis, Sherry L., 336
Wilson, C. W. M., 83
Wilson, Robert B., 88
Wilson, Robert N., 91

Wimmers, M. F., 96
Winch, Robert F., 43
Winsborough, Halliman H., 52
Wood, Vivian, 62, 64, 277
Woodruff, Diana S., 303
Wu, Frances Y. T., 263

Yankelovich, D., 359
Young, Anne McD., 359
Yudkin, John, 83

Zander, Mary, 207
Zimmerman, Michael, 269
Zuckerman, Harriet, 303

Index of Subjects

Cholesterol, 83
City, residence in, 261–62, 262t., 271, 272t., 274–75
Civil religion, 324
Cognitive consistency, 191, 325
Cognitive dissonance, 68, 325
Cohort(s), 33–34, 36–37, 49, 50, 51–52, 64, 70–71, 71t., 122, 189, 325
Cohort analysis, 27–29, 325
Cohort effects, 383
Communal living, 288
Community services, 168, 175, 222
Comparative analysis, 325
Comprehensive Employment and Training Act (CETA), 222
Congregate care facility, 169–70
Consanguine, definition of, 325
Conservatism, in old age, 228, 230. See also Attitudes, stability of
Consumer Price Index, 205
Consumers, old people as, 208, 209t.
Contentment, as measure of psychological well-being, 173–74
Counseling, preretirement, 314
Crime, and elderly, 275, 276t., 277
Critical mass, formation of, 6–11
Cross-cultural methods, 325–26
Cross-sectional data, 26, 325–26
Cultural development, 42, 43–44, 43. See also Sociology

Data. See Research methods
Day hospital program, 172, 173
Death, 58–61, 98–115
  attitudes toward and circumstances surrounding, 97, 109–15
  causes of, 105–109, 106t., 107t.
  fear of, 58–61
  after relocation, 166–67
  social, 111
  statistics on, 98–109
Death rates. See Mortality rate
Deinstitutionalization, 167–69
Dentures, 81
Dependency ratios, 197, 252, 326
Depression, 138–41. See also Psychological aspects
Deviance, 138–46
Diet, 83, 84t., 85, 101, 221
Disease. See also Health status
  deaths caused by, 105, 106t., 107–109, 107t.
  nutrition related to, 83, 85
  stress related to, 86–88
  type of, related to care before death, 114

Disengagement theory, 19, 20, 132–33, 285, 326
Drugs, for depression, 139

Economics of aging, 85, 87–88, 181–213. See also Socioeconomic aspects
Education, 298–306, 300t., 302t.
  aspects of old age related to level of, 129, 129t., 146–47, 159, 194
  levels of, 299–300, 300t.
  for older students, 300–304, 302t.
  study of gerontology included in, 304–305
Ego development, Erikson on, 23, 135, 139, 148
Ego identity. See also Self-esteem
  sick role and, 96–97
Egocentricity, 131–32
Emotional responses. See also Psychological aspects
  to birth and death, 111
Employee Retirement Income Security Act (ERISA), 203
Employment. See Labor force; Retirement; Work
Environment, age-segregated, 279
  change in, in relocation, 166–67
  variety in past, as aspect of mental health, 146–48
Esteem of old, 56–58. See also Self-esteem
Estrogen, 88–90
Ethnic aspects, 159–61, 280, 281t. See also Minority groups; Race
Ethology, 326
Exchange theory, 21, 286, 326
Extended expectations, 326

Facility, definition of, 176
Familism, 43, 43, 44, 326
Family, conjugal, 325
  cultural aspects of, 42–46, 57–58
  extended, 12, 242, 243, 326
  in later life, 241–67
  status of, as census classification, 249–50, 250t., 327
  stem, 45
  traditional, 334
Filial maturity, 265, 327
Filial piety, 46, 327
Foreign-born elderly, 160–61
Foster grandparents, 260, 312
Freudians, 45
Friendship, 277–79

Gemeinschaft, 287, 327

Generational ties. *See* Intergenerational relationships
Gerontology, social, 15–31
  increased study of, 3–6, 13–15, 304–305
Gerontophobia, 75
Gesellschaft, 287, 327
Golden Age Clubs, 284
Government programs, 163, 163*t.*, 164, 175–76, 192, 195, 198*t.*, 203, 205, 216–24. *See also* Medicaid; Medicare; Politics of aging; Social Security
Grandparents, 20, 22, 258–60. *See also* Intergenerational relationships
Gray Lobby, 219, 221, 233, 235–36, 238, 327
Gray Panthers, 192, 229, 234–35
Great Depression, 183, 231, 238, 273

Health Care Improvement Act, 263
Health insurance, 217
Health status, 90–96. *See also* Disease; Physical condition
  after institutionalization, 171–74
Hearing loss, 82
Heart disease, 103, 105, 106*t.*, 107, 108, 124
Hispanic aged, 94, 94*t. See also* Minorities
Historical aspects of aging, 42–48, 56–58, 152–53, 181–82, 214–17, 241–44, 269–70
Home care, 175
Homemakers, displaced, 200
  Social Security for, 199–200
Homes, adult, 176
  nonprofit, 176
  nursing, 176. *See also* Nursing homes
  old-age, 176
  personal care, 177
  proprietary, 177
Hospice, 111*n.*
Hospitals, 110–14, 154–57, 159–61, 164, 168–69, 172, 173, 176, 177
Hotels, 278
Housing, 208–11, 222–23. *See also* Living arrangements; Residence
Hypertension, related to stress, 87–88

Ideal type, definition of, 327
Illness. *See* Disease; Health status
Income, 94, 94*t.*, 158–59, 195–206, 212–13, 260–61. *See also* Socioeconomic aspects
Income maintenance programs, 216. *See also* Social Security; Supplemental Security Income

Indians. *See* Native Americans
Individual Retirement Account, 203, 327
Industrialization, 7, 11–12, 46–48, 47*t.*, 58, 59, 153, 181–82, 242, 243
Institution, as social system, 43, 46, 47*t.*, 328
Institutional sphere, definition of, 327–28
Institutionalization, 97, 151–77. *See also* Hospitals; Nursing homes
Institutions, 176, 177
  total, 170–74
Insurance, national health, 156, 158. *See also* Medicaid; Medicare
  social, 195–96. *See also* Social Security
Intelligence in old age, 121–25, 123, 136–37
Intergenerational relationships, 251–60
Interview, 25, 328
  depth, 326
  structured, 333
Interview schedule, 328
Involvement, 269–71, 277–85, 287–89
Isolation, 285–87. *See also* Single persons

Job performance, 187–88
Joking relationship, 260, 328

Keogh Plan, 203, 328

Labor force participation, 183–91. *See also* Work
Leisure, 306–16, 309*t.*, 310*t.*
Life course, 40, 48–54, 283
Life cycle squeeze, 254–55, 328
Life expectancy, 7–10, 9*t.*, 58, 98, 100–101, 100*t.*, 102*t.*, 102–103, 328
Life review, 135
Life span, 101–102
Life span development, 22–23, 328
Life stages, 48–49, 328
Living arrangements, 250–51, 251*t. See also* Isolation; Residence
Loneliness, 287, 288
Longitudinal, definition of, 25, 328
"Looking-glass" self, 66–68, 329

Marital status, 103–105, 104*t.*, 185, 186*t.*, 245–49, 246*t.*
Master status, 49, 329
Matriarchal, definition of, 44, 329
Matrilineal, definition of, 44, 329
Matrilocal, definition of, 44, 329
Mean, definition of, 329

Media, on growing old, 72–74
time spent with, 310t.
Median, definition of, 329
Medicaid, 156–57, 164, 218–19, 273, 275
Medical care. See Hospitals
Medicare, 12, 156–59, 164, 217–18, 273
Memory loss, 143–46, 174
Men, 44, 46, 57, 130. See also Sex Differences; Sex stereotypes
Menopause, 88–90
Menstruation, 89
Mental hospitals, 154–57, 159–61, 164, 168–69, 176, 177
Mental impairment, 28–29, 171–74. See also Neuroses
Mexican-Americans, 261, 263
Minority groups, 56, 94, 94t., 260–64, 271, 272t. See also Ethnic aspects; Racial aspects
Mode, definition of, 329
Models, 32
conceptual, 32, 325
Modernization, 329–30. See also Industrialization
Mortality rates, 98, 99t., 102–103, 104t., 105–109, 106t., 107t.
Motor responses, 121
Multidisciplinary, definition of, 330
Myths. See Beliefs

National Association of Retired Federal Employees (NARFE), 232, 233
National Council on Aging, 127–28, 128t., 129t., 187n.
National Council of Senior Citizens (NCSC), 232
National Institute of Aging (NIA), 223–24, 233
National Institute for Mental Health (NIMH), 224
National organizations, 232–36
National Retired Teachers Association (NRTA), 232–33
Native Americans, 100–101, 263
Necrophobia, 75, 330
Nepotism, 330
Neuroses, 131–32
Nonprofit homes, 176
Norms, 34, 36, 38–39, 41, 43, 61–64, 63t., 323, 330
Nursing homes, 154–55, 154t., 156, 156t., 157, 160–65, 162t., 163t., 168, 176. See also Institutionalization
Nutrition, 82–85, 221

Observation studies, 24, 330

Old age. See Aging
Old Age, Survivors, Disability, and Health Insurance Act (OASDHI), 195, 201, 202, 217
Old Age Assistance (OAA) programs, 195, 204
Old-age institution, definition of, 176–77
Older Americans Act, 12, 14, 17, 175, 219–22
Organizations, national, 232–36
Osteoporosis, 90

Parents, ancient, of aged offspring, 252–54. See also Intergenerational relationships
Participant observation, 24, 330
Patriarchy, 44, 330
Peers, 278–79, 330
Pensions, 203–204, 212. See also Social Security
Period effect, 27, 283, 330
Personal care home, definition of, 177
Personality, 103, 125–32, 134–35, 146–48
Physical condition, 80–82, 167
Physiological changes, 38, 79–90
Pluralistic ignorance, 331
Political behavior of old people, 224–39
Politics of aging, 214–40
Population data, 6–11, 35, 155–57
Poverty, 152–53, 160, 206–209, 264, 273–74, 278
Preliterate societies. See Simple societies
Primary group, 268–70, 331
Primary individual, 331
Proprietary homes, 163, 163t., 164, 177
Prosthetic device, 218, 331
Psychiatric problems. See Brain syndrome
Psychological aspects, 95–97, 119–50, 173–74
Psychosocial development, 37–38, 39, 331
Public assistance, 204
Puritan work ethic, 183, 306–307

Race differences, 9, 87–88, 94, 94t., 100–101, 100t., 108, 127–28, 128t., 159–61, 184t., 185–86, 190, 196t., 207–208, 207t., 280, 280t., 283–84. See also Minority groups
Reaction time, changes in, 121
Recreation, 308. See also Leisure
Religion, 46, 59–60, 293–98, 295t.
civil, 324
Relocation, 166–67
Replacement ratio, 202, 205
Reproductive capacity, changes in, 88–90
Research, 24–29, 219, 331

Residence, 271–75. *See also* Housing; Living arrangements
Retired persons, organizations for, 232–33
Retired Senior Volunteer Program (RSVP), 312
Retirement, 64, 191–99
  counseling before, 314
  early, 189, 194
  leisure time in, 313, 314, 315
  mandatory, 192–94, 329
Rites of passage, 48, 331
Role(s), 34, 34, 36, 41–42, 104, 147–48, 157–58, 331. *See also* Sex differences
Role clusters, 39, 40, 41
Role partner, 331
Role players, 21, 331
Role slack, 41, 331–32
Role strain, 41, 332
Role theory, 132
Rule of reciprocity, 21
Rural Health Service Clinics Act, 273
Rural residence, 271, 272t., 273–74

Secondary group, 268, 332
Secondary individual, 332
Secularization, 59, 332
Self-care, 80, 171–73
Self-concern, 131–32
Self-esteem and self-image, 67–70, 96–97, 126–31, 128t., 129t.
Self-fulfilling prophecy, 332
Self-help groups, 287–89, 332
Senility, 142, 143, 147. *See also* Memory loss
Senior Center movement, 284
Senior power, 236–39
Sensory motor responses, 121
Sex differences, 10, 92–94, 100–103, 108, 125, 129–31, 133–34, 161–63, 183–86, 207–208, 245–46, 249–51, 258–59, 277–78, 313–14
Sex stereotypes, 58, 72, 73, 79–80, 130–31
Sexuality, 72, 73–74, 89, 110, 248–49
"Shopping bag ladies," 278
Sick role in old age, 96–98
Simple societies, 6–7, 44–46, 57, 58, 214–15, 241–42, 269–70, 315
Single persons, 250, 251t. *See also* Isolation; Widowhood
Social aspects, 132–34. *See also* Psychosocial aspects; Sociology
"Social clocks," 62
Social construction, 332
Social control, 333
Social gerontology, 3–6, 13–31, 304–305

Social Security, 185, 195–97, 199–202, 261
Social Security Act. *See* Old Age, Survivors, Disability and Health Insurance Act
Social Security System, 12, 211, 212–13, 222, 223
Social stratification, 214, 333
Social structure, 36–37
Social structure differentiation, 43, 333
Sociobiology, 20, 25, 333
Socioeconomic aspects, 87–88, 94, 94t., 108, 112–14, 126–27, 146–48, 154, 158–59. *See also* Economics; Race
Sociology of aging, 32–54, 57. *See also* Simple societies
Special Committee on Aging, 223
Status, 33, 46–48, 47t., 333
Stereotypes, 66, 68, 72–74, 125
  sex, 58, 72, 73, 79–80, 130–31
Strata, 333. *See also* Age stratification
Stress, 86–88
Subculture of aging, 51, 53, 333
Suicide, 102, 104–105, 114, 140, 140t., 141t.
Supplemental Security Income (SSI), 195, 204–205, 207
Support systems, informal, 269, 277–82. *See also* Organizations; Self-help
Symbolic interaction, 21–22, 333

Tooth loss, 81–82
Trade associations, 233
Trade unions, 193
Transportation, 222, 274

Urban elderly, 261–62, 262t., 271, 272t., 274–75

Value, 334
Veteran's benefits, 204
Vision decrements, 82
Vitamins, 83
Voluntary associations, 282–85, 289, 334
Voting, 71, 71t., 224–25, 226t., 227t.

Welfare, 152–53, 156, 196, 198t., 200, 204–205
White House Conferences on Aging, 224, 233
Widowhood, 201, 278. *See also* Marital status